C000178589

Boxing

The Records

Ian Morrison

GUINNESS BOOKS

EDITOR: Beatrice Frei
DESIGN AND LAYOUT: Michael Morey

First edition 1986
Second edition © Ian Morrison and
Guinness Publishing Ltd 1988

Published in Great Britain by Guinness Publishing Ltd,
33 London Road, Enfield, Middlesex

All rights reserved. No part of this publication may be
reproduced, stored in a retrieval system, or transmitted in
any form or by any means, electronic, mechanical,
photocopying, recording or otherwise, without prior
permission in writing of the publisher.

Typeset in Sabon and Univers
by DP Press Ltd, Sevenoaks, Kent
Printed and bound in Great Britain by
Hazell Watson & Viney Ltd,
Member of the BPCC Group,
Aylesbury, Bucks

'Guinness' is a registered trade mark of
Guinness Superlatives Ltd

British Library Cataloguing in Publication Data

Morrison, Ian
    Guinness boxing: the records.
    1. Boxing—Records
    I. Title
    796.8'3   GV1137

ISBN 0–85112–345–7

Contents

Acknowledgements *4*

Abbreviations *4*

The History of Boxing *5*

The Weight Divisions *8*

The Bare-Knuckle Champions *8*
  English champions – American
  champions

World Title Fights *12*
  Results *12*
  The world champions in each division *60*
  World champions – nation-by-nation *65*
  Records and Statistics *67*

  Firsts – Undefeated champions – Longest
  reigning – Shortest reigning – Champions at
  more than one weight – Most successful title
  defences – Most fights engaged in – Regained
  world titles – Fights that ended in round one –
  Shortest fights – Disqualifications – Drawn
  fights – Most knockdowns – Fatalities –
  Record purses – Most fights – The
  champions – Venues – Referees – Managers –
  Trainers – The heavyweight champions

British Champions *120*

American Champions *124*

Commonwealth Champions *125*

European Champions *129*

The Olympic Games *134*

The Commonwealth Games *139*

World Amateur Championships
  141

ABA Champions *142*

Golden Gloves Champions *143*

Nicknames, Real Names
  and Name Changes *146*

Hall of Fame *148*

Fighters of the Year *150*

Miscellanea *151*
  Firsts – Career earnings – Attendances –
  Most fights – Most wins – Knock-outs –
  Worst records – Longest contests – Shortest
  contests – Longest careers – Shortest careers –
  Fatalities – Oldest fighters – Youngest
  fighters – The champions

Index to special features

The Queensberry Rules *88*

The First Champion –
  James Figg *90*

Jimmy Wilde *91*

Joe Louis *92*

Sugar Ray Robinson *94*

The Thrilla in Manilla *96*

Georges Carpentier *97*

Henry Cooper *98*

Rocky Marciano *100*

Madison Square Garden *102*

Bob Fitzsimmons *103*

Jack Dempsey *104*

Henry Armstrong *106*

Battle of the Long Count *108*

Archie Moore *109*

Mike Tyson *110*

Sugar Ray Leonard *112*

The Terry Lawless Stable *114*

Jack Johnson *115*

Ali's Three World Titles *116*

Larry Holmes *118*

Index *157*

Acknowledgements

John Grasso of the International Boxing Research Organization (IBRO) for his assistance with American records. *The Ring* for allowing permission to reproduce their Hall of Fame entrants and Fighters of the Year. Tony Boardman for assisting with the checking and collating of statistics. Manchester Central Library for their excellent microfilm facilities.

Abbreviations

SH	Super-heavyweight
H	Heavyweight
C	Cruiserweight
LH	Light-heavyweight
SM	Super-middleweight
M	Middleweight
LM	Light-middleweight/Junior-middleweight
W	Welterweight
LW	Light-welterweight/Junior-welterweight
L	Lightweight
JL	Junior-lightweight
Fe	Featherweight
SB	Super-bantamweight/Junior-featherweight
B	Bantamweight
SF	Super-flyweight/Junior-bantamweight
Fl	Flyweight
LF	Light-flyweight/Junior-flyweight
MF	Mini-flyweight

EBU	European Boxing Union
IBF	International Boxing Federation
IBU	International Boxing Union
NBA	National Boxing Association
NY	New York State Athletic Commission
WBA	World Boxing Association
WBC	World Boxing Council

D	Drew
DEF	Default
DIS	Disqualified
KO	Knock-out
NC	No contest
ND	No decision
PTS	Points
RSF	Referee stopped fight
RTD	Retired
TD	Technical decision
TKO	Technical knock-out

Countries

Alg	Algeria
Ant	Antigua
Arg	Argentina
Aus	Australia
Aut	Austria
Bah	Bahamas
Bar	Barbados
Bel	Belgium
Ber	Bermuda
Bra	Brazil
Bul	Bulgaria
CA	Costa Rica
Cam	Cameroon
Can	Canada
Cey	Ceylon
Chi	Chile
Chn	China
Col	Colombia
Cz	Czechoslovakia
Den	Denmark
Dom	Dominican Republic
Ecu	Ecuador
Eng	England
Est	Estonia
Fin	Finland
Fra	France
FRG	Federal Republic of Germany
GB	Great Britain
GDR	German Democratic Republic
Ger	Germany
Gha	Ghana
Gre	Greece
Guy	Guyana
Haw	Hawaii
Hol	Holland
IC	Ivory Coast
Ina	Indonesia
Ire	Ireland
Ita	Italy
Jam	Jamaica
Jap	Japan
Ken	Kenya
Mex	Mexico
Mon	Mongolia
Mor	Morocco
NG	New Guinea
Ngr	Nigeria
Nic	Nicaragua
N. Kor	North Korea
Nor	Norway
NZ	New Zealand
Pan	Panama
Par	Paraguay
Phi	Philippines
PNG	Papua New Guinea
Por	Portugal
PR	Puerto Rico
Rho	Rhodesia
Rom	Romania
SA	South Africa
Sco	Scotland
Sen	Senegal
S. Kor	South Korea
Spa	Spain
St.Vin	St. Vincent
Swe	Sweden
Swi	Switzerland
Syr	Syria
Tha	Thailand
Ton	Tonga
Tri	Trinidad and Tobago
Tun	Tunisia
Uga	Uganda
Uru	Uruguay
USA	United States of America
USSR	Union of Soviet Socialist Republics
Ven	Venezuela
VI	Virgin Islands (US)
Wal	Wales
Yug	Yugoslavia
Zai	Zaire

The History of Boxing

From the beginning of time men have fought one another, generally as a means of protecting their property. Over the years, as weapons developed, the use of fists in battle became redundant. The ancient Greeks and the Romans, however, were entertained by their gladiators engaging in fist battles but the first record of a boxing match in Britain was not until 1681 when the Duke of Albemarle organized a contest between his butler and his butcher. Precise details of the contest are not known, but it is believed to have taken place at the family home at New Hall in Essex.

It was not long after this that boxing, as we know it today, started to take shape.

In 1719 Oxfordshire-born James Figg, a renowned swordsman and cudgel fighter of his day, opened a school of arms at his amphitheatre in Oxford Road, London. This became boxing's first permanent home, and the following year Figg overcame a challenge from Gravesend pipemaker Ned Sutton to become boxing's first champion.

The 'Father of Boxing' John Broughton (GB), who devised the sport's first set of rules in 1743. Mary Evans Picture Library

Figg taught many aspiring boxers at his amphitheatre. He also staged contests there, and in 1733 he 'promoted' the first international bout when Bob Whittaker of England met Italy's Tito Alberto di Carini.

By this time, other amphitheatres had opened. One was at Tottenham Court Road, London, and was run by Jack Broughton.

Broughton, who became known as 'the Father of Boxing', fought Yorkshireman George Stevenson in 1741. Stevenson died as a result of injuries sustained and this caused Broughton to draw up the first set of boxing rules which were published in August 1743. These rules remained in force until the London Prize Ring rules were introduced nearly one hundred years later.

The first boxing club, formed in London in 1814, was called the Pugilistic Club. Its purpose was to control prize-fighting. And in 1838 the British Pugilists' Protective Association introduced the London Prize Ring rules, which replaced Broughton's rules. The London rules were revised in 1853 and 1866.

Prize-fighting was, by now, becoming popular in the United States. Jacob Hyer and Tom Beasley had, in 1816, engaged in the first American championship bout and in 1860 Tom Sayers of England and John C. Heenan of the United States met in the first international bout of any consequence. This heralded the start of international boxing.

The most important change in the sport's history was in 1865 when the 8th Marquess of Queensberry drew up his famous rules of boxing. They contained many new rules, not seen in the London rules, mainly because fighting with gloves had become more popular and it was to these fighters that Queensberry's Rules were directed.

The two most important rules, among the 12, were that each round should last for three minutes with a one-minute interval between each (previously a round ended only when a fighter was floored) and that wrestling or hugging was not allowed. The London rules permitted wrestling.

Prize-fighting still existed, however, and indeed the London rules were, as stated, revised the year after the introduction of the Queensberry Rules. But it was not long before the transition to glove fighting was complete and by the mid-1890s prize-fighting had virtually disappeared. The last bare-knuckle world heavyweight title fight was between John L. Sullivan (USA) and Jake Kilrain (USA) in 1889.

Many new organizations appeared following the introduction of the Queensberry Rules. The

Amateur Boxing Association (ABA) was formed in 1881 and held their first championships that year. The Pelican Club, a boxing club for the aristocracy, was founded by journalist William Goldberg, and opened at the Star Club, Denman Street, London in 1887. Four years later the sport's first governing body, the National Sporting Club, was opened at 43 King Street, Covent Garden, London.

Championship fights both sides of the Atlantic were commonplace. Charley Mitchell became the first British champion in 1882 and two years later Irish-born American Jack Dempsey became the first recognized world champion under Queensberry Rules when he took the middleweight title. James J. Corbett beat John L. Sullivan in 1892 to become the first of the new heavyweight world champions.

The introduction of the modern Olympic Games in 1896 saw a great upsurge in competitive amateur sporting tournaments. Boxing was no exception. It was, however, not included in the Olympic programme until the St Louis Games of 1904. The first European Amateur Championships were held in 1924 and boxing appeared at the first Empire Games in 1930. The European Amateur Junior Championships were next to appear in 1970 and, in 1974, the first Boxing World Amateur Championships were held in Cuba.

Safety in boxing has always been of paramount importance and everything has been done over the years to make the sport as safe as possible. In 1900 the New York Horton Law, which had only been passed four years earlier, was repealed. The law had stated that contests of unlimited duration could be held. The New York State's Frawley law, introduced in 1911 and repealed in 1917, stated that all bouts were mere exhibitions, and all results would be 'No Decision' unless one fighter was knocked out.

Boxing enjoyed a healthy growth period just before the First World War. The sport had seen the introduction of its first popular magazine, *Boxing* — the fore-runner to *Boxing News* — in 1909. The same year the National Sporting Club revised the Queensberry Rules and in 1911 the International Boxing Union (IBU) was formed in Paris.

But it was in the inter-war years that the sport enjoyed one of its healthiest growth periods. The British Boxing Board of Control was founded in 1918 and in 1920 the New York State Athletic Commission was formed. And in 1922 Nat Fleischer published the *Ring Magazine* — which has become boxing's Bible. Boxing was now well organized by strong governing bodies. It was also attracting big money and in 1921 the Jack Dempsey (USA)–Georges Carpentier (Fra) heavyweight fight attracted the sport's first $1 million gate. The first radio commentry of a fight, between Americans Johnny Ray and Johnny Dundee, was broadcast that same year on 11 April 1921 by KDKA, Pittsburgh, and helped increase the popularity of boxing, particularly in the United States. The first radio recording of part of a contest in Great Britain was by the BBC on 26 March 1926 and covered part of the

The Jack Dempsey (USA) (right) — Georges Carpentier (Fra) world heavyweight title fight, July 1921 — the first fight to attract a $million gate. Mary Evans Picture Library

First World Title Fights

The first world title fights under Queensberry Rules, as generally recognized, in each weight division were as follows:

HEAVYWEIGHT
7 Sep 1892 James J. Corbett (USA) v. John L. Sullivan (USA) New Orleans, USA

CRUISERWEIGHT
8 Dec 1979 Marvin Camel (USA) v. Mate Parlov (Yug) Split, Yugoslavia

LIGHT-HEAVYWEIGHT
22 Apr 1903 Jack Root (Aut) v. Charles 'Kid' McCoy (USA) Detroit, USA

SUPER-MIDDLEWEIGHT
28 Mar 1984 Murray Sutherland (GB) v. Ernie Singletary (USA) Atlantic City, USA

MIDDLEWEIGHT
30 Jul 1884 Jack Dempsey (Ire) v. George Fulljames (USA) New York, USA

LIGHT-MIDDLEWEIGHT
20 Oct 1962 Denny Moyer (USA) v. Joey Giambra (USA) Portland, USA

WELTERWEIGHT
30 Oct 1888 Paddy Duffy (USA) v. William McMillan (GB) Fort Foote, USA

LIGHT-WELTERWEIGHT
21 Sep 1926 Mushy Callahan (USA) v. Pinkey Mitchell (USA) Vernon, USA

LIGHTWEIGHT
16 Nov 1887 Jack McAuliffe (Ire) v. Jem Carney (GB) Revere, USA

JUNIOR-LIGHTWEIGHT
18 Nov 1921 Johnny Dundee (Ita) v. George Chaney (USA) New York, USA

FEATHERWEIGHT
31 Mar 1889 Ike Weir (GB) v. Frank Murphy (GB) Kouts, USA

SUPER-BANTAMWEIGHT
3 Apr 1976 Rigoberto Riasco (Pan) v. Waruinge Nakayama (Ken) Panama City, Panama

BANTAMWEIGHT
27 Jun 1890 George Dixon (Can) v. Nunc Wallace (GB) London, England

SUPER-FLYWEIGHT
2 Feb 1980 Rafael Orono (Ven) v. Seung-Hoon Lee (S. Kor) Caracas, Venezuela

FLYWEIGHT
18 Dec 1916 Jimmy Wilde (GB) v. Young Zulu Kid (Ita) London, England

LIGHT-FLYWEIGHT
4 Apr 1975 Franco Udella (Ita) v. Valentine Martinez (Mex) Milan, Italy

MINI-FLYWEIGHT
14 Jun 1987 Kyung-Yun Lee (S.Kor) v. Masaharu Kawakami (Jap) Bukok, South Korea

Johnny Curley–Harry Corbett contest at the National Sporting Club.

Attendances at contests, whether they were title fights or not, rose dramatically and in 1926 the largest-ever paid attendance, over 120 000, witnessed the American Gene Tunney–Jack Dempsey world heavyweight contest at the Sesquicentennial Stadium, Philadelphia.

The first televised bout was from the CBS Studios, New York on 25 August 1931. The first televised bout in Britain was from Broadcasting House on 22 August 1933 and involved two British boxers, Archie Sexton and Lauri Raiteri.

In 1927 the National Boxing Association (NBA) (forerunner of the World Boxing Association) was formed. At the time, world title fights fell under the jurisdiction of the New York State Commission, the NBA and IBU. The IBU changed its name to the European Boxing Union (EBU) in 1946 and the NBA changed to the World Boxing Association (WBA) in 1962.

Today there are three bodies who recognize world champions: the WBA, the World Boxing Council (WBC) which was formed in Mexico in 1963, and the International Boxing Federation (IBF), formed in the United States in 1983.

The WBA is largely an American organization which controls boxing throughout most of the United States, while the WBC is more international and attracts affiliation from, among others, the EBU and the British Boxing Board of Control (BBB of C).

The IBF initially started life as the United States Boxing Association International (USBAI) and their intention has been to oust the WBC and WBA. As yet they have not been successful.

In an attempt to clarify championship boxing in the United States, the North American Boxing Federation (NABF) was formed in 1969. Ten years later another American body, the United States Boxing Association (USBA) was formed.

Since the formation of the WBC in 1963 the number of weight divisions at which world champions are recognized has risen from 10 to 17 as a result of the introduction of junior divisions. The last significant change to world championship boxing was in 1982 when the WBC announced that all their title fights would be over 12 rounds, and not 15.

John Gully, English champion in 1807, spent part of his early life in a debtor's prison. Later, as a result of winning a bet, he won enough money to stand as a parliamentary candidate. He was duly elected to serve the Pontefract, West Yorkshire, constituency. He was also the owner of two Epsom Derby winners: Pyrrhus the First (1846) and Andover (1854). He died a very rich man.

The Weight Divisions

In the days of prize fighting, weight differences were not taken into consideration. One man fought another, irrespective of weight. In the mid-1850s, however, the following three divisions were formed, even though fighters could still meet men from different weight divisions:

Heavyweight	– over 156lb
Middleweight	– up to 156lb
Lightweight	– up to 133lb

Two further divisions were later added; they were:

Featherweight	– up to 119lb
Bantamweight	– up to 105lb

In 1910, following discussions between boxing authorities from Britain and the United States the following weight scale was draw up:

Heavyweight	– over 175lb
Light-heavyweight	– up to 175lb
Middleweight	– up to 154lb
Welterweight	– up to 142lb
Lightweight	– up to 133lb
Featherweight	– up to 122lb
Bantamweight	– up to 116lb
Flyweight	– up to 112lb
Paperweight	– up to 105lb

Following a meeting of the various boxing authorities on 1 September 1970, the weights in 11 divisions were standardized. Since then, five other divisions (cruiser, super-middle, super-bantam, super-fly and light-fly) have been created. The full list of current weight divisions is:

*	Heavyweight	– Any weight
*	Cruiserweight	– up to 195lb
	(also known as junior-heavyweight)	
*	Light-heavyweight	– up to 175lb
*	Super-middleweight	– up to 170lb
*	Middleweight	– up to 160lb
*	Light-middleweight	– up to 154lb
	(also known as junior-middleweight)	
*	Welterweight	– up to 147lb
*	Light-welterweight	– up to 140lb
	(also known as junior-welterweight)	
*	Lightweight	– up to 135lb
*	Junior-lightweight	– up to 130lb
	(also known as super-featherweight)	
*	Featherweight	– up to 126lb
	Super-bantamweight	– up to 122lb
	(also known as junior-featherweight)	
*	Bantamweight	– up to 118lb
	Super-flyweight	– up to 115lb
	(also known as junior-bantamweight)	
*	Flyweight	– up to 112lb
	Light-flyweight	– up to 108lb
	(also known as junior-flyweight)	
*	Mini-flyweight	– under 105lb

* Indicates weights at which British titles are contested.

The Association Internationale de Boxe Amateur (AIBA) recognizes 12 weight divisions, as follows:

Super-heavyweight	– over 200.5lb
Heavyweight	– up to 200.5lb
Light-heavyweight	– up to 179lb
Middleweight	– up to 165.5lb
Light-middleweight	– up to 156lb
Welterweight	– up to 148lb
Light-welterweight	– up to 140lb
Lightweight	– up to 132lb
Featherweight	– up to 126lb
Bantamweight	– up to 119.5lb
Flyweight	– up to 112.5lb
Light-flyweight	– up to 106lb

The Bare-Knuckle Champions

While men have had the instinct and desire to box with their fists for thousands of years it was only as recent as the early 18th century that it began to take shape as a sport. Oxfordshire-born James Figg established his amphitheatre in London and encouraged sportsmen to attend and participate in martial arts such as cudgelling and boxing.

Figg became an expert tutor and also the first recognized champion when he beat Gravesend pipemaker Ned Sutton. It was one of Figg's students, Jack Broughton, who drew up the first set of rules in 1743. The first organizing body, the Pugilistic Club, was formed in 1814 and they revised Broughton's Rules until bringing out their own set of rules — The London Prize Ring Rules — in 1838. Their rules were accepted both sides of the Atlantic, as the sport was by now popular in the United States. As more and more boxers were fighting in gloves, albeit a far distance from the gloves worn today, the 8th Marquess of Queensberry drew up a new set of rules designed for these new fighters, and by the end of the 19th century bare-knuckle fighting, or prize-fighting, was virtually obsolete.

English Champions

1719	James Figg
	Figg retired undefeated in 1730. Tom Pipes, Bill Gretting and Jack Broughton all claimed the title.
1734	George Taylor
1740	Jack Broughton
1750	Jack Slack
1760	Bill Stevens
1761	George Meggs
1762	George Milsom
1764	Bill Darts
1769	Tom Lyons
1771	Peter Corcoran
1776	Harry Sellars
1783	Tom Johnson
1791	Big Ben Brain
1794	Daniel Mendoza
1795	Gentleman John Jackson
1800	Jim Belcher

'The Gypsy' — Jem Mace (GB), who first won the English title in 1861 and was recognized as undisputed world heavyweight champion in 1870.
Syndication International

1803	Hen Pearce
1807	John Gully
1808	Tom Cribb
1821	Tom Spring
1824	Tom Cannon
1825	Jem Ward
1827	Peter Crawley
1827	Jem Ward (claimed title)
1833	Deaf James Burke
1839	Bendigo (William Thompson)
1839	Deaf James Burke (claimed title)
1840	Nick Ward
1841	Ben Gaunt
1845	Bendigo (William Thompson)
1850	William Perry
1851	Harry Broome
1856	Tom Paddock
1857	Tom Sayers
1860	Sam Hurst
1861	Jem Mace
1862	Tom King
1863	Jem Mace
1865	Joe Wormwald
1866	Jem Mace
1873	Tom Allen
1876	Joe Goss
1882	Charlie Mitchell
1885	Jem Smith

American Champions

1816	Jacob Hyer
1841	Tom Hyer
1852	John C. Morrissey (Ire)
1859	John C. Heenan
1863	Joe Coburn (Ire)
1865	Mike McCoole (Ire) (claimed title)
1869	Tom Allen (Eng) (claimed title)

Undisputed bare-knuckle world heavyweight champions

1863	Tom King (GB)
1869	Mike McCoole (Ire)
1870	Jem Mace (GB)
1873	Tom Allen (GB)
1876	Joe Goss (GB)
1880	Paddy Ryan (USA)
1882	John L. Sullivan (USA)

First world title fight

Generally regarded as:
Tom Sayers (GB) v. John C. Heenan (USA) at Farnborough, Hants, England, 17 April 1860. Contest was declared a draw after 37 rounds.

In 1884 Alex Agar (Aus) died as a result of injuries sustained in a bare-knuckle contest with Jim Lawson. Lawson was subsequently sent to prison for manslaughter and bare-knuckle fighting banned in Australia.

First world champion

Generally regarded as:
Tom King (GB) who beat John C. Heenan (USA) at Wadhurst, England, 10 December 1863.

Longest fights

6 hours 15 minutes
James Kelly v. Jonathan Smith at Dalesford, Victoria, NSW, Australia, 3 December 1855.

6 hours 3 minutes
Mike Madden v. Bill Hayes at Edenbridge, Kent, England, 17 July 1849.

5 hours 45 minutes
Mike Madden v. Jack Grant at Woking, Surrey, England, 12 December 1848.

5 hours 3 minutes
William Sheriff v. Jack Welsh at Philadelphia, USA, 4 April 1884.

Most recorded rounds

276 (in 4 hours 30 minutes)
Jack Jones beat Patsy Tunney at Cheshire, England, 1825. (Under Broughton's Rules, which existed at the time, a round ended when one fighter was knocked down.)

Shortest bare-knuckle fight

7 seconds
Tom Dow beat Ned Kiely at Kansas, USA, 4 January 1868.

Largest bare-knuckle purse

$22 500 Jack Cooper v. Wolf Bendoff at Port Elizabeth, South Africa, 1885.

First $20 000 stake

John L. Sullivan v. Jake Kilrain at Richburg, Mississippi, USA, 1885.

First $10 000 stake

Tom Hyer v. Yankee Sullivan at Rock Point, Maryland, USA, 1849.

First 1000 guineas stake ($5000 equivalent)

Hen Pearce v. John Gully at Hailsham, Sussex, England, 1805.

First fatality in prize-ring contest

George Stevenson (v. Jack Broughton) at Taylor's Booth, Tottenham Court Road, London, 24 April 1741.

First brothers to win title

Jem Ward (1825) and Nick Ward (1840) both won the English title.

First champion to regain his title

Jem Ward officially regained his title in 1831, although he reclaimed the title after losing it to Peter Crawley in 1827. Crawley announced his retirement a week after the fight.

Last bare-knuckle fight for British title

Jem Smith v. Jack Davies at London, 17 December 1885.

Last bare-knuckle championship contest in Europe

Jem Smith v. Frank Slavin at Bruges, Belgium, 23 December 1889.

Last bare-knuckle contest for world heavyweight title

John L. Sullivan v. Jake Kilrain at Richburg, Mississippi, USA, 8 July 1889.

First recipient of boxing belt

Following his defeat of Tom Molineaux at Copthall Common, England on 18 December 1810, Tom Cribb became the first recipient of a boxing belt. Since then it has been the practice to give belts to the winners of championships. The first belt was presented by George III.

Longest reigning champion

11 years (English title) — James Figg (1719–30).

Shortest reigning champion

7 days (English title) — Peter Crawley defeated Jem Ward, 2 January 1827. He declined the return fight, saying he had to concentrate on his business, and thus relinquished the title. The actual contest with Ward lasted just 26 minutes!

Nicknames of some famous bare-knuckle fighters

Benecia Boy	– John C. Heenan
Bendigo	– William Thompson
Big Ben	– Benjamin Brain
Black Diamond	– Jem Ward
Black Terror	– Bill Richmond
Black Wonder	– Bob Travers
Boston Strong Boy	– John L. Sullivan
Collier	– George Meggs
Game Chicken	– Henry 'Hen' Pearce
Gas Man	– Tom Hickman
Great Gun of Windsor	– Tom Cannon
(Ironically, Cannon shot himself in 1858!)	
Gypsy	– Jem Mace
Nailer	– Bill Stevens
Napolean of the Prize Ring	– Tom Sayers
Paviour	– Tom Juchua
Tipton Slasher	– William Perry
Waterman	– Tom Lyons
Young Rump Steak	– Peter Crawley

Jake Kilrain (USA) v. John L. Sullivan (USA), July 1889. The last bare-knuckle world heavyweight title fight.
Mary Evans Picture Library

World Title Fights

Results

The following is a list of all title fights generally accepted as being for world titles. Nationalities after fighters' names indicate their country of birth. Details of other claims to world titles are on pp. 57–65.

30 Jul 1884 *M* Jack Dempsey (Ire) KO –22 George Fulljames (USA) New York, USA

3 Feb 1886 *M* Jack Dempsey (Ire) KO –27 Jack Fogarty (USA) New York, USA

4 Mar 1886 *M* Jack Dempsey (Ire) KO –13 George LaBlanche (Can) New York, USA

16 Nov 1887 *L* Jack McAuliffe (Ire) D –74 Jem Carney (GB) Revere, USA. (Declared a draw after the ring had been invaded by spectators who tried to prevent Carney from knocking out McAuliffe.)

13 Dec 1887 *M* Jack Dempsey (Ire) KO –15 Johnny Reagan (USA) Long Island, USA

10 Oct 1888 *L* Jack McAuliffe (Ire) KO –10 Bill Dacey (USA) Dover, USA

30 Oct 1888 *W* Paddy Duffy (USA) KO –17 William McMillan (GB) Fort Foote, USA

29 Mar 1889 *W* Paddy Duffy (USA) DIS –45 Tom Meadows (Aus) San Francisco, USA

31 Mar 1889 *Fe* Ike Weir (GB) D –80 Frank Murphy (GB) Kouts, USA. (Police stopped fight.)

27 Aug 1889 *M* George La Blanche (Can) KO –32 Jack Dempsey (Ire) San Francisco, USA (LaBlanche knocked out Dempsey with illegal pivot blow. He was also over the weight limit. Consequently, Dempsey was deemed not to have lost his title.)

13 Jan 1890 *Fe* Billy Murphy (NZ) KO –14 Ike Weir (GB) San Francisco, USA

18 Feb 1890 *M* Jack Dempsey (Ire) KO –28 Billy McCarthy (Aus) San Francisco, USA

27 Jun 1890 *B* George Dixon (Can) KO –18 Nunc Wallace (GB) London, England

3 Sep 1890 *Fe* Young Griffo (Aus) PTS –15 Billy Murphy (NZ) Sydney, Australia

23 Oct 1890 *B* George Dixon (Can) PTS –40 Johnny Murphy (USA) Providence, USA

14 Jan 1891 *M* Bob Fitzsimmons (GB) RSF –15 Jack Dempsey (Ire) New Orleans, USA

31 Mar 1891 *B* George Dixon (Can) RSF –22 Cal McCarthy (USA) Troy, USA

28 Jul 1891 *Fe* George Dixon (Can) KO –5 Abe Willis (Aus) San Francisco, USA

27 Jun 1892 *Fe* George Dixon (Can) KO –14 Fred Johnson (USA) Coney Island, USA

5 Sep 1892 *L* Jack McAuliffe (Ire) KO –15 Billy Myer (USA) New Orleans, USA

6 Sep 1892 *Fe* George Dixon (Can) KO –8 Jack Skelly (USA) New Orleans, USA

7 Sep 1892 *H* James J. Corbett (USA) KO –21 John L. Sullivan (USA) New Orleans, USA

14 Dec 1892 *W* Mysterious Billy Smith (USA) KO –14 Danny Needham (USA) San Francisco, USA

17 Apr 1893 *W* Mysterious Billy Smith (USA) KO –2 Tom Williams (Aus) New York, USA

8 Aug 1893 *Fe* George Dixon (Can) KO –3 Eddie Pierce (USA) Coney Island, USA

25 Sep 1893 *Fe* George Dixon (Can) KO –7 Solly Smith (USA) Coney Island, USA

25 Jan 1894 *H* James J. Corbett (USA) KO –3 Charlie Mitchell (GB) Jacksonville, USA

26 Jul 1894 *W* Tommy Ryan (USA) PTS –20 Mysterious Billy Smith (USA) Minneapolis, USA

26 Sep 1894 *M* Bob Fitzsimmons (GB) KO –2 Dan Creedon (Aus) New Orleans, USA

26 Sep 1894 *Fe* George Dixon (Can) D –20 Young Griffo (Aus) Boston, USA

18 Jan 1895 *W* Tommy Ryan (USA) KO –3 Jack Dempsey (Ire) New York, USA

27 May 1895 *W* Tommy Ryan (USA) D –18 Mysterious Billy Smith (USA) New York, USA. (Police stopped fight.)

27 Aug 1895 *Fe* George Dixon (Can) PTS –25 Johnny Griffin (USA) Boston, USA

2 Mar 1896 *W* Charles 'Kid' McCoy (USA) KO –15 Tommy Ryan (USA) Long Island, USA

1 Jun 1896 *L* George 'Kid' Lavigne (USA) KO –17 Dick Burge (GB) London, England

27 Oct 1896 *L* George 'Kid' Lavigne (USA) KO –24 Jack Everhardt (USA) New York, USA

8 Feb 1897 *L* George 'Kid' Lavigne (USA) PTS –25 Kid McPartland (USA) New York, USA

17 Mar 1897 *H* Bob Fitzsimmons (GB) KO –14 James J. Corbett (USA) Carson City, USA

7 Apr 1897 *Fe* George Dixon (Can) PTS –25 Frank Erne (Swi) New York, USA

28 Apr 1897 *L* George 'Kid' Lavigne (USA) KO –11 Eddie Connolly (USA) New York, USA

4 Oct 1897 *Fe* Solly Smith (USA) PTS –20 George Dixon (Can) San Francisco, USA

29 Oct 1897 *L* George 'Kid' Lavigne (USA) PTS –12 Joe Walcott (Bar) San Francisco, USA

6 Dec 1897 *B* Jimmy Barry (USA) KO –20 Walter Croot (GB) London, England

25 Feb 1898 *M* Tommy Ryan (USA) KO –18 George Green (USA) San Francisco, USA

17 Mar 1898 *L* George 'Kid' Lavigne (USA) D –20 Jack Daly (USA) Cleveland, USA

30 May 1898 *B* Jimmy Barry (USA) D –20 Casper Leon (Ita) New York, USA

25 Aug 1898 *W* Mysterious Billy Smith (USA) PTS –25 Matty Matthews (USA) New York, USA

26 Sep 1898 *Fe* Dave Sullivan (Ire) RTD –5 Solly Smith (USA) Coney Island, USA

28 Sep 1898 *L* George 'Kid' Lavigne (USA) D –20 Franke Erne (Swi) Coney Island, USA

7 Oct 1898 *W* Mysterious Billy Smith (USA) PTS –25 Charley McKeever (USA) New York, USA

24 Oct 1898 *M* Tommy Ryan (USA) PTS –20 Jack Bonner (USA) Coney Island, USA

11 Nov 1898 *Fe* George Dixon (Can) DIS –10 Dave Sullivan (Ire) New York, USA

25 Nov 1898 *L* George 'Kid' Lavigne (USA) PTS –20 Tom Tracy (USA) San Francisco, USA

29 Nov 1898 *Fe* George Dixon (Can) PTS –25 Oscar Gardner (USA) New York, USA

6 Dec 1898 *W* Mysterious Billy Smith (USA) PTS –20 Joe Walcott (Bar) New York, USA

29 Dec 1898 *B* Jimmy Barry (USA) D –20 Casper Leon (Ita) Davenport, USA

17 Jan 1899 *Fe* George Dixon (Can) KO –10 Young Pluto (USA) New York, USA

23 Jan 1899 *W* Mysterious Billy Smith (USA) KO –15 Billy Edwards (Aus) New York, USA

10 Mar 1899 *W* Mysterious Billy Smith (USA) RSF –14 George 'Kid' Lavigne (USA) San Francisco, USA

15 May 1899 *Fe* George Dixon (Can) PTS –20 Kid Broad (USA) Buffalo, USA

2 Jun 1899 *Fe* George Dixon (Can) PTS –25 Joe Bernstein (USA) New York, USA

9 Jun 1899 *H* James J. Jeffries (USA) KO –11 Bob Fitzsimmons (GB) Coney Island, USA

30 Jun 1899 *W* Mysterious Billy Smith (USA) D –20 Charley McKeever (USA) New York, USA

1 Jul 1899 *Fe* George Dixon (Can) PTS –20 Tommy White (USA) Denver, USA

3 Jul 1899 *L* Frank Erne (Swi) PTS –20 George 'Kid' Lavigne (USA) Buffalo, USA

11 Aug 1899 *Fe* George Dixon (Can) D –20 Eddie Santry (USA) New York, USA

12 Sep 1899 *B* Terry McGovern (USA) KO –1 Pedlar Palmer (GB) New York, USA

18 Sep 1899 *M* Tommy Ryan (USA) KO –10 Frank Craig (USA) Coney Island, USA

2 Nov 1899 *Fe* George Dixon (Can) PTS –25 Will Curley (USA) New York, USA

3 Nov 1899 *H* James J. Jeffries (USA) PTS –25 Tom Sharkey (Ire) Coney Island, USA

8 Nov 1899 *W* Mysterious Billy Smith (USA) PTS –20 Charley McKeever (USA) New York, USA

21 Nov 1899 *Fe* George Dixon (Can) PTS –25 Eddie Lenny (USA) New York, USA

4 Dec 1899 *L* Frank Erne (Swi) D –25 Jack O'Brien (USA) Coney Island, USA

22 Dec 1899 *B* Terry McGovern (USA) KO –2 Harry Forbes (USA) New York, USA

9 Jan 1900 *Fe* Terry McGovern (USA) KO –8 George Dixon (Can) New York, USA

15 Jan 1900 *W* Rube Ferns (USA) DIS –21 Mysterious Billy Smith (USA) Buffalo, USA

1 Feb 1900 *Fe* Terry McGovern (USA) KO –5 Eddie Santry (USA) Chicago, USA

9 Mar 1900 *Fe* Terry McGovern (USA) KO –3 Oscar Gardner (USA) New York, USA

23 Mar 1900 *L* Frank Erne (Swi) KO –12 Joe Gans (USA) New York, USA

11 May 1900 *H* James J. Jeffries (USA) KO –23 James J. Corbett (USA) Coney Island, USA

12 Jun 1900 *Fe* Terry McGovern (USA) KO –3 Tommy White (USA) Coney Island, USA

6 Sep 1900 *B* Harry Forbes (USA) D –20 Casper Leon (Ita) St Joseph, USA

16 Oct 1900 *W* Matty Matthews (USA) PTS –15 Rube Ferns (USA) Detroit, USA

2 Nov 1900 *Fe* Terry McGovern (USA) KO –7 Joe Bernstein (USA) Louiseville, USA

4 Mar 1901 *M* Tommy Ryan (USA) KO –17 Tommy West (USA) Louiseville, USA

18 Mar 1901 *B* Harry Harris (USA) PTS –20 Pedlar Palmer (GB) London, England

2 Apr 1901 *B* Harry Forbes (USA) PTS –15 Casper Leon (Ita) Memphis, USA

29 Apr 1901 *W* Matty Matthews (USA) PTS –20 Tom Couhig (USA) Louiseville, USA

30 Apr 1901 *Fe* Terry McGovern (USA) KO –4 Oscar Gardner (USA) San Francisco, USA

24 May 1901 *W* Rube Ferns (USA) KO –10 Matty Matthews (USA) Toronto, Canada

29 May 1901 *Fe* Terry McGovern (USA) KO –5 Aurelio Herrera (USA) San Francisco, USA

23 Sep 1901 *W* Rube Ferns (USA) KO –9 Frank Erne (Swi) Fort Erie, USA

15 Nov 1901 *H* James J. Jeffries (USA) RTD –5 Gus Ruthlin (USA) San Francisco, USA

28 Nov 1901 *Fe* Young Corbett (USA) KO –2 Terry McGovern (USA) Hartford, USA

18 Dec 1901 *W* Joe Walcott (Bar) KO –5 Rube Ferns (USA) Fort Erie, USA

23 Jan 1902 *B* Harry Forbes (USA) KO –4 Dan Dougherty (USA) St Louis, USA

27 Feb 1902 *B* Harry Forbes (USA) PTS –15 Tommy Feltz (USA) St Louis, USA

12 May 1902 *L* Joe Gans (USA) KO –1 Frank Erne (Swi) Fort Erie, USA

23 Jun 1902 *W* Joe Walcott (Bar) PTS –15 Tommy West (GB) London, England

25 Jul 1902 *H* James J. Jeffries (USA) KO –8 Bob Fitzsimmons (GB) San Francisco, USA

15 Sep 1902 *M* Tommy Ryan (USA) KO –6 Kid Carter (USA) Fort Erie, USA

17 Sep 1902 *L* Joe Gans (USA) KO –5 Gus Gardner (USA) Baltimore, USA

23 Dec 1902 *B* Harry Forbes (USA) RSF –7 Frankie Neil (USA) Oakland, USA

27 Feb 1903 *B* Harry Forbes (USA) PTS –10 Andy Tokell (GB) Detroit, USA

11 Mar 1903 *L* Joe Gans (USA) KO –11 Steve Crosby (USA) Hot Springs, USA

'Nonpareil' Jack Dempsey (Ire) retained his world middleweight title in 1887 by knocking out his opponent, Johnny Reagan (USA). The contest took place in two rings. It started at Huntington, Long Island but, in the eighth round, the tide from a nearby river caused the ring to flood. The fighters and spectators boarded a tug and continued the bout some 25 miles away!

Charles 'Kid' McCoy (USA) can claim to be the most married of all world champions with ten marriages to his credit — three to the same woman.

McCoy is also famous for lending his name to a well-known saying. He was a master of tricking his opponents into believing he was ill or in difficulty. Consequently, his opponents were never sure whether he was 'real' or not. And so was born the saying: 'Is it the real McCoy?'

22 Apr 1903 *LH* Jack Root (Aut) PTS –10 Charles 'Kid' McCoy (USA) Detroit, USA

4 Jul 1903 *LH* George Gardner (Ire) KO –12 Jack Root (Aut) Fort Erie, USA

13 Aug 1903 *B* Frankie Neil (USA) KO –2 Harry Forbes (USA) San Francisco, USA

14 Aug 1903 *H* James J. Jeffries (USA) KO –10 James J. Corbett (USA) San Francisco, USA

4 Sep 1903 *B* Frankie Neil (USA) KO –15 Billy de Coursey (USA) Los Angeles, USA

16 Oct 1903 *B* Frankie Neil (USA) D –20 Johnny Reagan (USA) Los Angeles, USA

9 Nov 1903 *M* Tommy Ryan (USA) KO –3 Johnny Gorman (GB) London, England

25 Nov 1903 *LH* Bob Fitzsimmons (GB) PTS –20 George Gardner (Ire) San Francisco, USA

1 Feb 1904 *Fe* Abe Attell (USA) KO –4 Harry Forbes (USA) St Louis, USA

28 Mar 1904 *L* Joe Gans (USA) PTS –10 Gus Gardner (USA) Saginaw, USA

30 Apr 1904 *W* Dixie Kid (USA) DIS –20 Joe Walcott (Bar) San Francisco, USA

12 May 1904 *W* Dixie Kid (USA) D –20 Joe Walcott (Bar) San Francisco, USA

17 Jun 1904 *B* Frankie Neil (USA) KO –3 Harry Forbes (USA) Chicago, USA

26 Aug 1904 *H* James J. Jeffries (USA) KO –2 Jack Munro (USA) San Francisco, USA

17 Oct 1904 *B* Joe Bowker (GB) PTS –20 Frankie Neil (USA) London, England

31 Oct 1904 *L* Joe Gans (USA) DIS –5 Jimmy Britt (USA) San Francisco, USA

22 Feb 1905 *Fe* Abe Attell (USA) D –15 Kid Goodman (USA) Boston, USA

3 Jul 1905 *H* Marvin Hart (USA) RSF –12 Jack Root (Aut) Reno, USA

20 Oct 1905 *B* Jimmy Walsh (USA) PTS –15 Digger Stanley (GB) Chelsea, USA

20 Dec 1905 *LH* Philiadelphia Jack O'Brien (USA) KO –13 Bob Fitzsimmons (GB) San Francisco, USA

23 Feb 1906 *H* Tommy Burns (Can) PTS –20 Marvin Hart (USA) Los Angeles, USA

4 Jul 1906 *Fe* Abe Attell (USA) PTS –20 Frankie Neil (USA) Los Angeles, USA

3 Sep 1906 *L* Joe Gans (USA) DIS –42 Battling Nelson (Den) Goldfield, USA

2 Oct 1906 *H* Tommy Burns (Can) KO –15 Jim Flynn (USA) Los Angeles, USA

16 Oct 1906 *W* Honey Mellody (USA) PTS –15 Joe Walcott (Bar) Chelsea, USA

30 Oct 1906 *Fe* Abe Attell (USA) PTS –20 Harry Baker (USA) Los Angeles, USA

28 Nov 1906 *H/LH* Tommy Burns (Can) D –20 Philadelphia Jack O'Brien (USA) Los Angeles, USA

7 Dec 1906 *Fe* Abe Attell (USA) KO –8 Jimmy Walsh (USA) Los Angeles, USA

18 Jan 1907 *Fe* Abe Attell (USA) KO –8 Harry Baker (USA) Los Angeles, USA

23 Apr 1907 *W* Mike 'Twin' Sullivan (USA) PTS –20 Honey Mellody (USA) Los Angeles, USA

8 May 1907 *H* Tommy Burns (Can) PTS –20 Philadelphia Jack O'Brien (USA) Los Angeles, USA

24 May 1907 *Fe* Abe Attell (USA) PTS –20 Kid Solomon (USA) Los Angeles, USA

4 Jul 1907 *H* Tommy Burns (Can) KO –1 Bill Squires (Aus) Colma, USA

2 Sep 1907 *M* Stanley Ketchel (USA) KO –32 Joe Thomas (USA) Colma, USA

9 Sep 1907 *L* Joe Gans (USA) KO –6 Jimmy Britt (USA) San Francisco, USA

27 Sep 1907 *L* Joe Gans (USA) PTS –20 George Memsic (USA) Los Angeles, USA

29 Oct 1907 *Fe* Abe Attell (USA) KO –4 Freddie Weekes (USA) Los Angeles, USA

2 Dec 1907 *H* Tommy Burns (Can) KO –10 Gunner Moir (GB) London, England

12 Dec 1907 *M* Stanley Ketchel (USA) PTS –20 Joe Thomas (USA) San Francisco, USA

1 Jan 1908 *Fe* Abe Attell (USA) D –25 Owen Moran (GB) San Francisco, USA

10 Feb 1908 *H* Tommy Burns (Can) KO –4 Jack Palmer (GB) London, England

22 Feb 1908 *M* Stanley Ketchel (USA) KO –1 Mike 'Twin' Sullivan (USA) Colma, USA

17 Mar 1908 *H* Tommy Burns (Can) KO –1 Jem Roche (Ire) Dublin, Ireland

1 Apr 1908 *L* Joe Gans (USA) KO –3 Spike Robson (GB) Philadelphia, USA

18 Apr 1908 *H* Tommy Burns (Can) KO –5 Jewey Smith (GB) Paris, France

14 May 1908 *L* Joe Gans (USA) KO –11 Rudy Unholz (USA) San Francisco, USA

4 Jun 1908 *M* Stanley Ketchel (USA) PTS –10 Billy Papke (USA) Milwaukee, USA

13 Jun 1908 *H* Tommy Burns (Can) KO –8 Bill Squires (Aus) Paris, France

4 Jul 1908 *L* Battling Nelson (Den) KO –17 Joe Gans (USA) San Francisco, USA

31 Jul 1908 *M* Stanley Ketchel (USA) KO –3 Hugo Kelly (USA) San Francisco, USA

18 Aug 1908 *M* Stanley Ketchel (USA) KO –2 Joe Thomas (USA) San Francisco, USA

24 Aug 1908 *H* Tommy Burns (Can) KO –13 Bill Squires (Aus) Sydney, Australia

2 Sep 1908 *H* Tommy Burns (Can) KO –6 Bill Lang (Aus) Sydney, Australia

7 Sep 1908 *M* Billy Papke (USA) KO –12 Stanley Ketchel (USA) Vernon, USA

7 Sep 1908 *Fe* Abe Attell (USA) D –23 Owen Moran (GB) San Francisco, USA

9 Sep 1908 *L* Battling Nelson (Den) KO –21 Joe Gans (USA) Colma, USA

26 Nov 1908 *M* Stanley Ketchel (USA) KO –11 Billy Papke (USA) Colma, USA

26 Dec 1908 *H* Jack Johnson (USA) RSF –14 Tommy Burns (Can) Sydney, Australia

26 Mar 1909 *Fe* Abe Attell (USA) KO –8 Frankie White (USA) Dayton, USA

29 May 1909 *L* Battling Nelson (Den) KO –23 Dick Hyland (USA) Colma, USA

22 Jun 1909 *L* Battling Nelson (Den) KO –5 Jack Clifford (USA) Oklahoma, USA

5 Jul 1909 *M* Stanley Ketchel (USA) PTS –20 Billy Papke (USA) Colma, USA

16 Oct 1909 *H* Jack Johnson (USA) KO –12 Stanley Ketchel (USA) Colma, USA

22 Feb 1910 *L* Ad Wolgast (USA) KO –40 Battling Nelson (Den) Port Richmond, USA

28 Feb 1910 *Fe* Abe Attell (USA) KO –6 Harry Forbes (USA) New York, USA

6 Mar 1910 *B* Johnny Coulon (Can) KO –19 Jim Kendrick (GB) New Orleans, USA

19 Mar 1910 *M* Billy Papke (USA) KO –3 Willie Lewis (USA) Paris, France

4 Jul 1910 *H* Jack Johnson (USA) RSF –15 James J. Jeffries (USA) Reno, USA

19 Dec 1910 *B* Johnny Coulon (Can) PTS –15 Earl Denning (USA) Memphis, USA

11 Feb 1911 *M* Cyclone Johnny Thompson (USA) PTS –20 Billy Papke (USA) Sydney, Australia

7 Mar 1911 *L* Ad Wolgast (USA) KO –9 George Memsic (USA) Los Angeles, USA

27 May 1911 *L* Ad Wolgast (USA) KO –16 Frankie Burns (USA) San Francisco, USA

8 Jun 1911 *M* Billy Papke (USA) KO –9 Jim Sullivan (GB) London, England

4 Jul 1911 *L* Ad Wolgast (USA) KO –13 Owen Moran (GB) San Francisco, USA

3 Feb 1912 *B* Johnny Coulon (Can) PTS –20 Frankie Conley (USA) Vernon, USA

18 Feb 1912 *B* Johnny Coulon (Can) PTS –20 Frankie Burns (USA) New Orleans, USA

22 Feb 1912 *Fe* Johnny Kilbane (USA) PTS –20 Abe Attell (USA) Vernon, USA

21 May 1912 *Fe* Johnny Kilbane (USA) D –12 Jimmy Walsh (USA) Boston, USA

29 Jun 1912 *M* Billy Papke (USA) RTD –15 Marcel Moreau (Fra) Paris, France

4 Jul 1912 *H* Jack Johnson (USA) KO –9 Jim Flynn (USA) Las Vegas, USA

4 Jul 1912 *L* Ad Wolgast (USA) KO –13 Joe Rivers (Mex) Vernon, USA

18 Oct 1912 *B* Johnny Coulon (Can) ND –10 Kid Williams (Den) New York, USA

23 Oct 1912 *M* Billy Papke (USA) RTD –17 Georges Carpentier (Fra) Paris, France

28 Nov 1912 *L* Willie Ritchie (USA) DIS –16 Ad Wolgast (USA) Daly City, USA

George Bernard (Fra) suddenly fell asleep at the end of the sixth round of his world middleweight title fight with Billy Papke (USA) in 1912. He could not be revived in time to start the seventh round. He later alleged he had been drugged.

4 Dec 1912 *M* Billy Papke (USA) RTD –6 George Bernard (Fra) Paris, France

5 Mar 1913 *M* Frank Klaus (USA) DIS –15 Billy Papke (USA) Paris, France

29 Apr 1913 *Fe* Johnny Kilbane (USA) D –20 Johnny Dundee (Ita) Vernon, USA

4 Jul 1913 *L* Willie Ritchie (USA) KO –11 Joe Rivers (Mex) San Francisco, USA

11 Oct 1913 *M* George Chip (USA) KO –6 Frank Klaus (USA) Pittsburgh, USA

28 Nov 1913 *H* Jack Johnson (USA) KO –2 Andre Sproul (Fra) Paris, France

19 Dec 1913 *H* Jack Johnson (USA) D –20 Jim Johnson (USA) Paris, France

23 Dec 1913 *M* George Chip (USA) KO –5 Frankie Klaus (USA) Pittsburgh, USA

How The Daily Mirror *front page covered the Jack Johnson–James J. Jeffries (USA) world heavyweight title fight in 1910.* Syndication International

7 Apr 1914 *M* Al McCoy (USA) KO –1 George Chip (USA) Brooklyn, USA

17 Apr 1914 *L* Willie Ritchie (USA) PTS –20 Harlem Tommy Murphy (USA) San Francisco, USA

28 Apr 1914 *LH* Jack Dillon (USA) PTS –10 Al Norton (USA) Kansas City, USA

9 Jun 1914 *B* Kid Williams (Den) KO –3 Johnny Coulon (Can) Los Angeles, USA

27 Jun 1914 *H* Jack Johnson (USA) PTS –20 Frank Moran (USA) Paris, France

7 Jul 1914 *L* Freddie Welsh (GB) PTS –20 Willie Ritchie (USA) London, England

5 Apr 1915 *H* Jess Willard (USA) KO –26 Jack Johnson (USA) Havana, Cuba

31 Aug 1915 *W* Ted 'Kid' Lewis (GB) PTS –12 Jack Britton (USA) Boston, USA

10 Sep 1915 *B* Johnny Ertle (Aut) DIS –5 Kid Williams (Den) St Paul, USA. Williams argued that the bout took place in a town where decisions were prohibited. Consequently he claimed he could not be disqualified. He continued to be regarded as the champion.

27 Sep 1915 *W* Ted 'Kid' Lewis (GB) PTS –12 Jack Britton (USA) Boston, USA

6 Dec 1915 *B* Kid Williams (Den) D –20 Frankie Burns (USA) New Orleans, USA

7 Feb 1916 *B* Kid Williams (Den) D –29 Pete Herman (USA) New Orleans, USA

25 Mar 1916 *H* Jess Willard (USA) ND –10 Frank Moran (USA) New York, USA

24 Apr 1916 *W* Jack Britton (USA) PTS –20 Ted 'Kid' Lewis (GB) New Orleans, USA

25 Apr 1916 *LH* Jack Dillon (USA) PTS –15 Battling Levinsky (USA) Kansas City, USA

4 Jul 1916 *L* Freddie Welsh (GB) DIS –11 Ad Wolgast (USA) Denver, USA

4 Sep 1916 *L* Freddie Welsh (GB) PTS –20 Charlie White (GB) Colorado Springs, USA

4 Sep 1916 *Fe* Johnny Kilbane (USA) KO –3 George 'Kayo' Chaney (USA) Cedar Point, USA

17 Oct 1916 *LH* Jack Dillon (USA) PTS –10 Tim O'Neill (USA) New York, USA

24 Oct 1916 *LH* Battling Levinsky (USA) PTS –12 Jack Dillon (USA) Boston, USA

18 Dec 1916 *Fl* Jimmy Wilde (GB) KO –11 Young Zulu Kid (Ita) London, England

9 Jan 1917 *B* Pete Herman (USA) PTS –20 Kid Williams (Den) New Orleans, USA

12 Mar 1917 *Fl* Jimmy Wilde (GB) RTD –4 George Clark (GB) London, England

---

The last bout under the Frawley Law, which prohibited the giving of points decisions in contests in New York, was the world middleweight title fight between Americans Mike O'Dowd and Al McCoy on 14 November 1917. The result: O'Dowd won with a sixth round knock-out.

---

28 May 1917 *L* Benny Leonard (USA) KO –9 Freddie Welsh (GB) New York, USA

25 Jun 1917 *W* Ted 'Kid' Lewis (GB) PTS –20 Jack Britton (USA) Dayton, USA

4 Jul 1917 *W* Ted 'Kid' Lewis (GB) ND –15 Johnny Griffiths (USA) Akron, USA

25 Jul 1917 *L* Benny Leonard (USA) RTD –3 Johnny Kilbane (USA) Philadelphia, USA

31 Aug 1917 *W* Ted 'Kid' Lewis (GB) KO –1 Albert Badoud (Swe) New York, USA

5 Nov 1917 *B* Pete Herman (USA) PTS –20 Frankie Burns (USA) New Orleans, USA

14 Nov 1917 *M* Mike O'Dowd (USA) KO –6 Al McCoy (USA) Brooklyn, USA

17 May 1918 *W* Ted 'Kid' Lewis (GB) RTD –20 Johnny Tillman (USA) Denver, USA

4 Jul 1918 *W* Ted 'Kid' Lewis (GB) ND –20 Johnny Griffiths (USA) Akron, USA

17 Mar 1919 *W* Jack Britton (USA) KO –9 Ted 'Kid' Lewis (GB) Canton, USA

5 May 1919 *W* Jack Britton (USA) PTS –15 Johnny Griffiths (USA) Buffalo, USA

4 Jul 1919 *H* Jack Dempsey (USA) RTD –3 Jess Willard (USA) Toledo, USA

17 Jul 1919 *M* Mike O'Dowd (USA) KO –3 Al McCoy (USA) St Paul, USA

21 Apr 1920 *Fe* Johnny Kilbane (USA) KO –7 Alvie Miller (USA) Lorian, USA

6 May 1920 *M* Johnny Wilson (USA) PTS –12 Mike O'Dowd (USA) Boston, USA

31 May 1920 *W* Jack Britton (USA) PTS –15 Johnny Griffiths (USA) Akron, USA

5 Jul 1920 *L* Benny Leonard (USA) KO –8 Charlie White (USA) Benton Harbor, USA

23 Aug 1920 *W* Jack Britton (USA) D –12 Lou Bogash (USA) Bridgeport, USA

6 Sep 1920 *H* Jack Dempsey (USA) KO –3 Billy Miske (USA) Benton Harbor, USA

12 Oct 1920 *LH* Georges Carpentier (Fra) KO –4 Battling Levinsky (USA) Jersey City, USA

26 Nov 1920 *L* Benny Leonard (USA) RSF –14 Joe Welling (USA) New York, USA

14 Dec 1920 *H* Jack Dempsey (USA) KO –12 Bill Brennan (USA) New York, USA

22 Dec 1920 *B* Joe Lynch (USA) PTS –15 Pete Herman (USA) New York, USA

14 Jan 1921 *L* Benny Leonard (USA) RSF –6 Ritchie Mitchell (USA) New York, USA

17 Jan 1921 *M* Johnny Wilson (USA) ND –12 George Chip (USA) Pittsburgh, USA

7 Feb 1921 *W* Jack Britton (USA) PTS –15 Ted 'Kid' Lewis (GB) New York, USA

17 Mar 1921 *M* Johnny Wilson (USA) PTS –15 Mike O'Dowd (USA) New York, USA

2 Jul 1921 *H* Jack Dempsey (USA) KO –4 Georges Carpentier (Fra) New Jersey, USA

25 Jul 1921 *B* Pete Herman (USA) PTS –15 Joe Lynch (USA) Brooklyn, USA

5 Sep 1921 *M* Johnny Wilson (USA) ND –12 Bryan Downey (USA) Jersey City, USA

17 Sep 1921 *Fe* Johnny Kilbane (USA) KO –7 Danny Frush (GB) Cleveland, USA

23 Sep 1921 *B* Johnny Buff (USA) PTS –15 Pete Herman (USA) New York, USA

10 Nov 1921 *B* Johnny Buff (USA) PTS –15 Little Jack Sharkey (Ita) New York, USA

18 Nov 1921 *JL* Johnny Dundee (Ita) DIS –5 George Chaney (USA) New York, USA

10 Feb 1922 *L* Benny Leonard (USA) PTS –15 Rocky Kansas (USA) New York, USA

17 Feb 1922 *W* Jack Britton (USA) D –15 Dave Shade (USA) New York, USA

11 May 1922 *LH* Georges Carpentier (Fra) KO –1 Ted 'Kid' Lewis (GB) London, England

26 Jun 1922 *W* Jack Britton (USA) DIS –13 Benny Leonard (USA) New York, USA

4 Jul 1922 *L* Benny Leonard (USA) RTD –8 Rocky Kansas (USA) Michigan, USA

8 Jul 1922 *JL* Johnny Dundee (Ita) PTS –15 Little Jack Sharkey (Ita) New York, USA

10 Jul 1922 *B* Joe Lynch (USA) RTD –14 Johnny Buff (USA) New York, USA

14 Aug 1922 *M(NY)* Dave Rosenberg (USA) PTS –15 Phil Krug (USA) New York, USA

15 Aug 1922 *Fe(NY)* Johnny Dundee (Ita) KO –9 Danny Frush (GB) Brooklyn, USA

24 Sep 1922 *LH* Battling Siki (Sen) KO –6 Georges Carpentier (Fra) Paris, France

1 Nov 1922 *W* Mickey Walker (USA) PTS –15 Jack Britton (USA) New York, USA

30 Nov 1922 *M(NY)* Mike O'Dowd (USA) DIS –8 Dave Rosenberg (USA) New York, USA

22 Dec 1922 *B* Joe Lynch (USA) PTS –15 Midget Smith (USA) New York, USA

2 Feb 1923 *JL* Johnny Dundee (Ita) PTS –15 Elino Flores (Phi) New York, USA

17 Mar 1923 *LH* Mike McTigue (Ire) PTS –20 Battling Siki (Sen) Dublin, Ireland

22 Mar 1923 *W* Mickey Walker (USA) ND –12 Pete Latzo (USA) Newark, USA

30 May 1923 *JL* Jack Bernstein (USA) PTS –15 Johnny Dundee (Ita) New York, USA

2 Jun 1923 *Fe* Eugene Criqui (Fra) KO –6 Johnny Kilbane (USA) New York, USA

18 Jun 1923 *Fl* Pancho Villa (Phi) KO –7 Jimmy Wilde (GB) New York, USA

4 Jul 1923 *H* Jack Dempsey (USA) PTS –15 Tom Gibbons (USA) Shelby, USA

24 Jul 1923 *L* Benny Leonard (USA) PTS –15 Lew Tendler (USA) New York, USA

26 Jul 1923 *Fe* Johnny Dundee (Ita) PTS –15 Eugene Criqui (Fra) New York, USA

31 Aug 1923 *M* Harry Greb (USA) PTS –15 Johnny Wilson (USA) New York, USA

14 Sep 1923 *H* Jack Dempsey (USA) KO –2 Luis 'Angel' Firpo (Arg) New York, USA

13 Oct 1923 *Fl* Pancho Villa (Phi) PTS –15 Benny Schwartz (USA) Baltimore, USA

19 Oct 1923 *B(NY)* Abe Goldstein (USA) PTS –12 Joe Burman (USA) New York, USA

3 Dec 1923 *M* Harry Greb (USA) PTS –10 Bryan Downey (USA) Pittsburgh, USA

17 Dec 1923 *JL* Johnny Dundee (Ita) PTS –15 Jack Bernstein (USA) New York, USA

Georges Carpentier (left) unsuccessfully challenged Jack Dempsey (USA) for the world heavyweight crown in 1921. Dempsey knocked the Frenchman out in the fourth round. Mary Evans Picture Library

18 Jan 1924 *M* Harry Greb (USA) PTS –15 Johnny Wilson (USA) New York, USA

21 Mar 1924 *B* Abe Goldstein (USA) PTS –15 Joe Lynch (USA) New York, USA

24 Mar 1924 *M* Harry Greb (USA) KO –12 Fay Kaiser (USA) Baltimore, USA

20 May 1924 *Fl* Pancho Villa (Phi) PTS –15 Frankie Ash (USA) Brooklyn, USA

2 Jun 1924 *W* Mickey Walker (USA) PTS –10 Lew Tendler (USA) Philadelphia, USA

20 Jun 1924 *JL* Steve 'Kid' Sullivan (USA) PTS –15 Johnny Dundee (Ita) New York, USA

26 Jun 1924 *M* Harry Greb (USA) PTS –15 Ted Moore (GB) New York, USA

16 Jul 1924 *B* Abe Goldstein (USA) PTS –15 Charles Ledoux (Fra) New York, USA

8 Sep 1924 *B* Abe Goldstein (USA) PTS –15 Tommy Ryan (USA) New York, USA

12 Oct 1924 *W* Mickey Walker (USA) KO –6 Bobby Barrett (USA) Philadelphia, USA

15 Oct 1924 *JL* Steve 'Kid' Sullivan (USA) KO –5 Mike Ballerino (USA) New York, USA

19 Dec 1924 *B* Eddie 'Cannonball' Martin (USA) PTS –15 Abe Goldstein (USA) New York, USA

The only known instance of a boxer getting married on the morning of a world title fight was in 1917 when Pete Herman (USA) took his wedding vows on the morning of his bantamweight fight with Frankie Burns (USA).

2 Jan 1925 *Fe* Louis 'Kid' Kaplan (USSR) RTD –9 Danny Kramer (USA) New York, USA

20 Mar 1925 *B* Charley Phil Rosenberg (USA) PTS –15 Eddie 'Cannonball' Martin (USA) New York, USA

1 Apr 1925 *JL* Mike Ballerino (USA) PTS –10 Steve 'Kid' Sullivan (USA) Philadelphia, USA

31 May 1925 *LH* Paul Berlenbach (USA) PTS –15 Mike McTigue (Ire) New York, USA

2 Jul 1925 *M* Harry Greb (USA) PTS –15 Mickey Walker (USA) New York, USA

13 Jul 1925 *L* Jimmy Goodrich (USA) KO –2 Stanislaus Loayza (Chi) Long Island, USA

23 Jul 1925 *B* Charley Phil Rosenberg (USA) KO –4 Eddie Shea (USA) New York, USA

22 Aug 1925 *Fl* Fidel La Barba (USA) PTS –10 Frankie Genaro (USA) Los Angeles, USA

27 Aug 1925 *Fe* Louis 'Kid' Kaplan (USSR) D –15 Babe Herman (Por) Waterbury, USA

11 Sep 1925 *LH* Paul Berlenbach (USA) PTS –15 Jimmy Slattery (USA) New York, USA

12 Sep 1925 *W* Mickey Walker (USA) PTS –15 Dave Shade (USA) New York, USA

13 Nov 1925 *M* Harry Greb (USA) PTS –15 Tony Marullo (USA) New Orleans, USA

2 Dec 1925 *JL* Tod Morgan (USA) KO –10 Mike Ballerino (USA) Los Angeles, USA

8 Dec 1925 *L* Rocky Kansas (USA) PTS –15 Jimmy Goodrich (USA) New York, USA

11 Dec 1925 *LH* Paul Berlenbach (USA) PTS –15 Jack Delaney (Can) New York, USA

18 Dec 1925 *Fe* Louis 'Kid' Kaplan (USSR) PTS –15 Babe Herman (Por) New York, USA

26 Feb 1926 *M* Tiger Flowers (USA) PTS –15 Harry Greb (USA) New York, USA

2 Mar 1926 *B* Charley Phil Rosenberg (USA) PTS –10 George Butch (USA) St Louis, USA

20 May 1926 *W* Pete Latzo (USA) PTS –10 Mickey Walker (USA) Scranton, USA

10 Jun 1926 *LH* Paul Berlenbach (USA) PTS –15 Young Stribling (USA) New York, USA

29 Jun 1926 *W* Pete Latzo (USA) KO –5 Willie Harmon (USA) Newark, USA

3 Jul 1926 *L* Sammy Mandell (USA) PTS –10 Rocky Kansas (USA) Chicago, USA

9 Jul 1926 *W* Pete Latzo (USA) DIS –4 George Levine (USA) New York, USA

16 Jul 1926 *LH* Jack Delaney (Can) PTS –15 Paul Berlenbach (USA) New York, USA

19 Aug 1926 *M* Tiger Flowers (USA) PTS –15 Harry Greb (USA) New York, USA

21 Sep 1926 *LW* Mushy Callahan (USA) PTS –10 Pinkey Mitchell (USA) Vernon, USA

23 Sep 1926 *H* Gene Tunney (USA) PTS –10 Jack Dempsey (USA) Philadelphia, USA

19 Nov 1926 *JL* Tod Morgan (USA) PTS –15 Carl Duane (USA) New York, USA

3 Dec 1926 *M* Mickey Walker (USA) PTS –10 Tiger Flowers (USA) Chicago, USA

21 Jan 1927 *Fl* Fidel La Barba (USA) PTS –12 Elky Clark (GB) New York, USA

26 Mar 1927 *B(NBA)* Bud Taylor (USA) D –10 Tony Canzoneri (USA) Chicago, USA

3 Jun 1927 *W* Joe Dundee (Ita) PTS –15 Pete Latzo (USA) New York, USA

24 Jun 1927 *B(NBA)* Bud Taylor (USA) PTS –10 Tony Canzoneri (USA) Chicago, USA

30 Jun 1927 *M* Mickey Walker (USA) KO –10 Tommy Milligan (GB) London, England

30 Aug 1927 *LH(NBA)* Jimmy Slattery (USA) PTS –10 Maxie Rosenbloom (USA) Hartford, USA

19 Sep 1927 *Fe* Benny Bass (USSR) PTS –10 Red Chapman (USA) Philadelphia, USA

22 Sep 1927 *H* Gene Tunney (USA) PTS –10 Jack Dempsey (USA) Chicago, USA

7 Oct 1927 *LH* Tommy Loughran (USA) PTS –15 Mike McTigue (Ire) New York, USA

24 Oct 1927 *Fe(NY)* Tony Canzoneri (USA) PTS –15 Johnny Dundee (Ita) New York, USA

28 Nov 1927 *Fl(NBA)* Albert 'Frenchie' Belanger (Can) PTS –10 Frankie Genaro (USA) Toronto, Canada

12 Dec 1927 *LH* Tommy Loughran (USA) PTS –15 Jimmy Slattery (USA) New York, USA

16 Dec 1927 *Fl(NY)* Corporal Izzy Schwartz (USA) PTS –15 Newsboy Brown (USSR) New York, USA

19 Dec 1927 *Fl(NBA)* Albert 'Frenchie' Belanger (Can) PTS –10 Ernie Jarvis (GB) Toronto, Canada

6 Jan 1928 *LH* Tommy Loughran (USA) PTS –15 Leo Lomski (USA) New York, USA.

6 Feb 1928 *Fl(NBA)* Frankie Genaro (USA) PTS –10 Albert 'Frenchie' Belanger (Can) Toronto, Canada

10 Feb 1928 *Fe* Tony Canzoneri (USA) PTS –15 Benny Bass (USSR) New York, USA

9 Apr 1928 *Fl(NY)* Corporal Izzy Schwartz (USA) PTS –15 Routier Parra (Arg) New York, USA

21 May 1928 *L* Sammy Mandell (USA) PTS –15 Jimmy McLarnin (Ire) New York, USA

23 May 1928 *B(NY)* Bushy Graham (Ita) PTS –15 Corporal Izzy Schwartz (USA) Brooklyn, USA

1 Jun 1928 *LH* Tommy Loughran (USA) PTS –15 Pete Latzo (USA) Brooklyn, USA

21 Jun 1928 *M* Mickey Walker (USA) PTS –10 Ace Hudkins (USA) Chicago, USA

7 Jul 1928 *W* Joe Dundee (Ita) KO –8 Hilario Martinez (Spa) Barcelona, Spain

16 Jul 1928 *LH* Tommy Loughran (USA) PTS –10 Pete Latzo (USA) Wilkes-Barre, USA

18 Jul 1928 *JL* Tod Morgan (USA) PTS –15 Eddie 'Cannonball' Martin (USA) New York, USA

20 Jul 1928 *Fl(NY)* Corporal Izzy Schwartz (USA) DIS –4 Frisco Grande (Phi) New York, USA

23 Jul 1928 *H* Gene Tunney (USA) RSF –11 Tom Heeney (NZ) New York, USA

28 Sep 1928 *Fe* Andre Routis (Fra) PTS –15 Tony Canzoneri (USA) New York, USA

The last world heavyweight title fight over a scheduled ten rounds was the Gene Tunney–Jack Dempsey 'Battle of the Long Count' on 22 September 1927.

2 Mar 1929 *Fl(NBA)* Emile Pladner (Fra) KO –1 Frankie Genaro (USA) Paris, France

12 Mar 1929 *Fl(NY)* Corporal Izzy Schwartz (USA) PTS –12 Albert 'Frenchie' Belanger (Can) Toronto, Canada

25 Mar 1929 *W* Jackie Fields (USA) PTS –10 Young Jack Thompson (USA) Chicago, USA

28 Mar 1929 *LH* Tommy Loughran (USA) PTS –10 Mickey Walker (USA) Chicago, USA

5 Apr 1929 *JL* Tod Morgan (USA) PTS –10 Santiago Zorilla (Pan) Los Angeles, USA

18 Apr 1929 *Fl(NBA)* Frankie Genaro (USA) DIS –5 Emile Pladner (Fra) Paris, France

20 May 1929 *JL* Tod Morgan (USA) PTS –10 Baby Salsorio (Mex) Los Angeles, USA

18 Jun 1929 *B* Panama Al Brown (Pan) PTS –15 Vidal Gregorio (Spa) New York, USA

18 Jul 1929 *LH* Tommy Loughran (USA) PTS –15 Jimmy Braddock (USA) New York, USA

25 Jul 1929 *W* Jackie Fields (USA) DIS –2 Joe Dundee (Ita) Detroit, USA

25 Jul 1929 *Fe* Andre Routis (Fra) KO –3 Buster Brown (USA) Baltimore, USA

2 Aug 1929 *L* Sammy Mandell (USA) PTS –10 Tony Canzoneri (USA) Chicago, USA

23 Sep 1929 *Fe* Battling Battalino (USA) PTS –15 Andre Routis (Fra) Hartford, USA

17 Oct 1929 *Fl(NBA)* Frankie Genaro (USA) PTS –15 Ernie Jarvis (GB) London, England

29 Oct 1929 *M* Mickey Walker (USA) PTS –10 Ace Hudkins (USA) Los Angeles, USA

19 Dec 1929 *JL* Benny Bass (USSR) KO –2 Tod Morgan (USA) New York, USA

18 Jan 1930 *Fl(NBA)* Frankie Genaro (USA) RTD –12 Yvon Trevidic (Fra) Paris, France

10 Feb 1930 *LH(NY)* Jimmy Slattery (USA) PTS –15 Lou Scozza (USA) Buffalo, USA

18 Feb 1930 *LW(NY)* Jack 'Kid' Berg (GB) RTD –10 Mushy Callahan (USA) London, England

21 Mar 1930 *Fl(NY)* Midget Wolgast (USA) PTS –15 Black Bill (USA) New York, USA

9 May 1930 *W* Young Jack Thompson (USA) PTS –15 Jackie Fields (USA) Detroit, USA

16 May 1930 *Fl(NY)* Midget Wolgast (USA) RTD –5 Willie La Morte (USA) New York, USA

10 Jun 1930 *Fl(NBA)* Frankie Genaro (USA) PTS –10 Albert 'Frenchie' Belanger (Can) Toronto, Canada

12 Jun 1930 *H* Max Schmeling (Ger) DIS –4 Jack Sharkey (USA) New York, USA

12 June 1930 *LW(NY)* Jack 'Kid' Berg (GB) RSF –10 Herman Perlick (USA) New York, USA

25 Jun 1930 *LH(NY)* Maxie Rosenbloom (USA) PTS –15 Jimmy Slattery (USA) Buffalo, USA

17 Jul 1930 *L* Al Singer (USA) KO –1 Sammy Mandell (USA) New York, USA

6 Aug 1930 *Fl(NBA)* Frankie Genaro (USA) PTS –10 Willie La Morte (USA) Newark, USA

3 Sep 1930 *LW(NY)* Jack 'Kid' Berg (GB) PTS –10 Buster Brown (USA) Newark, USA

5 Sep 1930 *W* Tommy Freeman (USA) PTS –15 Young Jack Thompson (USA) Cleveland, USA

4 Oct 1930 *B* Panama Al Brown (Pan) PTS –15 Eugene Huat (Fra) Paris, France

22 Oct 1930 *LH(NY)* Maxie Rosenbloom (USA) KO –11 Abe Bain (USA) New York, USA

14 Nov 1930 *L* Tony Canzoneri (USA) KO –1 Al Singer (USA) New York, USA

2 Dec 1930 *Fe* Battling Battalino (USA) PTS –15 Kid Chocolate (Cuba) New York, USA

26 Dec 1930 *Fl* Frankie Genaro (USA) D –15 Midget Wolgast (USA) New York, USA

9 Jan 1931 *W* Tommy Freeman (USA) PTS –10 Pete August (USA) Hot Springs, USA

23 Jan 1931 *LW* Jack 'Kid' Berg (GB) PTS –10 Goldie Hess (Nor) Chicago, USA

26 Jan 1931 *W* Tommy Freeman (USA) PTS –10 Eddie Murdock (USA) Oklahoma, USA

5 Feb 1931 *W* Tommy Freeman (USA) KO –5 Duke Trammel (USA) Memphis, USA

9 Feb 1931 *W* Tommy Freeman (USA) KO –5 Al 'Kid' Kober (USA) New Orleans, USA

11 Feb 1931 *B* Panama Al Brown (Pan) PTS –10 Nick Bensa (Fra) Paris, France

1 Mar 1931 *W* Tommy Freeman (USA) KO –12 Alfredo Gaona (Mex) Mexico City, Mexico

25 Mar 1931 *Fl(NBA)* Frankie Genaro (USA) D –15 Victor Ferrand (Spa) Barcelona, Spain

14 Apr 1931 *W* Young Jack Thompson (USA) KO –12 Tommy Freeman (USA) Cleveland, USA

23 Apr 1931 *LW/L* Tony Canzoneri (USA) KO –3 Jack 'Kid' Berg (GB) Chicago, USA

22 May 1931 *Fe* Battling Battalino (USA) PTS –15 Fidel La Barba (USA) New York, USA

1 Jul 1931 *Fe* Battling Battalino (USA) PTS –10 Irish Bobby Brady (USA) Jersey City, USA

3 Jul 1931 *H* Max Schmeling (Ger) RSF –15 Young Stribling (USA) Cleveland, USA

13 Jul 1931 *LW* Tony Canzoneri (USA) PTS –10 Cecil Payne (USA) Los Angeles, USA

13 Jul 1931 *Fl(NY)* Midget Wolgast (USA) PTS –15 Ruby Bradley (USA) New York, USA

15 Jul 1931 *JL* Kid Chocolate (Cuba) RSF –7 Benny Bass (USSR) Philadelphia, USA

23 Jul 1931 *Fe* Battling Battalino (USA) PTS –15 Freddie Miller (USA) Cincinnati, USA

30 Jul 1931 *Fl(NBA)* Frankie Genaro (USA) KO –6 Jackie Harmon (USA) Waterbury, USA

5 Aug 1931 *LH(NY)* Maxie Rosenbloom (USA) PTS –15 Jimmy Slattery (USA) New York, USA

25 Aug 1931 *M(NBA)* Gorilla Jones (USA) PTS –10 Tiger Thomas (USA) Milwaukee, USA

25 Aug 1931 *B* Panama Al Brown (Pan) PTS –15 Pete Sanstol (Nor) Montreal, Canada

10 Sep 1931 *L* Tony Canzoneri (USA) PTS –15 Jack 'Kid' Berg (GB) New York, USA

3 Oct 1931 *Fl(NBA)* Frankie Genaro (USA) PTS –15 Valentin Angelmann (Fra) Paris, France

23 Oct 1931 *W* Lou Brouillard (Can) PTS –15 Young Jack Thompson (USA) Boston, USA

27 Oct 1931 *B* Panama Al Brown (Pan) PTS –15 Eugene Huat (Fra) Montreal, Canada

27 Oct 1931 *Fl(IBU)* Young Perez (Tun) KO –2 Frankie Genaro (USA) Paris, France

29 Oct 1931 *LW* Tony Canzoneri (USA) PTS –10 Phillie Griffin (USA) Newark, USA

Italy's Primo Carnera (here seen dressed as a caveman for a ball at the Royal Opera House!) was the heaviest man to hold the world heavyweight title, weighing in at 270lb in 1934. He was dressed more conventionally for his four world title fights! BBC Hulton Picture Library

4 Nov 1931 *Fe* Batting Battalino (USA) PTS –10 Eddie Mastro (USA) Chicago, USA

20 Nov 1931 *LW/L* Tony Canzoneri (USA) PTS –15 Kid Chocolate (Cuba) New York, USA

18 Jan 1932 *LW* Johnny Jadick (USA) PTS –10 Tony Canzoneri (USA) Philadelphia, USA

25 Jan 1932 *M(NBA)* Gorilla Jones (USA) KO –6 Oddone Piazza (Ita) Milwaukee, USA

28 Jan 1932 *W* Jackie Fields (USA) PTS –10 Lou Brouillard (Can) Chicago, USA

18 Mar 1932 *LH(NBA)* George Nichols (USA) PTS –10 Dave Maier (USA) Chicago, USA

26 Apr 1932 *M(NBA)* Gorilla Jones (USA) PTS –12 Young Terry (USA) Trenton, USA

26 May 1932 *Fe(NBA)* Tommy Paul (USA) PTS –15 Johnny Pena (USA) Detroit, USA

31 May 1932 *LH(NBA)* Lou Scozza (USA) PTS –10 George Nichols (USA) Buffalo, USA

11 Jun 1932 *M(NBA)* Marcel Thil (Fra) DIS –11 Gorilla Jones (USA) Paris, France

21 Jun 1932 *H* Jack Sharkey (USA) PTS –15 Max Schmeling (Ger) Long Island, USA

4 Jul 1932 *M(NBA)* Marcel Thil (Fra) PTS –15 Len Harvey (GB) London, England

10 Jul 1932 *B* Panama Al Brown (Pan) PTS –15 Kid Francis (Fra) Marseilles, France

14 Jul 1932 *LH* Maxie Rosenbloom (USA) PTS –15 Lou Scozza (USA) Buffalo, USA

18 Jul 1932 *LW* Johnny Jadick (USA) PTS –10 Tony Canzoneri (USA) Philadelphia, USA

4 Aug 1932 *Fe(NY)* Kid Chocolate (Cuba) PTS –10 Eddie Shea (USA) Chicago, USA

19 Sep 1932 *B* Panama Al Brown (Pan) KO –1 Emile Pladner (Fra) Toronto, Canada

13 Oct 1932 *Fe(NY)* Kid Chocolate (Cuba) KO –12 Lew Feldman (USA) New York USA

31 Oct 1932 *Fl(IBU)* Jackie Brown (GB) RSF –13 Young Perez (Tun) Manchester, England

4 Nov 1932 *L* Tony Canzoneri (USA) PTS –15 Billy Petrolle (USA) New York, USA

21 Nov 1932 *M(NY)* Ben Jeby (USA) PTS –15 Chick Devlin (USA) New York, USA

9 Dec 1932 *Fe(NY)* Kid Chocolate (Cuba) PTS –15 Fidel La Barba (USA) New York, USA

13 Jan 1933 *M(NY)* Ben Jeby (USA) KO –12 Frank Battaglia (Can) New York, USA

13 Jan 1933 *Fe(NBA)* Freddie Miller (USA) PTS –10 Tommy Paul (USA) Chicago, USA

30 Jan 1933 *M(NBA)* Gorilla Jones (USA) KO –7 Sammy Slaughter (USA) Cleveland, USA

20 Feb 1933 *LW* Battling Shaw (Mex) PTS –10 Johnny Jadick (USA) New Orleans, USA

22 Feb 1933 *LH* Maxie Rosenbloom (USA) PTS –10 Al Stillman (USA) St Louis, USA

22 Feb 1933 *W* Young Corbett III (Ita) PTS –10 Jackie Fields (USA) San Francisco, USA

24 Feb 1933 *Fe(NBA)* Freddie Miller (USA) PTS –10 Baby Arizmendi (Mex) Los Angeles, USA

10 Mar 1933 *LH* Maxie Rosenbloom (USA) PTS –15 Ad Heuser (Ger) New York, USA

17 Mar 1933 *M(NY)* Ben Jeby (USA) D –15 Vince Dundee (Ita) New York, USA

18 Mar 1933 *B* Panama Al Brown (Pan) PTS –12 Dom Bernasconi (Ita) Milan, Italy

21 Mar 1933 *Fe(NY)* Freddie Miller (USA) PTS –10 Speedy Dado (Phi) Los Angeles, USA

24 Mar 1933 *LH* Maxie Rosenbloom (USA) KO –4 Bob Godwin (USA) New York, USA

9 May 1933 *Fe(NY)* Kid Chocolate (Cuba) PTS –15 Seaman Tommy Watson (GB) New York, USA

21 May 1933 *LW* Tony Canzoneri (USA) PTS –10 Battling Shaw (Mex) New Orleans, USA

29 May 1933 *W* Jimmy McLarnin (Ire) KO –1 Young Corbett III (Ita) Los Angeles, USA

12 Jun 1933 *Fl(IBU)* Jackie Brown (GB) PTS –15 Valentin Angelmann (Fra) London, England

23 Jun 1933 *LW/L* Barney Ross (USA) PTS –10 Tony Canzoneri (USA) Chicago, USA

29 Jun 1933 *H* Primo Carnera (Ita) KO –6 Jack Sharkey (USA) Long Island, USA

3 Jul 1933 *B* Panama Al Brown (Pan) PTS –15 Johnny King (GB) Manchester, England

10 Jul 1933 *M(NY)* Ben Jeby (USA) PTS –15 Young Terry (USA) Newark, USA

9 Aug 1933 *M(NY)* Lou Brouillard (Can) KO –7 Ben Jeby (USA) New York, USA

11 Sep 1933 *Fl(IBU)* Jackie Brown (GB) PTS –15 Valentin Angelmann (Fra) Manchester, England

12 Sep 1933 *L* Barney Ross (USA) PTS –15 Tony Canzoneri (USA) New York, USA

2 Oct 1933 *M(NBA)* Marcel Thil (Fra) PTS –15 Kid Tunero (Cuba) Paris, France

22 Oct 1933 *H* Primo Carnera (Ita) PTS –15 Paulino Uzcudun (Spa) Rome, Italy

30 Oct 1933 *M(NY)* Vince Dundee (Ita) PTS –15 Lou Brouillard (Can) Boston, USA

3 Nov 1933 *LH* Maxie Rosenbloom (USA) PTS –15 Mickey Walker (USA) New York, USA

17 Nov 1933 *LW* Barney Ross (USA) PTS –10 Sammy Fuller (USA) Chicago, USA

8 Dec 1933 *M(NY)* Vince Dundee (Ita) PTS –15 Andy Callahan (USA) Boston, USA

11 Dec 1933 *Fl(IBU)* Jackie Brown (GB) PTS –15 Ginger Foran (GB) Manchester, England

26 Dec 1933 *JL* Frankie Klick (USA) KO –7 Kid Chocolate (Cuba) Philadelphia, USA

1 Jan 1934 *Fe(NBA)* Freddie Miller (USA) PTS –10 Little Jack Sharkey (USA) Chicago, USA

5 Feb 1934 *LH* Maxie Rosenbloom (USA) D –15 Joe Knight (USA) Miami, USA

7 Feb 1934 *LW* Barney Ross (USA) PTS –12 Pete Nebo (USA) Kansas City, USA

9 Feb 1934 *B* Panama Al Brown (Pan) PTS –15 Young Perez (Tun) Paris, France

26 Feb 1934 *M(NBA)* Marcel Thil (Fra) PTS –15 Ignacio Ara (Spa) Paris, France

1 Mar 1934 *H* Primo Carnera (Ita) PTS –15 Tommy Loughran (USA) Miami, USA

5 Mar 1934 *LW* Barney Ross (USA) D –10 Frankie Klick (USA) San Francisco, USA

1 May 1934 *M(NY)* Vince Dundee (Ita) PTS –15 Al Diamond (USA) Paterson, USA

3 May 1934 *M(NBA)* Marcel Thil (Fra) PTS –15 Gustave Roth (Bel) Paris, France

---

The first all-European world heavyweight title fight took place on 22 October 1933 when Italy's Primo Carnera fought Spain's Paulino Uzcudun.

---

28 May 1934 *W* Barney Ross (USA) PTS –15 Jimmy McLarnin (Ire) New York, USA

2 Jun 1934 *B(NBA)* Sixto Escobar (PR) KO –9 Baby Casanova (Mex) Montreal, Canada

14 Jun 1934 *H* Max Baer (USA) KO –11 Primo Carnera (Ita) Long Island, USA

18 Jun 1934 *Fl(IBU)* Jackie Brown (GB) D –15 Valentin Angelmann (Fra) Manchester, England

8 Aug 1934 *B(NBA)* Sixto Escobar (PR) PTS –15 Eugene Huat (Fra) Montreal, Canada

30 Aug 1934 *Fe(NY)* Baby Arizmendi (Mex) PTS –15 Mike Belloise (USA) New York, USA

11 Sep 1934 *M(NY)* Teddy Yarosz (USA) PTS –15 Vince Dundee (Ita) Pittsburgh, USA

17 Sep 1934 *W* Jimmy McLarnin (Ire) PTS –15 Barney Ross (USA) New York, USA

21 Sep 1934 *Fe(NBA)* Freddie Miller (USA) PTS –15 Nel Tarleton (GB) Liverpool England

15 Oct 1934 *M(NBA)* Marcel Thil (Fra) D –15 Carmelo Candel (Fra) Paris, France

16 Nov 1934 *LH* Bob Olin (USA) PTS –15 Maxie Rosenbloom (USA) New York, USA

10 Dec 1934 *LW* Barney Ross (USA) PTS –12 Bobby Pacho (Mex) Cleveland, USA

28 Jan 1935 *LW* Barney Ross (USA) PTS –10 Frankie Klick (USA) Miami, USA

17 Feb 1935 *Fe(NBA)* Freddie Miller (USA) KO –1 Jose Girones (Spa) Barcelona, Spain

9 Apr 1935 *LW* Barney Ross (USA) PTS –12 Henry Woods (USA) Seattle, USA

10 May 1935 *L* Tony Canzoneri (USA) PTS –15 Lou Ambers (USA) New York, USA

28 May 1935 *W* Barney Ross (USA) PTS –15 Jimmy McLarnin (Ire) New York, USA

1 Jun 1935 *B(NY)* Baltazar Sangchilli (Spa) PTS –15 Panama Al Brown (Pan) Valencia, Spain

2 Jun 1935 *M(NBA)* Marcel Thil (Fra) PTS –15 Ignacio Ara (Spa) Madrid, Spain

12 Jun 1935 *Fe(NBA)* Freddie Miller (USA) PTS –15 Nel Tarleton (GB) Liverpool, England

13 Jun 1935 *H* James J. Braddock (USA) PTS –15 Max Baer (USA) Long Island, USA

28 Jun 1935 *M(NBA)* Marcel Thil (Frac) PTS –10 Carmelo Candel (Fra) Paris, France

26 Aug 1935 *B(NBA)* Lou Salica (USA) PTS –15 Sixto Escobar (PR) New York, USA

9 Sep 1935 *Fl(IBU)* Benny Lynch (GB) RTD –2 Jackie Brown (GB) Manchester, England

16 Sep 1935 *Fl(NY)* Small Montana (Phi) PTS –10 Midget Wolgast (USA) Oakland, USA

19 Sep 1935 *M(NY)* Ed 'Babe' Risko (USA) PTS –15 Teddy Yarosz (USA) Pittsburgh, USA

4 Oct 1935 *L* Tony Canzoneri (USA) PTS –15 Al Roth (USA) New York, USA

22 Oct 1935 *Fe(NBA)* Freddie Miller (USA) PTS –15 Vernon Cormier (USA) Boston, USA

31 Oct 1935 *LH* John Henry Lewis (USA) PTS –15 Bob Olin (USA) St Louis, USA

15 Nov 1935 *B(NBA)* Sixto Escobar (PR) PTS –15 Lou Salica (USA) New York, USA

20 Jan 1936 *M(NBA)* Marcel Thil (Fra) DIS –4 Lou Brouillard (Can) Paris, France

10 Feb 1936 *M(NY)* Ed 'Babe' Risko (USA) PTS –15 Tony Fisher (USA) Newark, USA

18 Feb 1936 *Fe(NBA)* Freddie Miller (USA) PTS –12 Johnny Pena (USA) Seattle, USA

2 Mar 1936 *Fe(NBA)* Freddie Miller (USA) PTS –15 Petey Sarron (USA) Miami, USA

13 Mar 1936 *LH* John Henry Lewis (USA) PTS –15 Jock McAvoy (GB) New York, USA

11 May 1936 *Fe(NBA)* Petey Sarron (USA) PTS –15 Freddie Miller (USA) Washington, USA

29 Jun 1936 *B(NY)* Tony Marino (USA) KO –14 Baltazar Sangchilli (Spa) New York, USA

11 Jul 1936 *M(NY)* Freddie Steele (USA) PTS –15 Ed 'Babe' Risko (USA) Seattle, USA

22 Jul 1936 *Fe(NBA)* Petey Sarron (USA) PTS –15 Baby Manuel (Spa) Dallas, USA

31 Aug 1936 *B* Sixto Escobar (PR) RSF –13 Tony Marino (USA) New York, USA

3 Sep 1936 *L* Lou Ambers (USA) PTS –15 Tony Canzoneri (USA) New York, USA

4 Sep 1936 *Fe(NY)* Mike Belloise (USA) KO –9 Dave Crowley (GB) New York, USA

16 Sep 1936 *Fl(IBU)* Benny Lynch (GB) KO –8 Pat Palmer (GB) Glasgow, Scotland

13 Oct 1936 *B* Sixto Escobar (PR) KO –1 Carlos 'Indian' Quintana (Pan) New York, USA

9 Nov 1936 *LH* John Henry Lewis (USA) PTS –15 Len Harvey (GB) London, England

27 Nov 1936 *W* Barney Ross (USA) PTS –15 Izzy Jannazzo (USA) New York USA

1 Jan 1937 *M* Freddie Steele (USA) PTS –10 Gorilla Jones (USA) New York, USA

19 Jan 1937 *Fl* Benny Lynch (GB) PTS –15 Small Montana (USA) London, England

19 Feb 1937 *M* Freddie Steele (USA) PTS –15 Ed 'Babe' Risko (USA) New York, USA

21 Feb 1937 *B* Sixto Escobar (PR) PTS –15 Lou Salica (USA) San Juan, Puerto Rico

7 May 1937 *L* Lou Ambers (USA) PTS –15 Tony Canzoneri (USA) New York, USA

11 May 1937 *M* Freddie Steele (USA) KO –3 Frank Battaglia (Can) Seattle, USA

3 Jun 1937 *LH* John Henry Lewis (USA) KO –8 Bob Olin (USA) St Louis, USA

22 Jun 1937 *H* Joe Louis (USA) KO –8 James J. Braddock (USA) Chicago, USA

30 Aug 1937 *H* Joe Louis (USA) PTS –15 Tommy Farr (GB) New York, USA

4 Sep 1937 *Fe(NBA)* Petey Sarron (USA) PTS –12 Freddie Miller (USA) Johannesburg, South Africa

11 Sep 1937 *M* Freddie Steele (USA) KO –4 Ken Overlin (USA) Seattle, USA

23 Sep 1937 *W* Barney Ross (USA) PTS –15 Ceferino Garcia (Phi) New York, USA

23 Sep 1937 *L* Lou Ambers (USA) PTS –15 Pedro Montanez (PR) New York, USA

23 Sep 1937 *B* Harry Jeffra (USA) PTS –15 Sixto Escobar (PR) New York, USA

23 Oct 1937 *Fl* Benny Lynch (GB) KO –13 Peter Kane (GB) Glasgow, Scotland

29 Oct 1937 *Fe* Henry Armstrong (USA) KO –6 Petey Sarron (USA) New York, USA

19 Feb 1938 *M* Freddie Steele (USA) KO –7 Carmen Barth (USA) Cleveland, USA

20 Feb 1938 *B* Sixto Escobar (PR) PTS –15 Harry Jeffra (USA) San Juan, Puerto Rico

23 Feb 1938 *H* Joe Louis (USA) KO –3 Nathan Mann (USA) New York, USA

1 Apr 1938 *H* Joe Louis (USA) KO –5 Harry Thomas (USA) Chicago, USA

1 Apr 1938 *M(NY)* Fred Apostoli (USA) PTS –15 Glen Lee (USA) New York, USA

25 Apr 1938 *LH* John Henry Lewis (USA) KO –4 Emilio Martinez (USA) Minneapolis, USA

31 May 1938 *W* Henry Armstrong (USA) PTS –15 Barney Ross (USA) New York, USA

22 Jun 1938 *H* Joe Louis (USA) KO –1 Max Schmeling (Ger) New York, USA

26 Jul 1938 *M(NBA)* Al Hostak (USA) KO –1 Freddie Steele (USA) Seattle, USA

17 Aug 1938 *L* Henry Armstrong (USA) PTS –15 Lou Ambers (USA) New York, USA

22 Sep 1938 *Fl* Peter Kane (GB) PTS –15 Jackie Jurich (USA) Liverpool, England

17 Oct 1938 *Fe(NY)* Joey Archibald (USA) PTS –15 Mike Belloise (USA) New York, USA

28 Oct 1938 *LH* John Henry Lewis (USA) PTS –15 Al Gainer (USA) New Haven, USA

1 Nov 1938 *M(NBA)* Sol Kreiger (USA) PTS –15 Al Hostak (USA) Seattle, USA

18 Nov 1938 *M(NY)* Fred Apostoli (USA) KO –8 Young Corbett III (Ita) New York, USA

25 Nov 1938 *W* Henry Armstrong (USA) PTS –15 Ceferino Garcia (Phi) New York, USA

28 Nov 1938 *LH(NY)* Tiger Jack Fox (USA) PTS –15 Al Gainer (USA) New York, USA

5 Dec 1938 *W* Henry Armstrong (USA) KO –3 Al Manfredo (USA) Cleveland, USA

29 Dec 1938 *Fe(NBA)* Leo Rodak (USA) PTS –10 Leone Efrati (Ita) Chicago, USA

10 Jan 1939 *W* Henry Armstrong (USA) PTS –10 Baby Arizmendi (Mex) Los Angeles, USA

25 Jan 1939 *H* Joe Louis (USA) RSF –1 John Henry Lewis (USA) New York, USA

3 Feb 1939 *LH(NY)* Melio Bettina (USA) RSF –9 Tiger Jack Fox (USA) New York, USA

14 Mar 1939 *W* Henry Armstrong (USA) KO –4 Bobby Pacho (Mex) Havana, Cuba

16 Mar 1939 *W* Henry Armstrong (USA) KO –1 Lew Feldman (USA) St Louis, USA

31 Mar 1939 *W* Henry Armstrong (USA) KO –12 Davey Day (USA) New York, USA

2 Apr 1939 *B* Sixto Escobar (PR) PTS –15 Johnny 'Kayo' Morgan (USA) San Juan, Puerto Rico

The referee of the Benny Lynch–Peter Kane (both GB) world flyweight title fight at Glasgow in October 1937 was BBC radio commentator Barrington Dalby.

17 Apr 1939 *H* Joe Louis (USA) KO –1 Jack Roper (USA) Los Angeles, USA

18 Apr 1939 *Fe* Joey Archibald (USA) PTS –15 Leo Rodak (USA) Rhode Island, USA

25 May 1939 *W* Henry Armstrong (USA) PTS –15 Ernie Roderick (GB) London, England

27 Jun 1939 *M(NBA)* Al Hostak (USA) KO –4 Solly Kreiger (USA) Seattle, USA

28 Jun 1939 *H* Joe Louis (USA) RSF –4 Tony Galento (USA) New York, USA

13 Jul 1939 *LH* Billy Conn (USA) PTS –15 Melio Bettina (USA) New York, USA

22 Aug 1939 *L* Lou Ambers (USA) PTS –15 Henry Armstrong (USA) New York, USA

20 Sep 1939 *H* Joe Louis (USA) KO –11 Bob Pastor (USA) Detroit, USA

25 Sep 1939 *LH* Billy Conn (USA) PTS –15 Melio Bettina (USA) Pittsburgh, USA

28 Sep 1939 *Fe* Joey Archibald (USA) PTS –15 Harry Jeffra (USA) Washington, USA

2 Oct 1939 *M(NY)* Ceferino Garcia (Phi) KO –7 Fed Apostoli (USA) New York, USA

9 Oct 1939 *W* Henry Armstrong (USA) KO –4 Al Manfredo (USA) Des Moines, USA

13 Oct 1939 *W* Henry Armstrong (USA) KO –2 Howard Scott (USA) Minneapolis, USA

20 Oct 1939 *W* Henry Armstrong (USA) KO –3 Ritchie Fontaine (USA) Seattle, USA

24 Oct 1939 *W* Henry Armstrong (USA) PTS –10 Jimmy Garrison (USA) Los Angeles, USA

30 Oct 1939 *W* Henry Armstrong (USA) KO –4 Bobby Pacho (Mex) Denver, USA

17 Nov 1939 *LH* Billy Conn (USA) PTS –15 Gus Lesnevich (USA) New York, USA

11 Dec 1939 *M(NBA)* Al Hostak (USA) KO –1 Eric Seelig (Ger) Cleveland, USA

11 Dec 1939 *W* Henry Armstrong (USA) KO –7 Jimmy Garrison (USA) Cleveland, USA

23 Dec 1939 *M(NY)* Ceferino Garcia (Phi) KO –13 Glen Lee (USA) Manila, Philippines

4 Jan 1940 *W* Henry Armstrong (USA) KO –5 Joe Ghnouly (USA) St Louis, USA

24 Jan 1940 *W* Henry Armstrong (USA) KO –9 Pedro Montanez (PR) New York, USA

9 Feb 1940 *H* Joe Louis (USA) PTS –15 Arturo Godoy (Chi) New York, USA

1 Mar 1940 *M(NY)* Ceferino Garcia (Phi) D –10 Henry Armstrong (USA) Los Angeles, USA

4 Mar 1940 *B(NBA)* Georgie Pace (USA) D –15 Lou Salica (USA) Toronto, Canada

29 Mar 1940 *H* Joe Louis (USA) KO –2 Johnny Paycheck (USA) New York, USA

26 Apr 1940 *W* Henry Armstrong (USA) KO –7 Paul Junior (USA) Boston, USA

3 May 1940 *L(NBA)* Sammy Angott (USA) PTS –15 Davey Day (USA) Louiseville, USA

10 May 1940 *L(NY)* Lew Jenkins (USA) RSF –3 Lou Ambers (USA) New York, USA

20 May 1940 *Fe(NY)* Harry Jeffra (USA) PTS –15 Joey Archibald (USA) Baltimore, USA

23 May 1940 *M(NY)* Ken Overlin (USA) PTS –15 Ceferino Garcia (Phi) New York, USA

Between 9 and 30 October 1939 Henry Armstrong (USA) engaged in five world welterweight title fights. He won them all.

24 May 1940 *W* Henry Armstrong (USA) KO –5 Ralph Zanelli (USA) Boston, USA

5 Jun 1940 *LH* Billy Conn (USA) PTS –15 Gus Lesnevich (USA) Detroit, USA

20 Jun 1940 *H* Joe Louis (USA) RSF –8 Arturo Godoy (Chi) New York, USA

21 Jun 1940 *W* Henry Armstrong (USA) KO –3 Paul Junior (USA) Portland, USA

10 Jul 1940 *Fe(NBA)* Petey Scalzo (USA) RSF –15 Bobby 'Poison' Ivy (USA) Hartford, USA

19 Jul 1940 *M(NBA)* Tony Zale (USA) KO –13 Al Hostak (USA) Seattle, USA

29 Jul 1940 *Fe(NY)* Harry Jeffra (USA) PTS –15 Spider Armstrong (Can) Baltimore, USA

23 Sep 1940 *W* Henry Armstrong (USA) KO –4 Phil Furr (USA) Washington, USA

24 Sep 1940 *B* Lou Salica (USA) PTS –15 Georgie Pace (USA) New York, USA

4 Oct 1940 *W* Fritzie Zivic (USA) PTS –15 Henry Armstrong (USA) New York, USA

1 Nov 1940 *M(NY)* Ken Overlin (USA) PTS –15 Steve Belloise (USA) New York, USA

22 Nov 1940 *L(NY)* Lew Jenkins (USA) RSF –2 Pete Lello (USA) New York, USA

13 Dec 1940 *M(NY)* Ken Overlin (USA) PTS –15 Steve Belloise (USA) New York, USA

16 Dec 1940 *H* Joe Louis (USA) RTD –6 Al McCoy (USA) Boston, USA

13 Jan 1941 *LH(NBA)* Anton Christoforidis (Gre) PTS –15 Melio Bettina (USA) Cleveland, USA

13 Jan 1941 *B* Lou Salica (USA) PTS –15 Tommy Forte (USA) Philadelphia, USA

17 Jan 1941 *W* Fritzie Zivic (USA) KO –12 Henry Armstrong (USA) New York, USA

31 Jan 1941 *H* Joe Louis (USA) KO –5 Red Burman (USA) New York, USA

17 Feb 1941 *H* Joe Louis (USA) KO –2 Gus Dorazio (USA) Philadelphia, USA

21 Feb 1941 *M(NBA)* Tony Zale (USA) KO –14 Steve Mamakos (Gre) Chicago, USA

21 Mar 1941 *H* Joe Louis (USA) KO –13 Abe Simon (USA) Detroit, USA

8 Apr 1941 *H* Joe Louis (USA) RSF –9 Tony Musto (USA) St Louis, USA

25 Apr 1941 *B* Lou Salica (USA) PTS –15 Lou Transparenti (USA) Baltimore, USA

9 May 1941 *M(NY)* Billy Soose (USA) PTS –15 Ken Overlin (USA) New York, USA

12 May 1941 *Fe(NY)* Joey Archibald (USA) PTS –15 Harry Jeffra (USA) Washington, USA

19 May 1941 *Fe(NBA)* Petey Scalzo (USA) PTS –15 Phil Zwick (USA) Milwaukee, USA

22 May 1941 *LH* Gus Lesnevich (USA) PTS –15 Anton Christoforidis (Gre) New York, USA

23 May 1941 *H* Joe Louis (USA) DIS –7 Buddy Baer (USA) Washington, USA

28 May 1941 *M(NBA)* Tony Zale (USA) KO –2 Al Hostak (USA) Chicago, USA

16 Jun 1941 *B* Lou Salica (USA) PTS –15 Tommy Forte (USA) Philadelphia, USA

18 Jun 1941 *H* Joe Louis (USA) KO –13 Billy Conn (USA) New York, USA

1 Jul 1941 *Fe(NBA)* Ritchie Lemos (USA) KO –5 Petey Scalzo (USA) Los Angeles, USA

21 Jul 1941 *W* Freddie 'Red' Cochrane (USA) PTS –15 Fritzie Zivic (USA) Newark, USA

26 Aug 1941 *LH* Gus Lesnevich (USA) PTS –15 Tami Mauriello (USA) New York, USA

11 Sep 1941 *Fe(NY)* Chalky Wright (Mex) KO –11 Joey Archibald (USA) Washington, USA

29 Sep 1941 *H* Joe Louis (USA) RSF –6 Lou Nova (USA) New York, USA

14 Nov 1941 *LH* Gus Lesnevich (USA) PTS –15 Tami Mauriello (USA) New York, USA

18 Nov 1941 *Fe(NBA)* Jackie Wilson (USA) PTS –12 Ritchie Lemos (USA) Los Angeles, USA

28 Nov 1941 *M* Tony Zale (USA) PTS –15 Georgie Abrams (USA) New York, USA

12 Dec 1941 *Fe(NBA)* Jackie Wilson (USA) PTS –12 Ritchie Lemos (USA) Los Angeles, USA

19 Dec 1941 *L* Sammy Angott (USA) PTS –15 Lew Jenkins (USA) New York, USA

9 Jan 1942 *H* Joe Louis (USA) KO –1 Buddy Baer (USA) New York, USA

27 Mar 1942 *H* Joe Louis (USA) KO –6 Abe Simon (USA) New York, USA

15 May 1942 *L* Sammy Angott (USA) PTS –15 Allie Stolz (USA) New York USA

19 Jun 1942 *Fe(NY)* Chalky Wright (Mex) KO –10 Harry Jeffra (USA) Baltimore, USA

7 Aug 1942 *B* Manuel Ortiz (USA) PTS –12 Lou Salica (USA) Hollywood, USA

25 Sept 1942 *Fe(NY)* Chalky Wright (Mex) PTS –15 Charlie Constantino (USA) New York, USA

20 Nov 1942 *Fe(NY)* Willie Pep (USA) PTS –15 Chalky Wright (Mex) New York, USA

18 Dec 1942 *L(NY)* Beau Jack (USA) KO –3 Tippy Larkin (USA) New York, USA

1 Jan 1943 *B* Manuel Ortiz (USA) PTS –10 Kenny Lindsay (Can) Portland, USA

18 Jan 1943 *Fe(NBA)* Jackie Callura (Can) PTS –15 Jackie Wilson (USA) Providence, USA

27 Jan 1943 *B* Manuel Ortiz (USA) RSF –10 George Freitas (USA) Oakland, USA

10 Mar 1943 *B* Manuel Ortiz (USA) RSF –11 Lou Salica (USA) Oakland, USA

18 Mar 1943 *Fe(NBA)* Jackie Callura (Can) PTS –15 Jackie Wilson (USA) Boston, USA

28 Apr 1943 *B* Manuel Ortiz (USA) KO –6 Lupe Cordoza (USA) Fort Worth, USA

21 May 1943 *L(NY)* Bob Montgomery (USA) PTS –15 Beau Jack (USA) New York, USA

26 May 1943 *B* Manuel Ortiz (USA) PTS –15 Joe Robleto (USA) Long Beach, USA

8 Jun 1943 *Fe(NY)* Willie Pep (USA) PTS –15 Sal Bartolo (USA) Boston, USA

19 Jun 1943 *Fl* Jackie Paterson (GB) KO –1 Peter Kane (GB) Glasgow, Scotland

12 Jul 1943 *B* Manuel Ortiz (USA) KO –7 Joe Robleto (USA) Seattle, USA

16 Aug 1943 *Fe(NBA)* Phil Terranova (USA) KO –8 Jackie Callura (Can) New Orleans, USA

1 Oct 1943 *B* Manuel Ortiz (USA) KO –4 Leonardo Lopez (Mex) Hollywood, USA

27 Oct 1943 *L(NBA)* Sammy Angott (USA) PTS –15 Luther 'Slugger' White (USA) Hollywood, USA

19 Nov 1943 *L(NY)* Beau Jack (USA) PTS –15 Bob Montgomery (USA) New York, USA

23 Nov 1943 *B* Manuel Ortiz (USA) PTS –15 Benny Goldberg (USA) Los Angeles, USA

27 Dec 1943 *Fe(NBA)* Phil Terranova (USA) KO –6 Jackie Callura (Can) New Orleans, USA

3 Mar 1944 *L(NY)* Bob Montgomery (USA) PTS –15 Beau Jack (USA) New York, USA

8 Mar 1944 *L(NBA)* Juan Zurita (Mex) PTS –15 Sammy Angott (USA) Hollywood, USA

10 Mar 1944 *Fe(NBA)* Sal Bartolo (USA) PTS –15 Phil Terranova (USA) Boston, USA

14 Mar 1944 *B* Manuel Ortiz (USA) PTS –15 Ernesto Aguilar (Mex) Los Angeles, USA

4 Apr 1944 *B* Manuel Ortiz (USA) PTS –15 Tony Olivera (USA) Los Angeles, USA

5 May 1944 *Fe(NBA)* Sal Bartolo (USA) PTS –15 Phil Terranova (USA) Boston, USA

12 Sep 1944 *B* Manuel Ortiz (USA) RSF –4 Luis Castello (Mex) Los Angeles, USA

29 Sep 1944 *Fe(NY)* Willie Pep (USA) PTS –15 Chalky Wright (Mex) New York, USA

14 Nov 1944 *B* Manuel Ortiz (USA) RSF –9 Luis Castello (Mex) Los Angeles, USA

15 Dec 1944 *Fe(NBA)* Sal Bartolo (USA) PTS –15 Willie Roche (USA) Boston, USA

19 Feb 1945 *Fe(NY)* Willie Pep (USA) PTS –15 Phil Terranova (USA) New York, USA

18 Apr 1945 *L(NBA)* Ike Williams (USA) KO –2 Juan Zurita (Mex) Mexico City, Mexico

1 Feb 1946 *W* Marty Servo (USA) KO –4 Freddie 'Red' Cochrane (USA) New York, USA

25 Feb 1946 *B* Manuel Ortiz (USA) KO –13 Luis Castello (Mex) San Francisco, USA

29 Apr 1946 *LW* Tippy Larkin (USA) PTS –12 Willie Joyce (USA) Boston, USA

3 May 1946 *Fe(NBA)* Sal Bartolo (USA) KO –6 Spider Armstrong (Can) Boston, USA

14 May 1946 *LH* Gus Lesnevich (USA) RSF –10 Freddie Mills (GB) London, England

18 May 1946 *B* Manuel Ortiz (USA) KO –5 Kenny Lindsay (Can) Los Angeles, USA

7 Jun 1946 *Fe* Willie Pep (USA) KO –12 Sal Bartolo (USA) New York, USA

10 Jun 1946 *B* Manuel Ortiz (USA) KO –11 Jackie Jurich (USA) San Francisco, USA

19 Jun 1946 *H* Joe Louis (USA) KO –8 Billy Conn (USA) New York, USA

28 Jun 1946 *L(NY)* Bob Montgomery (USA) KO –13 Allie Stolz (USA) New York, USA

10 Jul 1946 *Fl* Jackie Paterson (GB) PTS –15 Joe Curran (GB) Glasgow, Scotland

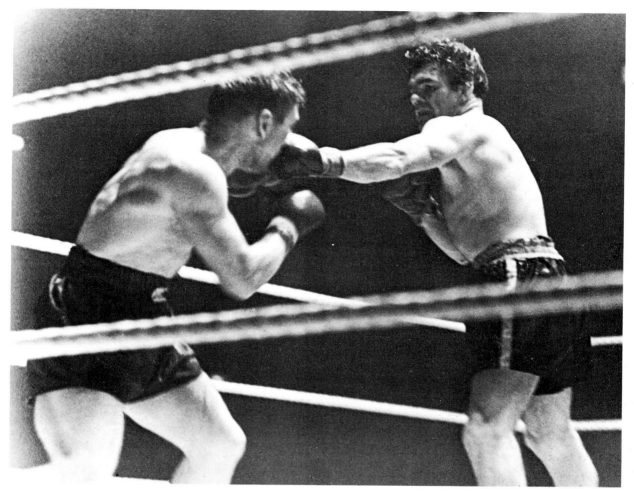

Freddie Mills (right) on his way to defeat by Gus Lesnevich (USA) in a world light-heavyweight title fight at Harringay in 1946. Two years later Mills (GB) beat Lesnevich to win the crown. Syndication International

4 Sep 1946 *L(NBA)* Ike Williams (USA) KO –9 Ronnie James (GB) Cardiff, Wales

13 Sep 1946 *LW* Tippy Larkin (USA) PTS –12 Willie Joyce (USA) New York, USA

18 Sep 1946 *H* Joe Louis (USA) KO –1 Tami Mauriello (USA) New York, USA

27 Sep 1946 *M* Tony Zale (USA) KO –6 Rocky Graziano (USA) New York, USA

26 Nov 1946 *L(NY)* Bob Montgomery (USA) KO –8 Wesley Mouzon (USA) Philadelphia, USA

20 Dec 1946 *W* Sugar Ray Robinson (USA) PTS –15 Tommy Bell (USA) New York, USA

6 Jan 1947 *B* Harold Dade (USA) PTS –15 Manuel Ortiz (USA) San Francisco, USA

28 Feb 1947 *LH* Gus Lesnevich (USA) KO –10 Billy Fox (USA) New York, USA

11 Mar 1947 *B* Manuel Ortiz (USA) PTS –15 Harold Dade (USA) Los Angeles, USA

30 May 1947 *B* Manuel Ortiz (USA) PTS –15 David Kui Kong Young (Haw) Honolulu, Hawaii

24 Jun 1947 *W* Sugar Ray Robinson (USA) KO –8 Jimmy Doyle (USA) Cleveland, USA

16 Jul 1947 *M* Rocky Graziano (USA) KO –6 Tony Zale (USA) Chicago, USA

4 Aug 1947 *L* Ike Williams (USA) KO –6 Bob Montgomery (USA) Philadelphia, USA

22 Aug 1947 *Fe* Willie Pep (USA) KO –12 Jock Leslie (USA) Flint, USA

20 Oct 1947 *Fl(NBA)* Rinty Monaghan (GB) PTS –15 Dado Marino (Haw) London, England

5 Dec 1947 *H* Joe Louis (USA) PTS –15 Jersey Joe Walcott (USA) New York, USA

19 Dec 1947 *W* Sugar Ray Robinson (USA) KO –6 Chuck Taylor (USA) Detroit, USA

20 Dec 1947 *B* Manuel Ortiz (USA) PTS –15 Tirso Del Rosario (Phi) Manila, Philippines

24 Feb 1948 *Fe* Willie Pep (USA) RSF –10 Humberto Sierra (Cuba) Miami, USA

5 Mar 1948 *LH* Gus Lesnevich (USA) KO –1 Billy Fox (USA) New York, USA

23 Mar 1948 *Fl* Rinty Monaghan (GB) KO –7 Jackie Paterson (GB) Belfast, Ireland

25 May 1948 *L* Ike Williams (USA) PTS –15 Enrique Bolanos (USA) Los Angeles, USA

10 Jun 1948 *M* Tony Zale (USA) KO –3 Rocky Graziano (USA) Newark, USA

25 Jun 1948 *H* Joe Louis (USA) KO –11 Jersey Joe Walcott (USA) New York, USA

28 Jun 1948 *W* Sugar Ray Robinson (USA) PTS –15 Bernard Docusen (Phi) Chicago, USA

4 Jul 1948 *B* Manuel Ortiz (USA) KO –8 Memo Valero (Mex) Mexicali, Mexico

12 Jul 1948 *L* Ike Williams (USA) KO –6 Beau Jack (USA) Philadelphia, USA

26 Jul 1948 *LH* Freddie Mills (GB) PTS –15 Gus Lesnevich (USA) London, England

21 Sep 1948 *M* Marcel Cerdan (Alg) KO –12 Tony Zale (USA) Jersey City, USA

23 Sep 1948 *L* Ike Williams (USA) KO –10 Jesse Flores (USA) New York, USA

29 Oct 1948 *Fe* Sandy Saddler (USA) KO –4 Willie Pep (USA) New York, USA

11 Feb 1949 *Fe* Willie Pep (USA) PTS –15 Sandy Saddler (USA) New York, USA

1 Mar 1949 *B* Manuel Ortiz (USA) PTS –15 Dado Marino (Haw) Honolulu, Hawaii

5 Apr 1949 *Fl* Rinty Monaghan (GB) PTS –15 Maurice Sandeyron (Fra) Belfast, Ireland

16 Jun 1949 *M* Jake La Motta (USA) RTD –10 Marcel Cerdan (Alg) Detroit, USA

22 Jun 1949 *H(NBA)* Ezzard Charles (USA) PTS –15 Jersey Joe Walcott (USA) Chicago, USA

11 Jul 1949 *W* Sugar Ray Robinson (USA) PTS –15 Kid Gavilan (Cuba) Philadelphia, USA

21 Jul 1949 *L* Ike Williams (USA) KO –4 Enrique Bolanos (USA) Los Angeles, USA

10 Aug 1949 *H(NBA)* Ezzard Charles RSF –7 Gus Lesnevich (USA) New York, USA

20 Sep 1949 *Fe* Willie Pep (USA) RSF –7 Eddie Compo (USA) Waterbury, USA

30 Sep 1949 *Fl* Rinty Monaghan (GB) D –15 Terry Allen (GB) Belfast, Ireland

14 Oct 1949 *H(NBA)* Ezzard Charles (USA) KO –8 Pat Velentino (USA) San Francisco, USA

5 Dec 1949 *L* Ike Williams (USA) PTS –15 Freddie Dawson (USA) Philadelphia, USA

16 Jan 1950 *Fe* Willie Pep (USA) KO –5 Charley Riley (USA) St Louis, USA

24 Jan 1950 *LH* Joey Maxim (USA) KO –10 Freddie Mills (GB) London, England

17 Mar 1950 *Fe* Willie Pep (USA) PTS –15 Ray Famechon (Fra) New York, USA

25 Apr 1950 *Fl* Terry Allen (GB) PTS –15 Honore Pratesi (Fra) London, England

31 May 1950 *B* Vic Toweel (SA) PTS –15 Manuel Ortiz (USA) Johannesburg, South Africa

12 Jul 1950 *M* Jake La Motta (USA) PTS –15 Tiberio Mitri (Ita) New York, USA

1 Aug 1950 *Fl* Dado Marino (Haw) PTS –15 Terry Allen (GB) Honolulu, Hawaii

9 Aug 1950 *W* Sugar Ray Robinson (USA) PTS –15 Charley Fusari (USA) Jersey City, USA

15 Aug 1950 *H(NBA)* Ezzard Charles (USA) RSF –14 Freddy Beshore (USA) Buffalo, USA

8 Sep 1950 *Fe* Sandy Saddler (USA) RTD –7 Willie Pep (USA) New York, USA

13 Sep 1950 *M* Jake La Motta (USA) KO –15 Laurent Dauthuille (Fra) Detroit, USA

27 Sep 1950 *H* Ezzard Charles (USA) PTS –15 Joe Louis (USA) New York, USA

2 Dec 1950 *B* Vic Toweel (SA) RTD –10 Danny O'Sullivan (GB) Johannesburg, South Africa

5 Dec 1950 *H* Ezzard Charles (USA) KO –11 Nick Barone (USA) Cincinnati, USA

12 Jan 1951 *H* Ezzard Charles (USA) RSF –10 Lee Oma (USA) New York, USA

14 Feb 1951 *M* Sugar Ray Robinson (USA) RSF –13 Jake La Motta (USA) Chicago, USA

7 Mar 1951 *H* Ezzard Charles (USA) PTS –15 Jersey Joe Walcott (USA) Detroit, USA

14 Mar 1951 *W(NBA)* Johnny Bratton (USA) PTS –15 Charley Fusari (USA) Chicago, USA

18 May 1951 *W* Kid Gavilan (Cuba) PTS –15 Johnny Bratton (USA) New York, USA

25 May 1951 *L* Jimmy Carter (USA) RSF –14 Ike Williams (USA) New York, USA

30 May 1951 *H* Ezzard Charles (USA) PTS –15 Joey Maxim (USA) Chicago, USA

10 Jul 1951 *M* Randolph Turpin (GB) PTS –15 Sugar Ray Robinson (USA) London, England

18 Jul 1951 *H* Jersey Joe Walcott (USA) KO –7 Ezzard Charles (USA) Pittsburgh, USA

22 Aug 1951 *LH* Joey Maxim (USA) PTS –15 Irish Bob Murphy (USA) New York, USA

29 Aug 1951 *W* Kid Gavilan (Cuba) PTS –15 Billy Graham (USA) New York, USA

12 Sep 1951 *M* Sugar Ray Robinson (USA) RSF –10 Randolph Turpin (GB) New York, USA

26 Sep 1951 *Fe* Sandy Saddler (USA) RTD –9 Willie Pep (USA) New York, USA

1 Nov 1951 *Fl* Dado Marino (Haw) PTS –15 Terry Allen (GB) Honolulu, Hawaii

14 Nov 1951 *L* Jimmy Carter (USA) PTS –15 Art Aragon (USA) Los Angeles, USA

17 Nov 1951 *B* Vic Toweel (SA) PTS –15 Luis Romero (Spa) Johannesburg, South Africa

26 Jan 1952 *B* Vic Toweel (SA) PTS –15 Peter Keenan (GB) Johannesburg, South Africa

4 Feb 1952 *W* Kid Gavilan (Cuba) PTS –15 Bobby Dykes (USA) Miami, USA

13 Mar 1952 *M* Sugar Ray Robinson (USA) PTS –15 Carl 'Bobo' Olson (Haw) San Francisco, USA

1 Apr 1952 *L* Jimmy Carter (USA) PTS –15 Lauro Salas (Mex) Los Angeles, USA

(Opposite above) *Two men who fought on Jack Solomons' promotions — Freddie Mills (GB) (left) and Joey Maxim (USA).* The Photo Source

(Opposite below) *Jersey Joe Walcott (USA) falling to the canvas during his world title fight with Ezzard Charles (USA) in March 1951. He got up, but only to lose on points to the defending champion.* The Photo Source

Having won the world welter and middleweight titles, Sugar Ray Robinson (USA) went for this third title in 1952 when he attempted to win the light-heavyweight crown. His hopes were dashed when intense heat forced him to retire at the end of round 13 and Joey Maxim (USA) retained his title. Six months later Robinson announced his first retirement. The Photo Source.

16 Apr 1952 *M* Sugar Ray Robinson (USA) KO –3 Rocky Graziano (USA) Chicago, USA

14 May 1952 *L* Lauro Salas (Mex) PTS –15 Jimmy Carter (USA) Los Angeles, USA

19 May 1952 *Fl* Yoshio Shirai (Jap) PTS –15 Dado Marino (Haw) Tokyo, Japan

5 Jun 1952 *H* Jersey Joe Walcott (USA) PTS –15 Ezzard Charles (USA) Philadelphia, USA

25 Jun 1952 *LH* Joey Maxim (USA) RTD –14 Sugar Ray Robinson (USA) New York, USA

7 Jul 1952 *W* Kid Gavilan (Cuba) KO –11 Gil Turner (USA) Philadelphia, USA

23 Sep 1952 *H* Rocky Marciano (USA) KO –13 Jersey Joe Walcott (USA) Philadelphia, USA

5 Oct 1952 *W* Kid Gavilan (Cuba) PTS –15 Billy Graham (USA) Havana, Cuba

15 Oct 1952 *L* Jimmy Carter (USA) PTS –15 Lauro Salas (Mex) Chicago, USA

15 Nov 1952 *B* Jimmy Carruthers (Aus) KO –1 Vic Toweel (SA) Johannesburg, South Africa

15 Nov 1952 *Fl* Yoshio Shirai (Jap) PTS –15 Dado Marino (Haw) Tokyo, Japan

17 Dec 1952 *LH* Archie Moore (USA) PTS –15 Joey Maxim (USA) St Louis, USA

11 Feb 1953 *W* Kid Gavilan (Cuba) KO –10 Chuck Davey (USA) Chicago, USA

21 Mar 1953 *B* Jimmy Carruthers (Aus) KO –10 Vic Toweel (SA) Johannesburg, South Africa

24 Apr 1953 *L* Jimmy Carter (USA) RSF –4 Tommy Collins (USA) Boston, USA

15 May 1953 *H* Rocky Marciano (USA) KO –1 Jersey Joe Walcott (USA) Chicago, USA

18 May 1953 *Fl* Yoshio Shirai (Jap) PTS –15 Tanny Campo (Phi) Tokyo, Japan

12 Jun 1953 *L* Jimmy Carter (USA) RSF –15 George Araujo (USA) New York, USA

24 Jun 1953 *LH* Archie Moore (USA) PTS –15 Joey Maxim (USA) Ogden, USA

18 Sep 1953 *W* Kid Gavilan (Cuba) PTS –15 Carmen Basilio (USA) Syracuse, USA

24 Sep 1953 *H* Rocky Marciano (USA) RSF –11 Roland LaStarza (USA) New York, USA

21 Oct 1953 *M* Carl 'Bobo' Olson (Haw) PTS –15 Randolph Turpin (GB) New York, USA

27 Oct 1953 *Fl* Yoshio Shirai (Jap) PTS –15 Terry Allen (GB) Tokyo, Japan

11 Nov 1953 *L* Jimmy Carter (USA) KO –5 Armand Savoi (Can) Montreal, Canada

13 Nov 1953 *W* Kid Gavilan (Cuba) PTS –15 Johnny Bratton (USA) Chicago, USA

13 Nov 1953 *B* Jimmy Carruthers (Aus) PTS –15 Henry 'Pappy' Gault (USA) Sydney, Australia

27 Jan 1954 *LH* Archie Moore (USA) PTS –15 Joey Maxim (USA) Miami, USA

5 Mar 1954 *L* Paddy de Marco (USA) PTS –15 Jimmy Carter (USA) New York, USA

2 Apr 1954 *M* Carl 'Bobo' Olson (Haw) PTS –15 Kid Gavilan (Cuba) Chicago, USA

2 May 1954 *B* Jimmy Carruthers (Aus) PTS –12 Chamrern Songkitrat (Tha) Bangkok, Thailand

24 May 1954 *Fl* Yoshio Shirai (Jap) PTS –15 Leo Espinosa (Phi) Tokyo, Japan

American Willie Pep's career lasted 26 years. In 1947 he was told he would most probably never walk again without crutches following an aeroplane accident. Nineteen years after the accident he had his last professional fight! The Photo Source

The following fighters overcame physical disabilities to go on to win world titles: Mario D'Agata (bantamweight 1956–7) was a deaf and dumb mute Harry Greb (middleweight 1923–6) was virtually blind in one eye Eugene Criqui (featherweight 1923) had no jaw bone. A silver plate, held together by wire, had been inserted in its place Willie Pep (featherweight 1942–8 and 1949–50), although he did not suffer from any physical disability, was severely injured in a plane crash in January 1947. He was told he would never box again, and it was unlikely he would walk without crutches. Five months after the crash he was back in the ring, winning the first of 26 consecutive contests. And, in the August, he beat Jock Leslie to retain his world title.

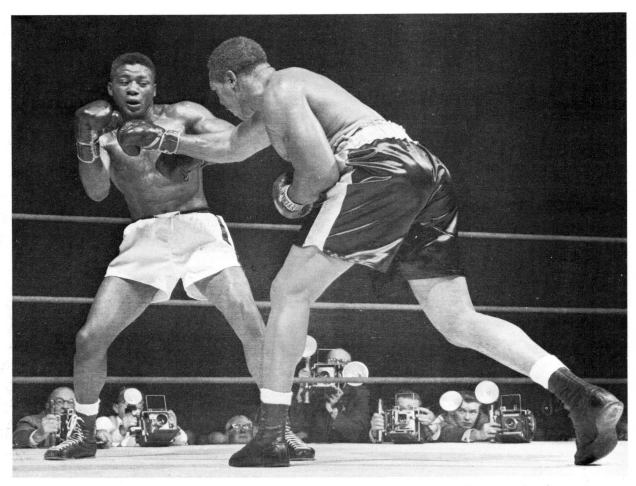

Floyd Patterson (left) taunting Archie Moore (USA) during their fight for the vacant world heavyweight title in 1956. Patterson (USA) won the title, and Moore failed, for the second time, in his bid to add the heavyweight title to his light-heavyweight crown. UPI/Bettmann Newsphotos

17 Jun 1954 *H* Rocky Marciano (USA) PTS –15 Ezzard Charles (USA) New York, USA

11 Aug 1954 *LH* Archie Moore (USA) KO –14 Harold Johnson (USA) New York, USA

20 Aug 1954 *M* Carl 'Bobo' Olson (Haw) PTS –15 Rocky Castellani (USA) San Francisco, USA

17 Sep 1954 *H* Rocky Marciano (USA) KO –8 Ezzard Charles (USA) New York, USA

18 Sep 1954 *B* Robert Cohen (Alg) PTS –15 Chamrern Songkitrat (Tha) Bangkok, Thailand

20 Oct 1954 *W* Johnny Saxton (USA) PTS –15 Kid Gavilan (Cuba) Philadelphia, USA

17 Nov 1954 *L* Jimmy Carter (USA) RSF –15 Paddy de Marco (USA) San Francisco, USA

26 Nov 1954 *Fl* Pascual Perez (Arg) PTS –15 Yoshio Shirai (Jap) Tokyo, Japan

15 Dec 1954 *M* Carl 'Bobo' Olson (Haw) KO –11 Pierre Langlois (Fra) San Francisco, USA

25 Feb 1955 *Fe* Sandy Saddler (USA) PTS –15 Teddy 'Red Top' Davis (USA) New York, USA

9 Mar 1955 *B(NBA)* Raton Macias (Mex) KO –11 Chamrern Songkitrat (Tha) San Francisco, USA

1 Apr 1955 *W* Tony de Marco (USA) RSF –14 Johnny Saxton (USA) Boston, USA

16 May 1955 *H* Rocky Marciano (USA) RSF –9 Don Cockell (GB) San Francisco, USA

30 May 1955 *Fl* Pascual Perez (Arg) KO –5 Yoshio Shirai (Jap) Tokyo, Japan

10 Jun 1955 *W* Carmen Basilio (USA) RSF –12 Tony de Marco (USA) Syracuse, USA

22 Jun 1955 *LH* Archie Moore (USA) KO –3 Carl 'Bobo' Olson (Haw) New York, USA

29 Jun 1955 *L* Wallace 'Bud' Smith (USA) PTS –15 Jimmy Carter (USA) Boston, USA

3 Sep 1955 *B(NY)* Robert Cohen (Alg) D –15 Willie Toweel (SA) Johannesburg, South Africa

21 Sep 1955 *H* Rocky Marciano (USA) KO –9 Archie Moore (USA) New York, USA

19 Oct 1955 *L* Wallace 'Bud' Smith (USA) PTS –15 Jimmy Carter (USA) Cincinnati, USA

30 Nov 1955 *W* Carmen Basilio (USA) KO –12 Tony de Marco (USA) Boston, USA

9 Dec 1955 *M* Sugar Ray Robinson (USA) KO –2 Carl 'Bobo' Olson (Haw) Chicago, USA

11 Jan 1956 *Fl* Pascual Perez (Arg) PTS –15 Leo Espinosa (Phil) Buenos Aires, Argentina

18 Jan 1956 *Fe* Sandy Saddler (USA) RSF –13 Flash Elorde (Phi) San Francisco, USA

14 Mar 1956 *W* Johnny Saxton (USA) PTS –15 Carmen Basilio (USA) Chicago, USA

25 Mar 1956 *B(NBA)* Raton Macias (Mex) KO –10 Leo Espinosa (Phi) Mexico City, Mexico

18 May 1956 *M* Sugar Ray Robinson (USA) KO –4 Carl 'Bobo' Olson (Haw) Los Angeles, USA

5 Jun 1956 *LH* Archie Moore (USA) RSF –10 Yolande Pompey (Tri) London, England

29 Jun 1956 *B(NY)* Mario D'Agata (Ita) RTD –6 Robert Cohen (Alg) Rome, Italy

30 Jun 1956 *Fl* Pascual Perez (Arg) RTD –11 Oscar Suarez (Cuba) Montevideo, Uruguay

24 Aug 1956 *L* Joe Brown (USA) PTS –15 Wallace 'Bud' Smith (USA) New Orleans, USA

12 Sep 1956 *W* Carmen Basilio (USA) KO –9 Johnny Saxton (USA) Syracuse, USA

30 Nov 1956 *H* Floyd Patterson (USA) KO –5 Archie Moore (USA) Chicago, USA

2 Jan 1957 *M* Gene Fullmer (USA) PTS –15 Sugar Ray Robinson (USA) New York, USA

13 Feb 1957 *L* Joe Brown (USA) RSF –10 Wallace 'Bud' Smith (USA) Miami, USA

22 Feb 1957 *W* Carmen Basilio (USA) KO –2 Johnny Saxton (USA) Cleveland, USA

30 Mar 1957 *Fl* Pascual Perez (Arg) KO –1 Dai Dower (GB) Buenos Aires, Argentina

11 Apr 1957 *B(NY)* Alphonse Halimi (Alg) PTS –15 Mario D'Agata (Ita) Paris, France

1 May 1957 *M* Sugar Ray Robinson (USA) KO –5 Gene Fullmer (USA) Chicago, USA

15 Jun 1957 *B(NBA)* Raton Macias (Mex) RSF –11 Dommy Ursua (Phi) San Francisco, USA

19 Jun 1957 *L* Joe Brown (USA) RSF –15 Orlando Zulueta (Cuba) Denver, USA

24 Jun 1957 *Fe* Hogan 'Kid' Bassey (Ngr) RSF –10 Cherif Hamia (Alg) Paris, France

29 Jul 1957 *H* Floyd Patterson (USA) RSF –10 Tommy Jackson (USA) New York, USA

22 Aug 1957 *H* Floyd Patterson (USA) KO –6 Pete Rademacher (USA) Seattle, USA

20 Sep 1957 *LH* Archie Moore (USA) KO –7 Tony Anthony (USA) Los Angeles, USA

23 Sep 1957 *M* Carmen Basilio (USA) PTS –15 Sugar Ray Robinson (USA) New York, USA

6 Nov 1957 *B* Alphonse Halimi (Alg) PTS –15 Raton Macias (Mex) Los Angeles, USA

4 Dec 1957 *L* Joe Brown (USA) RSF –11 Joey Lopes (USA) Chicago, USA

7 Dec 1957 *Fl* Pascual Perez (Arg) KO –3 Young Martin (Spa) Buenos Aires, Argentina

25 Mar 1958 *M* Sugar Ray Robinson (USA) PTS –15 Carmen Basilio (USA) Chicago, USA

1 Apr 1958 *Fe* Hogan 'Kid' Bassey (Ngr) KO –3 Ricardo Moreno (Mex) Los Angeles, USA

19 Apr 1958 *Fl* Pascual Perez (Arg) PTS –15 Ramon Arias (Ven) Caracas, Venezuela

7 May 1958 *L* Joe Brown (USA) RSF –8 Ralph Dupas (USA) Houston, USA

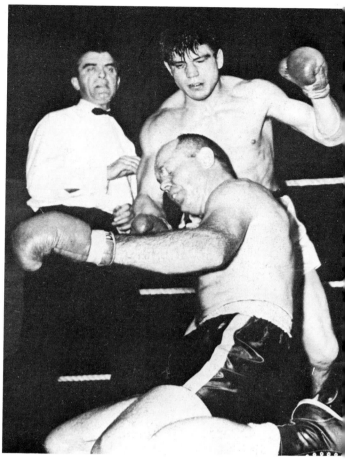

Pete Rademacher (USA) falling to the canvas against Karl Mildenberger (Ger) fought Floyd Patterson (USA) for the world heavyweight title in August 1957. The Photo Source

6 Jun 1958 *W* Virgil Atkins (USA) RSF –4 Vince Martinez (USA) Los Angeles, USA

23 Jul 1958 *L* Joe Brown (USA) PTS –15 Kenny Lane (USA) Houston, USA

18 Aug 1958 *H* Floyd Patterson (USA) RTD –12 Roy Harris (USA) Los Angeles, USA

5 Dec 1958 *W* Don Jordan (USA) PTS –15 Virgil Atkins (USA) Los Angeles, USA

10 Dec 1958 *LH* Archie Moore (USA) KO –11 Yvon Durelle (Can) Montreal, Canada

Pete Rademacher (USA), the 1956 Olympic heavyweight champion, was knocked out by Floyd Patterson (USA) when he challenged Patterson for the world heavyweight title in 1957. It was Rademacher's first professional fight.

15 Dec 1958 *Fl* Pascual Perez (Arg) PTS –15 Dommy Ursua (Phi) Manila, Philippines

11 Feb 1959 *L* Joe Brown (USA) PTS –15 Johnny Busso (USA) Houston, USA

18 Mar 1959 *Fe* Davey Moore (USA) RTD –13 Hogan 'Kid' Bassey (Ngr) Los Angeles, USA

24 Apr 1959 *W* Don Jordan (USA) PTS –15 Virgil Atkins (USA) St Louis, USA

1 May 1959 *H* Floyd Patterson (USA) KO –11 Brian London (GB) Indianapolis, USA

3 Jun 1959 *L* Joe Brown (USA) RTD –8 Paolo Rosi (Ita) Washington, USA

12 Jun 1959 *LW* Carlos Ortiz (PR) RSF –12 Kenny Lane (USA) New York, USA

26 Jun 1959 *H* Ingemar Johansson (Swe) RSF –3 Floyd Patterson (USA) New York, USA

8 Jul 1959 *B* Joe Becerra (Mex) KO –8 Alphonse Halimi (Alg) Los Angeles, USA

10 Jul 1959 *W* Don Jordan (USA) PTS –15 Denny Moyer (USA) Portland, USA

20 Jul 1959 *JL* Harold Gomes (USA) PTS –15 Paul Jorgensen (USA) Providence, USA

10 Aug 1959 *Fl* Pascual Perez (Arg) PTS –15 Kenji Yonekura (Jap) Tokyo, Japan

12 Aug 1959 *LH* Archie Moore (USA) KO –3 Yvon Durelle (Can) Montreal, Canada

19 Aug 1959 *Fe* Davey Moore (USA) RTD –10 Hogan 'Kid' Bassey (Ngr) Los Angeles, USA

28 Aug 1959 *M(NBA)* Gene Fullmer (USA) KO –14 Carmen Basilio (USA) San Francisco, USA

5 Nov 1959 *Fl* Pascual Perez (Arg) KO –13 Sadao Yaoita (Jap) Osaka, Japan

2 Dec 1959 *L* Joe Brown (USA) RTD –5 Dave Charnley (GB) Houston, USA

4 Dec 1959 *M(NBA)* Gene Fullmer (USA) PTS –15 Spider Webb (USA) Logan, USA

22 Jan 1960 *M* Paul Pender (USA) PTS –15 Sugar Ray Robinson (USA) Boston, USA

4 Feb 1960 *LW* Carlos Ortiz (PR) KO –10 Battling Torres (Mex) Los Angeles, USA

4 Feb 1960 *B* Joe Becerra (Mex) KO –9 Alphonse Halimi (Alg) Los Angeles, USA

16 Mar 1960 *JL* Flash Elorde (Phi) RSF –7 Harold Gomes (USA) Manila, Philippines

16 Apr 1960 *Fl* Pone Kingpetch (Tha) PTS –15 Pascual Perez (Arg) Bangkok, Thailand

20 Apr 1960 *M(NBA)* Gene Fullmer (USA) D –15 Joey Giardello (USA) Bozeman, USA

23 May 1960 *B* Joe Becerra (Mex) PTS –15 Kenji Yonekura (Jap) Tokyo, Japan

27 May 1960 *W* Benny 'Kid' Paret (Cuba) PTS –15 Don Jordan (USA) Las Vegas, USA

10 Jun 1960 *M* Paul Pender (USA) PTS –15 Sugar Ray Robinson (USA) Boston, USA

Las Vegas, now very much part of the fight scene, staged its first world title fight bout on 27 May 1960. Benny Paret (Cuba) took the welterweight title from Don Jordan (USA).

---

15 Jun 1960 *LW* Carlos Ortiz (PR) PTS –15 Duilio Loi (Ita) San Francisco, USA

20 Jun 1960 *H* Floyd Patterson (USA) KO –5 Ingemar Johansson (Swe) New York, USA

29 Jun 1960 *M(NBA)* Gene Fullmer (USA) KO –12 Carmen Basilio (USA) Salt Lake City, USA

17 Aug 1960 *JL* Flash Elorde (Phi) KO –1 Harold Gomes (USA) San Francisco, USA

29 Aug 1960 *Fe* Davey Moore (USA) PTS –15 Kazuo Takayama (Jap) Tokyo, Japan

1 Sep 1960 *LW* Duilio Loi (Ita) PTS –15 Carlos Ortiz (PR) Milan, Italy

22 Sep 1960 *Fl* Pone Kingpetch (Tha) RSF –8 Pascual Perez (Arg) Los Angeles, USA

25 Oct 1960 *B(EBU)* Alphonse Halimi (Alg) PTS –15 Freddie Gilroy (GB) London, England

28 Oct 1960 *L* Joe Brown (USA) PTS –15 Cisco Andrade (USA) Los Angeles, USA

18 Nov 1960 *B(NBA)* Eder Jofre (Bra) KO –6 Eloy Sanchez (Mex) Los Angeles, USA

3 Dec 1960 *M(NBA)* Gene Fullmer (USA) D –15 Sugar Ray Robinson (USA) Los Angeles, USA

10 Dec 1960 *W* Benny 'Kid' Paret (Cuba) PTS –15 Frederico Thompson (Pan) New York, USA

14 Jan 1961 *M* Paul Pender (USA) RSF –7 Terry Downes (GB) Boston, USA

7 Feb 1961 *LH(NBA)* Harold Johnson (USA) KO –9 Jesse Bowdry (USA) Miami, USA

4 Mar 1961 *M(NBA)* Gene Fullmer (USA) PTS –15 Sugar Ray Robinson (USA) Las Vegas, USA

13 Mar 1961 *H* Floyd Patterson (USA) KO –6 Ingemar Johansson (Swe) Miami, USA

19 Mar 1961 *JL* Flash Elorde (Phi) PTS –15 Joey Lopes (USA) Manila, Philippines

25 Mar 1961 *B(NBA)* Eder Jofre (Bra) RTD –9 Piero Rollo (Ita) Rio De Janeiro, Brazil

1 Apr 1961 *W* Emile Griffith (VI) KO –13 Benny 'Kid' Paret (Cuba) Miami, USA

8 Apr 1961 *Fe* Davey Moore (USA) KO –1 Danny Valdez (USA) Los Angeles, USA

18 Apr 1961 *L* Joe Brown (USA) PTS –15 Dave Charnley (GB) London, England

22 Apr 1961 *M* Paul Pender (USA) PTS –15 Carmen Basilio (USA) Boston, USA

24 Apr 1961 *LH(NBA)* Harold Johnson (USA) KO –2 Von Clay (USA) Philiadelphia, USA

10 May 1961 *LW* Duilio Loi (Ita) PTS –15 Carlos Ortiz (PR) Milan, Italy

27 May 1961 *B(EBU)* Johnny Caldwell (GB) PTS –15 Alphonse Halimi (Alg) London, England

3 Jun 1961 *W* Emile Griffith (VI) RSF –12 Gaspar 'Indian' Ortega (Mex) Los Angeles, USA

10 Jun 1961 *LH* Archie Moore (USA) PTS –15 Giulio Rinaldi (Ita) New York, USA

27 Jun 1961 *Fl* Pone Kingpetch (Tha) PTS –15 Mitsunori Seki (Jap) Tokyo, Japan

11 Jul 1961 *M* Terry Downes (GB) RTD –9 Paul Pender (USA) London, England

5 Aug 1961 *M(NBA)* Gene Fullmer (USA) PTS –15 Florentino Fernandez (Cuba) Ogden, USA

19 Aug 1961 *B(NBA)* Eder Jofre (Bra) RTD –7 Ramon Arias (Ven) Caracas, Venezuela

DESCRIPTION OF A BOXING MATCH. June 9th 1812

Battle between Ward and Quirk for 100 Guineas aside — Remarks, A more determined and spirited contest than this has seldom been witnessed. the first twelve Rounds were exceedingly hard fought without the slightest attempt to shift on either side. Ward had a decided advantage over his opponent in the science of the art of boxing, and he shewed himself a much better hitter than Quirk. The lose of the contest might in a great measure be attributed to his gaity for he was full of fight until his strength failed him. which with an accidental hit deprived him altogether of defending himself. the beating he received was nothing in comparison to what he had given, for his opponents head was swelled hideously, and his eyes were invisible. Quirks greatest perfection is being a bottom man - equal to Ward. He threw away numberless hits and was always slow. His superior strength as we have before observed, supported him until his opponent was exhausted. when his Blows however slow told forcibly and well. Gulley seconded Ward and Elias Spray Quirk.

A Thomas Rowlandson etching of a 19th-century bare-knuckle contest. Mary Evans

Left *There is no mistaking this king . . . Mike Tyson (USA) after being crowned undisputed heavyweight champion of the world in 1987. He was the first unified heavyweight champion since Leon Spinks (USA) nine years earlier.* All Sport

Opposite above *Lloyd Honeyghan (GB, right) ready to pounce in his WBC welterweight title bout against Jorge Vaca (Mex) at Wembley in 1987. The fight was stopped in the 8th round after Vaca received a bad cut. Under a new rule the contest was awarded to the Mexican because he was ahead on points at the time.* All Sport

Opposite below *Marvin Hagler (left) during his world middleweight title fight with Sugar Ray Leonard at Las Vegas in 1987. Leonard gained a disputed points decision to win his third world title.* All Sport

Below *Mike Tyson (left) shows his usual determination on his way to beating Tony Tucker (USA) to add the IBF title to his WBA and WBC titles and thus become the undisputed heavyweight champion of the world. Tucker didn't let go of his crown too easily: the bout went the full 12 rounds.* All Sport

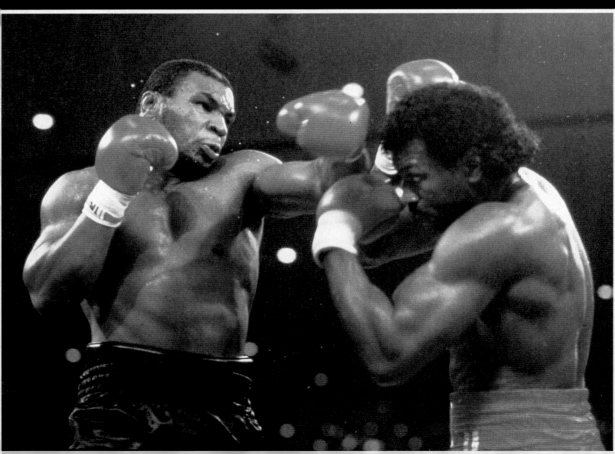

Muhammad Ali (white shorts) is inviting Leon Spinks to 'come and get him' during their second world title fight in 1978. Seven months earlier Spinks dethroned Ali as champion but the 'Louisville Lip' became the first man to regain the title a second time with a unanimous 15-round points decision. All Sport

Floyd Patterson (USA) (right) became the first man in history to regain the world heavyweight title when he knocked out Sweden's Ingemar Johansson in the fourth round of this fight at the New York Polo Grounds in 1960. The Photo Source

29 Aug 1961 *LH(NBA)* Harold Johnson (USA) PTS –15 Eddie Cotton (USA) Seattle, USA

30 Sep 1961 *W* Benny 'Kid' Paret (Cuba) PTS –15 Emile Griffith (VI) New York, USA

21 Oct 1961 *LW* Duilio Loi (Ita) D –15 Eddie Perkins (USA) Milan, Italy

28 Oct 1961 *L* Joe Brown (USA) PTS –15 Bert Somodio (Phi) Quezon City, Philippines

31 Oct 1961 *B(EBU)* Johnny Caldwell (GB) PTS –15 Alphonse Halimi (Alg) London, England

13 Nov 1961 *Fe* Davey Moore (USA) PTS –15 Kazuo Takayama (Jap) Tokyo, Japan

4 Dec 1961 *H* Floyd Patterson (USA) KO –4 Tom McNeeley (USA) Toronto, Canada

9 Dec 1961 *M(NBA)* Gene Fullmer (USA) KO –10 Benny 'Kid' Paret (Cuba) Las Vegas, USA

16 Dec 1961 *JL* Flash Elorde (Phi) KO –1 Sergio Caprari (Ita) Manila, Philippines

18 Jan 1962 *B* Eder Jofre (Bra) RTD –10 Johnny Caldwell (GB) Sao Paulo, Brazil

24 Mar 1962 *W* Emile Griffith (VI) RSF –12 Benny 'Kid' Paret (Cuba) New York, USA

7 Apr 1962 *M* Paul Pender (USA) PTS –15 Terry Downes (GB) Boston, USA

21 Apr 1962 *L* Carlos Ortiz (PR) PTS –15 Joe Brown (USA) Las Vegas, USA

4 May 1962 *B* Eder Jofre (Bra) RSF –10 Herman Marques (USA) San Francisco, USA

12 May 1962 *LH* Harold Johnson (USA) PTS –15 Doug Jones (USA) Philadelphia, USA

30 May 1962 *Fl* Pone Kingpetch (Tha) PTS –15 Kyo Noguchi (Jap) Tokyo, Japan

23 Jun 1962 *LH* Harold Johnson (USA) PTS –15 Gustav Scholz (FRG) Berlin, West Germany

23 Jun 1962 *JL* Flash Elorde (Phi) PTS –15 Auburn Copeland (USA) Manila, Philippines

13 Jul 1962 *W* Emile Griffith (VI) PTS –15 Ralph Dupas (USA) Las Vegas, USA

17 Aug 1962 *Fe* Davey Moore (USA) RSF –2 Olli Makim (Fin) Helsinki, Finland

11 Sep 1962 *B* Eder Jofre (Bra) KO –6 Joe Medel (Mex) Sao Paulo, Brazil

14 Sep 1962 *LW* Eddie Perkins (USA) PTS –15 Duilio Loi (Ita) Milan, Italy

25 Sep 1962 *H* Sonny Liston (USA) KO –1 Floyd Patterson (USA) Chicago, USA

10 Oct 1962 *Fl* Fighting Harada (Jap) KO –11 Pone Kingpetch (Tha) Tokyo, Japan

20 Oct 1962 *LM* Denny Moyer (USA) PTS –15 Joey Giambra (USA) Portland, USA

23 Oct 1962 *M(NBA)* Dick Tiger (Ngr) PTS –15 Gene Fullmer (USA) San Francisco, USA

2 Dec 1962 *L* Carlos Ortiz (PR) KO –5 Teruo Kosaka (Jap) Tokyo, Japan

8 Dec 1962 *W* Emile Griffith (VI) RSF –9 Jorge Fernandez (Arg) Las Vegas, USA

15 Dec 1962 *LW* Duilio Loi (Ita) PTS –15 Eddie Perkins (USA) Milan, Italy

12 Jan 1963 *Fl* Pone Kingpetch (Tha) PTS –15 Fighting Harada (Jap) Bangkok, Thailand

16 Feb 1963 *JL* Flash Elorde (Phi) PTS –15 Johnny Bizzaro (USA) Manila, Philippines

19 Feb 1963 *LM* Denny Moyer (USA) PTS –15 Stan Harrington (USA) Honolulu, Hawaii

23 Feb 1963 *M* Dick Tiger (Ngr) D –15 Gene Fullmer (USA) Las Vegas, USA

21 Mar 1963 *W* Luis Rodriguez (Cuba) PTS –15 Emile Grittith (VI) Los Angeles, USA

21 Mar 1963 *LW* Roberto Cruz (Phi) KO –1 Battling Torres (Mex) Los Angeles, USA

21 Mar 1963 *Fe* Ultiminio 'Sugar' Ramos (Cuba) RTD –10 Davey Moore (USA) Los Angeles, USA

4 Apr 1963 *B* Eder Jofre (Bra) KO –3 Katsutoshi Aoki (Jap) Tokyo, Japan

7 Apr 1963 *L* Carlos Ortiz (PR) RSF –13 Doug Vaillant (Cuba) San Juan, Puerto Rico

29 Apr 1963 *LM* Ralph Dupas (USA) PTS –15 Denny Moyer (USA) New Orleans, USA

18 May 1963 *B* Eder Jofre (Bra) RTD –11 Johnny Jamito (Phi) Manila, Philippines

1 Jun 1963 *LH* Willie Pastrano (USA) PTS –15 Harold Johnson (USA) Las Vegas, USA

8 Jun 1963 *W* Emile Griffith (VI) PTS –15 Luis Rodriguez (Cuba) New York, USA

15 Jun 1963 *LW* Eddie Perkins (USA) PTS –15 Roberto Cruz (Phi) Manila, Philippines

17 Jun 1963 *LM* Ralph Dupas (USA) PTS –15 Denny Moyer (USA) Baltimore, USA

13 Jul 1963 *Fe* Ultiminio 'Sugar' Ramos (Cuba) PTS –15 Rafiu King (Ngr) Mexico City, Mexico

22 Jul 1963 *H* Sonny Liston (USA) KO –1 Floyd Patterson (USA) Las Vegas, USA

10 Aug 1963 *M* Dick Tiger (Ngr) KO –7 Gene Fullmer (USA) Ibadan, Nigeria

7 Sep 1963 *LM* Sandro Mazzinghi (Ita) KO –9 Ralph Dupas (USA) Milan, Italy

18 Sep 1963 *Fl* Hiroyuki Ebihara (Jap) KO –1 Pone Kingpetch (Tha) Tokyo, Japan

16 Nov 1963 *JL* Flash Elorde (Phi) DIS –11 Love Allotey (Gha) Manila, Philippines

2 Dec 1963 *LM* Sandro Mazzinghi (Ita) KO –13 Ralph Dupas (USA) Sydney, Australia

7 Dec 1963 *M* Joey Giardello (USA) PTS –15 Dick Tiger (Ngr) New York, USA

4 Jan 1964 *LW* Eddie Perkins (USA) RSF –13 Yoshinori Takahashi (Jap) Tokyo, Japan

23 Jan 1964 *Fl* Pone Kingpetch (Tha) PTS –15 Hiroyuki Ebihara (Jap) Bangkok, Thailand

15 Feb 1964 *L* Carlos Ortiz (PR) RSF –14 Flash Elorde (Phi) Manila, Philippines

25 Feb 1964 *H* Cassius Clay (USA) RTD –6 Sonny Liston (USA) Miami, USA

28 Feb 1964 *Fe* Ultiminio 'Sugar' Ramos (Cuba) RTD –6 Mitsonuri Seki (Jap) Tokyo, Japan

10 Apr 1964 *LH* Willie Pastrano (USA) KO –6 Gregorio Peralta (Arg) New Orleans, USA

11 Apr 1964 *L* Carlos Ortiz (PR) PTS –15 Kenny Lane (USA) San Juan, Puerto Rico

19 Apr 1964 *LW* Eddie Perkins (USA) PTS –15 Bunny Grant (Jam) Kingston, Jamaica

9 May 1964 *Fe* Ultiminio 'Sugar' Ramos (Cuba) PTS –15 Floyd Robertson (Gha) Accra, Ghana

12 Jun 1964 *W* Emile Griffith (VI) PTS –15 Luis Rodriguez (Cuba) Las Vegas, USA

27 Jul 1964 *JL* Flash Elorde (Phi) RSF –12 Teruo Kosaka (Jap) Tokyo, Japan

22 Sep 1964 *W* Emile Griffith (VI) PTS –15 Brian Curvis (GB) London, England

26 Sep 1964 *Fe* Vicente Saldivar (Mex) RTD –11 Ultiminio 'Sugar' Ramos (Cuba) Mexico City, Mexico

3 Oct 1964 *LM* Sandro Mazzinghi (Ita) RSF –12 Tony Montano (USA) Genoa, Italy

27 Nov 1964 *B* Eder Jofre (Bra) KO –7 Bernardo Carabello (Col) Bogotá, Colombia

30 Nov 1964 *LH* Willie Pastrano (USA) RSF –11 Terry Downes (GB) Manchester, England

11 Dec 1964 *LM* Sandro Mazzinghi (Ita) PTS –15 Fortunato Manca (Ita) Rome, Italy

14 Dec 1964 *M* Joey Giardello (USA) PTS –15 Rubin Carter (USA) Philadelphia, USA

Missed me! Cassius Clay (USA) (right) on his way to first winning the world title. Sonny Liston (USA) never came out for the seventh round. The Photo Source

18 Jan 1965 *LW* Carlos Hernandez (Ven) PTS –15 Eddie Perkins (USA) Caracas, Venezuela

5 Mar 1965 *H(WBA)* Ernie Terrell (USA) PTS –15 Eddie Machen (USA) Chicago, USA

30 Mar 1965 *LH* Jose Torres (PR) KO –9 Willie Pastrano (USA) New York, USA

30 Mar 1965 *W* Emile Griffith (VI) PTS –15 Jose Stable (Cuba) New York, USA

10 Apr 1965 *L* Ismael Laguna (Pan) PTS –15 Carlos Ortiz (PR) Panama City, Panama

23 Apr 1965 *Fl* Salvatore Burruni (Ita) PTS –15 Pone Kingpetch (Tha) Rome, Italy

7 May 1965 *Fe* Vicente Saldivar (Mex) RSF –15 Raul Rojas (USA) Los Angeles, USA

16 May 1965 *LW* Carlos Hernandez (Ven) RSF –4 Mario Rossito (Col) Maracaibo, Venezuela

18 May 1965 *B* Fighting Harada (Jap) PTS –15 Eder Jofre (Bra) Nagoya, Japan

25 May 1965 *H* Muhammad Ali (USA) KO –1 Sonny Liston (USA) Lewiston, USA

5 Jun 1965 *JL* Flash Elorde (Phi) KO –13 Teruo Kosaka (Jap) Manila, Philippines

18 Jun 1965 *LM* Nino Benvenuti (Ita) KO –6 Sandro Mazzinghi (Ita) Milan, Italy

10 Jul 1965 *LW* Carlos Hernandez (Ven) KO –3 Percy Hayles (Jam) Kingston, Jamaica

7 Sep 1965 *Fe* Vicente Saldivar (Mex) PTS –15 Howard Winstone (GB) London, England

21 Oct 1965 *M* Dick Tiger (Ngr) PTS –15 Joey Giardello (USA) New York, USA

1 Nov 1965 *H(WBA)* Ernie Terrell (USA) PTS –15 George Chuvalo (Can) Toronto, Canada

13 Nov 1965 *L* Carlos Ortiz (PR) PTS –15 Ismael Laguna (Pan) San Juan, Puerto Rico

22 Nov 1965 *H* Muhammad Ali (USA) RSF –12 Floyd Patterson (USA) Las Vegas, USA

30 Nov 1965 *B* Fighting Harada (Jap) PTS –15 Alan Rudkin (GB) Tokyo, Japan

2 Dec 1965 *Fl(WBC)* Salvatore Burruni (Ita) KO –13 Rocky Gattelleri (Ita) Sydney, Australia

4 Dec 1965 *JL* Flash Elorde (Phi) PTS –15 Kang-Il Suh (S. Kor) Manila, Philippines

10 Dec 1965 *W* Emile Griffith (VI) PTS –15 Manuel Gonzalez (USA) New York, USA

17 Dec 1965 *LM* Nino Benvenuti (Ita) PTS –15 Sandro Mazzinghi (Ita) Rome, Italy

12 Feb 1966 *Fe* Vicente Saldivar (Mex) KO –2 Floyd Robertson (Gha) Mexico City, Mexico

29 Mar 1966 *H* Muhammad Ali (USA) PTS –15 George Chuvalo (Can) Toronto, Canada

1 Apr 1966 *Fl(WBA)* Horacio Accavallo (Arg) PTS –15 Katsuyoshi Takayama (Jap) Tokyo, Japan

25 Apr 1966 *M* Emile Griffith (VI) PTS –15 Dick Tiger (Ngr) New York, USA

29 Apr 1966 *LW* Sandro Lopopolo (Ita) PTS –15 Carlos Hernandez (Ven) Rome, Italy

21 May 1966 *H* Muhammad Ali (USA) RSF –6 Henry Cooper (GB) London, England

21 May 1966 *LH* Jose Torres (PR) PTS –15 Wayne Thornton (USA) New York, USA

31 May 1966 *B* Fighting Harada (Jap) PTS –15 Eder Jofre (Bra) Tokyo, Japan

14 Jun 1966 *Fl(WBC)* Walter McGowan (GB) PTS –15 Salvatore Burruni (Ita) London, England

20 Jun 1966 *L* Carlos Ortiz (PR) RSF –12 Johnny Bizzaro (USA) Pittsburgh, USA

25 Jun 1966 *LM* Ki-Soo Kim (S. Kor) PTS –15 Nino Benvenuti (Ita) Seoul, South Korea

28 Jun 1966 *H(WBA)* Ernie Terrell (USA) PTS –15 Doug Jones (USA) Houston, USA

13 Jul 1966 *M* Emile Griffith (VI) PTS –15 Joey Archer (USA) New York, USA

15 Jul 1966 *Fl(WBA)* Horacio Accavallo (Arg) PTS –15 Hiroyuki Ebihara (Jap) Buenos Aires, Argentina

6 Aug 1966 *H* Muhammad Ali (USA) KO –3 Brian London (GB) London, England

7 Aug 1966 *Fe* Vicente Saldivar (Mex) PTS –15 Mitsunori Seki (Jap) Mexico City, Mexico

15 Aug 1966 *LH* Jose Torres (PR) PTS –15 Eddie Cotton (USA) Las Vegas, USA

24 Aug 1966 *W(WBA)* Curtis Cokes (USA) PTS –15 Manuel Gonzalez (USA) New Orleans, USA

10 Sep 1966 *H* Muhammad Ali (USA) RSF –12 Karl Mildenberger (FRG) Frankfurt, West Germany

15 Oct 1966 *LH* Jose Torres (PR) KO –2 Chic Calderwood (GB) San Juan, Puerto Rico

21 Oct 1966 *LW* Sandro Lopopolo (Ita) RSF –7 Vicente Rivas (Ven) Rome, Italy

22 Oct 1966 *L* Carlos Ortiz (PR) RSF –5 Ultiminio 'Sugar' Ramos (Cuba) Mexico City, Mexico

23 Oct 1966 *JL* Flash Elorde (Phi) PTS –15 Vicente Derado (Arg) Manila, Philippines

14 Nov 1966 *H* Muhammad Ali (USA) RSF –3 Cleveland Williams (USA) Houston, USA

28 Nov 1966 *W* Curtis Cokes (USA) PTS –15 Jean Josselin (Fra) Dallas, USA

28 Nov 1966 *L(WBA)* Carlos Ortiz (PR) KO –14 Flash Elorde (Phi) New York, USA

10 Dec 1966 *Fl(WBA)* Horacio Accavallo (Arg) PTS –15 Efren Torres (Mex) Buenos Aires, Argentina

16 Dec 1966 *LH* Dick Tiger (Ngr) PTS –15 Jose Torres (PR) New York, USA

17 Dec 1966 *LM* Ki-Soo Kim (S. Kor) PTS –15 Stan Harrington (USA) Seoul, South Korea

30 Dec 1966 *Fl(WBC)* Chartchai Chionoi (Tha) RSF –9 Walter McGowan (GB) Bangkok, Thailand

3 Jan 1967 *B* Fighting Harada (Jap) PTS –15 Joe Medel (Mex) Nagoya, Japan

23 Jan 1967 *M* Emile Griffith (VI) PTS –15 Joey Archer (USA) New York, USA

29 Jan 1967 *Fe* Vicente Saldivar (Mex) RSF –7 Mitsunori Seki (Jap) Mexico City, Mexico

6 Feb 1967 *H* Muhammad Ali (USA) PTS –15 Ernie Terrell (USA) Houston, USA

22 Mar 1967 *H* Muhammad Ali (USA) KO –7 Zora Folley (USA) New York, USA

17 Apr 1967 *M* Nino Benvenuti (Ita) PTS –15 Emile Griffith (VI) New York, USA

30 Apr 1967 *LW* Paul Fuji (Haw) RTD –2 Sandro Lopopolo (Ita) Tokyo, Japan

16 May 1967 *LH* Dick Tiger (Ngr) PTS –15 Jose Torres (PR) New York, USA

19 May 1967 *W* Curtis Cokes (USA) RSF –10 François Pavilla (Fra) Dallas, USA

15 Jun 1967 *JL* Yoshiaki Numata (Jap) PTS –15 Flash Elorde (Phi) Tokyo, Japan

15 Jun 1967 *Fe* Vicente Saldivar (Mex) PTS –15 Howard Winstone (GB) Cardiff, Wales

1 Jul 1967 *L* Carlos Ortiz (PR) RSF –4 Ultiminio 'Sugar' Ramos (Cuba) Mexico City, Mexico

4 Jul 1967 *B* Fighting Harada (Jap) PTS –15 Bernardo Carabello (Col) Tokyo, Japan

26 Jul 1967 *Fl(WBC)* Chartchai Chionoi (Tha) KO –3 Puntip Keosuriya (Tha) Bangkok, Thailand

13 Aug 1967 *Fl(WBA)* Horacio Accavallo (Arg) PTS –15 Hiroyuki Ebihara (Jap) Buenos Aires, Argentina

16 Aug 1967 *L* Carlos Ortiz (PR) PTS –15 Ismael Laguna (Pan) New York, USA

19 Sep 1967 *Fl(WBC)* Chartchai Chionoi (Tha) RSF –7 Walter McGowan (GB) London, England

29 Sep 1967 *M* Emile Griffith (VI) PTS –15 Nino Benvenuti (Ita) New York, USA

2 Oct 1967 *W* Curtis Cokes (USA) RSF –8 Charley Shipes (USA) Oakland, USA

14 Oct 1967 *Fe* Vicente Saldivar (Mex) RTD –12 Howard Winstone (GB) Mexico City, Mexico

31 Oct 1967 *LM* Ki-Soo Kim (S. Kor) PTS –15 Freddie Little (USA) Seoul, South Korea

16 Nov 1967 *LW* Paul Fuji (Haw) KO –4 Willi Quator (FRG) Tokyo, Japan

17 Nov 1967 *LH* Dick Tiger (Ngr) KO –12 Roger Rouse (USA) Las Vegas, USA

14 Dec 1967 *JL* Hiroshi Kobayashi (Jap) KO –12 Yoshiaki Numata (Jap) Tokyo, Japan

23 Jan 1968 *Fe(WBC)* Howard Winstone (GB) RSF –9 Mitsunori Seki (Jap) London, England

28 Jan 1968 *Fl(WBC)* Chartchai Chionoi (Tha) RSF –13 Efren Torres (Mex) Mexico City, Mexico

27 Feb 1968 *B* Lionel Rose (Aus) PTS –15 Fighting Harada (Jap) Tokyo, Japan

4 Mar 1968 *H(NY)* Joe Frazier (USA) RSF –11 Buster Mathis (USA) New York, USA

4 Mar 1968 *M* Nino Benvenuti (Ita) PTS –15 Emile Griffith (VI) New York, USA

28 Mar 1968 *Fe(WBA)* Raul Rojas (USA) PTS –15 Enrique Higgins (Col) Los Angeles, USA

30 Mar 1968 *JL* Hiroshi Kobayashi (Jap) D –15 Rene Barrientos (Phi) Tokyo, Japan

16 Apr 1968 *W* Curtis Cokes (USA) RSF –5 Willie Ludick (SA) Dallas, USA

27 Apr 1968 *H(WBA)* Jimmy Ellis (USA) PTS –15 Jerry Quarry (USA) Oakland, USA

24 May 1968 *LH* Bob Foster (USA) KO –4 Dick Tiger (Ngr) New York, USA

26 May 1968 *LM* Sandro Mazzinghi (Ita) PTS –15 Ki-Soo Kim (S. Kor) Milan, Italy

Despite taking this right from Joey Archer (USA), Emile Griffith (VI) still went on successfully to defend his world middleweight title at Madison Square Garden in 1967. The Photo Source

This was the first of Howard Winstone's two attempts at taking the world featherweight title off Vicente Saldivar (Mexico), in 1967. Winstone (GB) lost on points over 15 rounds. Syndication International

24 Jun 1968 *H(NY)* Joe Frazier (USA) RTD –2 Manuel Ramos (Mex) New York, USA

29 Jun 1968 *L* Carlos Cruz (Dom) PTS –15 Carlos Ortiz (PR) Santo Domingo, Dominican Republic

2 Jul 1968 *B* Lionel Rose (Aus) PTS –15 Takao Sakurai (Jap) Tokyo, Japan

24 July 1968 *Fe(WBC)* Jose Legra (Cuba) RSF –5 Howard Winstone (GB) Porthcawl, Wales

14 Sep 1968 *H(WBA)* Jimmy Ellis (USA) PTS –15 Floyd Patterson (USA) Stockholm, Sweden

27 Sep 1968 *L* Carlos Cruz (Dom) PTS –15 Mando Ramos (USA) Los Angeles, USA

28 Sep 1968 *Fe(WBA)* Sho Saijyo (Jap) PTS –15 Raul Rojas (USA) Los Angeles, USA

15 Oct 1968 *JL* Hiroshi Kobayashi (Jap) PTS –15 Jaime Valladares (Ecu) Tokyo, Japan

21 Oct 1968 *W* Curtis Cokes (USA) PTS –15 Ramon LaCruz (Arg) New Orleans, USA

25 Oct 1968 *LM* Sandro Mazzinghi (Ita) NC –8 Freddie Little (USA) Rome, Italy

10 Nov 1968 *Fl(WBC)* Chartachai Chionoi (Tha) PTS –15 Bernabe Villacampo (Phi) Bangkok, Thailand

6 Dec 1968 *H(NY)* Joe Frazier (USA) PTS –15 Oscar Bonavena (Arg) Philadelphia, USA

6 Dec 1968 *B* Lionel Rose (Aus) PTS –15 Chucho Castillo (Mex) Inglewood, USA

12 Dec 1968 *LW(WBA)* Nicolino Loche (Arg) RTD –9 Paul Fuji (Haw) Tokyo, Japan

14 Dec 1968 *M* Nino Benvenuti (Ita) PTS –15 Don Fullmer (USA) San Remo, Italy

14 Dec 1968 *LW(WBC)* Pedro Adigue (Phi) PTS –15 Adolph Pruitt (USA) Manila, Philippines

12 Jan 1969 *Fe(WBC)* Johnny Famechon (Fra) PTS –15 Jose Legra (Cuba) London, England

22 Jan 1969 *LH* Bob Foster (USA) KO –1 Frank de Paula (USA) New York, USA

9 Feb 1969 *Fe(WBA)* Sho Saijyo (Jap) PTS –15 Pedro Gomez (Ven) Tokyo, Japan

15 Feb 1969 *JL(WBC)* Rene Barrientos (Phi) PTS –15 Ruben Navarro (Mex) Manila, Philippines

18 Feb 1969 *L* Mando Ramos (USA) RSF –11 Carlos Cruz (Dom) Los Angeles, USA

23 Feb 1969 *Fl(WBC)* Efren Torres (Mex) RSF –8 Chartchai Chionoi (Tha) Mexico City, Mexico

8 Mar 1969 *B* Lionel Rose (Aus) PTS –15 Alan Rudkin (GB) Melbourne, Australia

17 Mar 1969 *LM* Freddie Little (USA) PTS –15 Stan Hayward (USA) Las Vegas, USA

30 Mar 1969 *Fl(WBA)* Hiroyuki Ebihara (Jap) PTS –15 Jose Severino (Bra) Sapporo, Japan

6 Apr 1969 *JL(WBA)* Hiroshi Kobayashi (Jap) PTS –15 Antonio Amaya (Pan) Tokyo, Japan

18 Apr 1969 *W* Jose Napoles (Cuba) RSF –13 Curtis Cokes (USA) Los Angeles, USA

22 Apr 1969 *H(NY)* Joe Frazier (USA) KO –1 Dave Zyglewicz (USA) Houston, USA

3 May 1969 *LW(WBA)* Nicolino Loche (Arg) PTS –15 Carlos Hernandez (Ven) Buenos Aires, Argentina

24 May 1969 *LH* Bob Foster (USA) KO –4 Andy Kendall (USA) West Springfield, USA

23 Jun 1969 *H(NY)* Joe Frazier (USA) RSF –7 Jerry Quarry (USA) New York, USA

29 Jun 1969 *W* Jose Napoles (Cuba) RTD –10 Curtis Cokes (USA) Mexico City, Mexico

28 Jul 1969 *Fe(WBC)* Johnny Famechon (Fra) PTS –15 Fighting Harada (Jap) Sydney, Australia

22 Aug 1969 *B* Ruben Olivares (Mex) KO –5 Lionel Rose (Aus) Inglewood, USA

7 Sep 1969 *Fe(WBA)* Sho Saijyo (Jap) KO –2 Jose Luis Pimentel (Mex) Sapporo, Japan

9 Sep 1969 *LM* Freddie Little (USA) KO –2 Hisao Minami (Jap) Osaka, Japan

4 Oct 1969 *M* Nino Benvenuti (Ita) DIS –7 Fraser Scott (USA) Naples, Italy

4 Oct 1969 *L* Mando Ramos (USA) KO –6 Yoshiaki Numata (Jap) Los Angeles, USA

11 Oct 1969 *LW(WBA)* Nicolino Loche (Arg) PTS –15 Joao Henrique (Bra) Buenos Aires, Argentina

17 Oct 1969 *W* Jose Napoles (Cuba) PTS –15 Emile Griffith (VI) Los Angeles, USA

19 Oct 1969 *Fl(WBA)* Bernabe Villacampo (Phi) PTS –15 Hiroyuki Ebihara (Jap) Osaka, Japan

9 Nov 1969 *JL(WBA)* Hiroshi Kobayashi (Jap) PTS –15 Carlos Canete (Arg) Tokyo, Japan

22 Nov 1969 *M* Nino Benvenuti (Ita) KO –11 Luis Rodriguez (Cuba) Rome, Italy

28 Nov 1969 *Fl(WBC)* Efren Torres (Mex) PTS –15 Susumu Hanagata (Jap) Guadalajara, Mexico

12 Dec 1969 *B* Ruben Olivares (Mex) RSF –2 Alan Rudkin (GB) Inglewood, USA

6 Jan 1970 *Fe(WBC)* Johnny Famechon (Fra) KO –14 Fighting Harada (Jap) Tokyo, Japan

31 Jan 1970 *LW(WBC)* Bruno Arcari (Ita) PTS –15 Pedro Adigue (Phi) Rome, Italy

8 Feb 1970 *Fe(WBA)* Sho Saijyo (Jap) PTS –15 Godfrey Stevens (Chi) Tokyo, Japan

14 Feb 1970 *W* Jose Napoles (Cuba) RSF –15 Ernie Lopez (USA) Inglewood, USA

16 Feb 1970 *H* Joe Frazier (USA) RTD –4 Jimmy Ellis (USA) New York, USA

3 Mar 1970 *L* Ismael Laguna (Pan) RTD –9 Mando Ramos (USA) Los Angeles, USA

20 Mar 1970 *LM* Freddie Little (USA PTS –15 Gerhard Piaskowy (FRG) Berlin, West Germany

20 Mar 1970 *Fl(WBC)* Chartchai Chionoi (Tha) PTS –15 Efren Torres (Mex) Bangkok, Thailand

4 Apr 1970 *LH* Bob Foster (USA) RSF –3 Roger Rouse (USA) Missoula, USA

5 Apr 1970 *JL(WBC)* Yoshiaki Numata (Jap) PTS –15 Rene Barrientos (Phi) Tokyo, Japan

14 Apr 1970 *Fl(WBC)* Berkrerk Chartvanchai (Tha) PTS –15 Bernabe Villacampo (Phi) Bangkok, Thailand

9 May 1970 *Fe(WBC)* Vicente Saldivar (Mex) PTS –15 Johnny Famechon (Fra) Rome, Italy

16 May 1970 *LW(WBA)* Nicolino Loche (Arg) PTS –15 Adolph Pruitt (USA) Buenos Aires, Argentina

23 May 1970 *M* Nino Benvenuti (Ita) KO –8 Tom Bethea (USA) Umag, Yugoslavia

6 Jun 1970 *L* Ismael Laguna (Pan) RSF –13 Ishimatsu Susuki (Jap) Panama City, Panama

27 Jun 1970 *LH* Bob Foster (USA) KO –10 Mark Tessman (USA) Baltimore, USA

5 Jul 1970 *Fe(WBA)* Sho Saijyo (Jap) PTS –15 Frankie Crawford (USA) Sendai, Japan

9 July 1970 *LM* Carmen Bossi (Ita) PTS –15 Freddie Little (USA) Monza, Italy

10 Jul 1970 *LW(WBC)* Bruno Arcari (Ita) DIS –6 Rene Roque (Fra) Lignano Sabbiadoro, Italy

23 Aug 1970 *JL(WBA)* Hiroshi Kobayashi (Jap) PTS –15 Antonio Amaya (Pan) Tokyo, Japan

26 Sep 1970 *L* Ken Buchanan (GB) PTS –15 Ismael Laguna (Pan) San Juan, Puerto Rico

27 Sep 1970 *JL(WBC)* Yoshiaki Numata (Jap) KO –5 Raul Rojas (USA) Tokyo, Japan

16 Oct 1970 *B* Jesus Chucho Castillo (Mex) RSF –14 Ruben Olivares (Mex) Inglewood, USA

21 Oct 1970 *FI(WBA)* Masao Ohba (Jap) RSF –13 Berkrerk Chartvanchai (Tha) Tokyo, Japan

30 Oct 1970 *LW(WBC)* Bruno Arcari (Ita) KO –3 Raimundo Dias (Bra) Genoa, Italy

7 Nov 1970 *M* Carlos Monzon (Arg) KO –12 Nino Benvenuti (Ita) Rome, Italy

18 Nov 1970 *H* Joe Frazier (USA) KO –2 Bob Foster (USA) Detroit, USA

3 Dec 1970 *W* Billy Backus (USA) RSF –4 Jose Napoles (Cuba) Syracuse, USA

7 Dec 1970 *FI(WBC)* Erbito Salavarria (Phi) RSF –2 Chartchai Chionoi (Tha) Bangkok, Thailand

11 Dec 1970 *Fe(WBC)* Kuniaki Shibata (Jap) RSF –12 Vicente Saldivar (Mex) Tijuana, Mexico

3 Jan 1971 *JL(WBC)* Yoshiaki Numata (Jap) PTS –15 Rene Barrientos (Phi) Shizuoka, Japan

12 Feb 1971 *L* Ken Buchanan (GB) PTS –15 Ruben Navarro (USA) Los Angeles, USA

27 Feb 1971 *LH(WBA)* Vicente Paul Rondon (Ven) RSF –6 Jimmy Dupree (USA) Caracas, Venezuela

2 Mar 1971 *LH(WBC)* Bob Foster (USA) KO –4 Hal Carroll (USA) Scranton, USA

4 Mar 1971 *JL(WBA)* Hiroshi Kobayashi (Jap) PTS –15 Ricardo Arredondo (Mex) Utsunomija, Japan

6 Mar 1971 *LW(WBC)* Bruno Arcari (Ita) PTS –15 Joao Henrique (Bra) Genoa, Italy

8 Mar 1971 *H* Joe Frazier (USA) PTS –15 Muhammad Ali (USA) New York, USA

1 Apr 1971 *FI(WBA)* Masao Ohba (Jap) PTS –15 Betulio Gonzalez (Ven) Tokyo, Japan

2 Apr 1971 *B* Ruben Olivares (Mex) PTS –15 Jesus Chucho Castillo (Mex) Inglewood, USA

3 Apr 1971 *LW(WBA)* Nicolino Loche (Arg) PTS –15 Domingo Barrera (Spa) Buenos Aires, Argentina

24 Apri 1971 *LH(WBC)* Bob Foster (USA) PTS –15 Ray Anderson (USA) Tampa, USA

29 Apr 1971 *LM* Carmen Bossi (Ita) D –15 Jose Hernandez (Spa) Madrid, Spain

30 Apr 1971 *FI(WBC)* Erbito Salavarria (Phi) PTS –15 Susumu Hanagata (Jap) Manila, Philippines

8 May 1971 *M* Carlos Monzon (Arg) RSF –3 Nino Benvenuti (Ita) Monte Carlo, Monaco

31 May 1971 *JL(WBC)* Yoshiaki Numata (Jap) PTS –15 Lionel Rose (Aus) Hiroshima, Japan

3 Jun 1971 *Fe(WBC)* Kuniaki Shibata (Jap) KO –1 Raul Cruz (Mex) Tokyo, Japan

4 Jun 1971 *W* Jose Napoles (Cuba) RSF –8 Billy Backus (USA) Inglewood, USA

5 Jun 1971 *LH(WBA)* Vicente Paul Rondon (Ven) KO –1 Piero del Papa (Ita) Caracas, Venezuela

26 Jun 1971 *LW(WBC)* Bruno Arcari (Ita) RSF –9 Enrique Jana (Arg) Palermo, Italy

29 Jul 1971 *JL(WBA)* Alfredo Marcano (Ven) RTD –10 Hiroshi Kobayashi (Jap) Aomoni, Japan

21 Aug 1971 *LH(WBA)* Vicente Paul Rondon (Ven) PTS –15 Eddie Jones (USA) Caracas, Venezuela

2 Sep 1971 *Fe(WBA)* Antonio Gomez (Ven) RSF –5 Sho Saijyo (Jap) Tokyo, Japan

13 Sep 1971 *L* Ken Buchanan (GB) PTS –15 Ismael Laguna (Pan) New York, USA

25 Sep 1971 *M* Carlos Monzon (Arg) RSF –14 Emile Griffith (VI) Buenos Aires, Argentina

9 Oct 1971 *LW(WBC)* Bruno Arcari (Ita) KO –10 Domingo Barrera Corpas (Spa) Genoa, Italy

10 Oct 1971 *JL(WBC)* Ricardo Arredondo (Mex) KO –10 Yoshiaki Numata (Jap) Sendai, Japan

23 Oct 1971 *FI(WBA)* Masao Ohba (Jap) PTS –15 Fernando Cabanela (Phi) Tokyo, Japan

25 Oct 1971 *B* Ruben Olivares (Mex) RSF –14 Kazuyoshi Kanazawa (Jap) Nagoya, Japan

26 Oct 1971 *LH(WBA)* Vincente Paul Rondon (Ven) RSF –12 Gomeo Brennan (Bah) Miami, USA

30 Oct 1971 *LH(WBC)* Bob Foster (USA) RSF –8 Tommy Hicks (USA) Scranton, USA

31 Oct 1971 *LM* Koichi Wajima (Jap) PTS –15 Carmen Bossi (Ita) Tokyo, Japan

5 Nov 1971 *L(WBC)* Pedro Carrasco (Spa) DIS–11 Mando Ramos (USA) Madrid, Spain

6 Nov 1971 *JL(WBA)* Alfredo Marcano (Ven) RSF –4 Kenji Iwata (Jap) Caracas, Venezuela

11 Nov 1971 *Fe(WBC)* Kuniaki Shibata (Jap) D –15 Ernesto Marcel (Pan) Matsuyama, Japan

20 Nov 1971 *FI(WBC)* Erbito Salavarria (Phi) D –15 Betulio Gonzalez (Ven) Maracaibo, Venezuela

11 Dec 1971 *LW(WBA)* Nicolino Loche (Arg) PTS –15 Antonio Cervantes (Col) Buenos Aires, Argentina

14 Dec 1971 *W* Jose Napoles (Cuba) PTS –15 Hedgemon Lewis (USA) Inglewood, USA

14 Dec 1971 *B* Ruben Olivares (Mex) RSF –11 Jesus Pimentel (Mex) Inglewood, USA

15 Dec 1971 *LH(WBA)* Vicente Paul Rondon (Ven) KO –8 Doyle Baird (USA) Cleveland, USA

16 Dec 1971 *LH(WBC)* Bob Foster (USA) RSF –4 Brian Kelly (USA) Oklahoma City, USA

15 Jan 1972 *H* Joe Frazier (USA) RSF –4 Terry Daniels (USA) New Orleans, USA

29 Jan 1972 *JL(WBC)* Ricardo Arredondo (Mex) PTS –15 Jose Isaac Marin (CR) San Jose, Costa Rica

5 Feb 1972 *Fe(WBA)* Antonio Gomez (Ven) KO –7 Raul Martinez (Mex) Maracay, Venezuela

18 Feb 1972 *L(WBC)* Mando Ramos (USA) PTS –15 Pedro Carrasco (Spa) Los Angeles, USA

4 Mar 1972 *M* Carlos Monzon (Arg) RSF –5 Denny Moyer (USA) Rome, Italy

4 Mar 1972 *FI(WBA)* Masao Ohba (Jap) PTS –15 Susumu Hanagata (Jap) Tokyo, Japan

10 Mar 1972 *LW(WBA)* Alfonso Frazer (Pan) PTS –15 Nicolino Loche (Arg) Panama City, Panama

19 Mar 1972 *B* Rafael Herrera (Mex) KO –8 Ruben Olivares (Mex) Mexico City, Mexico

28 Mar 1972 *W* Jose Napoles (Cuba) KO –7 Ralph Charles (GB) London, England

7 Apr 1972 *LH* Bob Foster (USA) KO –2 Vicente Paul Rondon (Ven) Miami, USA

22 Apr 1972 *JL(WBC)* Ricardo Arredondo (Mex) KO –5 William Martinez (Nic) Mexico City, Mexico

25 Apr 1972 *JL(WBA)* Ben Villaflor (Phi) PTS –15 Alfredo Marcano (Ven) Honolulu, USA

7 May 1972 *LM* Koichi Wajima (Jap) KO –1 Domenico Tiberia (Ita) Fukuoka, Japan

9 May 1972 *Fe(WBC)* Clemente Sanchez (Mex) KO –3 Kuniaki Shibata (Jap) Tokyo, Japan

25 May 1972 *H* Joe Frazier (USA) RSF –4 Ron Stander (USA) Omaha, USA

3 Jun 1972 *Fl(WBC)* Betulio Gonzalez (Ven) KO –4 Socrates Batoto (Phi) Caracas, Venezuela

10 Jun 1972 *W* Jose Napoles (Cuba) RSF –2 Adolph Pruitt (USA) Monterrey, Mexico

10 Jun 1972 *LW(WBC)* Bruno Arcari (Ita) KO –12 Joao Henrique (Bra) Genoa, Italy

17 Jun 1972 *M* Carlos Monzon (Arg) RTD –12 Jean-Claude Boutier (Fra) Paris, France

26 Jun 1972 *L(WBA)* Roberto Duran (Pan) RSF –13 Ken Buchanan (GB) New York, USA

27 Jun 1972 *LH* Bob Foster (USA) KO –4 Mike Quarry (USA) Las Vegas, USA

28 Jun 1972 *L(WBC)* Mando Ramos (USA) PTS –15 Pedro Carrasco (Spa) Madrid, Spain

29 Jul 1972 *B* Enrique Pinder (Pan) PTS –15 Rafael Herrera (Mex) Panama City, Panama

19 Aug 1972 *M* Carlos Monzon (Arg) RSF –5 Tom Bogs (Den) Copenhagen, Denmark

19 Aug 1972 *Fe(WBA)* Ernesto Marcel (Pan) PTS –15 Antonio Gomez (Ven) Maracay, Venezuela

5 Sep 1972 *JL(WBA)* Ben Villaflor (Phi) D –15 Victor Echegaray (Arg) Honolulu, USA

15 Sep 1972 *L(WBC)* Erubey 'Chango' Carmona (Mex) RSF –8 Mando Ramos (USA) Los Angeles, USA

15 Sep 1972 *JL(WBC)* Ricardo Arredondo (Mex) KO –12 Susumu Okabe (Jap) Tokyo, Japan

26 Sep 1972 *LH* Bob Foster (USA) KO –14 Chris Finnegan (GB) London, England

29 Sep 1972 *Fl(WBC)* Venice Borkorsor (Tha) RTD –10 Betulio Gonzalez (Ven) Bangkok, Thailand

3 Oct 1972 *LM* Koichi Wajima (Jap) KO –3 Matt Donovan (Tri) Tokyo, Japan

29 Oct 1972 *LW(WBA)* Antonio Cervantes (Col) KO –10 Alfonso Frazer (Pan) Panama City, Panama

10 Nov 1972 *L(WBC)* Rodolfo Gonzalez (Mex) RTD –12 Erubey 'Chango' Carmona (Mex) Los Angeles, USA

11 Nov 1972 *M* Carlos Monzon (Arg) PTS –15 Bennie Briscoe (USA) Buenos Aires, Argentina

2 Dec 1972 *LW(WBC)* Bruno Arcari (Ita) PTS –15 Everaldo Costa Azevedo (Bra) Turin, Italy

16 Dec 1972 *Fe(WBC)* Jose Legra (Cuba) RSF –10 Clemente Sanchez (Mex) Monterrey, Mexico

21 Dec 1972 *Fe(WBA)* Ernesto Marcel (Pan) RSF –6 Enrique Garcia (Mex) Panama City, Panama

9 Jan 1973 *LM* Koichi Wajima (Jap) D –15 Miguel de Oliveira (Bra) Tokyo, Japan

20 Jan 1973 *L(WBA)* Roberto Duran (Pan) KO –5 Jimmy Robertson (USA) Panama City, Panama

20 Jan 1973 *B(WBA)* Romeo Anaya (Mex) KO –3 Enrique Pinder (Pan) Panama City, Panama

21 Jan 1973 *Fl(WBA)* Masao Ohba (Jap) RSF –12 Chartchai Chionoi (Tha) Tokyo, Japan

22 Jan 1973 *H* George Foreman (USA) RSF –2 Joe Frazier (USA) Kingston, Jamaica

9 Feb 1973 *Fl(WBC)* Venice Borkorsor (Tha) PTS –15 Erbito Salavarria (Phi) Bangkok, Thailand

15 Feb 1973 *LW(WBA)* Antonio Cervantes (Col) PTS –15 Jose Marquez (PR) San Juan, Puerto Rico

28 Feb 1973 *W* Jose Napoles (Cuba) KO –7 Ernie Lopez (USA) Inglewood, USA

6 Mar 1973 *JL(WBC)* Ricardo Arredondo (Mex) PTS –15 Apollo Yoshio (Jap) Fukuoka, Japan

12 Mar 1973 *JL(WBA)* Kuniaki Shibata (Jap) PTS –15 Ben Villaflor (Phi) Honolulu, USA

17 Mar 1973 *LW(WBA)* Antonio Cervantes (Col) RTD –9 Nicolino Loche (Arg) Maracay, Venezuela

17 Mar 1973 *L(WBC)* Rodolfo Gonzalez (Mex) RSF –9 Ruben Navarro (USA) Los Angeles, USA

14 Apr 1973 *B(WBC)* Rafael Herrera (Mex) RSF –12 Rodolfo Martinez (Mex) Monterrey, Mexico

20 Apr 1973 *LM* Koichi Wajima (Jap) PTS –15 Ryu Sorimachi (Jap) Tokyo, Japan

28 Apr 1973 *B(WBA)* Romeo Anaya (Mex) PTS –15 Rogelio Lara (Mex) Inglewood, USA

5 May 1973 *Fe(WBC)* Eder Jofre (Bra) PTS –15 Jose Legra (Cuba) Brasilia, Brazil

17 May 1973 *Fl(WBC)* Chartchai Chionoi (Tha) RSF –4 Fritz Chervet (Swi) Bangkok, Thailand

19 May 1973 *LW(WBA)* Antonio Cervantes (Col) RSF –5 Alfonso Frazer (Pan) Panama City, Panama

2 Jun 1973 *M* Carlos Monzon (Arg) PTS –15 Emile Griffith (VI) Monte Carlo, Monaco

2 Jun 1973 *L(WBA)* Roberto Duran (Pan) RSF –8 Hector Thompson (Aus) Panama City, Panama

19 Jun 1973 *JL(WBA)* Kuniaki Shibata (Jap) PTS –15 Victor Echegaray (Arg) Tokyo, Japan

23 Jun 1973 *W* Jose Napoles (Cuba) PTS –15 Roger Menetrey (Fra) Grenoble, France

14 Jul 1973 *Fe(WBA)* Ernesto Marcel (Pan) RTD –11 Antonio Gomez (Ven) Panama City, Panama

4 Aug 1973 *Fl(WBC)* Betulio Gonzalez (Ven) PTS –15 Miguel Canto (Mex) Maracaibo, Venezuela

14 Aug 1973 *LM* Koichi Wajima (Jap) RTD –12 Silvano Bertini (Ita) Sapporo, Japan

18 Aug 1973 *B(WBA)* Romeo Anaya (Mex) KO –5 Enrique Pinder (Pan) Inglewood, USA

21 Aug 1973 *LH* Bob Foster (USA) PTS –15 Pierre Fourie (SA) Albuquerque, USA

1 Sep 1973 *H* George Foreman (USA) KO –1 Joe Roman (PR) Tokyo, Japan

1 Sep 1973 *JL(WBC)* Ricardo Arredondo (Mex) RSF –6 Morita Kashiwaba (Jap) Tokyo, Japan

8 Sep 1973 *LW(WBA)* Antonio Cervantes (Col) RSF –5 Carlos Giminez (Arg) Bogotá, Colombia

8 Sep 1973 *L(WBA)* Roberto Duran (Pan) RSF –10 Ishimatsu Susuki (Jap) Panama City, Panama

8 Sep 1973 *Fe(WBA)* Ernesto Marcel (Pan) KO –9 Shig Nemoto (Jap) Panama City, Panama

22 Sep 1973 *W* Jose Napoles (Cuba) PTS –15 Clyde Gray (Can) Toronto, Canada

29 Sep 1973 *M* Carlos Monzon (Arg) RTD –6 Jose Napoles (Cuba) Paris, France

13 Oct 1973 *B(WBC)* Rafael Herrera (Mex) PTS –15 Venice Borkorsor (Tha) Inglewood, USA

17 Oct 1973 *JL(WBA)* Ben Villaflor (Phi) KO –1 Kuniaki Shibata (Jap) Honolulu, USA

21 Oct 1973 *Fe(WBC)* Eder Jofre (Bra) KO –4 Vicente Saldivar (Mex) Salvador, Brazil

27 Oct 1973 *L(WBC)* Rodolfo Gonzalez (Mex) RTD –10 Antonio Puddu (Ita) Los Angeles, USA

27 Oct 1973 *Fl(WBA)* Chartchai Chionoi (Tha) PTS –15 Susumu Hanagata (Jap) Bangkok, Thailand

1 Nov 1973 *LW(WBC)* Bruno Arcari (Ita) KO –5 Jorgen Hansen (Den) Copenhagen, Denmark

13 Nov 1973 *B(WBA)* Arnold Taylor (SA) KO –14 Romeo Anaya (Mex) Johannesburg, South Africa

17 Nov 1973 *Fl(WBC)* Betulio Gonzalez (Ven) RSF –11 Alberto Morales (Mex) Caracas, Venezuela

1 Dec 1973 *LH* Bob Foster (USA) PTS –15 Pierre Fourie (SA) Johannesburg, South Africa

5 Dec 1973 *LW(WBA)* Antonio Cervantes (Col) PTS –15 Tetsuo Furuyama (Jap) Panama City, Panama

5 Feb 1974 *LM* Koichi Wajima (Jap) PTS –15 Miguel de Oliveira (Bra) Tokyo, Japan

16 Feb 1974 *LW(WBC)* Bruno Arcari (Ita) DIS –8 Tony Ortiz (Spa) Turin, Italy

16 Feb 1974 *Fe(WBA)* Ernesto Marcel (Pan) PTS –15 Alexis Arguello (Nic) Panama City, Panama

28 Feb 1974 *JL(WBC)* Kuniaki Shibata (Jap) PTS –15 Ricardo Arredondo (Mex) Tokyo, Japan

2 Mar 1974 *LW(WBC)* Antonio Cervantes (Col) KO –6 Chang Kil-Lee (S. Kor) Cartagena, Colombia

14 Mar 1974 *JL(WBA)* Ben Villaflor (Phi) D –15 Apollo Yoshio (Jap) Toyama, Japan

16 Mar 1974 *L(WBA)* Roberto Duran (Pan) KO –11 Esteban de Jesus (PR) Panama City, Panama

26 Mar 1974 *H* George Foreman (USA) RSF –2 Ken Norton (USA) Caracas, Venezuela

11 Apr 1974 *L(WBC)* Guts Ishimatsu (Jap) KO –8 Rodolfo Gonzalez (Mex) Tokyo, Japan

27 Apr 1974 *Fl(WBA)* Chartchai Chionoi (Tha) PTS –15 Fritz Chervet (Swi) Zurich, Switzerland

23 May 1974 *M(WBC)* Rodrigo Valdez (Col) KO –7 Bennie Briscoe (USA) Monte Carlo, Monaco

25 May 1974 *B(WBC)* Rafael Herrera (Mex) KO –6 Romeo Anaya (Mex) Mexico City, Mexico

4 Jun 1974 *LM* Oscar Albarado (USA) KO –15 Koichi Wajima (Jap) Tokyo, Japan

17 Jun 1974 *LH* Bob Foster (USA) D –15 Jorge Ahumada (Arg) Albuquerque, USA

27 Jun 1974 *JL(WBC)* Kuniaki Shibata (Jap) PTS –15 Antonio Amaya (Pan) Tokyo, Japan

3 Jul 1974 *B(WBA)* Soo-Hwan Hong (S. Kor) PTS –15 Arnold Taylor (SA) Durban, South Africa

9 Jul 1974 *Fe(WBA)* Ruben Olivares (Mex) RSF –7 Zensuke Utagawa (Jap) Inglewood, USA

20 Jul 1974 *Fl(WBC)* Betulio Gonzalez (Ven) RSF –10 Franco Udella (Ita) Sabbiardoro, Italy

27 July 1974 *LW(WBA)* Antonio Cervantes (Col) KO –2 Victor Ortiz (PR) Cartagena, Colombia

3 Aug 1974 *W* Jose Napoles (Cuba) RSF –9 Hedgemon Lewis (USA) Mexico City, Mexico

24 Aug 1974 *JL(WBA)* Ben Villaflor (Phi) RSF –2 Yasatsune Uehara (Jap) Honolulu, USA

7 Sep 1974 *Fe(WBC)* Bobby Chacon (USA) RSF –9 Alfredo Marcano (Ven) Los Angeles, USA

12 Sep 1974 *L(WBC)* Guts Ishimatsu (Jap) D –15 Arturo Pineda (USA) Nagoya, Japan

21 Sep 1974 *LW(WBC)* Perico Fernandez (Spa) PTS –15 Lion Furuyama (Jap) Rome, Italy

1 Oct 1974 *LH(WBC)* John Conteh (GB) PTS –15 Jorge Ahumada (Arg) London, England

1 Oct 1974 *Fl(WBC)* Shoji Oguma (Jap) PTS –15 Betulio Gonzalez (Ven) Tokyo, Japan

3 Oct 1974 *JL(WBC)* Kuniaki Shibata (Jap) RSF –15 Ramiro Clay Bolanos (Ecu) Tokyo, Japan

5 Oct 1974 *M(WBA)* Carlos Monzon (Arg) KO –7 Tony Mundine (Aus) Buenos Aires, Argentina

8 Oct 1974 *LM* Oscar Albarado (USA) RSF –7 Ryu Sorimachi (Jap) Tokyo, Japan

18 Oct 1974 *Fl(WBA)* Susumu Hanagata (Jap) RSF –6 Chartchai Chionoi (Tha) Yokohama, Japan

26 Oct 1974 *LW(WBA)* Antonio Cervantes (Col) KO –8 Yasuaki Kadota (Jap) Tokyo, Japan

30 Oct 1974 *H* Muhammad Ali (USA) KO –8 George Foreman (USA) Kinshasa, Zaire

13 Nov 1974 *M(WBC)* Rodrigo Valdez (Col) KO –11 Gratien Tonna (Fra) Paris, France

23 Nov 1974 *Fe(WBA)* Alexis Arguello (Nic) KO –13 Ruben Olivares (Mex) Inglewood, USA

28 Nov 1974 *L(WBC)* Guts Ishimatsu (Jap) KO –12 Rodolfo Gonzalez (Mex) Osaka, Japan

7 Dec 1974 *LH(WBA)* Victor Galindez (Arg) RTD –12 Len Hutchins (USA) Buenos Aires, Argentina

7 Dec 1974 *B(WBC)* Rodolfo Martinez (Mex) RSF –4 Rafael Herrera (Mex) Merida, Mexico

14 Dec 1974 *W* Jose Napoles (Cuba) KO –3 Horacio Saldano (Arg) Mexico City, Mexico

21 Dec 1974 *L(WBA)* Roberto Duran (Pan) RSF –1 Mastaka Takayama (Jap) San Jose, Costa Rica

28 Dec 1974 *B(WBA)* Soo-Hwan Hong (S. Kor) PTS –15 Fernando Cabanela (Phi) Seoul, South Korea

18 Jan 1975 *Fl(WBC)* Miguel Canto (Mex) PTS –15 Shoji Oguma (Jap) Sendai, Japan

21 Jan 1975 *LM* Koichi Wajima (Jap) PTS –15 Oscar Albarado (USA) Tokyo, Japan

27 Feb 1975 *L(WBC)* Guts Ishimatsu (Jap) PTS –15 Ken Buchanan (GB) Tokyo, Japan

1 Mar 1975 *Fe(WBC)* Bobby Chacon (USA) KO –2 Jesus Estrada (Mex) Los Angeles, USA

2 Mar 1975 *L(WBA)* Roberto Duran (Pan) KO –14 Ray Lampkin (USA) Panama City, Panama

11 Mar 1975 *LH(WBC)* John Conteh (GB) RSF –5 Lonnie Bennett (USA) London, England

14 Mar 1975 *JL(WBA)* Ben Villaflor (Phi) PTS –15 Hyun-Chi Kim (S. Kor) Manila, Philippines

14 Mar 1975 *B(WBA)* Alfonso Zamora (Mex) KO –4 Soo-Hwan Hong (S. Kor) Inglewood, USA

15 Mar 1975 *Fe(WBA)* Alexis Arguello (Nic) RSF –8 Leonel Hernandez (Ven) Caracas, Venezuela

23 Mar 1975 *JL(WBC)* Kuniaki Shibata (Jap) PTS –15 Ould Makloufi (Alg) Fukuoka, Japan

24 Mar 1975 *H* Muhammad Ali (USA) RSF –15 Chuck Wepner (USA) Cleveland, USA

29 Mar 1975 *W* Jose Napoles (Cuba) TD –12 Armando Muniz (Mex) Acapulco, Mexico

1 Apr 1975 *Fl(WBA)* Erbito Salavarria (Phi) PTS –15 Susumu Hanagata (Jap) Toyama, Japan

4 Apr 1975 *LF(WBC)* Franco Udella (Ita) DIS –12 Valentine Martinez (Mex) Milan, Italy

7 Apr 1975 *LH(WBA)* Victor Galindez (Arg) RTD –12 Len Hutchins (USA) Buenos Aires, Argentina

19 Apr 1975 *LW(WBC)* Perico Fernandez (Spa) KO –9 Joao Henrique (Bra) Barcelona, Spain

10 May 1975 *LM(WBC)* Miguel de Oliveira (Bra) PTS –15 Jose Duran (Spa) Madrid, Spain

16 May 1975 *H* Muhammad Ali (USA) RSF –11 Ron Lyle (USA) Las Vegas, USA

17 May 1975 *LW(WBA)* Antonio Cervantes (Col) PTS –15 Esteban de Jesus (PR) Panama City, Panama

21 May 1975 *B(WBC)* Rodolfo Martinez (Mex) RSF –7 Nestor Jiminez (Col) Bogotá, Colombia

24 May 1975 *Fl(WBC)* Miguel Canto (Mex) PTS –15 Betulio Gonzalez (Ven) Monterrey, Mexico

31 May 1975 *M(WBC)* Rodrigo Valdez (Col) KO –8 Ramon Mendez (Arg) Cali, Colombia

31 May 1975 *Fe(WBA)* Alexis Arguello (Nic) RSF –2 Rigoberto Riasco (Pan) Granada, Nicaragua

5 Jun 1975 *L(WBC)* Guts Ishimatsu (Jap) PTS –15 Arturo Pineda (Mex) Osaka, Japan

7 Jun 1975 *LM(WBA)* Jae-Do Yuh (S. Kor) KO –7 Koichi Wajima (Jap) Kitsakyushu, Japan

20 Jun 1975 *Fe(WBC)* Ruben Olivares (Mex) RSF –2 Bobby Chacon (USA) Inglewood, USA

28 Jun 1975 *W(WBA)* Angel Espada (PR) PTS –15 Clyde Gray (Can) San Juan, Puerto Rico

30 Jun 1975 *LH(WBA)* Victor Galindez (Arg) PTS –15 Jorge Ahumada (Arg) New York, USA

30 Jun 1975 *M(WBA)* Carlos Monzon (Arg) KO –10 Tony Licata (USA) New York, USA

1 Jul 1975 *H* Muhammad Ali (USA) PTS –15 Joe Bugner (GB) Kuala Lumpur, Malaysia

5 Jul 1975 *JL(WBC)* Alfredo Escalera (PR) KO –2 Kuniaki Shibata (Jap) Mito, Japan

12 Jul 1975 *W(WBC)* Jose Napoles (Cuba) PTS –15 Armando Muniz (Mex) Mexico City, Mexico

15 Jul 1975 *LW(WBC)* Saensak Muangsurin (Tha) RTD –8 Perico Fernandez (Spa) Bangkok, Thailand

16 Aug 1975 *M(WBC)* Rodrigo Valdez (Col) PTS –15 Rudy Robles (Mex) Cartagena, Colombia

23 Aug 1975 *Fl(WBC)* Miguel Canto (Mex) RSF –11 Jiro Takada (Jap) Merida, Mexico

23 Aug 1975 *LF(WBA)* Jaime Rios (Pan) PTS –15 Rigoberto Marcano (Ven) Panama City, Panama

30 Aug 1975 *B(WBA)* Alfonso Zamora (Mex) KO –4 Thanomjit Sukothai (Tha) Anaheim, USA

13 Sep 1975 *LF(WBC)* Luis Estaba (Ven) KO –4 Rafael Lovera (Par) Caracas, Venezuela

13 Sep 1975 *LH(WBA)* Victor Galindez (Arg) PTS –15 Pierre Fourie (SA) Johannesburg, South Africa

20 Sep 1975 *JL(WBC)* Alfredo Escalera (PR) D –15 Leonel Hernandez (Ven) Caracas, Venezuela

20 Sep 1975 *Fe(WBC)* David Kotey (Gha) PTS –15 Ruben Olivares (Mex) Inglewood, USA

1 Oct 1975 *H* Muhammad Ali (USA) RTD –14 Joe Frazier (USA) Manila, Philippines

8 Oct 1975 *B(WBC)* Rodolfo Martinez (Mex) PTS –15 Hisami Numata (Jap) Sendai, Japan

11 Oct 1975 *W(WBA)* Angel Espada (PR) PTS –15 Johnny Gant (USA) San Juan, Puerto Rico

12 Oct 1975 *Fe(WBA)* Alexis Arguello (Nic) KO –5 Royal Kobayashi (Jap) Tokyo, Japan

17 Oct 1975 *Fl(WBA)* Erbito Salavarria (Phi) PTS –15 Susumu Hanagata (Jap) Yokohama, Japan

11 Nov 1975 *LM(WBA)* Jae-Do Yuh (S. Kor) KO –6 Masahiro Misako (Jap) Shizuoko, Japan

13 Nov 1975 *LM(WBC)* Elisha Obed (Bah) RTD –10 Miguel de Oliveira (Bra) Paris, France

15 Nov 1975 *LW(WBA)* Antonio Cervantes (Col) RTD –7 Hector Thompson (Aus) Panama City, Panama

4 Dec 1975 *L(WBC)* Guts Ishimatsu (Jap) KO –14 Alvaro Rojas (CR) Tokyo, Japan

6 Dec 1975 *W(WBC)* John H. Stracey (GB) RSF –6 Jose Napoles (Cuba) Mexico City, Mexico

6 Dec 1975 *B(WBA)* Alfonso Zamora (Mex) KO –2 Socrates Batoto (Phi) Mexico City, Mexico

12 Dec 1975 *JL(WBC)* Alfredo Escalera (PR) RSF –9 Svein-Erik Paulsen (Nor) Oslo, Norway

13 Dec 1975 *M(WBA)* Carlos Monzon (Arg) KO –5 Gratien Tonna (Fra) Paris, France

13 Dec 1975 *Fl(WBC)* Miguel Canto (Mex) PTS –15 Ignacio Espinal (Dom) Merida, Mexico

17 Dec 1975 *LF(WBC)* Luis Estaba (Ven) RSF –10 Takenobu Shimabukuro (Jap) Okinawa, Japan

20 Dec 1975 *L(WBA)* Roberto Duran (Pan) KO –15 Leoncio Ortiz (Mex) San Juan, Puerto Rico

3 Jan 1976 *LF(WBC)* Jaime Rios (Pan) PTS –15 Kazunori Tenryu (Jap) Kagoshima, Japan

12 Jan 1976 *JL(WBA)* Ben Villaflor (Phi) RSF –13 Morito Kashiwaba (Jap) Tokyo, Japan

25 Jan 1976 *LW(WBC)* Saensak Muangsurin (Tha) PTS –15 Lion Furuyama (Jap) Tokyo, Japan

30 Jan 1976 *B(WBC)* Rodolfo Martinez (Mex) PTS –15 Venice Borkorsor (Tha) Bangkok, Thailand

14 Feb 1976 *LF(WBC)* Luis Estaba (Ven) PTS –15 Leo Palacios (Mex) Caracas, Venezuela

17 Feb 1976 *LM(WBA)* Koichi Wajima (Jap) KO –15 Jae-Do Yuh (S. Kor) Tokyo, Japan

20 Feb 1976 *H* Muhammad Ali (USA) KO –5 Jean-Pierre Coopman (Bel) San Juan, Puerto Rico

20 Feb 1976 *JL(WBC)* Alfredo Escalera (PR) KO –13 Jose Fernandez (Dom) San Juan, Puerto Rico

27 Feb 1976 *Fl(WBA)* Alfonso Lopez (Pan) RSF –15 Erbito Salavarria (Phi) Manila, Philippines

28 Feb 1976 *LM(WBC)* Elisha Obed (Bah) KO –2 Tony Gardner (USA) Nassau, Bahamas

6 Mar 1976 *LW(WBA)* Wilfredo Benitez (USA) PTS –15 Antonio Cervantes (Col) San Juan, Puerto Rico

6 Mar 1976 *Fe(WBC)* David Kotey (Gha) RSF –12 Flipper Uehara (Jap) Accra, Ghana

28 Mar 1976 *M(WBA)* Victor Galindez (Arg) RTD –3 Harald Skog (Nor) Oslo, Norway

28 Mar 1976 *LH(WBC)* Rodrigo Valdez (Col) KO –4 Max Cohen (Mor) Paris, France

30 Mar 1976 *W* (WBC) John H. Stracey (GB) RSF –10 Hedgemon Lewis (USA) London, England

1 Apr 1976 *JL(WBC)* Alfredo Escalera (PR) RSF –6 Buzzsaw Yamabe (Jap) Nara, Japan

3 Apr 1976 *SB(WBC)* Rigoberto Riasco (Pan) RTD –8 Waruinge Nakayama (Ken) Panama City, Panama

3 Apr 1976 B(WBA) Alfonso Zamora (Mex) KO –2 Eusebio Pedroza (Pan) Mexicali, Mexico

13 Apr 1976 JL(WBA) Ben Villaflor (Phi) D –15 Sam Serrano (PR) Honolulu, USA

21 Apr 1976 Fl(WBA) Alfonso Lopez (Pan) PTS –15 Shoji Oguma (Jap) Tokyo, Japan

24 Apr 1976 LM(WBC) Elisha Obed (Bah) PTS –15 Sea Robinson (IC) Abidjan, Ivory Coast

27 Apr 1976 W(WBA) Angel Espada (PR) RSF –8 Alfonso Hayman (USA) San Juan, Puerto Rico

30 Apr 1976 H Muhammad Ali (USA) PTS –15 Jimmy Young (USA) Landover, USA

1 May 1976 LF(WBC) Luis Estaba (Ven) PTS –15 Juan Alvarez (Mex) Caracas, Venezuela

8 May 1976 L(WBC) Esteban de Jesus (PR) PTS –15 Guts Ishimatsu (Jap) San Juan, Puerto Rico

8 May 1976 B(WBC) Carlos Zarate (Mex) KO –9 Rodolfo Martinez (Mex) Inglewood, USA

15 May 1976 Fl(WBC) Miguel Canto (Mex) PTS –15 Susumu Hanagata (Jap) Merida, Mexico

18 May 1976 LM(WBA) Jose Duran (Spa) KO –14 Koichi Wajima (Jap) Tokyo, Japan

22 May 1976 LH(WBA) Victor Galindez (Arg) KO –15 Richie Kates (USA) Johannesburg, South Africa

23 May 1976 L(WBA) Roberto Duran (Pan) KO –14 Lou Bizzaro (USA) Erie, USA

24 May 1976 H Muhammad Ali (USA) KO –5 Richard Dunn (GB) Munich, West Germany

31 May 1976 LW(WBA) Wilfredo Benitez (USA) PTS –15 Emiliano Villa (Col) San Juan, Puerto Rico

12 Jun 1976 SB(WBC) Rigoberto Riasco (Pan) RSF –10 Livio Nolasco (Dom) Panama City, Panama

18 Jun 1976 LM (WBC) Eckhard Dagge (FRG) RTD –10 Elisha Obed (Bah) Berlin, West Germany

19 Jun 1976 Fe(WBA) Alexis Arguello (Nic) KO –3 Salvador Torres (Mex) Inglewood, USA

22 Jun 1976 W(WBC) Carlos Palomino (Mex) RSF –12 John H. Stracey (GB) London, England

26 Jun 1976 M Carlos Monzon (Arg) PTS –15 Rodrigo Valdez (Col) Monte Carlo, Monaco

30 Jun 1976 LW(WBC) Miguel Velasquez (Spa) DIS –4 Saensak Muangsurin (Tha) Madrid, Spain

1 Jul 1976 JL(WBC) Alfredo Escalera (PR) PTS –15 Buzzsaw Yamabe (Jap) Nara, Japan

1 Jul 1976 LF(WBA) Juan Jose Guzman (Dom) PTS –15 Jaime Rios (Pan) Santo Domingo, Dominican Republic

10 Jul 1976 B(WBA) Alfonso Zamora (Mex) KO –3 Gilberto Illueca (Pan) Juarez, Mexico

16 Jul 1976 Fe(WBC) David Kotey (Gha) RSF –3 Shig Fukuyama (Jap) Tokyo, Japan

17 Jul 1976 W(WBA) Jose Pipino Cuevas (Mex) RSF –2 Angel Espada (PR) Mexicali, Mexico

18 Jul 1976 LF(WBC) Luis Estaba (Ven) KO –3 Franco Udella (Ita) Caracas, Venezuela

1 Aug 1976 SB(WBC) Rigoberto Riasco (Pan) PTS –15 Dong-Kyun Yum (S. Kor) Seoul, South Korea

28 Aug 1976 B(WBC) Carlos Zarate (Mex) RSF –12 Paul Ferreri (Ita) Inglewood, USA

11 Sep 1976 L(WBC) Esteban de Jesus (PR) KO –7 Hector Medina (Dom) Bayamon, Puerto Rico

18 Sep 1976 LM(WBC) Eckhard Dagge (FRG) PTS –15 Emile Griffith (VI) Berlin, West Germany

18 Sep 1976 JL(WBC) Alfredo Escalera (PR) RTD –12 Ray Lunny (USA) San Juan, Puerto Rico

26 Sep 1976 LF(WBC) Luis Estaba (Ven) RTD –10 Rodolfo Rodriguez (Arg) Caracas, Venezuela

28 Sep 1976 H Muhammad Ali (USA) PTS –15 Ken Norton (USA) New York, USA

2 Oct 1976 Fl(WBA) Guty Espadas (Mex) RSF –13 Alfonso Lopez (Pan) Los Angeles, USA

3 Oct 1976 Fl(WBC) Miguel Canto (Mex) PTS –15 Betulio Gonzalez (Ven) Caracas, Venezuela

5 Oct 1976 LH(WBA) Victor Galindez (Arg) PTS –15 Kosie Smith (SA) Johannesburg, South Africa

8 Oct 1976 LM(WBA) Miguel Angel Castellini (Arg) PTS –15 Jose Duran (Spa) Madrid, Spain

9 Oct 1976 LH(WBC) John Conteh (GB) PTS –15 Alvaro Lopez (Mex) Copenhagen, Denmark

9 Oct 1976 SB(WBC) Royal Kobayashi (Jap) RSF –8 Rigoberto Riasco (Pan) Tokyo, Japan

10 Oct 1976 LF(WBA) Yoko Gushiken (Jap) KO –7 Juan Jose Guzman (Dom) Kofu, Japan

15 Oct 1976 L(WBA) Roberto Duran (Pan) KO –1 Alvaro Rojas (CR) Hollywood, USA

16 Oct 1976 LW(WBA) Wilfredo Benitez (USA) RSF –3 Tony Petronelli (USA) San Juan, Puerto Rico

16 Oct 1976 JL(WBA) Sam Serrano (PR) PTS –15 Ben Villaflor (Phi) San Juan, Puerto Rico

16 Oct 1976 B(WBA) Alfonso Zamora (Mex) RSF –12 Soo-Hwan Hong (S. Kor) Inchon, South Korea

27 Oct 1976 W(WBA) Jose Pipino Cuevas (Mex) KO –6 Shoji Tsujimoto (Jap) Kanazawa, Japan

29 Oct 1976 LW(WBC) Saensak Muangsurin (Tha) RSF –2 Miguel Velasquez (Spa) Segovia, Spain

5 Nov 1976 Fe(WBC) Danny Lopez (USA) PTS –15 David Kotey (Gha) Accra, Ghana

13 Nov 1976 B(WBC) Carlos Zarate (Mex) KO –4 Waruinge Nakayama (Ken) Culiacan, Mexico

19 Nov 1976 Fl(WBC) Miguel Canto (Mex) PTS –15 Orlando Javierto (Phi) Los Angeles, USA

21 Nov 1976 LF(WBC) Luis Estaba (Ven) RSF –10 Valentin Martinez (Mex) Caracas, Venezuela

24 Nov 1976 SB(WBC) Dong-Kyun Yum (S. Kor) PTS –15 Royal Kobayashi (Jap) Seoul, South Korea

30 Nov 1976 JL(WBC) Alfredo Escalera (PR) PTS –15 Tyrone Everett (USA) Philadelphia, USA

1 Jan 1977 Fl(WBA) Guty Espadas (Mex) RTD –7 Jiro Takada (Jap) Tokyo, Japan

15 Jan 1977 LW(WBC) Saensak Muangsurin (Tha) RSF –15 Monroe Brooks (USA) Chian-Mai, Thailand

15 Jan 1977 JL(WBA) Sam Serrano (PR) KO –11 Alberto Herrera (Ecu) Guayaquil, Ecuador

15 Jan 1977 Fe(WBA) Rafael Ortega (Pan) PTS –15 Francisco Coronado (Nic) Panama City, Panama

22 Jan 1977 W(WBC) Carlos Palomino (Mex) RSF –15 Armando Muniz (Mex) Los Angeles, USA

29 Jan 1977 L(WBA) Roberto Duran (Pan) KO –13 Vilomar Fernandez (Dom) Miami, USA

30 Jan 1977 LF(WBA) Yoko Gushiken (Jap) PTS –15 Jaime Rios (Pan) Tokyo, Japan

5 Feb 1977 B(WBC) Carlos Zarate (Mex) RSF –3 Fernando Cabanela (Phi) Mexico City, Mexico

12 Feb 1977 L(WBC) Esteban de Jesus (PR) RSF –4 Buzzsaw Yamabe (Jap) Bayamon, Puerto Rico

13 Feb 1977 *SB(WBC)* Dong-Kyun Yum (S. Kor) PTS –15 Jose Cervantes (Col) Seoul, South Korea

5 Mar 1977 *LH(WBC)* John Conteh (GB) RSF –3 Len Hutchins (USA) Liverpool, England

6 Mar 1977 *LM(WBA)* Eddie Gazo (Nic) PTS –15 Miguel Angel Castellini (Arg) Managua, Nicaragua

12 Mar 1977 *W(WBA)* Jose Pipino Cuevas (Mex) RSF –2 Miguel Campanino (Arg) Mexico City, Mexico

15 Mar 1977 *LM(WBC)* Eckhard Dagge (FRG) D –15 Maurice Hope (Ant) Berlin, West Germany

17 Mar 1977 *JL(WBC)* Alfredo Escalera (PR) RSF –6 Ron McGarvey (USA) San Juan, Puerto Rico

2 Apr 1977 *LW(WBC)* Saensak Muangsurin (Tha) KO –6 Guts Ishumatsu (Jap) Tokyo, Japan

24 Apr 1977 *Fl(WBC)* Miguel Canto (Mex) PTS –15 Reyes Arnal (Ven) Caracas, Venezuela

30 Apr 1977 *Fl(WBA)* Guty Espadas (Mex) RSF –13 Alfonso Lopez (Pan) Merida, Mexico

2 May 1977 *LF(WBA)* Yoko Gushiken (Jap) PTS –15 Rigoberto Marcano (Ven) Sapporo, Japan

15 May 1977 *LF(WBC)* Luis Estaba (Ven) PTS –15 Rafael Pedroza (Pan) Caracas, Venezuela

16 May 1977 *H* Muhammad Ali (USA) PTS –15 Alfredo Evangelista (Uru) Landover, USA

16 May 1977 *JL(WBC)* Alfredo Escalera (PR) KO –8 Carlos Becceril (Mex) Landover, USA

21 May 1977 *LH(WBC)* Miguel Cuello (Arg) KO –9 Jesse Burnett (USA) Monte Carlo, Monaco

21 May 1977 *SB(WBC)* Wilfredo Gomez (PR) KO –12 Dong-Kyun Yum (S. Kor) San Juan, Puerto Rico

29 May 1977 *Fe(WBA)* Rafael Ortega (Pan) PTS –15 Flipper Uehara (Jap) Okinawa, Japan

7 Jun 1977 *LM(WBA)* Eddie Gazo (Nic) RSF –11 Koichi Wajima (Jap) Tokyo, Japan

14 Jun 1977 *W(WBC)* Carlos Palomino (Mex) KO –11 Dave 'Boy' Green (GB) London, England

15 Jun 1977 *L(WBC)* Esteban de Jesus (PR) KO –11 Vicente Saldivar Mijares (Mex) Bayamon, Puerto Rico

15 Jun 1977 *Fl(WBC)* Miguel Canto (Mex) PTS –15 Kimio Furesawa (Jap) Tokyo, Japan

17 Jun 1977 *LW(WBC)* Saensak Muangsurin (Tha) PTS –15 Perico Fernandez (Spa) Madrid, Spain

18 Jun 1977 *LH(WBA)* Victor Galindez (Arg) PTS –15 Richie Kates (USA) Rome, Italy

25 Jun 1977 *LW(WBA)* Antonio Cervantes (Col) RSF –5 Carlos Maria Giminez (Arg) Maracaibo, Venezuela

26 Jun 1977 *JL(WBA)* Sam Serrano (PR) PTS –15 Leonel Hernandez (Ven) Puerto de la Cruz, Venezuela

11 Jul 1977 *SB(WBC)* Wilfredo Gomez (PR) KO –5 Raul Tirado (Mex) San Juan, Puerto Rico

17 Jul 1977 *LF(WBC)* Luis Estaba (Ven) PTS –15 Ricardo Estupinan (Col) Puerto de la Cruz, Venezuela

30 Jul 1977 *M* Carlos Monzon (Arg) PTS –15 Rodrigo Valdez (Col) Monte Carlo, Monaco

6 Aug 1977 *LM(WBC)* Rocky Mattioli (Ita) KO –5 Eckhard Dagge (FRG) Berlin, West Germany

6 Aug 1977 *W(WBA)* Jose Pipino Cuevas (Mex) KO –2 Clyde Gray (Can) Los Angeles, USA

20 Aug 1977 *LW(WBC)* Saensak Muangsurin (Tha) RSF –6 Mike Everett (USA) Roi-Et, Thailand

27 Aug 1977 *JL(WBA)* Sam Serrano (PR) PTS –15 Apollo Yoshio (Jap) San Juan, Puerto Rico

28 Aug 1977 *LF(WBC)* Luis Estaba (Ven) RSF –11 Juan Alvarez (Mex) Puerto de la Cruz, Venezuela

10 Sep 1977 *JL(WBC)* Alfredo Escalera (PR) PTS –15 Sigfrido Rodriguez (Mex) San Juan, Puerto Rico

13 Sep 1977 *LM(WBA)* Eddie Gazo (Nic) PTS –15 Kenji Shibata (Jap) Tokyo, Japan

13 Sep 1977 *W(WBC)* Carlos Palomino (Mex) PTS –15 Everaldo Costa Azevedo (Bra) Los Angeles, USA

13 Sep 1977 *Fe(WBC)* Danny Lopez (USA) RSF –7 Jose Torres (Mex) Los Angeles, USA

15 Sep 1977 *L(WBA)* Roberto Duran (Pan) PTS –15 Edwin Viruet (PR) Philadelphia, USA

17 Sep 1977 *LH(WBA)* Victor Galindez (Arg) PTS –15 Alvaro Lopez (Mex) Rome, Italy

17 Sep 1977 *Fl(WBC)* Miguel Canto (Mex) PTS –15 Martin Vargas (Chi) Merida, Mexico

18 Sep 1977 *LF(WBC)* Luis Estaba (Ven) KO –15 Orlando Hernandez (CR) Caracas, Venezuela

29 Sep 1977 *H* Muhammad Ali (USA) PTS –15 Earnie Shavers (USA) New York, USA

9 Oct 1977 *LF(WBA)* Yoko Gushiken (Jap) KO –4 Montsayarm Mahachai (Tha) Oita, Japan

22 Oct 1977 *LW(WBC)* Saensak Muangsurin (Tha) PTS –15 Saoul Mamby (Jam) Bangkok, Thailand

29 Oct 1977 *B(WBC)* Carlos Zarate (Mex) RSF –6 Danilo Batista (Bra) Los Angeles, USA

29 Oct 1977 *LF(WBC)* Luis Estaba (Ven) PTS –15 Netrnoi Vorasingh (Tha) Caracas, Venezuela

5 Nov 1977 *M* Rodrigo Valdez (Col) PTS –15 Bennie Briscoe (USA) Campione d'Italia, Switzerland

5 Nov 1977 *LW(WBA)* Antonio Cervantes (Col) PTS –15 Adriano Marrero (Dom) Maracay, Venezuela

19 Nov 1977 *LH(WBA)* Victor Galindez (Arg) PTS –15 Eddie Gregory (USA) Turin, Italy

19 Nov 1977 *W(WBA)* Jose Pipino Cuevas (Mex) RSF –11 Angel Espada (PR) San Juan, Puerto Rico

19 Nov 1977 *JL(WBA)* Sam Serrano (PR) RSF –10 Tae-Ho Kim (S. Kor) San Juan, Puerto Rico

19 Nov 1977 *B(WBA)* Jorge Lujan (Pan) KO –10 Alfonso Zamora (Mex) Los Angeles, USA

19 Nov 1977 *Fl(WBA)* Guty Espadas (Mex) KO –8 Alex Santana (Nic) Los Angeles, USA

26 Nov 1977 *SB(WBA)* Soo-Hwan Hong (S. Kor) KO –3 Hector Carrasquilla (Pan) Panama City, Panama

30 Nov 1977 *Fl(WBC)* Miguel Canto (Mex) PTS –15 Martin Vargas (Chi) Santiago, Chile

2 Dec 1977 *B(WBC)* Carlos Zarate (Mex) RSF –5 Juan Francisco Rodriguez (Spa) Madrid, Spain

10 Dec 1977 *W(WBC)* Carlos Palomino (Mex) KO –13 Jose Palacios (Mex) Los Angeles, USA

17 Dec 1977 *Fe(WBA)* Cecilio Lastra (Spa) PTS –15 Rafael Ortega (Pan) Torrelavega, Spain

18 Dec 1977 *LM(WBA)* Eddie Gazo (Nic) PTS –15 Lim-Jao Keun (S. Kor) Inchon, South Korea

30 Dec 1977 *LW(WBC)* Saensak Muangsurin (Tha) RTD –13 Jo Kimpuani (Zai) Chantaburi, Thailand

2 Jan 1978 *Fl(WBA)* Guty Espadas (Mex) RSF –7 Kimio Furesawa (Jap) Tokyo, Japan

4 Jan 1978 *Fl(WBC)* Miguel Canto (Mex) PTS –15 Shoji Oguma (Jap) Koriyama, Japan

7 Jan 1978 *LH(WBC)* Mate Parlov (Yug) KO –9 Miguel Cuello (Arg) Milan, Italy

19 Jan 1978 *SB(WBC)* Wilfredo Gomez (PR) KO –3 Royal Kobayashi (Jap) Kitakyushu, Japan

21 Jan 1978 *L* Roberto Duran (Pan) KO –12 Esteban de Jesus (PR) Las Vegas, USA

28 Jan 1978 *JL(WBC)* Alexis Arguello (Nic) RSF –13 Alfredo Escalera (PR) San Juan, Puerto Rico

29 Jan 1978 *LF(WBA)* Yoko Gushiken (Jap) KO –14 Anecito Vargas (Phi) Nagoya, Japan

1 Feb 1978 *SB(WBA)* Soo-Hwan Hong (S. Kor) PTS –15 Yu Kasahara (Jap) Tokyo, Japan

11 Feb 1978 *W(WBC)* Carlos Palomino (Mex) KO –7 Ryu Sorimachi (Jap) Las Vegas, USA

15 Feb 1978 *Fe(WBC)* Danny Lopez (USA) RSF –6 David Kotey (Gha) Las Vegas, USA

18 Feb 1978 *H* Leon Spinks (USA) PTS –15 Muhammad Ali (USA) Las Vegas, USA

18 Feb 1978 *JL(WBA)* Sam Serrano (PR) PTS –15 Mario Martinez (Nic) San Juan, Puerto Rico

19 Feb 1978 *LF(WBC)* Freddie Castillo (Mex) RSF –14 Luis Estaba (Ven) Caracas, Venezuela

25 Feb 1978 *B(WBC)* Carlos Zarate (Mex) RSF –8 Albert Davila (USA) Los Angeles, USA

4 Mar 1978 *W(WBA)* Jose Pipino Cuevas (Mex) RSF –10 Harold Weston (USA) Los Angeles, USA

11 Mar 1978 *LM(WBC)* Rocky Mattioli (Ita) KO –7 Elisha Obed (Bah) Melbourne, Australia

18 Mar 1978 *W(WBC)* Carlos Palomino (Mex) RSF –9 Mimoun Mohatar (Mor) Las Vegas, USA

18 Mar 1978 *B(WBA)* Jorge Lujan (Pan) RTD –11 Roberto Rubaldino (Mex) San Antonio, USA

8 Apr 1978 *LW(WBC)* Saensak Muangsurin (Tha) RSF –13 Francis Moreno (Ven) Hat Yai, Thailand

8 Apr 1978 *SB(WBC)* Wilfredo Gomez (PR) RSF –7 Juan Antonio Lopez (Mex) Bayamon, Puerto Rico

16 Apr 1978 *Fe(WBA)* Eusebio Pedroza (Pan) KO –13 Cecilio Lastra (Spa) Panama City, Panama

18 Apr 1978 *Fl(WBC)* Miguel Canto (Mex) PTS –15 Shoji Oguma (Jap) Tokyo, Japan

22 Apr 1978 *M* Hugo Corro (Arg) PTS –15 Rodrigo Valdez (Col) San Remo, Italy

22 Apr 1978 *B(WBA)* Carlos Zarate (Mex) RSF –13 Andres Hernandez (PR) San Juan, Puerto Rico

25 Apr 1978 *Fe(WBC)* Danny Lopez (USA) RSF –6 Jose Paula (Bra) Los Angeles, USA

28 Apr 1978 *LW(WBA)* Antonio Cervantes (Col) KO –6 Tongta Kiatvayupak (Tha) Udon-Thani, Thailand

29 Apr 1978 *JL(WBC)* Alexis Arguello (Nic) RSF –5 Rey Tam (Phi) Los Angeles, USA

6 May 1978 *LH(WBA)* Victor Galindez (Arg) PTS –15 Alvaro Lopez (Mex) Via Reggio, Italy

6 May 1978 *SB(WBA)* Ricardo Cardona (Col) RSF –12 Soo-Hwan Hong (S. Kor) Seoul, South Korea

6 May 1978 *LF(WBC)* Netrnoi Vorasingh (Tha) PTS –15 Freddie Castillo (Mex) Bangkok, Thailand

14 May 1978 *LM(WBC)* Rocky Mattioli (Ita) RSF –5 Jose Duran (Spa) Pescara, Italy

20 May 1978 *W(WBA)* Jose Pipino Cuevas (Mex) RSF –2 Billy Backus (USA) Los Angeles, USA

27 May 1978 *W(WBC)* Carlos Palomino (Mex) PTS –15 Armando Muniz (Mex) Los Angeles, USA

2 Jun 1978 *SB(WBC)* Wilfredo Gomez (PR) RSF –3 Sakad Porntavee (Tha) Korat, Thailand

3 Jun 1978 *JL(WBC)* Alexis Arguello (Nic) KO –1 Diego Alcala (Pan) San Juan, Puerto Rico

10 Jun 1978 *H(WBC)* Larry Holmes (USA) PTS –15 Ken Norton (USA) Las Vegas, USA

10 Jun 1978 *B(WBC)* Carlos Zarate (Mex) KO –4 Emilio Hernandez (Ven) Las Vegas, USA

17 Jun 1978 *LH(WBC)* Mate Parlov (Yug) PTS –15 John Conteh (GB) Belgrade, Yugoslavia

2 Jul 1978 *Fe(WBA)* Eusebio Pedroza (Pan) RSF –12 Ernesto Herrera (Mex) Panama City, Panama

8 Jul 1978 *JL(WBA)* Sam Serrano (PR) RSF –9 Yung-Ho Oh (S. Kor) San Juan, Puerto Rico

5 Aug 1978 *M* Hugo Corro (Arg) PTS –15 Ronnie Harris (USA) Buenos Aires, Argentina

9 Aug 1978 *LM(WBA)* Masashi Kudo (Jap) PTS –15 Eddie Gazo (Nic) Akita, Japan

13 Aug 1978 *Fl(WBA)* Betulio Gonzalez (Ven) PTS –15 Guty Espadas (Mex) Maracay, Venezuela

26 Aug 1978 *LW(WBA)* Antonio Cervantes (Col) KO –9 Norman Sekgapane (SA) Mmabatho, South Africa

2 Sep 1978 *SB(WBA)* Ricardo Cardona (Col) PTS –15 Ruben Valdes (Col) Cartagena, Colombia

9 Sep 1978 *W(WBA)* Jose Pipino Cuevas (Mex) RSF –2 Pete Ranzany (USA) Sacramento, USA

9 Sep 1978 *SB(WBC)* Wilfredo Gomez (PR) RSF –13 Leonardo Cruz (Dom) San Juan, Puerto Rico

15 Sep 1978 *H(WBA)* Muhammad Ali (USA) PTS –15 Leon Spinks (USA) New Orleans, USA

15 Sep 1978 *LH(WBA)* Mike Rossman (USA) RSF –13 Victor Galindez (Arg) New Orleans, USA

15 Sep 1978 *Fe(WBC)* Danny Lopez (USA) KO –2 Juan Malvarez (Arg) New Orleans, USA

15 Sep 1978 *B(WBA)* Jorge Lujan (Pan) PTS –15 Albert Davila (USA) New Orleans, USA

30 Sep 1978 *LF(WBC)* Sung-Jun Kim (S. Kor) KO –3 Netrnoi Vorasingh (Tha) Seoul, South Korea

15 Oct 1978 *LF(WBA)* Yoko Gushiken (Jap) KO –5 Sang-Il Chung (S. Kor) Tokyo, Japan

21 Oct 1978 *Fe(WBC)* Danny Lopez (USA) DIS –4 Pel Clemente (Phi) Pessaro, Italy

29 Oct 1978 *SB(WBC)* Wilfredo Gomez (PR) RSF –5 Carlos Zarate (Mex) San Juan, Puerto Rico

2 Nov 1978 *SB(WBA)* Ricardo Cardona (Col) PTS –15 Soon-Hyun Chung (S. Kor) Seoul, South Korea

4 Nov 1978 *Fl(WBA)* Betulio Gonzalez (Ven) RSF –12 Martin Vargas (Chi) Maracay, Venezuela

10 Nov 1978 *H(WBC)* Larry Holmes (USA) KO –7 Alfredo Evangelista (Uru) Las Vegas, USA

10 Nov 1978 *JL(WBC)* Alexis Arguello (Nic) PTS –15 Arturo Leon (Mex) Las Vegas, USA

11 Nov 1978 *M* Hugo Corro (Arg) PTS –15 Rodrigo Valdez (Col) Buenos Aires, Argentina

20 Nov 1978 *Fl(WBC)* Miguel Canto (Mex) PTS –15 Tacomron Viboonchai (Tha) Houston, USA

27 Nov 1978 *Fe(WBA)* Eusebio Pedroza (Pan) PTS –15 Enrique Solis (PR) San Juan, Puerto Rico

29 Nov 1978 *JL(WBA)* Sam Serrano (PR) PTS –15 Takeo Maruki (Jap) Nagoya, Japan

2 Dec 1978 *LH(WBC)* Marvin Johnson (USA) RSF –10 Mate Parlov (Yug) Marsala, Italy

5 Dec 1978 *LH(WBA)* Mike Rossman (USA) RSF –6 Aldo Traversaro (Ita) Philadelphia, USA

14 Dec 1978 *LM(WBA)* Masashi Kudo (Jap) PTS –15 Ho-In Joo (S. Kor) Osaka, Japan

30 Dec 1978 *LW(WBC)* Sang-Hyun Kim (S. Kor) RSF –13 Saensak Muangsurin (Tha) Seoul, South Korea

7 Jan 1979 *LF(WBA)* Yoko Gushiken (Jap) KO –7 Rigoberto Marcano (Ven) Kawasaki, Japan

9 Jan 1979 *Fe(WBA)* Eusebio Pedroza (Pan) RTD –13 Royal Kobayashi (Jap) Tokyo, Japan

14 Jan 1979 *W(WBC)* Wilfred Benitez (USA) PTS –15 Carlos Palomino (Mex) San Juan, Puerto Rico

26 Jan 1979 *LW(WBA)* Antonio Cervantes (Col) PTS –15 Miguel Montilla (Dom) New York, USA

29 Jan 1979 *W(WBA)* Jose Pipino Cuevas (Mex) RSF –2 Scott Clark (USA) Los Angeles, USA

29 Jan 1979 *Fl(WBA)* Betulio Gonzalez (Ven) D –15 Shoji Oguma (Jap) Hamatsu, Japan

4 Feb 1979 *JL(WBC)* Alexis Arguello (Nic) KO –13 Alfredo Escalera (PR) Rimini, Italy

10 Feb 1979 *Fl(WBC)* Miguel Canto (Mex) PTS –15 Antonio Avelar (Mex) Merida, Mexico

18 Feb 1979 *JL(WBA)* Sam Serrano (PR) PTS –15 Julio Valdez (Dom) San Juan, Puerto Rico

4 Mar 1979 *LM(WBC)* Maurice Hope (Ant) RTD –8 Rocky Mattioli (Ita) San Remo, Italy

9 Mar 1979 *SB(WBC)* Wilfredo Gomez (PR) RSF –5 Nestor Jiminez (Col) New York, USA

10 Mar 1979 *Fe(WBC)* Danny Lopez (USA) KO –2 Roberto Castanon (Spa) Salt Lake City, USA

10 Mar 1979 *B(WBC)* Carlos Zarate (Mex) KO –3 Mensah Kpalongo (Ton) Los Angeles, USA

14 Mar 1979 *LM(WBA)* Masashi Kudo (Jap) PTS –15 Manuel Gonzalez (Arg) Tokyo, Japan

18 Mar 1979 *Fl(WBC)* Chan-Hee Park (S. Kor) PTS –15 Miguel Canto (Mex) Pusan, South Korea

25 Mar 1979 *W(WBC)* Wilfredo Benitez (USA) PTS –15 Harold Weston (USA) San Juan, Puerto Rico

29 Mar 1979 *H(WBC)* Larry Holmes (USA) RSF –7 Ossie Ocasio (PR) Las Vegas, USA

31 Mar 1979 *LF(WBC)* Sung-Jun Kim (S. Kor) D –15 Ray Melandez (Dom) Seoul, South Korea

8 Apr 1979 *Fe(WBA)* Eusebio Pedroza (Pan) RSF –11 Hector Carrasquilla (Pan) Panama City, Panama

8 Apr 1979 *B(WBA)* Jorge Lujan (Pan) RSF –15 Cleo Garcia (Nic) Los Angeles, USA

8 Apr 1979 *LF(WBA)* Yoko Gushiken (Jap) KO –7 Alfonso Lopez (Pan) Tokyo, Japan

15 Apr 1979 *LH(WBA)* Victor Galindez (Arg) RTD –9 Mike Rossman (USA) New Orleans, USA

15 Apr 1979 *JL(WBA)* Sam Serrano (PR) RSF –8 Nkosana 'Happy Boy' Mgxaji (SA) Cape Town, South Africa

17 Apr 1979 *L(WBC)* Jim Watt (GB) RSF –12 Alfredo Pitalua (Col) Glasgow, Scotland

22 Apr 1979 *LH(WBC)* Matt Franklin (USA) RSF –8 Marvin Johnson (USA) Indianapolis, USA

19 May 1979 *Fl(WBC)* Chan-Hee Park (S. Kor) PTS –15 Tsutomo Igerishi (Jap) Seoul, South Korea

1 Jun 1979 *LW(WBC)* Sang-Hyun Kim (S. Kor) PTS –15 Fitzroy Guisseppi (Tri) Seoul, South Korea

3 Jun 1979 *B(WBC)* Lupe Pintor (Mex) PTS –15 Carlos Zarate (Mex) Las Vegas, USA

16 Jun 1979 *L(WBA)* Ernesto Espana (Ven) KO –13 Claude Noel (Tri) San Juan, Puerto Rico

Mike Ayala (USA) was knocked-out twice during his world featherweight title fight against Danny Lopez (USA) in 1979. He was counted out in the 11th round by referee Carlos Padilla. The Ayala camp protested that their man was up on the count of nine. Padilla conferred with the timekeeper who confirmed that as being correct. The fight continued and Ayala was knocked out for the second time in the 15th round.

16 Jun 1979 *SB(WBC)* Wilfredo Gomez (PR) KO –5 Julio Hernandez (Nic) San Juan, Puerto Rico

17 Jun 1979 *Fe(WBC)* Danny Lopez (USA) KO –15 Mike Ayala (USA) San Antonio, USA

20 Jun 1979 *LM(WBA)* Masashi Kudo (Jap) RTD –12 Manuel Gonzalez (Arg) Yokkaichi, Japan

22 Jun 1979 *H(WBC)* Larry Holmes (USA) RSF –12 Mike Weaver (USA) New York, USA

23 Jun 1979 *SB(WBA)* Ricardo Cardona (Col) PTS –15 Soon-Hyun Chung (S. Kor) Seoul, South Korea

30 Jun 1979 *M* Vito Antuofermo (Ita) PTS –15 Hugo Corro (Arg) Monte Carlo, Monaco

8 Jul 1979 *JL(WBC)* Alexis Arguello (Nic) RSF –11 Rafael Limon (Mex) New York, USA

13 Jul 1979 *Fl(WBA)* Betulio Gonzalez (Ven) KO –12 Shoji Oguma (Jap) Utsonomiya, Japan

21 Jul 1979 *Fe(WBA)* Eusebio Pedroza (Pan) RSF –12 Ruben Olivares (Mex) Houston, USA

28 Jul 1979 *LF(WBC)* Sung-Jun Kim (S. Kor) PTS –15 Siony Carupo (Phi) Seoul, South Korea

30 Jul 1979 *W(WBA)* Jose Pipino Cuevas (Mex) PTS –15 Randy Shields (USA) Chicago, USA

4 Aug 1979 *L(WBA)* Ernesto Espana (Ven) RSF –9 Johnny Lira (USA) Chicago, USA

18 Aug 1979 *LH(WBC)* Matt Franklin (USA) PTS –15 John Conteh (GB) Atlantic City, USA

25 Aug 1979 *LW(WBA)* Antonio Cervantes (Col) PTS –15 Kwang-Min Kim (S. Kor) Seoul, South Korea

6 Sep 1979 *SB(WBA)* Ricardo Cardona (Col) PTS –15 Yukio Segawa (Jap) Hacinohe, Japan

9 Sep 1979 *Fl(WBC)* Chan-Hee Park (S. Kor) D –15 Miguel Canto (Mex) Seoul, South Korea

25 Sep 1979 *LM(WBC)* Maurice Hope (Ant) RSF –7 Mike Baker (USA) London, England

25 Sep 1979 *Fe(WBC)* Danny Lopez (USA) KO –3 Jose Caba (Dom) Los Angeles, USA

28 Sep 1979 *H(WBC)* Larry Holmes (USA) RSF –11 Earnie Shavers (USA) Las Vegas, USA

28 Sep 1979 *SB(WBC)* Wilfredo Gomez (PR) KO –10 Carlos Mendoza (Pan) Las Vegas, USA

3 Oct 1979 *LW(WBC)* Sang-Hyun Kim (S. Kor) KO –11 Masahiro Yokai (Jap) Tokyo, Japan

6 Oct 1979 *B(WBA)* Jorge Lujan (Pan) RSF –15 Roberto Rubaldino (Mex) McAllen, USA

20 Oct 1979 *H(WBA)* John Tate (USA) PTS –15 Gerrie Coetzee (SA) Johannesburg, South Africa

24 Oct 1979 *LM(WBA)* Ayub Kalule (Uga) PTS –15 Masashi Kudo (Jap) Akita, Japan

26 Oct 1979 *SB(WBC)* Wilfredo Gomez (PR) KO –5 Nicky Perez (USA) New York, USA

28 Oct 1979 *LF(WBA)* Yoko Gushiken (Jap) RSF –7 Tito Abbella (Phi) Tokyo, Japan

3 Nov 1979 *L(WBC)* Jim Watt (GB) RSF –9 Roberto Vasquez (USA) Glasgow, Scotland

16 Nov 1979 *JL(WBC)* Alexis Arguello (Nic) RTD –7 Bobby Chacon (USA) Los Angeles, USA

16 Nov 1979 *Fl(WBA)* Luis Ibarra (Pan) PTS –15 Betulio Gonzalez (Ven) Maracay, Venezuela

17 Nov 1979 *Fe(WBA)* Eusebio Pedroza (Pan) KO –11 Johnny Aba (NG) Port Moresby, New Guinea

30 Nov 1979 *LH(WBA)* Marvin Johnson (USA) KO –11 Victor Galindez (Arg) New Orleans, USA

30 Nov 1979 *M* Vito Antuofermo (Ita) D –15 Marvin Hagler (USA) Las Vegas, USA

30 Nov 1979 *W(WBC)* Sugar Ray Leonard (USA) RSF –15 Wilfredo Benitez (USA) Las Vegas, USA

6 Dec 1979 *LM(WBA)* Ayub Kalule (Uga) PTS –15 Steve Gregory (USA) Copenhagen, Denmark

8 Dec 1979 *W(WBA)* Jose Pipino Cuevas (Mex) RSF –10 Angel Espada (PR) Los Angeles, USA

8 Dec 1979 *C(WBC)* Marvin Camel (USA) D –15 Mate Parlov (Yug) Split, Yugoslavia

15 Dec 1979 *SB(WBA)* Ricardo Cardona (Col) PTS –15 Sergio Palma (Arg) Barranquilla, Colombia

16 Dec 1979 *Fl(WBC)* Chan-Hee Park (S. Kor) KO –5 Guty Espadas (Mex) Seoul, South Korea

3 Jan 1980 *LF(WBC)* Shigeo Nakajima (Jap) PTS –15 Sung-Jun Kim (S. Kor) Tokyo, Japan

20 Jan 1980 *JL(WBC)* Alexis Arguello (Nic) RSF –11 Ruben Castillo (USA) Tucson, USA

22 Jan 1980 *Fe(WBA)* Eusebio Pedroza (Pan) PTS –15 Shig 'Spider' Nemoto (Jap) Tokyo, Japan

27 Jan 1980 *LF(WBA)* Yoko Gushiken (Jap) PTS –15 Yung-Hyun Kim (S. Kor) Osaka, Japan

2 Feb 1980 *Fe(WBC)* Salvador Sanchez (Mex) RSF –13 Danny Lopez (USA) Phoenix, USA

2 Feb 1980 *SF(WBC)* Rafael Orono (Ven) PTS –15 Seung-Hoon Lee (S. Kor) Caracas, Venezuela

3 Feb 1980 *H(WBC)* Larry Holmes (USA) KO –6 Lorenzo Zanon (Ita) Las Vegas, USA

3 Feb 1980 *SB(WBA)* Wilfredo Gomez (PR) KO –6 Ruben Valdez (Col) Las Vegas, USA

9 Feb 1980 *B(WBC)* Lupe Pintor (Mex) RSF –12 Alberto Sandoval (USA) Los Angeles, USA

10 Feb 1980 *Fl(WBC)* Chan-Hee Park (S. Kor) PTS –15 Arnel Arrozal (Phi) Seoul, South Korea

16 Feb 1980 *Fl(WBA)* Tae-Shik Kim (S. Kor) KO –2 Luis Ibarra (Pan) Seoul, South Korea

2 Mar 1980 *L(WBA)* Hilmer Kenty (USA) RSF –9 Ernesto Espana (Ven) Detroit, USA

14 Mar 1980 *L(WBC)* Jim Watt (GB) RSF –4 Charlie Nash (GB) Glasgow, Scotland

16 Mar 1980 *M* Alan Minter (GB) PTS –15 Vito Antuofermo (Ita) Las Vegas, USA

23 Mar 1980 *LW(WBC)* Saoul Mamby (Jam) RSF –14 Sang-Hyun Kim (S. Kor) Seoul, South Korea

23 Mar 1980 *LF(WBC)* Hilario Zapata (Pan) PTS –15 Shigeo Nakajima (Jap) Tokyo, Japan

29 Mar 1980 *LH(WBC)* Matt Saad Muhammad (USA) RSF –4 John Conteh (GB) Atlantic City, USA

29 Mar 1980 *LW(WBA)* Antonio Cervantes (Col) RSF –7 Miguel Montilla (Dom) Cartagena, Colombia

29 Mar 1980 *Fe(WBA)* Eusebio Pedroza (Pan) KO –9 Juan D. Malvares (Arg) Panama City, Panama

31 Mar 1980 *H(WBC)* Larry Holmes (USA) RSF –8 Leroy Jones (USA) Las Vegas, USA

31 Mar 1980 *H(WBA)* Mike Weaver (USA) KO –15 John Tate (USA) Knoxville, USA

31 Mar 1980 *C(WBC)* Marvin Camel (USA) PTS –15 Mate Parlov (Yug) Las Vegas, USA

31 Mar 1980 *LH(WBA)* Eddie Gregory (USA) RSF –11 Marvin Johnson (USA) Knoxville, USA

31 Mar 1980 *W(WBC)* Sugar Ray Leonard (USA) KO –4 Dave 'Boy' Green (GB) Landover, USA

2 Apr 1980 *B(WBA)* Jorge Lujan (Pan) RSF –9 Shuichi Isogami (Jap) Tokyo, Japan

3 Apr 1980 *JL(WBA)* Sam Serrano (PR) RSF –13 Kiyoshi Kazama (Jap) Nara, Japan

6 Apr 1980 *W(WBA)* Jose Cuevas (Mex) KO –5 Harold Volbrecht (SA) Houston, USA

12 Apr 1980 *Fe(WBC)* Salvador Sanchez (Mex) PTS –15 Ruben Castillo (USA) Tucson, USA

12 Apr 1980 *SF(WBC)* Rafael Orono (Ven) PTS –15 Ramon Soria (Arg) Caracas, Venezuela

18 Apr 1980 *LM(WBA)* Ayub Kalule (Uga) RSF –11 Emilianno Villa (Col) Copenhagen, Denmark

27 Apr 1980 *JL(WBC)* Alexis Arguello (Nic) RSF –4 Rolando Navarrete (Phi) San Juan, Nicaragua

4 May 1980 *SB(WBA)* Leo Randolph (USA) RSF –15 Ricardo Cardona (Col) Seattle, USA

11 May 1980 *LH(WBC)* Matt Saad Muhammad (USA) RSF –5 Louis Pergaud (Cam) Halifax, Canada

18 May 1980 *Fl(WBC)* Shoji Oguma (Jap) KO –9 Chan-Hee Park (S. Kor) Seoul, South Korea

1 Jun 1980 *LF(WBA)* Yoko Gushiken (Jap) RSF –8 Martin Vargas (Chi) Kochi, Japan

7 Jun 1980 *L(WBC)* Jim Watt (GB) PTS –15 Howard Davis (USA) Glasgow, Scotland

7 Jun 1980 *LF(WBC)* Hilario Zapata (Pan) PTS –15 Chi-Bok Kim (S. Kor) Seoul, South Korea

11 Jun 1980 *B(WBC)* Lupe Pintor (Mex) D –15 Eijiro Murata (Jap) Tokyo, Japan

13 Jun 1980 *LM(WBA)* Ayub Kalule (Uga) PTS –15 Marijan Benes (Yug) Randers, Denmark

20 Jun 1980 *W(WBC)* Roberto Duran (Pan) PTS –15 Sugar Ray Leonard (USA) Montreal, Canada

21 Jun 1980 *Fe(WBC)* Salvador Sanchez (Mex) RSF –14 Danny Lopez (USA) Las Vegas, USA

28 Jun 1980 *M* Alan Minter (GB) KO –8 Vito Antuofermo (Ita) London, England

29 Jun 1980 *Fl(WBA)* Tae-Shik Kim (S. Kor) PTS –15 Arnel Arrozal (Phi) Seoul, South Korea

7 Jul 1980 *H(WBC)* Larry Holmes (USA) RSF –7 Scott Ledoux (USA) Minneapolis, USA

7 Jul 1980 *LW(WBC)* Saoul Mamby (Jam) KO –13 Esteban de Jesus (PR) Minneapolis, USA

12 Jul *LM(WBC)* Maurice Hope (Ant) RSF –11 Rocky Mattioli (Ita) London, England

13 Jul 1980 *LH(WBC)* Matt Saad Muhammad (USA) RSF – 14 Alvaro Lopez (Mex) Great George, USA

20 Jul 1980 *LH(WBA)* Eddie Mustaffa Muhammad (USA) RSF – 10 Jerry Martin (Ant) McAfee, USA

20 Jul 1980 *Fe(WBA)* Eusebio Pedroza (Pan) KO – 9 Sa-Wang Kim (S. Kor) Seoul, South Korea

28 Jul 1980 *SF(WBC)* Rafael Orono (Ven) D – 15 Willie Jensen (USA) Caracas, Venezuela

28 Jul 1980 *Fl(WBC)* Shoji Oguma (Jap) PTS – 15 Sun-Jung Kim (S. Kor) Tokyo, Japan

2 Aug 1980 *W(WBA)* Thomas Hearns (USA) RSF – 2 Jose Cuevas (Mex) Detroit, USA

2 Aug 1980 *LW(WBA)* Aaron Pryor (USA) KO – 4 Antonio Cervantes (Col) Cincinatti, USA

2 Aug 1980 *L(WBA)* Hilmer Kenty (USA) RSF – 9 Yung-Ho Oh (S. Kor) Detroit, USA

2 Aug 1980 *JL(WBA)* Yasatsune Uehara (Jap) KO – 6 Sam Serrano (PR) Detroit, USA

9 Aug 1980 *SB(WBA)* Sergio Palma (Arg) KO – 6 Leo Randolph (USA) Spokane, USA

16 Aug 1980 *LF(WBC)* Hilario Zapata (Pan) PTS – 15 Hector Ray Melendez (Dom) Caracas, Venezuela

22 Aug 1980 *SB(WBC)* Wilfredo Gomez (PR) RSF – 5 Derrick Holmes (USA) Las Vegas, USA

29 Aug 1980 *B(WBA)* Julian Solis (PR) PTS – 15 Jorge Lujan (Pan) Miami, USA

6 Sep 1980 *LM(WBA)* Ayub Kalule (Uga) PTS – 15 Bushy Bester (SA) Aarhus, Denmark

13 Sep 1980 *Fe(WBC)* Salvador Sanchez (Mex) PTS – 15 Pat Ford (Guy) San Antonio, USA

15 Sep 1980 *SF(WBC)* Rafael Orono (Ven) KO – 3 Jovita Rengifo (Ven) Barquisimento, Venezuela

17 Sep 1980 *LF(WBC)* Hilario Zapata (Pan) RSF – 11 Shigeo Nakajima (Jap) Tokyo, Japan

19 Sep 1980 *B(WBC)* Lupe Pintor (Mex) KO – 12 Johnny Owen (GB) Los Angeles, USA

20 Sep 1980 *L(WBA)* Hilmer Kenty (USA) KO – 4 Ernesto Espana (Ven) San Juan, Puerto Rico

27 Sep 1980 *M* Marvin Hagler (USA) RSF – 3 Alan Minter (GB) London, England

2 Oct 1980 *H(WBC)* Larry Holmes (USA) RTD – 10 Muhammad Ali (USA) Las Vegas, USA

2 Oct 1980 *LW(WBC)* Saoul Mamby (Jam) PTS – 15 Maurice 'Termite' Watkins (USA) Las Vegas, USA

4 Oct 1980 *Fe(WBA)* Eusebio Pedroza (Pan) PTS – 15 Rocky Lockridge (USA) Great George, USA

12 Oct 1980 *LF(WBA)* Yoko Gushiken (Jap) PTS – 15 Pedro Flores (Mex) Kanazawa, Japan

18 Oct 1980 *Fl(WBC)* Shoji Oguma (Jap) PTS – 15 Chan-Hee Park (S. Kor) Tokyo, Japan

25 Oct 1980 *H(WBA)* Mike Weaver (USA) KO – 13 Gerrie Coetzee (SA) Sun City, South Africa

1 Nov 1980 *L(WBC)* Jim Watt (GB) RSF – 12 Sean O'Grady (USA) Glasgow, Scotland

8 Nov 1980 *L(WBA)* Hilmer Kenty (USA) PTS – 15 Vilomar Fernandez (Dom) Detroit, USA

8 Nov 1980 *SB(WBA)* Sergio Palma (Arg) KO – 9 Ulisses Morales (Pan) Buenos Aires, Argentina

14 Nov 1980 *B(WBA)* Jeff Chandler (USA) RSF – 14 Julian Solis (PR) Miami, USA

20 Nov 1980 *JL(WBA)* Yasatsune Uehara (Jap) PTS – 15 Leonel Hernandez (Ven) Tokyo, Japan

22 Nov 1980 *LW(WBA)* Aaron Pryor (USA) RSF – 6 Gaetan Hart (Can) Cincinatti, USA

26 Nov 1980 *C(WBC)* Carlos de Leon (PR) PTS – 15 Marvin Camel (USA) New Orleans, USA

26 Nov 1980 *LM(WBC)* Maurice Hope (Ant) PTS – 15 Carlos Herrera (Mex) London, England

28 Nov 1980 *LH(WBC)* Matt Saad Muhammad (USA) KO – 3 Lotte Mwale (Zam) San Diego, USA

28 Nov 1980 *W(WBC)* Sugar Ray Leonard (USA) RTD – 8 Roberto Duran (Pan) New Orleans, USA

29 Nov 1980 *LH(WBA)* Eddie Mustaffa Muhammad (USA) RSF – 3 Rudi Koopmans (Hol) Los Angeles, USA

1 Dec 1980 *LF(WBC)* Hilario Zapata (Pan) PTS – 15 Reinaldo Beccerra (Ven) Caracas, Venezuela

6 Dec 1980 *W(WBA)* Thomas Hearns (USA) KO – 6 Luis Primera (Ven) Detroit, USA

11 Dec 1980 *JL(WBC)* Rafael Limon (Mex) RSF – 15 Idefonso Bethelmy (Ven) Los Angeles, USA

13 Dec 1980 *Fe(WBC)* Salvador Sanchez (Mex) PTS – 15 Juan Laporte (PR) El Paso, USA

13 Dec 1980 *SB(WBC)* Wilfredo Gomez (PR) KO – 3 Jose Cervantes (Col) Miami, USA

13 Dec 1980 *Fl(WBA)* Peter Mathebula (SA) PTS – 15 Tae-Shik Kim (S. Kor) Los Angeles, USA

19 Dec 1980 *B(WBC)* Lupe Pintor (Mex) PTS – 15 Albert Davila (USA) Los Angeles, USA

17 Jan 1981 *M* Marvin Hagler (USA) RSF – 8 Fulgencio Obelmejias (Ven) Boston, USA

24 Jan 1981 *SF(WBC)* Chul-Ho Kim (S. Kor) KO – 9 Rafael Orono (Ven) San Cristobal, Venezuela

31 Jan 1981 *B(WBA)* Jeff Chandler (USA) PTS – 15 Jorge Lujan (Pan) Philadelphia, USA

3 Feb 1981 *Fl(WBC)* Shoji Oguma (Jap) PTS – 15 Chan-Hee Park (S. Kor) Tokyo, Japan

8 Feb 1981 *LF(WBC)* Hilario Zapata (Pan) RTD – 13 Joey Olivo (USA) Panama City, Panama

14 Feb 1981 *Fe(WBA)* Eusebio Pedroza (Pan) KO – 13 Pat Ford (Guy) Panama City, Panama

22 Feb 1981 *B(WBC)* Lupe Pintor (Mex) PTS – 15 Jose Uziga (Arg) Houston, USA

28 Feb 1981 *LH(WBC)* Matt Saad Muhammad (USA) RSF – 11 Vonzell Johnson (USA) Atlantic City, USA

8 Mar 1981 *JL(WBC)* Cornelius Boza-Edwards (Uga) PTS – 15 Rafael Limon (Mex) Stockton, USA

8 Mar 1981 *LF(WBA)* Pedro Flores (Mex) TKO – 12 Yoko Gushiken (Jap) Nama, Japan

22 Mar 1981 *Fe(WBC)* Salvador Sanchez (Mex) RSF – 10 Roberto Castanon (Spa) Las Vegas, USA

28 Mar 1981 *W(WBC)* Sugar Ray Leonard (USA) RSF – 10 Larry Bonds (USA) Syracuse, USA

28 Mar 1981 *Fl(WBA)* Santos Laciar (Arg) KO – 7 Peter Mathebula (SA) Johannesburg, South Africa

4 Apr 1981 *SB(WBA)* Sergio Palma (Arg) PTS – 15 Leonardo Cruz (Dom) Buenos Aires, Argentina

4 Apr 1981 *B(WBA)* Jeff Chandler (USA) D – 15 Eijiro Murata (Jap) Tokyo, Japan

9 Apr 1981 JL(WBA) Sam Serrano (PR) PTS – 15 Yasatsune Uehara (Jap) Wakayama, Japan

11 Apr 1981 *H(WBC)* Larry Holmes (USA) PTS – 15 Trevor Berbick (Can) Las Vegas, USA

12 Apr 1981 *L(WBA)* Sean O'Grady (USA) PTS – 15 Hilmer Kenty (USA) Atlantic City, USA

24 Apr 1981 *SF(WBC)* Chul-Ho Kim (S. Kor) PTS –15 Jiro Watanabe (Jap) Seoul, South Korea

24 Apr 1981 *LF(WBC)* Hilario Zapata (Pan) PTS –15 Rudy Crawford (USA) San Francisco, USA

25 Apr 1981 *LH(WBC)* Matt Saad Muhammad (USA) KO –9 Murray Sutherland (GB) Atlantic City, USA

25 Apr 1981 *W(WBA)* Thomas Hearns (USA) RSF –12 Randy Shields (USA) Phoenix, USA

12 May 1981 *Fl(WBC)* Antonio Avelar (Mex) KO –7 Shoji Oguma (Jap) Tokyo, Japan

23 May 1981 *LM(WBC)* Wilfred Benitez (USA) KO –12 Maurice Hope (Ant) Las Vegas, USA

30 May 1981 *JL(WBC)* Cornelius Boza-Edwards (Uga) RTD –13 Bobby Chacon (USA) Las Vegas, USA

6 Jun 1981 *Fl(WBA)* Luis Ibarra (Pan) PTS –15 Santos Laciar (Arg) Buenos Aires, Argentina

12 Jun 1981 *H(WBC)* Larry Holmes (USA) RSF –3 Leon Spinks (USA) Detroit, USA

12 Jun 1981 *LW(WBC)* Saoul Mamby (Jam) PTS –15 Jo Kimpuani (Zai) Detroit, USA

13 Jun 1981 *M* Marvin Hagler (USA) RTD –4 Vito Antuofermo (Ita) Boston, USA

20 Jun 1981 *JL(WBA)* Sam Serrano (PR) PTS –15 Leonel Hernandez (Ven) Caracas, Venezuela

21 Jun 1981 *L(WBC)* Alexis Arguello (Nic) PTS –15 Jim Watt (GB) London, England

25 Jun 1981 *LM(WBA)* Sugar Ray Leonard (USA) KO –9 Ayub Kalule (Uga) Houston, USA

25 Jun 1981 *W(WBA)* Thomas Hearns (USA) KO –4 Juan Pablo Baez (Dom) Houston, USA

27 Jun 1981 *LW(WBA)* Aaron Pryor (USA) RSF –2 Lennox Blackmore (Guy) Las Vegas, USA

18 Jul 1981 *LH(WBA)* Michael Spinks (USA) PTS –15 Eddie Mustaffa Muhammad (USA) Las Vegas, USA

19 Jul 1981 *LF(WBA)* Hwan-Jim Kim (S. Kor) RSF –13 Pedro Flores (Mex) Seoul, South Korea

25 Jul 1981 *B(WBA)* Jeff Chandler (USA) KO –7 Julian Solis (PR) Atlantic City, USA

26 Jul 1981 *B(WBC)* Lupe Pintor (Mex) RSF –8 Jovito Rengifo (Ven) Las Vegas, USA

29 Jul 1981 *SF(WBC)* Chul-Ho Kim (S. Kor) KO –13 Willie Jensen (USA) Pusan, South Korea

1 Aug 1981 *Fe(WBA)* Eusebio Pedroza (Pan) KO –7 Carlos Pinango (Ven) Caracas, Venezuela

15 Aug 1981 *SB(WBA)* Sergio Palma (Arg) RSF –12 Ricardo Cardona (Col) Buenos Aires, Argentina

15 Aug 1981 *LF(WBC)* Hilario Zapata (Pan) PTS –15 German Torres (Phi) Panama City, Panama

21 Aug 1981 *Fe(WBC)* Salvador Sanchez (Mex) RSF –8 Wilfredo Gomez (PR) Las Vegas, USA

29 Aug 1981 *LW(WBC)* Saoul Mamby (Jam) PTS –15 Thomas Americo (Ina) Djakarta, Indonesia

29 Aug 1981 *JL(WBC)* Rolando Navarrete (Phi) KO –5 Cornelius Boza-Edwards (Uga) Via Reggio, Italy

30 Aug 1981 *Fl(WBC)* Antonio Avelar (Mex) KO –2 Tae-Shik Kim (S. Kor) Seoul, South Korea

12 Sep 1981 *L(WBA)* Claude Noel (Tri) PTS –15 Rodolfo Gonzalez (Mex) Atlantic City, USA

12 Sep 1981 *SF(WBA)* Gustavo Ballas (Arg) RSF –8 Suk-Chul Bae (S. Kor) Buenos Aires, Argentina

16 Sep 1981 *W* Sugar Ray Leonard (USA) RSF –14 Thomas Hearns (USA) Las Vegas, USA

22 Sep 1981 *B(WBC)* Lupe Pintor (Mex) KO –15 Hurricane Teru (Jap) Tokyo, Japan

26 Sep 1981 *LH(WBC)* Matt Saad Muhammad (USA) RSF –11 Jerry Martin (Ant) Atlantic City, USA

26 Sep 1981 *Fl(WBA)* Juan Herrera (Mex) KO –11 Luis Ibarra (Pan) Mexico City, Mexico

3 Oct 1981 *H(WBA)* Mike Weaver (USA) PTS –15 James Tillis (USA) Rosemont, USA

3 Oct 1981 *M* Marvin Hagler (USA) RSF –11 Mustapha Hamsho (Syr) Rosemont, USA

3 Oct 1981 *L(WBC)* Alexis Arguello (Nic) RSF –14 Ray Mancini (USA) Atlantic City, USA

3 Oct 1981 *SB(WBA)* Sergio Palma (Arg) PTS –15 Vichit Muangroi-Et (Tha) Buenos Aires, Argentina

11 Oct 1981 *LF(WBA)* Hwan-Jim Kim (S. Kor) PTS –15 Alphonso Lopez (Pan) Seoul, South Korea

6 Nov 1981 *H(WBC)* Larry Holmes (USA) RSF –11 Renaldo Snipes (USA) Pittsburgh, USA

7 Nov 1981 *LH(WBA)* Michael Spinks (USA) KO –7 Vonzell Johnson (USA) Atlantic City, USA

7 Nov 1981 *LM(WBA)* Tadashi Mihara (Jap) PTS –15 Rocky Fratto (USA) Rochester, USA

7 Nov 1981 *LF(WBC)* Hilario Zapata (Pan) RSF –10 Netrnoi Vorasingh (Tha) Korat, Thailand

14 Nov 1981 *LW(WBA)* Aaron Pryor (USA) RSF –7 Dujuan Johnson (USA) Cleveland, USA

15 Nov 1981 *LM(WBC)* Wilfred Benitez (USA) PTS –15 Carlos Santos (USA) Las Vegas, USA

18 Nov 1981 *SF(WBC)* Chul-Ho Kim (S. Kor) RSF –9 Ryotsu Maruyama (Jap) Pusan, South Korea

21 Nov 1981 *L(WBC)* Alexis Arguello (Nic) KO –7 Roberto Elizondo (USA) Las Vegas, USA

5 Dec 1981 *L(WBA)* Arturo Frias (USA) KO –8 Claude Noel (Tri) Las Vegas, USA

5 Dec 1981 *Fe(WBA)* Eusebio Pedroza (Pan) KO –5 Bashew Sibaca (SA) Panama City, Panama

5 Dec 1981 *SF(WBA)* Rafael Pedroza (Pan) PTS –15 Gustavo Ballas (Arg) Panama City, Panama

9 Dec 1981 *LH(WBC)* Dwight Braxton (USA) RSF –10 Matt Saad Muhammad (USA) Atlantic City, USA

10 Dec 1981 *JL(WBA)* Sam Serrano (PR) RSF –12 Hikaru Tomonari (Jap) San Juan, Puerto Rico

10 Dec 1981 *B(WBA)* Jeff Chandler (USA) RSF –13 Eijiro Murata (Jap) Atlantic City, USA

12 Dec 1981 *Fe(WBC)* Salvador Sanchez (Mex) PTS –15 Pat Cowdell (GB) Houston, USA

16 Dec 1981 *LF(WBA)* Katsuo Tokashiki (Jap) PTS –15 Hwan-Jim Kim (S. Kor) Sendai, Japan

19 Dec 1981 *LW(WBC)* Saoul Mamby (Jam) PTS –15 Obisia Nwankpa (Ngr) Lagos, Nigeria

20 Dec 1981 *Fl(WBA)* Juan Herrera (Mex) RSF –7 Betulio Gonzalez (Ven) Mexico City, Mexico

15 Jan 1982 *SB(WBA)* Sergio Palma (Arg) PTS –15 Jorge Lujan (Pan) Cordoba, Argentina

16 Jan 1982 *JL(WBC)* Rolando Navarrete (Phi) KO –11 Chung-Il Choi (S. Kor) Manila, Philippines

24 Jan 1982 *Fe(WBA)* Eusebio Pedroza (Pan) PTS –15 Juan Laporte (PR) Atlantic City, USA

27 Jan 1982 *B(WBA)* Jeff Chandler (USA) RSF –6 Johnny Carter (USA) Philadelphia, USA

30 Jan 1982 *LM(WBC)* Wilfred Benitez (USA) PTS –15 Roberto Duran (Pan) Las Vegas, USA

30 Jan 1982 *L(WBA)* Arturo Frias (USA) TKO –9 Ernesto Espana (Ven) Los Angeles, USA

2 Feb 1982 *LM(WBA)* Davey Moore (USA) RSF –6 Tadashi Mihara (Jap) Tokyo, Japan

6 Feb 1982 *LF(WBC)* Amado Ursua (Mex) KO –2 Hilario Zapata (Pan) Panama City, Panama

10 Feb 1982 *SF(WBC)* Chul-Ho Kim (S. Kor) KO –8 Koki Ishii (Jap) Taegu, South Korea

13 Feb 1982 *C(WBA)* Ossie Ocasio (PR) PTS –15 Robbie Williams (SA) Johannesburg, South Africa

13 Feb 1982 *LH(WBA)* Michael Spinks (USA) RSF –6 Mustapha Wasajja (Uga) Atlantic City, USA

13 Feb 1982 *L(WBC)* Alexis Arguello (Nic) RSF –6 James Busceme (USA) Beaumont, USA

15 Feb 1982 *W(WBC)* Sugar Ray Leonard (USA) RSF –3 Bruce Finch (USA) Reno, USA

24 Feb 1982 *C(WBC)* Carlos de Leon (PR) RSF –7 Marvin Camel (USA) Atlantic City, USA

7 Mar 1982 *M* Marvin Hagler (USA) RSF –1 William 'Caveman' Lee (USA) Atlantic City, USA

20 Mar 1982 *Fl(WBC)* Prudencio Cardona (Col) KO –1 Antonio Avelar (Mex) Tampico, Mexico

21 Mar 1982 *LH(WBC)* Dwight Braxton (USA) RSF –6 Jerry Martin (Ant) Las Vegas, USA

21 Mar 1982 *LW(WBA)* Aaron Pryor (USA) RSF –12 Miguel Montilla (Dom) Atlantic City, USA

27 Mar 1982 *SB(WBC)* Wilfredo Gomez (PR) RSF –6 Juan 'Kid' Meza (Mex) Atlantic City, USA

4 Apr 1982 *LF(WBC)* Katsuo Tokashiki (Jap) PTS –15 Lupe Madera (Mex) Sendai, Japan

8 Apr 1982 *SF(WBA)* Jiro Watanabe (Jap) PTS –15 Rafael Pedroza (Pan) Osaka, Japan

11 Apr 1982 *LH(WBA)* Michael Spinks (USA) KO –8 Murray Sutherland (GB) Atlantic City, USA

13 Apr 1982 *LF(WBC)* Tadashi Tomori (Jap) PTS –15 Amado Ursua (Mex) Tokyo, Japan

26 Apr 1982 *LM(WBA)* Davey Moore (USA) KO –5 Charlie Weir (SA) Johannesburg, South Africa

1 May 1982 *Fl(WBA)* Santos Laciar (Arg) RSF –13 Juan Herrera (Mex) Merida, Mexico

8 May 1982 *L(WBA)* Ray Mancini (USA) RSF –1 Arturo Frias (USA) Las Vegas, USA

8 May 1982 *Fe(WBC)* Salvador Sanchez (Mex) PTS –15 Jorge 'Rocky' Garcia (Mex) Dallas, USA

22 May 1982 *L(WBC)* Alexis Arguello (Nic) KO –5 Andy Ganigan (USA) Las Vegas, USA

29 May 1982 *JL(WBC)* Rafael Limon (Mex) KO –12 Rolando Navarrete (Phi) Las Vegas, USA

3 Jun 1982 *B(WBC)* Lupe Pintor (Mex) RSF –11 Seung-Hoon Lee (S. Kor) Los Angeles, USA

5 Jun 1982 *JL(WBA)* Sam Serrano (PR) TKO –10 Ben Villablanca (Chi) Santiago, Chile

11 Jun 1982 *SB(WBC)* Wilfredo Gomez (PR) KO –10 Juan Antonio Lopez (Mex) Las Vegas, USA

12 Jun 1982 *H(WBC)* Larry Holmes (USA) RTD –13 Gerry Cooney (USA) Las Vegas, USA

12 Jun 1982 *LH(WBA)* Michael Spinks (USA) RSF –8 Jerry Celestine (USA) Atlantic City, USA

12 Jun 1982 *SB(WBA)* Leonardo Cruz (Dom) PTS –15 Sergio Palma (Arg) Miami, USA

26 Jun 1982 *LW(WBC)* Leroy Haley (USA) PTS –15 Saoul Mamby (Jam) Ohio, USA

27 Jun 1982 *C(WBC)* S. T. Gordon (USA) RSF –2 Carlos de Leon (PR) Ohio, USA

4 Jul 1982 *LW(WBA)* Aaron Pryor (USA) RSF –6 Akio Kameda (Jap) Cincinatti, USA

4 Jul 1982 *SF(WBC)* Chul-Ho Kim (S. Kor) D –15 Raul Valdez (Mex) Taejon, South Korea

7 Jul 1982 *LF(WBA)* Katsuo Tokashiki (Jap) KO –8 Masaharu Ina (Jap) Tokyo, Japan

17 Jul 1982 *LM(WBA)* Davey Moore (USA) RSF –10 Ayub Kalule (Uga) Atlantic City, USA

20 Jul 1982 *LF(WBC)* Hilario Zapata (Pan) PTS –15 Tadashi Tomori (Jap) Kamazawa, Japan

21 Jul 1982 *Fe(WBC)* Salvador Sanchez (Mex) RSF –15 Azumah Nelson (Gha) New York, USA

24 Jul 1982 *L(WBA)* Ray Mancini (USA) RSF –6 Ernesto Espana (Ven) Warren, USA

25 Jul 1982 *Fl(WBC)* Freddie Castillo (Mex) PTS –15 Prudencio Cardona (Col) Merida, Mexico

29 Jul 1982 *SF(WBA)* Jiro Watanabe (Jap) RSF –9 Gustavo Ballas (Arg) Osaka, Japan

8 Aug 1982 *LH(WBC)* Dwight Braxton (USA) RSF –6 Matt Saad Muhammad (USA) Philadelphia, USA

14 Aug 1982 *Fl(WBA)* Santos Laciar (Arg) PTS –15 Betulio Gonzalez (Ven) Maracaibo, Venezuela

18 Aug 1982 *SB(WBC)* Wildredo Gomez (PR) RTD –7 Roberto Rubaldino (Mex) San Juan, Puerto Rico

15 Sep 1982 *Fe(WBC)* Juan Laporte (PR) RSF –10 Mario Miranda (Col) New York, USA

18 Sep 1982 *LH(WBA)* Michael Spinks (USA) KO –9 Johnny Davis (USA) Atlantic City, USA

18 Sep 1982 *JL(WBC)* Rafael Limon (Mex) KO –7 Chung-Il Choi (S. Kor) Los Angeles, USA

18 Sep 1982 *LF(WBC)* Hilario Zapata (Pan) PTS –15 Jung-Koo Chang (S. Kor) Seoul, South Korea

10 Oct 1982 *LF(WBA)* Katsuo Tokashiki (Jap) PTS –15 Sung-Nam Kim (S. Kor) Tokyo, Japan

16 Oct 1982 *Fe(WBA)* Eusebio Pedroza (Pan) D –15 Bernard Taylor (USA) Charlotte, USA

20 Oct 1982 *LW(WBC)* Leroy Haley (USA) PTS –15 Juan Jose Giminez (Arg) Cleveland, USA

27 Oct 1982 *B(WBA)* Jeff Chandler (USA) RSF –9 Miguel Iriarte (Pan) Atlantic City, USA

31 Oct 1982 *M* Marvin Hagler (USA) KO –5 Fulgencio Obelmejias (Ven) San Remo, Italy

5 Nov 1982 *Fl(WBA)* Santos Laciar (Arg) RSF –13 Steve Muchoki (Ken) Copenhagen, Denmark

7 Nov 1982 *Fl(WBC)* Eleoncio Mercedes (Dom) PTS –15 Freddie Castillo (Mex) Los Angeles, USA

11 Nov 1982 *SF(WBA)* Jiro Watanabe (Jap) RTD –12 Shoji Oguma (Jap) Hamamatsu, Japan

12 Nov 1982 *LW(WBA)* Aaron Pryor (USA) RSF –14 Alexis Arguello (Nic) Miami, USA

13 Nov 1982 *L(WBA)* Ray Mancini (USA) RSF –14 Duk-Koo Kim (S. Kor) Las Vegas, USA

20 Nov 1982 *LH(WBC)* Dwight Muhammad Qawi (USA) RSF –11 Eddie Davis (USA) Atlantic City, USA

25 Nov 1982 *H(WBC)* Larry Holmes (USA) PTS –15 Randall Cobb (USA) Houston, USA

28 Nov 1982 *SF(WBC)* Rafael Orono (Ven) RSF –6 Chul-Ho Kim (S. Kor) Seoul, South Korea

30 Nov 1982 *LF(WBC)* Hilario Zapata (Pan) RSF –8 Tadashi Tomori (Jap) Tokyo, Japan

3 Dec 1982 *LM(WBC)* Thomas Hearns (USA) PTS –15 Wilfred Benitez (USA) New Orleans, USA

3 Dec 1982 *SB(WBC)* Wilfredo Gomez (PR) RSF –14 Lupe Pintor (Mex) New Orleans, USA

10 Dec 1982 *H(WBA)* Mike Dokes (USA) RSF –1 Mike Weaver (USA) Las Vegas, USA

11 Dec 1982 *JL(WBC)* Bob Chacon (USA) PTS –15 Rafael Limon (Mex) Sacramento, USA

15 Dec 1982 *C(WBA)* Ossie Ocasio (PR) PTS –15 Young Joe Louis (USA) Chicago, USA

19 Jan 1983 *JL(WBA)* Roger Mayweather (USA) KO –8 Sam Serrano (PR) San Juan, Puerto Rico

29 Jan 1983 *LM(WBA)* Davey Moore (USA) KO –4 Gary Guiden (USA) Atlantic City, USA

1 Feb 1983 *SF(WBA)* Rafael Orono (Ven) KO –4 Pedro Romero (Pan) Caracas, Venezuela

11 Feb 1983 *M* Marvin Hagler (USA) RSF –6 Tony Sibson (GB) Worcester, USA

13 Feb 1983 *W(WBA)* Don Curry (USA) PTS –15 Jun-Sok Hwang (S. Kor) Fort Worth, USA

13 Feb 1983 *LW(WBC)* Leroy Haley (USA) PTS –12 Saoul Mamby (Jam) Ohio, USA

17 Feb 1983 *C(WBC)* S. T. Gordon (USA) RSF –8 Jesse Burnett (USA) New Jersey, USA

20 Feb 1983 *Fe(WBC)* Juan Laporte (PR) PTS –12 Ruben Castillo (USA) San Juan, Puerto Rico

24 Feb 1983 *SF(WBA)* Jiro Watanabe (Jap) KO –8 Luis Ibanez (Peru) Hamamatsu, Japan

4 Mar 1983 *Fl(WBA)* Santos Laciar (Arg) KO –9 Ramon Neri (Dom) Cordoba, Argentina

13 Mar 1983 *B(WBA)* Jeff Chandler (USA) PTS –15 Jose Canizales (USA) Atlantic City, USA

15 Mar 1983 *Fl(WBC)* Charlie Magri (Tun) RSF –7 Eleoncio Mercedes (Dom) London, England

16 Mar 1983 *SB(WBA)* Leonardo Cruz (Dom) PTS –15 Soon-Hyun Chung (S. Kor) San Juan, Puerto Rico

19 Mar 1983 *LH* Michael Spinks (USA) PTS –15 Dwight Muhammad Qawi (USA) Atlantic City, USA

19 Mar 1983 *W(WBC)* Milton McCrory (USA) D –12 Colin Jones (GB) Reno, USA

26 Mar 1983 *H(WBC)* Larry Holmes (USA) PTS –12 Lucien Rodriguez (Mor) Scranton, USA

26 Mar 1983 *LF(WBC)* Chang-Jung Ko (S. Kor) RSF –3 Hilario Zapata (Pan) Seoul, South Korea

2 Apr 1983 *LW(WBA)* Aaron Pryor (USA) RSF –3 San-Hyun Kim (S. Kor) Atlantic City, USA

9 Apr 1983 *LF(WBA)* Katsuo Tokashiki (Jap) D –15 Lupe Madera (Mex) Tokyo, Japan

21 Apr 1983 *JL(WBA)* Roger Mayweather (USA) RSF –8 Jorge Alvarado (Pan) San Juan, Costa Rica

24 Apr 1983 *Fe(WBA)* Eusebio Pedroza (Pan) PTS –15 Rocky Lockridge (USA) San Remo, Italy

2 May 1983 *L(WBC)* Edwin Rosario (PR) PTS –12 Jose Luis Ramirez (Mex) San Juan, Puerto Rico

5 May 1983 *Fl(WBA)* Santos Laciar (Arg) RSF –2 Shuichi Hozumi (Jap) Shizuoka, Japan

18 May 1983 *LW(WBC)* Bruce Curry (USA) PTS –12 Leroy Haley (USA) Las Vegas, USA

20 May 1983 *H(WBC)* Larry Holmes (USA) PTS –12 Tim Witherspoon (USA) Las Vegas, USA

20 May 1983 *H(WBA)* Mike Dokes (USA) D –15 Mike Weaver (USA) Las Vegas, USA

20 May 1983 *C(WBA)* Ossie Ocasio (PR) PTS –15 Randy Stephens (USA) Las Vegas, USA

21 May 1983 *C(IBF)* Marvin Camel (USA) KO –9 Rocky Sekorski (USA) Billings, USA

27 May 1983 *M* Marvin Hagler (USA) KO –4 Wilford Scypion (USA) Rhode Island, USA

11 Jun 1983 *LF(WBC)* Chang-Jung Ko (S. Kor) RSF –2 Masaharu Iha (Jap) Taegu, South Korea

15 Jun 1983 *SB(WBC)* Jaime Garza (USA) RSF –2 Bobby Berna (Phi) Los Angeles, USA

16 Jun 1983 *LM(WBA)* Roberto Duran (Pan) RSF –8 Davey Moore (USA) New York, USA

23 Jun 1983 *SF(WBA)* Jiro Watanabe (Jap) PTS –15 Roberto Ramirez (Mex) Miyagi-Kew, Japan

25 Jun 1983 *Fe(WBC)* Juan Laporte (PR) PTS –12 Johnny De La Rosa (Dom) San Juan, Puerto Rico

7 July 1983 *LW(WBC)* Bruce Curry (USA) KO –7 Hidekazu Akai (Jap) Osaka, Japan

10 Jul 1983 *LF(WBA)* Lupe Madera (Mex) RSF –4 Katsuo Tokashiki (Jap) Tokyo, Japan

16 July 1983 *Fl(WBA)* Santos Laciar (Arg) RST –1 Shin-Hi Sop (S. Kor) Cheju, South Korea

17 Jul 1982 *C(WBC)* Carlos de Leon (PR) PTS –12 S. T. Gordon (USA) Las Vegas, USA

8 Aug 1983 *JL(WBC)* Hector Camacho (PR) RSF –5 Rafael Limon (Mex) San Juan, Puerto Rico

13 Aug 1983 *W(WBC)* Milton McCrory (USA) PTS –12 Colin Jones (GB) Las Vegas, USA

19 Aug 1983 *JL(WBA)* Roger Mayweather (USA) KO –1 Ben Villablanca (Chi) Las Vegas, USA

26 Aug 1983 *SB(WBA)* Leonardo Cruz (Dom) PTS –15 Cleo Garcia (Nic) Santo Domingo, Dominican Republic

31 Aug 1983 *B(WBC)* Albert Davila (USA) KO –12 Kiko Bejines (Mex) Los Angeles, USA

2 Sep 1983 *W(WBA)* Don Curry (USA) KO –1 Roger Stafford (USA) Sicily, Italy

9 Sep 1983 *LW(WBA)* Aaron Pryor (USA) KO –10 Alexis Arguello (Nic) Las Vegas, USA

10 Sep 1983 *H(WBC)* Larry Holmes (USA) RSF –5 Scott Frank (USA) Atlantic City, USA

10 Sep 1983 *B(WBA)* Jeff Chandler (USA) RSF –10 Eijiro Murata (Jap) Tokyo, Japan

10 Sep 1983 *LF(WBC)* Chang-Jung Ko (S. Kor) PTS –12 German Torres (Phi) Taejon, South Korea

15 Sep 1983 *L(WBA)* Ray Mancini (USA) KO –9 Orlando Romero (Peru) New York, USA

21 Sep 1983 *C(WBC)* Carlos de Leon (PR) RSF –4 Alvaro Lopez (Mex) San Jose, USA

24 Sep 1983 *H(WBA)* Gerrie Coetzee (SA) KO –10 Mike Dokes (USA) Cleveland, USA

27 Sep 1983 *Fl(WBC)* Frank Cedeno (Phi) RSF –6 Charlie Magri (Tun) London, England

5 Oct 1983 *SF(WBA)* Jiro Watanabe (Jap) TKO –11 Chung-Soon Kwon (S. Kor) Osaka, Japan

20 Oct 1983 *LW(WBC)* Bruce Curry (USA) PTS –12 Leroy Haley (USA) Las Vegas, USA

22 Oct 1983 *Fe(WBA)* Eusebio Pedroza (Pan) PTS –15 Jose Caba (Dom) St Vincent, West Indies

23 Oct 1983 *LF(WBA)* Lupe Madera (Mex) PTS –15 Katsuo Tokashiki (Jap) Saporro, Japan

29 Oct 1983 *SF(WBC)* Rafael Orono (Ven) KO –5 Orlando Maldonado (PR) Caracas, Venezuela

10 Nov 1983 *M* Marvin Hagler (USA) PTS –15 Roberto Duran (Pan) Las Vegas, USA

18 Nov 1983 *JL(WBC)* Hector Camacho (PR) KO –5 Rafael Solis (PR) San Juan, Puerto Rico

25 Nov 1983 *H(WBC)* Larry Holmes (USA) TKO –1 Marvis Frazier (USA) Las Vegas, USA

25 Nov 1983 *LH* Michael Spinks (USA) RSF –10 Oscar Rivadeneyra (USA) Vancouver, Canada

26 Nov 1983 *SF(WBC)* Payao Poontarat (Tha) PTS –12 Rafael Orono (Ven) Bangkok, Thailand

4 Dec 1983 *SB(IBF)* Bobby Berna (Phi) KO –9 Seung-In Suh (S. Kor) Seoul, South Korea

10 Dec 1983 *SF(IBF)* Joo-Do Chun (S. Kor) RSF –5 Ken Kasugai (Jap) Osaka, Japan

10 Dec 1983 *LF(IBF)* Dodie Penalosa (Phi) RSF –12 Satoshi Shingaki (Jap) Osaka, Japan

13 Dec 1983 *C(IBF)* Marvin Camel (USA) KO –5 Roddy McDonald (Can) Halifax, Canada

17 Dec 1983 *B(WBA)* Jeff Chandler (USA) RSF –7 Oscar Muniz (USA) Atlantic City, USA

24 Dec 1983 *Fl(IBF)* Soon-Chun Kwon (S. Kor) KO –5 Rene Busayong (Phi) Seoul, South Korea

14 Jan 1984 *L(WBA)* Ray Mancini (USA) RSF –3 Bobby Chacon (USA) Reno, USA

15 Jan 1984 *W(WBC)* Milton McCrory (USA) RSF –6 Milton Guest (USA) Detroit, USA

18 Jan 1984 *Fl(WBC)* Koji Kobayashi (Jap) RSF –2 Frank Cedeno (Phi) Tokyo, Japan

21 Jan 1984 *LW(WBA)* Johnny Bumphus (USA) PTS –15 Lorenzo Garcia (Arg) Atlantic City, USA

28 Jan 1984 *SF(IBF)* Joo-Do Chun (S. Kor) KO –12 Prayurasak Muangsurin (Tha) Seoul, South Korea

28 Jan 1984 *Fl(WBA)* Santos Laciar (Arg) PTS –15 Juan Herrera (Mex) Marsala, Italy

29 Jan 1984 *LW(WBC)* Billy Costello (USA) RSF –10 Bruce Curry (USA) Beaumont, USA

30 Jan 1984 *L(IBF)* Charlie 'Choo Choo' Brown (USA) PTS –15 Melvin Paul (USA) Atlantic City, USA

4 Feb 1984 *W(WBA)* Don Curry (USA) PTS –15 Marlon Starling (USA) Atlantic City, USA

11 Feb 1984 *LM(WBC)* Thomas Hearns (USA) PTS –12 Luigi Minchillo (Ita) Detroit, USA

22 Feb 1984 *SB(WBA)* Loris Stecca (Ita) RSF –12 Leonardo Cruz (Dom) Milan, Italy

25 Feb 1984 *LH* Michael Spinks (USA) PTS –12 Eddie Davis (USA) Atlantic City, USA

25 Feb 1984 *JL(WBA)* Rocky Lockridge (USA) KO –1 Roger Mayweather (USA) Beaumont, USA

25 Feb 1984 *Fl(IBF)* Soon-Chun Kwon (S. Kor) PTS –15 Roger Castillo (Phi) Seoul, South Korea

3 Mar 1984 *LF(WBC)* Chang-Jung Ko (S. Kor) PTS –12 Sot Chitalada (Tha) Pusan, South Korea

4 Mar 1984 *Fe(IBF)* Min-Keum Oh (S. Kor) KO –2 Joko Arter (Phi) Seoul, South Korea

9 Mar 1984 *H(WBC)* Tim Witherspoon (USA) PTS –12 Greg Page (USA) Las Vegas, USA

9 Mar 1984 *C(WBC)* Carlos de Leon (PR) PTS –12 Anthony Davis (USA) Las Vegas, USA

11 Mar 1984 *LM(IBF)* Mark Medal (USA) RSF –5 Earl Hargrove (USA) Atlantic City, USA

15 Mar 1984 *SF(WBA)* Jiro Watanabe (Jap) RSF –15 Celso Chavez (Pan) Osaka, Japan

17 Mar 1984 *L(WBC)* Edwin Rosario (PR) RSF –1 Roberto Elizondo (USA) San Juan, Puerto Rico

17 Mar 1984 *SF(IBF)* Joo-Do Chun (S. Kor) KO –1 Diego de Villa (Phi) Kwangju, South Korea

27 Mar 1984 *SF(WBC)* Payao Poontarat (Tha) TKO –10 Gustavo Espadas (Mex) Bangkok, Thailand

28 Mar 1984 *SM(IBF)* Murray Sutherland (GB) PTS –15 Ernie Singletary (USA) Atlantic City, USA

30 Mar 1984 *M* Marvin Hagler (USA) RSF –10 Juan Domingo Roldan (Arg) Las Vegas, USA

31 Mar 1984 *Fe(WBC)* Wilfredo Gomez (PR) PTS –12 Juan Laporte (PR) San Juan, Puerto Rico

7 Apr 1984 *B(WBA)* Richard Sandoval (USA) RSF –15 Jeff Chandler (USA) Atlantic City, USA

9 Apr 1984 *Fl(WBC)* Gabriel Bernal (Mex) RSF –2 Koji Kobayashi (Jap) Tokyo, Japan

15 Apr 1984 *W(WBC)* Milton McCrory (USA) RSF –6 Gilles Elbilla (Fra) Detroit, USA

15 Apr 1984 *L(IBF)* Harry Arroyo (USA) RSF –4 Charlie 'Choo Choo' Brown (USA) Atlantic City, USA

15 Apr 1984 *SB(IBF)* Seung-In Suh (S. Kor) KO –10 Bobby Berna (Phi) Seoul, South Korea

15 Apr 1984 *B(IBF)* Satoshi Shingaki (Jap) KO –8 Elmer Magallano (USA) Kashiwara, Japan

21 Apr 1984 *W(WBA)* Don Curry (USA) RTD –7 Elio Diaz (Ven) Fort Worth, USA

22 Apr 1984 *JL(IBF)* Hwan-Kil Yuh (S. Kor) PTS –15 Rod Sequenan (Phi) Seoul, South Korea

5 May 1984 *C(WBA)* Ossie Ocasio (PR) RSF –15 John Odhiambo (Uga) San Juan, Puerto Rico

12 May 1984 *LF(WBA)* Francisco Quiroz (Dom) KO –9 Lupe Madera (Mex) Maracaibo, Venezuela

13 May 1984 *LF(IBF)* Dodie Penalosa (Phi) KO –9 Jae-Hong Kim (S. Kor) Seoul, South Korea

19 May 1984 *Fl(IBF)* Soon-Chun Kwon (S. Kor) PTS –15 Ian Clyde (USA) Taejon, South Korea

26 May 1984 *SB(WBC)* Jaime Garza (USA) KO –3 Felipe Orozco (Col) Miami, USA

26 May 1984 *SF(IBF)* Joo-Do Chun (S. Kor) KO –6 Felix Marquez (PR) Chonju, South Korea

27 May 1984 *Fe(WBA)* Eusebio Pedroza (Pan) PTS –15 Angel Levy Meyor (Ven) Maracaibo, Venezuela

27 May 1984 *SB(WBA)* Victor Callejas (PR) KO –8 Loris Stecca (Ita) San Juan, Puerto Rico

27 May 1984 *B(WBC)* Albert Davila (USA) RSF –11 Enrique Sanchez (Dom) Miami, USA

1 Jun 1984 *LW(WBA)* Gene Hatcher (USA) RSF –11 Johnny Bumphus (USA) Buffalo, USA

1 Jun 1984 *L(WBA)* Livingstone Bramble (VI) RSF –14 Ray Mancini (USA) Buffalo, USA

1 Jun 1984 *Fl(WBC)* Gabriel Bernal (Mex) RSF –11 Antoine Montero (Fra) Nimes, France

3 Jun 1984 *C(WBC)* Carlos de Leon (PR) PTS –12 Bashiru Ali (Nig) Oakland, USA

10 Jun 1984 *Fe(IBF)* Min-Keum Oh (S. Kor) PTS –15 Kelvin Lampkin (USA) Seoul, South Korea

12 Jun 1984 *JL(WBA)* Rocky Lockridge (USA) RSF –11 Tae-Jin Moon (S. Kor) Anchorage, USA

16 Jun 1984 *LM(WBC)* Thomas Hearns (USA) RSF –2 Roberto Duran (Pan) Las Vegas, USA

22 Jun 1984 *LW(IBF)* Aaron Pryor (USA) PTS –15 Nicky Furlano (Can) Toronto, Canada

23 Jun 1984 *L(WBC)* Edwin Rosario (PR) PTS –12 Howard Davis (USA) San Juan, Puerto Rico

5 Jul 1984 *SF(WBC)* Jiro Watanabe (Jap) PTS –12 Payao Poontarat (Tha) Osaka, Japan

16 Jul 1984 *LW(WBC)* Billy Costello (USA) PTS –12 Ronnie Shields (USA) New York, USA

20 Jul 1984 *SF(IBF)* Joo-Do Chun (S. Kor) KO –7 William Develos (Phi) Pusan, South Korea

22 Jul 1984 *SM(IBF)* Chong-Pal Park (S. Kor) KO –11 Murray Sutherland (GB) Seoul, South Korea

4 Aug 1984 *B(IBF)* Satoshi Shingaki (Jap) PTS –15 Horves de la Puz (Phi) Naha, Japan

18 Aug 1984 *LF(WBA)* Francisco Quiroz (Dom) KO –2 Victor Sierra (Pan) Panama City, Panama

18 Aug 1984 *LF(WBC)* Chang-Jung Ko (S. Kor) RSF –9 Katsuo Tokashiki (Jap) Pohang, South Korea

31 Aug 1984 *H(WBC)* Pinklon Thomas (USA) PTS –12 Tim Witherspoon (USA) Las Vegas, USA

1 Sep 1984 *L(IBF)* Harry Arroyo (USA) RSF –8 Charlie 'White Lightning' Brown (USA) Youngstown, USA

7 Sep 1984 *Fl(IBF)* Soon-Chun Kwon (S. Kor) RSF –12 Joaquin Flores (Col) Seoul, South Korea

13 Sep 1984 *JL(WBC)* Julio-Cesar Chavez (Mex) RSF –8 Mario Martinez (Mex) Los Angeles, USA

15 Sep 1984 *LM(WBC)* Thomas Hearns (USA) RSF –3 Fred Hutchings (USA) Saginaw, USA

15 Sep 1984 *Fl(WBA)* Santos Laciar (Arg) KO –10 Prudencio Cardona (Col) Cordoba, Argentina

16 Sep 1984 *JL(IBF)* Hwan-Kil Yuh (S. Kor) KO –6 Sakda Galexi (Tha) Pohang, South Korea

22 Sep 1984 *W(WBA)* Don Curry (USA) KO –6 Nino La Rocca (Mau) Monte Carlo, Monaco

22 Sep 1984 *B(WBA)* Richard Sandoval (USA) PTS –15 Edgar Roman (Ven) Monte Carlo, Monaco

6 Oct 1984 *C(IBF)* Leroy Murphy (USA) RSF –14 Marvin Camel (USA) Billings, USA

8 Oct 1984 *Fl(WBC)* Sot Chitalada (Tha) PTS –12 Gabriel Bernal (Mex) Bangkok, Thailand

20 Oct 1984 *M* Marvin Hagler (USA) RSF –3 Mustapha Hamsho (Syr) New York, USA

20 Oct 1984 *LM(WBA)* Mike McCallum (Jam) PTS –15 Sean Mannion (USA) New York, USA

2 Nov 1984 *JM(IBF)* Carlos Santos (PR) PTS –15 Mark Medal (USA) New York, USA

3 Nov 1984 *LW(WBC)* Billy Costello (USA) PTS –12 Saoul Mamby (Jam) New York USA

3 Nov 1984 *L(WBC)* Jose Luis Ramirez (Mex) RSF –4 Edwin Rosario (PR) San Juan, Puerto Rico

3 Nov 1984 *SB(WBC)* Juan 'Kid' Meza (Mex) KO –1 Jaime Garza (USA) New York, USA

9 Nov 1984 *H(IBF)* Larry Holmes (USA) RSF –12 James 'Bonecrusher' Smith (USA) Las Vegas, USA

16 Nov 1984 *LF(IBF)* Dodie Penalosa (Phi) PTS –15 Chun-Hwan Choi (S. Kor) Manila, Philippines

21 Nov 1984 *SF(WBA)* Kaosai 'Galaxy' (Tha) KO –6 Eusebio Espinal (Dom) Bangkok, Thailand

29 Nov 1984 *SF(WBC)* Jiro Watanabe (Jap) RSF –11 Payao Poontarat (Tha) Kumamoto, Japan

1 Dec 1984 *H(WBA)* Greg Page (USA) KO –8 Gerrie Coetzee (SA) Sun City, South Africa

1 Dec 1984 *C(WBA)* Piet Crous (SA) PTS –15 Ossie Ocasio (PR) Sun City, South Africa

2 Dec 1984 *LM(WBA)* Mike McCallum (Jam) TKO –13 Luigi Minchillo (Ita) Milan, Italy

8 Dec 1984 *Fe(WBC)* Azumah Nelson (Gha) RSF –11 Wilfredo Gomez (PR) San Juan, Puerto Rico

8 Dec 1984 *Fl(WBA)* Santos Laciar (Arg) PTS –15 Hilario Zapata (Pan) Buenos Aires, Argentina

15 Dec 1984 *LW(WBA)* Gene Hatcher (USA) PTS –15 Ubaldo Sacco (Arg) Fort Worth, USA

15 Dec 1984 *B(WBA)* Richard Sandoval (USA) RSF –8 Gardeno Villoa (Chi) Miami, USA

15 Dec 1984 *LF(WBC)* Chang-Jung Ko (S. Kor) PTS –12 Tadashi Kuromochi (Jap) Pusan, South Korea

20 Dec 1984 *C(IBF)* Leroy Murphy (USA) RSF –12 Young Joe Louis (USA) Chicago, USA

2 Jan 1985 *SM(IBF)* Chong-Pal Park (S. Kor) KO –2 Roy Gumbs (Jam) Seoul, South Korea

2 Jan 1985 *SB(IBF)* Chi-Won Kim (S. Kor) KO –2 Seung-In Suh (S. Kor) Seoul, South Korea

6 Jan 1985 *SF(IBF)* Joo-Do Chun (S. Kor) KO –15 Park-Kwang Gu (S. Kor) Ulsan, South Korea

12 Jan 1985 *L(IBF)* Harry Arroyo (USA) RSF –11 Terence Alli (Guy) Atlantic City, USA

19 Jan 1985 *W(WBA)* Don Curry (USA) RSF –4 Colin Jones (GB) Birmingham, England

26 Jan 1985 *JL(WBA)* Rocky Lockridge (USA) RSF –6 Kamel Bou Ali (Tun) Riva Del Garda, Italy

2 Feb 1985 *Fe(WBA)* Eusebio Pedroza (Pan) PTS –15 Jorge Lujan (Pan) Panama City, Panama

2 Feb 1985 *SB(WBA)* Victor Callejas (PR) PTS –15 Seung-Hoon Lee (S. Kor) San Juan, Puerto Rico

16 Feb 1985 *LW(WBC)* Billy Costello (USA) PTS –12 Leroy Haley (USA) New York, USA

16 Feb 1985 *L(WBA)* Livingstone Bramble (VI) PTS –15 Ray Mancini (USA) Reno, USA

16 Feb 1985 *JL(IBF)* Lester Ellis (Aus) PTS –15 Hwan-Kil Yuh (S. Kor) Melbourne, Australia

20 Feb 1985 *Fl(WBC)* Sot Chitalada (Tha) RSF –4 Charlie Magri (Tun) London, England

23 Feb 1985 *LH* Michael Spinks (USA) RSF –3 David Sears (USA) Atlantic City, USA

2 Mar 1985 *LW(IBF)* Aaron Pryor (USA) PTS –15 Garry Hinton (USA) Atlantic City, USA

6 Mar 1985 *SF(WBA)* Kaosai 'Galaxy' (Tha) KO –7 Dong-Chun Lee (S. Kor) Bangkok, Thailand

9 Mar 1985 *W(WBC)* Milton McCrory (USA) PTS –12 Pedro Vilella (USA) Paris, France

9 Mar 1985 *SF(WBC)* Jiro Watanabe (Jap) PTS –12 Juliosoto Solano (Dom) Tokyo, Japan

15 Mar 1985 *H(IBF)* Larry Holmes (USA) RSF –10 David Bey (USA) Las Vegas, USA

29 Mar 1985 *LF(WBA)* Joey Olivo (USA) PTS –15 Francisco Quiroz (Dom) Miami, USA

30 Mar 1985 *C(WBA)* Piet Crous (SA) RSF –3 Randy Stephens (USA) Sun City, South Africa

6 Apr 1985 *L(IBF)* Jimmy Paul (USA) PTS –15 Harry Arroyo (USA) Atlantic City, USA

7 Apr 1985 *Fe(IBF)* Min-Keum Oh (S. Kor) PTS –15 Irving Mitchell (USA) Seoul, South Korea

14 Apr 1985 *Fl(IBF)* Soon-Chun Kwon (S. Kor) KO –3 Shinobu Kawashima (Jap) Seoul, South Korea

15 Apr 1985 *M* Marvin Hagler (USA) RSF –3 Thomas Hearns (USA) Las Vegas, USA

19 Apr 1985 *JL(WBC)* Julio-Cesar Chavez (Mex) RSF –6 Ruben Castillo (USA) Los Angeles, USA

19 Apr 1985 *SB(WBC)* Juan 'Kid' Meza (Mex) RSF –6 Mike Ayala (USA) Los Angeles, USA

26 Apr 1985 *JL(IBF)* Lester Ellis (Aus) RSF –13 Rod Sequenan (Phi) Melbourne, Australia

26 Apr 1985 *B(IBF)* Jeff Fenech (Aus) RSF –9 Satoshi Shingaki (Jap) Sydney, Australia

29 Apr 1985 *H(WBA)* Tony Tubbs (USA) PTS –15 Greg Page (USA) Buffalo, USA

3 May 1985 *SF(IBF)* Ellyas Pical (Ina) KO –8 Joo-Do Chun (S. Kor) Djakarta, Indonesia

4 May 1985 *B(WBC)* Daniel Zaragoza (Mex) DIS –7 Freddie Jackson (USA) Aruba, Dutch West Indies

4 May 1985 *LF(WBC)* Chang-Jung Ko (S. Kor) PTS –12 German Torres (Phi) Ulsan, South Korea

6 May 1985 *Fl(WBA)* Santos Laciar (Arg) PTS –15 Antoine Montero (Fra) Grenoble, France

19 May 1985 *JL(WBA)* Wilfredo Gomez (PR) PTS –15 Rocky Lockridge (USA) San Juan, Puerto Rico

20 May 1985 *H(IBF)* Larry Holmes (USA) PTS –15 Carl Williams (USA) Reno, USA

1 Jun 1985 *JM(IBF)* Carlos Santos (PR) PTS –15 Louis Acaries (Fra) Paris, France

3 Jun 1985 *L(IBF)* Jimmy Paul (USA) RSF –14 Robin Blake (USA) Las Vegas, USA

6 Jun 1985 *C(WBC)* Alphonso Ratliff (USA) PTS –12 Carlos de Leon (PR) Las Vegas, USA

6 Jun 1985 *LH* Michael Spinks (USA) RSF –8 Jim McDonald (USA) Las Vegas, USA

8 Jun 1985 *Fe(WBA)* Barry McGuigan (Ire) PTS –15 Eusebio Pedroza (Pan) London, England

15 Jun 1985 *H(WBC)* Pinklon Thomas (USA) RSF –8 Mike Weaver (USA) Las Vegas, USA

22 Jun 1985 *Fl(WBC)* Sot Chitalada (Tha) D –12 Gabriel Bernal (Mex) Bangkok, Thailand

28 Jun 1985 *SB(IBF)* Chi-Won Kim (S. Kor) KO –4 Bobby Berna (Phi) Pusan, South Korea

29 Jun 1985 *SM(IBF)* Chong-Pal Park (S. Kor) PTS –15 Vinnie Curto (USA) Seoul, South Korea

2 Jul 1985 *LF(WBA)* Joey Olivo (USA) PTS –15 Mun-Jin Choi (S. Kor) Seoul, South Korea

6 Jul 1985 *JL(WBC)* Julio-Cesar Chavez (Mex) RSF –2 Roger Mayweather (USA) Las Vegas, USA

12 Jul 1985 *JL(IBF)* Barry Michael (GB) PTS –15 Lester Ellis (Aus) Melbourne, Australia

14 Jul 1985 *W(WBC)* Milton McCrory (USA) KO –3 Carlos Trujillo (Pan) Monte Carlo, Monaco

17 Jul 1985 *SF(WBA)* Kaosai 'Galaxy' (Tha) RSF –5 Rafael Orono (Ven) Bangkok, Thailand

21 Jul 1985 *LW(WBA)* Ubaldo Sacco (Arg) RSF –9 Gene Hatcher (USA) Campione de Italia, Italy

28 Jul 1985 *C(WBA)* Dwight Muhammad Qawi (USA) KO –11 Piet Crous (SA) Sun City, South Africa

28 Jul 1985 *LM(WBA)* Mike McCallum (Jam) RSF –8 David Braxton (USA) Miami, USA

4 Aug 1985 *LF(WBC)* Chang-Jung Ko (S. Kor) PTS –12 Francisco Montiel (Mex) Seoul, South Korea

9 Aug 1985 *B(WBC)* Miguel 'Happy' Lora (Col) PTS –12 Daniel Zaragoza (Mex) Miami, USA

10 Aug 1985 *L(WBC)* Hector Camacho (PR) PTS –12 Jose Luis Ramirez (Mex) Las Vegas, USA

19 Aug 1985 *SB(WBC)* Lupe Pintor (Mex) PTS –12 Juan 'Kid' Meza (Mex) Mexico City, Mexico

22 Aug 1985 *LW(WBC)* Lonnie Smith (USA) RSF –8 Billy Costello (USA) New York, USA

23 Aug 1985 *B(IBF)* Jeff Fenech (Aus) RSF –3 Satoshi Shingaki (Jap) Sydney, Australia

25 Aug 1985 *SF(IBF)* Ellyas Pical (Ind) RSF –3 Wayne Mulholland (Aus) Djakarta, Indonesia

6 Sep 1985 *Fe(WBC)* Azumah Nelson (Gha) KO –5 Juvenal Ordenes (Chi) Miami, USA

17 Sep 1985 *SF(WBC)* Jiro Watanabe (Jap) RSF –7 Kazuo Katsuma (Jap) Osaka, Japan

20 Sep 1985 *H(IBF)* Michael Spinks (USA) PTS –15 Larry Holmes (USA) Las Vegas, USA

20 Sep 1985 *JL(WBC)* Julio Cesar Chavez (Mex) PTS –12 Dwight Pratchett (USA) Las Vegas, USA

22 Sep 1985 *C(WBC)* Bernard Benton (USA) PTS –12 Alphonso Ratliff (USA) Las Vegas, USA

28 Sep 1985 *Fe(WBA)* Barry McGuigan (Ire) RTD –7 Bernard Taylor (USA) Belfast, Ireland

5 Oct 1985 *Fl(WBA)* Hilario Zapata (Pan) PTS –15 Alonso Gonzalez (USA) Panama City, Panama

8 Oct 1985 *SB(IBF)* Chi-Won Kim (S. Kor) KO –1 Song-In Suh (S. Kor) Seoul, South Korea

12 Oct 1985 *Fe(WBC)* Azumah Nelson (Gha) KO –1 Pat Cowdell (GB) Birmingham, England

18 Oct 1985 *JL(IBF)* Barry Michael (GB) RSF –4 Jin-Sik Choi (S. Kor) Darwin, Australia

19 Oct 1985 *C(IBF)* Leroy Murphy (USA) KO –12 Chisanda Mutti (Zam) Monte Carlo, Monaco

9 Nov 1985 *SB(WBA)* Victor Callejas (PR) RSF –6 Loris Stecca (Ita) Rimini, Italy

10 Nov 1985 *LF(WBC)* Chang Jung-Ko (S. Kor) PTS –12 Jorge Cano (Mex) Taejon, South Korea

29 Nov 1985 *Fe(IBF)* Chung-Ki Yung (S. Kor) KO –15 Min-Keum Oh (S. Kor) Seoul, South Korea

1 Dec 1985 *B(IBF)* Jeff Fenech (Aus) PTS –15 Jerome Coffee (USA) Sydney, Australia

6 Dec 1985 *W* Don Curry (USA) KO –2 Milton McCrory (USA) Las Vegas, USA

8 Dec 1985 *LF(WBA)* Myung-Woo Yuh (S. Kor) PTS –15 Joey Olivo (USA) Taeku, South Korea

11 Dec 1985 *LH(WBC)* J.B. Williamson (USA) PTS –12 Prince Mohammed (Gha) Inglewood, USA

12 Dec 1985 *SF(WBC)* Jiro Watanabe (Jap) RSF –5 Suk-Huan Yun (S. Kor) Seoul, South Korea

21 Dec 1985 *M(IBF)* Slobodan Kacar (Yug) PTS –15 Eddie Mustafa Mohammad (USA) Pesaro, Italy

23 Dec 1985 *SF(WBA)* Kaosai Galaxy (Tha) KO –2 Edgar Monserrat (Pan) Bangkok, Thailand

17 Jan 1986 *H(WBA)* Tim Witherspoon (USA) PTS –15 Tony Tubbs (USA) Atlanta, USA

18 Jan 1986 *SB(WBC)* Samart Payakaroon (Tha) KO –5 Lupe Pintor (Mex) Bangkok, Thailand

31 Jan 1986 *Fl(WBA)* Hilario Zapata (Pan) PTS –15 Javier Lucas (Mex) Panama City, Panama

8 Feb 1986 *B(WBC)* Miguel Lora (Col) PTS –12 Wilfredo Vasquez (PR) Miami, USA

9 Feb 1986 *LH(WBA)* Marvin Johnson (USA) RSF –7 Leslie Stewart (Tri) Indianapolis, USA

15 Feb 1986 *Fe(WBA)* Barry McGuigan (Ire) RSF –14 Danilo Cabrera (Dom) Dublin, Ireland

15 Feb 1986 *SF(IBF)* Cesar Pelonco (Dom) PTS –15 Ellyas Pical (Ina) Djakarta, Indonesia

16 Feb 1986 *L(WBA)* Livingstone Bramble (VI) RSF–13 Tyrone Crawley (USA) Reno, USA

16 Feb 1986 *Fe(IBF)* Chung-Ki Young (S. Kor) KO –6 Tyrone Jackson (USA) Ulsan, South Korea

22 Feb 1986 *Fl(WBC)* Sot Chitalada (Tha) PTS –12 Freddie Castillo (Mex) Kuwait

25 Feb 1986 *Fe(WBC)* Azumah Nelson (Gha) PTS –12 Marcos Villasana (Mex) Inglewood, USA

3 Mar 1986 *W* Don Curry (USA) KO –2 Eduardo Rodriguez (Pan) Forth Worth, USA

9 Mar 1986 *LF(WBA)* Myung-Woo Yuh (S. Kor) PTS –15 Jose de Jesus (PR) Suwon, South Korea

10 Mar 1986 *M* Marvin Hagler (USA) KO –11 John Mugabi (Uga) Las Vegas, USA

10 Mar 1986 *B(WBA)* Gaby Canizales (USA) KO –7 Richie Sandoval (USA) Las Vegas, USA

15 Mar 1986 *LW(WBA)* Patrizio Oliva (Ita) PTS –15 Ubaldo Sacco (Arg) Monte Carlo, Monaco

20 Mar 1986 *SF(WBC)* Gilberto Roman (Mex) PTS –12 Jiro Watanabe (Jap) Osaka, Japan

22 Mar 1986 *H(WBC)* Trevor Berbick (Jam) PTS –12 Pinklon Thomas (USA) Las Vegas, USA

22 Mar 1986 *C(WBC)* Carlos de Leon (PR) PTS –12 Bernard Benton (USA) Las Vegas, USA

23 Mar 1986 *C(WBA)* Dwight Qawi (USA) RSF –6 Leon Spinks (USA) Reno, USA

7 Apr 1986 *Fl(WBA)* Hilario Zapata (Pan) PTS –15 Shuichi Hozumi (Jap) Hirosaki, Japan

11 Apr 1986 *SM(IBF)* Chong-Pal Park (S. Kor) KO –15 Vinnie Curto (USA) Los Angeles, USA

13 Apr 1986 *LF(WBC)* Chang-Jung Koo (S. Kor) PTS –12 German Torres (Mex) Seoul, South Korea

19 Apr 1986 *H(IBF)* Michael Spinks (USA) PTS –15 Larry Holmes (USA) Las Vegas, USA

19 Apr 1986 *C(IBF)* Leroy Murphy (USA) KO –9 Dorcy Gaymon (USA) San Remo, USA

26 Apr 1986 *LW(IBF)* Garry Hinton (USA) PTS –15 Antonio Reyes (Mex) Lucca, Italy

27 Apr 1986 *Fl(IBF)* Chung-Bi Won (S. Kor) PTS –15 Soon-Chun Kwon (S. Kor) Pusan, South Korea

30 Apr 1986 *LH(WBC)* Dennis Andries (Guy) PTS –12 J.B. Williamson (USA) London, England

5 May 1986 *LW(WBC)* Rene Arredondo (Mex) KO –5 Lonnie Smith (USA) Los Angeles, USA

15 May 1986 *JL(WBC)* Julio Cesar Chavez (Mex) RSF –5 Faustino Barrios (Arg) Paris, France

15 May 1986 *SF(WBC)* Gilberto Roman (Mex) PTS –12 Edgar Montserrat (Pan) Paris, France

18 May 1986 *F(IBF)* Chung-Ki Yung (S. Kor) PTS –15 Richard Savage (USA) Seoul, South Korea

22 May 1986 *JL(IBF)* Barry Michael (GB) RSF –4 Mark Fernandez (USA) Melbourne, Australia

24 May 1986 *JL(WBA)* Alfredo Layne (Pan) RSF –9 Wilfredo Gomez (PR) San Juan, Puerto Rico

1 Jun 1986 *SB(IBF)* Chi-Wan Kim (S. Kor) RSF –2 Ruby Casicas (Phi) Seoul, South Korea

4 Jun 1986 *LM(IBF)* Buster Drayton (USA) PTS –15 Carlos Santos (PR) New Jersey, USA

4 Jun 1986 *L(IBF)* Jimmy Paul (USA) PTS–15 Irleis Perez (USA) New Jersey, USA

4 Jun 1986 *B(WBA)* Bernardo Pinango (Ven) PTS –15 Gaby Canizales (USA) New Jersey, USA

13 Jun 1986 *L(WBC)* Hector Camacho (PR) PTS –12 Edwin Rosario (PR) New York, USA

13 Jun 1986 *JL(WBC)* Julio Cesar Chavez (Mex) RSF –7 Raul Rojas (USA), New York, USA

14 Jun 1986 *LF(WBA)* Myung-Woo Yuh (S. Kor) KO –12 Tomohiri Kiyuna (Jap) Inchon, South Korea

22 Jun 1986 *F(WBC)* Azumah Nelson (Gha) RSF –10 Danilo Cabrera (Dom) San Juan, Puerto Rico

23 Jun 1986 *LM(WBC)* Thomas Hearns (USA) RSF –8 Mark Medal (USA) Las Vegas, USA

23 Jun 1986 *F(WBA)* Steve Cruz (USA) PTS –15 Barry McGuigan (Ire) Las Vegas, USA

5 Jul 1986 *Fl(WBA)* Hilario Zapata (Pan) PTS –15 Dodie Penalosa (Phi) Manila, Phillippines

6 Jul 1986 *SM(IBF)* Chong-Pal Park (S. Kor) TD –12 Lindell Holmes (USA) Seoul, South Korea

6 Jul 1986 *SF(IBF)* Ellyas Pical (Ina) KO –3 Cesar Pelonco (Dom) Djakarta, Indonesia

12 Jul 1986 *C(WBA)* Evander Holyfield (USA) PTS –15 Dwight Qawi (USA) Atlanta, USA

18 Jul 1986 *SF(IBF)* Jeff Fenech (Aus) RSF –14 Steve McCrory (USA) Sydney, Australia

18 Jul 1986 *JB(WBC)* Gilberto Roman (Mex) PTS –12 Ruben Condori (Arg) Salta, Argentina

20 Jul 1986 *H(WBA)* Tim Witherspoon (USA) KO –11 Frank Bruno (GB) London, England

24 Jul 1986 *LW(WBC)* Tsuyoshsi Hamada (Jap) KO –1 Rene Arredondo (Mex) Tokyo, Japan

2 Aug 1986 *Fl(IBF)* Hi-Sop Shin (S. Kor) KO –15 Chung-Bi Won (S. Kor) Incheon, South Korea

3 Aug 1986 *JL(WBC)* Julio Cesar Chavez (Mex) PTS –12 Rocky Lockridge (USA) Monte Carlo, Monaco

10 Aug 1986 *C(WBC)* Carlos de Leon (PR) RSF –8 Michael Greer (USA) Giardini Naxos, Italy

15 Aug 1986 *L(IBF)* Jimmy Paul (USA) PTS –15 Darryl Tyson (USA) Detroit, USA

23 Aug 1986 *LM(WBA)* Mike McCallum (Jam) RSF –2 Julian Jackson (VI) Miami Beach, USA

23 Aug 1986 *JL(IBF)* Barry Michael (GB) PTS –15 Najib Daho (Mor) Manchester, England

23 Aug 1986 *B(WBC)* Miguel Lora (Col) RSF –6 Enrique Sanchez (Dom) Miami Beach, USA

24 Aug 1986 *LM(IBF)* Buster Drayton (USA) RSF –10 Davey Moore (USA) Juan les Pins, France

30 Aug 1986 *SF(WBC)* Gilberto Roman (Mex) PTS –12 Santos Laciar (Arg) Cordoba, Mexico

30 Aug 1986 *F(IBF)* Antonio Rivera (PR) RET –10 Chung-Ki Yung (S. Kor) Seoul, South Korea

6 Sep 1986 *H(IBF)* Michael Spinks (USA) RSF –4 Steffen Tangstad (Nor) Las Vegas, USA

6 Sep 1986 *LH(IBF)* Bobby Czyz (USA) RSF –5 Slobodan Kacar (Yug) Las Vegas, USA

6 Sep 1986 *LW(WBA)* Patrizio Oliva (Ita) RSF –3 Brian Brunette (USA) Naples, Italy

10 Sep 1986 *LH(WBC)* Dennis Andries (Guy) RSF –9 Tony Sibson (GB) London, England

12 Sep 1986 *Fl(WBA)* Hilario Zapata (Pan) PTS –15 Alberto Castro (Col) Panama City, Panama

13 Sep 1986 *LF(WBC)* Chang-Jung Koo (S. Kor) PTS –12 Francisco Montiel (Mex) Seoul, South Korea

14 Sep 1986 *SM(IBF)* Chong-Pal Park (S. Kor) PTS –15 Marvin Mack (USA) Seoul, South Korea

20 Sep 1986 *LH(WBA)* Marvin Johnson (USA) RSF –13 Jean Marie Emebe (Cam) Indianapolis, USA

26 Sep 1986 *L(WBA)* Edwin Rosario (PR) KO –2 Livingstone Bramble (VI) Miami Beach, USA

27 Sep 1986 *W* Lloyd Honeyghan (Jam) RET –6 Don Curry (USA) Atlantic City, USA

27 Sep 1986 *L(WBC)* Hector Camacho (PR) PTS –12 Cornelius Boza-Edwards (Uga) Miami Beach, USA

27 Sep 1986 *JL(WBA)* Brian Mitchell (SA) RSF –10 Alfredo Layne (Pan) Sun City, South Africa

4 Oct 1986 *B(WBA)* Bernardo Pinango (Ven) RET –10 Ciro de Leva (Ita) Turin, Italy

25 Oct 1986 *C(IBF)* Rickey Parkey (USA) RSF –10 Leroy Murphy (USA) Marsala, Italy

25 Oct 1986 *LM(WBA)* Mike McCallum (Jam) KO –9 Said Skouma (Fra) Paris, France

30 Oct 1986 *LW(IBF)* Joe Louis Manley (USA) KO –10 Gary Hinton (USA) Hartford, USA

15 Nov 1986 *B(WBC)* Miguel Lora (Col) PTS –12 Albert Davila (USA) Barranquilla, Colombia

22 Nov 1986 *H(WBC)* Mike Tyson (USA) RSF –2 Trevor Berbick (Jam) Las Vegas, USA

22 Nov 1986 *B(WBA)* Bernardo Pinango (Ven) RSF –15 Simon Skosana (SA) Johannesburg, South Africa

22 Nov 1986 *Fl(IBF)* Hi-Sop Shin (S. Kor) KO –13 Henry Brent (USA) Chunchon, South Korea

30 Nov 1986 *LF(WBA)* Myung-Woo Yuh (S. Kor) PTS –15 Mario deMarco (Arg) Seoul, South Korea

2 Dec 1986 *LW(WBC)* Tsuyoshi Hamada (Jap) PTS –12 Ronnie Shields (USA) Tokyo, Japan

3 Dec 1986 *SF(IBF)* Tae-Il Chang (S. Kor) KO –10 Lee-Dong Choon (S. Kor) Seoul, South Korea

5 Dec 1986 *LM(WBC)* Duane Thomas (USA) RSF –3 John Mugabi (Uga) Las Vegas, USA

6 Dec 1986 *L(IBF)* Greg Haugen (USA) PTS –15 Jimmy Paul (USA) Las Vegas, USA

6 Dec 1986 *Fl(WBA)* Hilario Zapata (Pan) PTS –15 Claudemir Dias (Bra) Salvador, Brazil

7 Dec 1986 *LF(IBF)* Chong-Hwan Choi (S. Kor) PTS –15 Choo-Woon Park (S. Kor) Seoul, South Korea

10 Dec 1986 *SB(WBC)* Samart Payakaroon (Tha) KO –12 Juan Meza (Mex) Bangkok, Thailand

10 Dec 1986 *Fl(WBC)* Sot Chitalada (Tha) PTS –12 Gabriel Bernal (Mex) Bangkok, Thailand

12 Dec 1986 *H(WBA)* James Smith (USA) RSF –1 Tim Witherspoon (USA) New York, USA

12 Dec 1986 *JL(WBC)* Julio Cesar Chavez (Mex) PTS –12 Juan Laporte (PR) New York, USA

15 Dec 1986 *SF(WBC)* Gilberto Roman (Mex) PTS –12 Kongtoranee Payakaroon (Tha) Bangkok, Thailand

26 Dec 1986 *LH(IBF)* Bobby Czyz (USA) KO –1 David Sears (USA) West Orange, USA

10 Jan 1987 *LW(WBA)* Patrizio Oliva (Ita) PTS –15 Rodolfo Gonzalez (Mex) Agrigento, Italy

16 Jan 1987 *SB(WBA)* Louie Espinoza (USA) RSF –4 Tommy Valoy (Dom) Pheonix, USA

18 Jan 1987 *SB(IBF)* Seung-Hoon Lee (S. Kor) KO –9 Prayurasak Muangsurin (Tha) Pohang, South Korea

25 Jan 1987 *SM(IBF)* Chong-Pal Park (S. Kor) RSF –15 Doug Sam (Aus) Seoul, South Korea

31 Jan 1987 *SF(WBC)* Gilberto Roman (Mex) RSF –9 Antoine Montero (Fra) Montpellier, France

3 Feb 1987 *B(WBA)* Bernardo Pinango (Ven) PTS –15 Frankie Duarte (USA) Los Angeles, USA

6 Feb 1987 *W(WBA)* Mark Breland (USA) KO –7 Harold Volbrecht (SA) Atlantic City, USA

13 Feb 1987 *Fl(WBA)* Fidel Bassa (Col) PTS –15 Hilario Zapata (Pan) Barranquilla, Colombia

14 Feb 1987 *C(WBA)* Evander Holyfield (USA) RSF –7 Henry Tillman (USA) Reno, USA

21 Feb 1987 *C(WBC)* Carlos de Leon (PR) RSF –4 Angelo Rottoli (Ita) Bergamo, Italy

21 Feb 1987 *LH(IBF)* Bobby Czyz (USA) KO –2 Willie Edwards (USA) Atlantic City, USA

22 Feb 1987 *W(WBC/IBF)* Lloyd Honeyghan (Jam) RSF –2 Johnny Bumphus (USA) London, England

22 Feb 1987 *Fl(IBF)* Dodie Penalosa (Phi) KO –5 Hi-Sop Shin (S. Kor) Inchon, South Korea

28 Feb 1987 *SF(WBA)* Kaosai Galaxy (Tha) KO –14 Ellyas Pical (Ina) Djakarta, Indonesia

1 Mar 1987 *LF(WBA)* Myung-Woo Yuh (S. Kor) KO –1 Eduardo Tunon (Pan) Seoul, South Korea

4 Mar 1987 *LM(IBF)* Terry Marsh (GB) RSF –10 Joe Louis Manley (USA) Basildon, England

6 Mar 1987 *Fe(WBA)* Antonio Esparragoza (Ven) RSF –12 Steve Cruz (USA) Fort Worth, USA

7 Mar 1987 *H(WBC/WBA)* Mike Tyson (USA) PTS –12 James Smith (USA) Las Vegas, USA

7 Mar 1987 *LH(WBC)* Thomas Hearns (USA) RSF –10 Dennis Andries (Guy) Detroit, USA

7 Mar 1987 *Fe(WBC)* Azumah Nelson (Gha) KO –6 Mauro Gutierrez (Mex) Las Vegas, USA

19 Mar 1987 *SF(WBC)* Gilberto Roman (Mex) PTS –12 Frank Cedeno (Phi) Mexicali, Mexico

27 Mar 1987 *JL(WBA)* Brian Mitchell (SA) D –15 Jose Rivera (PR) San Juan, Puerto Rico

28 Mar 1987 *C(IBF)* Rickey Parkey (USA) RSF –12 Chisanda Mutti (Zam) Lido di Camiore, Italy

29 Mar 1987 *B(WBA)* Takuya Muguruma (Jap) KO –5 Azael Moran (Pan) Moriguchi, Japan

29 Mar 1987 *LF(IBF)* Chong-Hwan Choi (S. Kor) PTS –15 Tracy Macalas (Phi) Seoul, South Korea

5 Apr 1987 *SB(IBF)* Seung-Hoon Lee (S. Kor) KO –10 Jorge Urbina Diaz (Mex) Seoul, South Korea

6 Apr 1987 *M(WBC)* Sugar Ray Leonard (USA) PTS –12 Marvin Hagler (USA) Las Vegas, USA

18 Apr 1987 *W(WBC/IBF)* Lloyd Honeyghan (Jam) PTS –12 Maurice Blocker (USA) London, England

18 Apr 1987 *JL(WBC)* Julio Cesar Chavez (Mex) RSF –4 Francisco da Cruz (Bra) Nimes, France

19 Apr 1987 *LM(WBA)* Mike McCallum (Jam) RSF –10 Milton McCrory (USA) Pheonix, USA

19 Apr 1987 *LF(WBC)* Chang-Jung Koo (S. Kor) RSF –6 Efren Pinto (Mex) Seoul, South Korea

25 Apr 1987 *Fl(WBA)* Fidel Bassa (Col) RSF –13 Dave McAuley (GB) Belfast, N. Ireland

2 May 1987 *SM(IBF)* Chong-Pal Park (S. Kor) PTS –15 Lindell Holmes (USA) Inchon, South Korea

4 May 1987 *LH(IBF)* Bobby Czyz (USA) RSF –6 Jim McDonald (USA) Atlantic City, USA

8 May 1987 *SB(WBC)* Jeff Fenech (Aus) RSF –4 Samart Payakaroon (Tha) Sydney, Australia

16 May 1987 C(IBF) Evander Holyfield (USA) RSF –3 Rickey Parkey (USA) Las Vegas, USA

16 May 1987 B(IBF) Kelvin Seabrooks (USA) KO –5 Miguel Maturana (Col) Cartagena, Colombia

16 May 1987 SF(WBC) Santos Laciar (Arg) RSF –11 Gilberto Roman (Mex) Reims, France

17 May 1987 JL(WBA) Brian Mitchell (SA) RSF –2 Aurelio Benitez (Ven) Sun City, S. Africa

17 May 1987 SF(IBF) Tae-Il Chang (S. Kor) PTS –15 Kwon-Sun Chon (S. Kor) Seoul, South Korea

23 May 1987 LH(WBA) Leslie Stewart (Tri) RSF –8 Marvin Johnson (USA) Port of Spain, Trinidad

24 May 1987 B(WBA) Chang-Yung Park (S. Kor) RSF –11 Takuya Muguruma (Jap) Osaka, Japan

30 May 1987 H(WBC/WBA) Mike Tyson (USA) RSF –6 Pinklon Thomas (USA) Las Vegas, USA

30 May 1987 H(IBF) Tony Tucker (USA) RSF –10 James Douglas (USA) Las Vegas, USA

2 Jun 1987 L(IBF) Vinny Pazienza (USA) PTS –15 Greg Haugen (USA) Providence, USA

7 Jun 1987 LF(WBA) Myung-Woo Yuh (S. Kor) RSF –15 Benedicto Murillo (Pan) Pusan, South Korea

14 Jun 1987 MF(IBF) Kyung-Yun Lee (S. Kor) RSF –2 Masaharu Kawakami (Jap) Bukok, South Korea

27 Jun LM(IBF) Matthew Hilton (Can) PTS –15 Buster Drayton (USA) Montreal, Canada

28 Jun LF(WBC) Chang-Jung Koo (S. Kor) KO–10 Augstin Garcia (Col) Inchon, South Korea

1 Jul 1987 LW(IBF) Terry Marsh (GB) RSF –6 Akio Kameda (Jap) London, England

4 Jul 1987 LW(WBA) Juan Martin Coggi (Arg) KO –3 Patrizio Oliva (Ita) Ribera, Italy

4 Jul 1987 B(IBF) Kelvin Seabrooks (USA) RTD –9 Thierry Jacob (Fra) Calais, France

4 Jul 1987 LF(IBF) Chong Hwan Choi (S. Kor) KO –4 Toshihiko Matsuda (Jap) Seoul, South Korea

10 Jul 1987 SB(WBC) Jeff Fenech (Aus) RSF –5 Greg Richardson (USA) Sydney, Australia

12 Jul 1987 LM(WBC) Lupe Aquino (Mex) PTS –12 Duane Thomas (USA) Bordeaux, France

15 Jul 1987 SM(IBF) Chong-Pal Park (S. Kor) KO –4 Emmanuel Otti (Uga) Kwangju, South Korea

15 Jul 1987 SB(WBA) Louie Espinoza (USA) RSF –15 Manuel Vilchez (Ven) Pheonix, USA

18 Jul 1987 LM(WBA) Mike McCallum (Jam) KO –5 Don Curry (USA) Las Vegas, USA

18 Jul 1987 SB(IBF) Seung-Hoon Lee (S. Kor) KO –5 Leo Collins (Phi) Pohang, South Korea

19 Jul 1987 L(WBC) Jose Luis Ramirez (Mex) PTS –12 Terrence Alli (Guy) St. Tropez, France

22 Jul 1987 LW(WBC) Rene Arredondo (Mex) RSF –6 Tsuyoshi Hamada (Jap) Tokyo, Japan

25 Jul 1987 B(WBC) Miguel Lora (Col) RSF –4 Antonio Avelar (Mex) Miami, USA

26 Jul 1987 Fe(WBA) Antonio Esparragoza (Ven) KO –10 Pascual Aranda (Mex) Houston, USA

1 Aug 1987 JL(WBA) Brian Mitchell (SA) RSF –14 Francisco Fernandez (Pan) Panama City, Panama

2 Aug 1987 H Mike Tyson (USA) PTS –12 Tony Tucker (USA) Las Vegas, USA

8 Aug 1987 SF(WBC) Jesus Rojas (Col) PTS –12 Santos Laciar (Arg) Miami, USA

9 Aug 1987 JL(IBF) Rocky Lockridge (USA) RET –8 Barry Michael (GB) Windsor, England

9 Aug 1987 LF(IBF) Chong-Hwan Choi (S. Kor) KO –3 Azadin Anhar (Ina) Djakarta, Indonesia

11 Aug 1987 L(WBA) Edwin Rosario (PR) RSF –8 Juan Nazario (PR) Chicago, USA

15 Aug 1987 C(WBA/IBF) Evander Holyfield (USA) RSF –11 Osvaldo Ocasio (PR) St. Tropez, France

15 Aug 1987 Fl(WBA) Fidel Bassa (Col) D –15 Hilario Zapata (Pan) Panama City, Panama

15 Aug 1987 SB(WBA) Louie Espinoza (USA) KO –9 Mike Ayala (USA) San Antonio, USA

21 Aug 1987 JL(WBC) Julio Cesar Chavez (Mex) PTS –12 Danilo Cabrera (Dom) Tijuana, Mexico

22 Aug 1987 W(WBA) Marlon Starling (USA) RSF –11 Mark Breland (USA) Columbia, USA

30 Aug 1987 W(WBC/IBF) Lloyd Honeyghan (Jam) KO –1 Gene Hatcher (USA) Marbella, Spain

30 Aug 1987 Fe(WBC) Azumah Nelson (Gha) PTS –12 Marcos Vilasana (Mex) Los Angeles, USA

5 Sep 1987 LH(WBA) Virgil Hill (USA) RSF –4 Leslie Stewart (Tri) New Jersey, USA

6 Sep 1987 Fl(WBC) Sot Chitalada (Tha) KO –4 Rae-Ki Ahn (S. Kor) Bangkok, Thailand

6 Sep 1987 Fl(IBF) Chang-Ho Choi (S. Kor) KO–11 Dodie Penalosa (Phi) Manila, Phillippines

20 Sep 1987 LF(WBA) Myung-Woo Yuh (S. Kor) KO–8 Ricardo Blanco (Col) Pohang, South Korea

---

World titles—other notable claimants

Over the years there have been many other claimants to world titles apart from the ones listed above, which are regarded as undisputed title claims. The following is a list of claimants to titles, many of whom were never taken seriously.

HEAVYWEIGHT

In 1913, during Jack Johnson's (USA) reign, a 'White Heavyweight' championship was held in Los Angeles and Luther McCarty (USA) was proclaimed champion. Arthur Pelkey (Can) , Gunboat Smith (USA) and Georges Carpentier (Fra) all subsequently claimed the crown.

In 1950 Lee Savold (USA) beat Bruce Woodcock (GB) at London for the title which was only recognized by the British Board. Savold's claim was not taken seriously elsewhere.

LIGHT-HEAVYWEIGHT

Jack Dillon (USA) claimed the title in 1912 following his win over Hugo Kelly (Ita). This was two years before his official recognition as champion.

Bob Godwin (USA) made a dubious claim to the NBA version of the title in 1933.

Between 1935 and 1938 Heinz Lazek (Aut), Gustave Roth (Bel) and Adolph Heuser (Ger) were all recognized as world champions by the IBU.

In 1939 and 1942, respectively, the British Boxing Board of Control recognized Len Harvey (GB) and Freddie Mills (GB) as world champions.

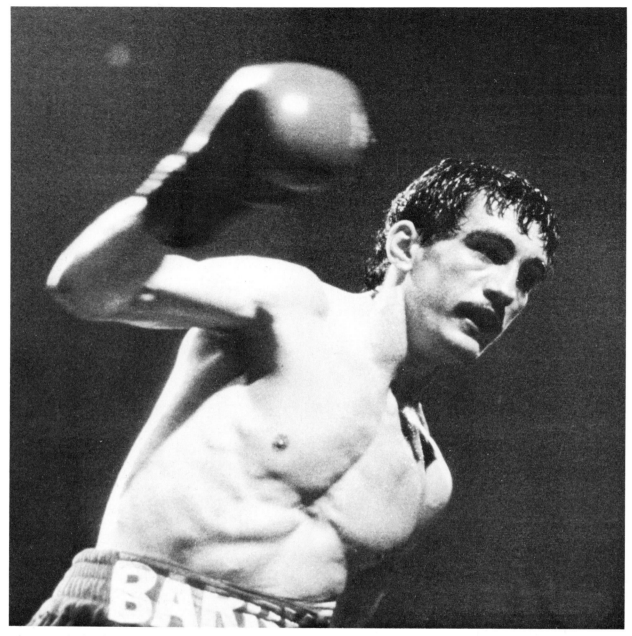

The man who has helped unite Ireland, Barry McGuigan (Ire), who beat Eusebio Pedroza (Pan) to win the world featherweight title in 1985. All Sport

Eddie Cotton (USA) was recognized as champion by the Michigan State Athletic Commission in 1963.

MIDDLEWEIGHT

Charles 'Kid' McCoy (USA) staked a claim as champion in 1897 following his victory over Dan Creedon (NZ). McCoy's claim was never taken seriously.

Hugo Kelly (Ita) claimed the title in 1907 after Tommy Ryan (USA) retired, but Kelly's claim was never taken seriously.

The claims of Billy Papke (USA) and Frank Klaus (USA) between 1911 and 1913 are both dubious claims to the title.

Jeff Smith (USA), Mick King (Aus) and Les Darcy (Aus) all claimed the title between 1914 and 1916 but they were only recognized as world champions in Australia.

Frank Mantell (Ger) claimed the title from 1912 to 1915 but he was not recognized outside California.

Marcel Thil (Fra) was recognized as champion in 1937, but only in Europe.

Fred Apostoli (USA) gained European recognition as champion in 1937 after he beat Marcel Thil (Fra). The New York champion Freddie Steele then refused to meet Apostoli and consequently Apostoli also gained their recognition.

Randolph Turpin (GB) also gained European recognition following his victory over Charles Humez (Fra) in 1953.

LIGHT-MIDDLEWEIGHT

Emile Griffith (VI) beat Teddy Wright (USA) at Vienna, Austria in 1962 to become the first claimant to the light-middleweight title. The fight, however, was only recognized by the Austrian Board of Control. After one successful defence, Griffith let his claim lapse.

WELTERWEIGHT

Joe Walcott (Bar) re-claimed the title in 1904 after Dixie Kid (USA) had outgrown the division. Walcott in his first 'defence' lost to Honey Mellody in 1906.

After Mike 'Twin' Sullivan reliquished the title the welterweight division was thrown into confusion between 1908 and 1915 with many claimants to the title. None were substantiated until Ted 'Kid' Lewis (GB) became recognized as champion in 1915. The men who claimed the title during the period of uncertainty were: Harry Lewis (USA), Jimmy Gardner (Ire), Jimmy Clabby (USA), Waldemar Holberg (Den), Tom McCormick (Ire), Matt Wells (GB), Mike Glover (USA) and Jack Britton (USA).

Charley Shipes (USA) beat Percy Manning (USA) in 1966 but the contest was recognized as a world title fight only by the Californian State Athletic Commission.

Hedgemon Lewis (USA) twice beat Billy Backus (USA) in 1972 to gain New York State recognition as champion.

LIGHT-WELTERWEIGHT

Pinkey Mitchell (USA) is often referred to as being the first world light-welterweight champion, but he only assumed that title after being nominated by readers of a boxing magazine in 1922.

LIGHTWEIGHT

Jimmy Britt (USA) claimed the 'White Lightweight' title in 1902 after beating Frank Erne (Swi). He made two successful defences before losing the 'title' to Battling Nelson (Den) in 1905.

Freddie Welsh (GB) claimed the title in 1912, four years before he became officially recognized, following his victory over Hughie Mehegan (Aus).

Following Sammy Angott's (USA) retirement in 1942 Luther 'Slugger' White (USA) became recognized as world champion, but only by the Maryland State Commission.

Kenny Lane (USA) won recognition by the Michigan State Athletic Commission as world champion in 1963 following his points win over Paul Armstead (USA).

JUNIOR-LIGHTWEIGHT

Sandy Saddler (USA) gained recognition in Cleveland in 1949. He made one successful defence of the title before the weight division fell into disuse, until 1959.

FEATHERWEIGHT

Ben Jordan (GB) claimed the title in 1898 after he beat George Dixon (Can). Dixon claimed his title was not at stake. Jordan subsequently lost to Eddie Santry (USA) who then claimed the title in 1899.

Tommy Sullivan (USA) claimed the title after beating Abe Attell (USA) in a non-title fight in 1904.

Jim Driscoll (GB) claimed the title in 1909 after he outclassed reigning champion Abe Attell (USA) in a no-decision 10-round contest. Despite Driscoll's claim, most authorities continued to recognize Attell as champion.

Tommy Noble (GB) was presented with a world-title belt in 1920 after his win over Johnny Murray (USA) but Noble's claim was never taken seriously.

Dick 'Honeyboy' Finnegan (USA) was recognized as world champion in 1926, but only by the Massachusetts State Boxing Commission.

Baby Arizmendi (Mex) claimed the title in 1934 after the New York Commission withdrew its recognition of champion Kid Chocolate.

Maurice Holtzer (Fra) gained IBU recognition as champion in 1937.

Jimmy Perrin (USA) gained Louisiana State recognition as champion in1940.

While Sandy Sadler was serving in the US Forces (1952–4) Percy Bassett (USA) beat Ray Famechon (Fra) for the 'interim' title in 1952. Bassett subsequently lost the title to Teddy 'Red Top' Davis (USA) in 1953.

SUPER-BANTAMWEIGHT

Although the weight division was introduced by the WBC in 1976, Jack Wolfe (USA) beat Joe Lynch in 1922 in a contest billed as being for the 'world junior featherweight' title. The following year Carl Duane (USA) took the 'title' from Wolfe. No further contests took place in the division until revived by the WBC.

BANTAMWEIGHT

George Dixon (Can) claimed the title in 1888, two years before he was internationally recognized as champion.

Upon Dixon's relinquishment of the title Tommy Kelly (USA) and Chappie Moran (GB) both claimed the title in 1888 and 1889, respectively. Billy Plimmer (GB) also staked a good claim in 1892 as a result of outpointing Kelly over ten rounds.

Jimmy Barry (USA) claimed his title in 1894 following his win over Caspar Leon (Ita). Three years later Barry was internationally recognized as champion but, in the meantime Pedlar Palmer (GB) joined Billy Plimmer as a good claimant to the title.

After Joe Bowker (GB) relinquished the title in 1904 Digger Stanley (GB) and Jimmy Walsh (USA) both claimed the title. Walsh relinquished his claim which left Stanley with the best claim but Walsh then reclaimed his title in 1908. Less than twelve months later he had relinquished it yet again. The division was thrown into a state of confusion. Stanley reclaimed the title in 1909 but other claimants at this time were: Eddie Campi (USA), Monte Attell (USA), Johnny Coulon (Can), Frankie Conley (Ita), Kid Murphy (USA) and Charles Ledoux (Fra).

Johnny Ertle (Aut) claimed the title in 1915 after he beat the then champion Kid Williams on a foul. Ertle's claim was never taken seriously.

Joe Burman (GB) claimed the title after beating reigning champion Pete Herman (USA) in 1919. Herman, however, claimed his title was not at stake. This was generally accepted and he continued to be recognized as champion.

When the title was declared vacant in 1927 Teddy Baldock (GB) and Willie Smith (SA) claimed the British version of the title.

Pete Sanstol (Nor) was recognized in Canada as the world champion in 1931.

FLYWEIGHT

Although Jimmy Wilde (GB) was the first officially recognized world flyweight champion in 1916 Sid Smith, Bill Ladbury, Percy Jones and Joe Symonds (all GB) were claimants to the title between 1913 and 1916. Following Pancho Villa's death in 1925 the title was claimed by Frankie Genaro (USA).

Following Fidel La Barba's retirement in 1927 the division was thrown into confusion. Several men claimed the title between 1927 and 1929, including: Johnny McCoy (USA), Newsboy Brown (USSR), Johnny Hill (GB), and Willie Le Morte (USA). Valentin Angelmann (Fra) was recognized as world champion by the IBU for a short while in 1937 but their recognition was withdrawn following the success of Benny Lynch (GB).

The world champions in each division

HEAVYWEIGHT

UNDISPUTED CHAMPIONS

James J. Corbett	USA	1892
Bob Fitzsimmons	GB	1897
James J. Jeffries	USA	1899
Marvin Hart	USA	1905
Tommy Burns	Can	1906
Jack Johnson	USA	1908
Jess Willard	USA	1915
Jack Dempsey	USA	1919
Gene Tunney	USA	1926
Max Schmeling	Ger	1930
Jack Sharkey	USA	1932
Primo Carnera	Ita	1933
Max Baer	USA	1934
James J. Braddock	USA	1935
Joe Louis	USA	1937
Ezzard Charles	USA	1950
Jersey Joe Walcott	USA	1951
Rocky Marciano	USA	1952
Floyd Patterson	USA	1956
Ingemar Johansson	Swe	1959
Floyd Patterson	USA	1960
Sonny Liston	USA	1962
Cassius Clay	USA	1964
Joe Frazier	USA	1970
George Foreman	USA	1973
Muhammad Ali (formerly Cassius Clay)	USA	1974
Leon Spinks	USA	1978
Mike Tyson	USA	1987

WBC

Ken Norton	USA	1978
Larry Holmes	USA	1978
Tim Witherspoon	USA	1984
Pinklon Thomas	USA	1984
Trevor Berbick	Jam	1986
Mike Tyson	USA	1986

WBA

Ernie Terrell	USA	1965
Jimmy Ellis	USA	1968
Muhammad Ali	USA	1978
John Tate	USA	1979
Mike Weaver	USA	1980
Mike Dokes	USA	1982
Gerrie Coetzee	SA	1983
Greg Page	USA	1984
Tony Tubbs	USA	1985
Tim Witherspoon	USA	1986
James Smith	USA	1986
Mike Tyson	USA	1987

IBF

Larry Holmes	USA	1984
Michael Spinks	USA	1985
Tony Tucker	USA	1987
Mike Tyson	USA	1987

NBA

Ezzard Charles	USA	1949

NEW YORK STATE

Joe Frazier	USA	1968

OTHER CLAIMANTS

Luther McCarty	USA	1913
Arthur Pelkey	Can	1913
Gunboat Smith	USA	1914
Georges Carpentier	Fra	1914
Lee Savold	USA	1950

CRUISERWEIGHT

WBC

Marvin Camel	USA	1980
Carlos de Leon	PR	1980
S. T. Gordon	USA	1982
Carlos de Leon	PR	1983
Alphonso Ratliff	USA	1985
Bernard Benton	USA	1985
Carlos de Leon	PR	1986

WBA

Ossie Ocasio	PR	1982
Piet Crous	SA	1984
Dwight Qawi (formerly Dwight Braxton)	USA	1985
Evander Holyfield	USA	1986

IBF

Marvin Camel	USA	1983
Leroy Murphy	USA	1984
Rickey Parkey	USA	1986
Evander Holyfield	USA	1987

LIGHT-HEAVYWEIGHT

UNDISPUTED CHAMPIONS

Jack Root	Aut	1903
George Gardner	Ire	1903
Bob Fitzsimmons	GB	1903
Philadelphia Jack O'Brien	USA	1905
Jack Dillon	USA	1914
Battling Levinsky	USA	1916
Georges Carpentier	Fra	1920
Battling Siki	Sen	1922
Mike McTigue	Ire	1923
Paul Berlenbach	USA	1925
Jack Delaney	Can	1926
Tommy Loughran	USA	1927
Maxie Rosenbloom	USA	1932
Bob Olin	USA	1934
John Henry Lewis	USA	1935
Billy Conn	USA	1939
Gus Lesnevich	USA	1941
Freddie Mills	GB	1948
Joey Maxim	USA	1950
Archie Moore	USA	1952
Harold Johnson	USA	1962
Willie Pastrano	USA	1963
Jose Torres	PR	1965
Dick Tiger	Ngr	1966
Bob Foster	USA	1968
Michael Spinks	USA	1983

WBC

Bob Foster	USA	1970
John Conteh	GB	1974
Miguel Cuello	Arg	1977
Mate Parlov	Yug	1978
Marvin Johnson	USA	1978
Matt Saad Muhammad (formerly Matt Franklin)	USA	1979
Dwight Braxton	USA	1981
J.B. Williamson	USA	1985
Dennis Andries	Guy	1986
Thomas Hearns	USA	1987

WBA

Vicente Rondon	Ven	1971
Victor Galindez	Arg	1974
Mike Rossman	USA	1978
Victor Galindez	Arg	1979
Marvin Johnson	USA	1979
Eddie Mustaffa Muhammad (formerly Eddie Gregory)	USA	1980
Michael Spinks	USA	1981
Marvin Johnson	USA	1986
Leslie Stewart	Tri	1987
Virgil Hill	USA	1987

IBF

Slobodan Kacar	Yug	1985
Bobby Czyz	USA	1987

NBA

Jimmy Slattery	USA	1927
George Nichols	USA	1932
Lou Scozza	USA	1932
Anton Christoforidis	Gre	1941
Harold Johnson	USA	1961

NEW YORK STATE

Jimmy Slattery	USA	1930
Maxie Rosenbloom	USA	1930
Tiger Jack Fox	USA	1938
Melio Bettina	USA	1939

OTHER CLAIMANTS

Jack Dillon	USA	1912
Bob Godwin	USA	1933
Heinz Lazek	Aut	1935
Gustave Roth	Bel	1936
Adolph Heuser	Ger	1938
Len Harvey	GB	1939
Freddie Mills	GB	1942
Eddie Cotton	USA	1963

SUPER-MIDDLEWEIGHT

UNDISPUTED CHAMPIONS

None (weight only recognized by IBF)

IBF

Murray Sutherland	GB	1984
Chong-Pal Park	S. Kor	1984

MIDDLEWEIGHT
UNDISPUTED CHAMPIONS

Jack Dempsey	Ire	1884
Bob Fitzsimmons	GB	1891
Charles 'Kid' McCoy	USA	1897
Tommy Ryan	USA	1898
Stanley Ketchel	USA	1907
Billy Papke	USA	1908
Stanley Ketchel	USA	1908
Billy Papke	USA	1910
Cyclone Johnny Thompson	USA	1911
George Chip	USA	1913
Al McCoy	USA	1914
Mike O'Dowd	USA	1917
Johnny Wilson	USA	1921
Harry Greb	USA	1923
Tiger Flowers	USA	1926
Mickey Walker	USA	1926
Freddie Steele	USA	1936
Tony Zale	USA	1941
Rocky Graziano	USA	1947
Tony Zale	USA	1948
Marcel Cerdan	Alg	1948
Jake La Motta	USA	1949
Sugar Ray Robinson	USA	1951
Randolph Turpin	GB	1951
Sugar Ray Robinson	USA	1951
Carl 'Bobo' Olson	Haw	1953
Sugar Ray Robinson	USA	1955
Gene Fullmer	USA	1957
Sugar Ray Robinson	USA	1957
Carmen Basilio	USA	1957
Sugar Ray Robinson	USA	1958
Paul Pender	USA	1960
Terry Downes	GB	1961
Paul Pender	USA	1962
Dick Tiger	Ngr	1963
Joey Giardello	USA	1963
Dick Tiger	Ngr	1965
Emile Griffith	VI	1966
Nino Benvenuti	Ita	1967
Emile Griffith	VI	1967
Nino Benvenuti	Ita	1968
Carlos Monzon	Arg	1970
Carlos Monzon	Arg	1976
Rodrigo Valdez	Col	1977
Hugo Corro	Arg	1978
Vito Antuofermo	Ita	1979
Alan Minter	GB	1980
Marvin Hagler	USA	1980
Marvin Hagler	USA	1986

WBC

Rodrigo Valdez	Col	1974
Sugar Ray Leonard	USA	1987

WBA

Carlos Monzon	Arg	1974

IBF

Slobodan Kacar	Yug	1985

NBA

Gorilla Jones	USA	1931
Marcel Thil	Fra	1932
Gorilla Jones	USA	1933
Marcel Thil	Fra	1933
Al Hostak	USA	1938
Sol Kreiger	USA	1938
Al Hostak	USA	1939
Tony Zale	USA	1940
Gene Fullmer	USA	1959
Dick Tiger	Ngr	1962

NEW YORK STATE

Dave Rosenberg	USA	1922
Mike O'Dowd	USA	1922
Ben Jeby	USA	1932
Lou Brouillard	Can	1933
Vince Dundee	Ita	1933
Teddy Yarosz	USA	1934
Ed 'Babe' Risko	USA	1935
Freddie Steele	USA	1936
Fred Apostoli	USA	1938
Ceferino Garcia	Phi	1939
Ken Overlin	USA	1940
Billy Soose	USA	1941

OTHER CLAIMANTS

Hugo Kelly	Ita	1907
Billy Papke	USA	1911
Frank Mantell	USA	1912
Frank Klaus	USA	1912
Jeff Smith	USA	1914
Mick King	Aus	1914
Les Darcy	Aus	1915
Marcel Thil	Fra	1937
Fred Apostoli	USA	1937
Randolph Turpin	GB	1953

LIGHT-MIDDLEWEIGHT
UNDISPUTED CHAMPIONS

Denny Moyer	USA	1962
Ralph Dupas	USA	1963
Sandro Mazzinghi	Ita	1963
Nino Benvenuti	Ita	1965
Ki-Soo Kim	S. Kor	1966
Sandro Mazzinghi	Ita	1968
Freddie Little	USA	1969
Carmelo Bossi	Ita	1970
Koichi Wajima	Jap	1971
Oscar Albarado	USA	1974
Koichi Wajima	Jap	1975

WBC

Miguel de Oliveira	Bra	1975
Elisha Obed	Bah	1975
Eckhard Dagge	FRG	1976
Rocky Mattioli	Ita	1977
Maurice Hope	Ant	1979
Wilfred Benitez	USA	1981
Thomas Hearns	USA	1982
Duane Thomas	USA	1986
Lupe Aquino	Mex	1987

WBA

Jae-Do Yuh	S. Kor	1975
Koichi Wajima	Jap	1976
Jose Duran	Spa	1976
Miguel Castellini	Arg	1976
Eddie Gazo	Nic	1977
Masashi Kudo	Jap	1978
Ayub Kalule	Uga	1979
Sugar Ray Leonard	USA	1981
Tadashi Mihara	Jap	1981
Davey Moore	USA	1982
Roberto Duran	Pan	1983

Mike McCallum	Jam	1984

IBF

Mark Medal	USA	1984
Carlos Santos	PR	1984
Buster Drayton	USA	1986
Matthew Hilton	Can	1987

OTHER CLAIMANTS

Emile Griffith	VI	1962

WELTERWEIGHT
UNDISPUTED CHAMPIONS

Paddy Duffy	USA	1888
Mysterious Billy Smith	USA	1892
Tommy Ryan	USA	1894
Charles 'Kid' McCoy	USA	1896
Mysterious Billy Smith	USA	1898
Rube Ferns	USA	1900
Matty Matthews	USA	1900
Rube Ferns	USA	1901
Joe Walcott	Bar	1901
Dixie Kid	USA	1904
Honey Mellody	USA	1906
Mike 'Twin' Sullivan	USA	1907
Ted 'Kid' Lewis	GB	1915
Jack Britton	USA	1916
Ted 'Kid' Lewis	GB	1917
Jack Britton	USA	1919
Mickey Walker	USA	1922
Pete Latzo	USA	1926
Joe Dundee	Ita	1927
Jackie Fields	USA	1929
Young Jack Thompson	USA	1930
Tommy Freeman	USA	1930
Young Jack Thompson	USA	1931
Lou Brouillard	Can	1931
Jackie Fields	USA	1932
Young Corbett III	Ita	1933
Jimmy McLarnin	Ire	1933
Barney Ross	USA	1934
Jimmy McLarnin	Ire	1934
Barney Ross	USA	1935
Henry Armstrong	USA	1938
Fritzie Zivic	USA	1940
Freddie 'Red' Cochrane	USA	1941
Marty Servo	USA	1946
Sugar Ray Robinson	USA	1946
Kid Gavilan	Cuba	1951
Johnny Saxton	USA	1954
Tony de Marco	USA	1955
Carmen Basilio	USA	1955
Johnny Saxton	USA	1956
Carmen Basilio	USA	1956
Virgil Atkins	USA	1958
Don Jordan	USA	1958
Benny 'Kid' Paret	Cuba	1960
Emile Griffith	VI	1961
Benny 'Kid' Paret	Cuba	1961
Emile Griffith	VI	1962
Luis Rodriguez	Cuba	1963
Emile Griffith	VI	1963
Curtis Cokes	USA	1967
Jose Napoles	Cuba	1969
Billy Backus	USA	1970
Jose Napoles	Cuba	1971
Sugar Ray Leonard	USA	1981
Don Curry	USA	1985
Lloyd Honeyghan	Jam	1986

WBC

John H. Stracey	GB	1975
Carlos Palomino	Mex	1976
Wilfred Benitez	USA	1979
Sugar Ray Leonard	USA	1979
Roberto Duran	Pan	1980
Sugar Ray Leonard	USA	1980
Milton McCrory	USA	1983
Lloyd Honeyghan	Jam	1987

WBA

Curtis Cokes	USA	1966
Angel Espada	PR	1975
Jose Cuevas	Mex	1976
Thomas Hearns	USA	1980
Don Curry	USA	1983
Mark Breland	USA	1987
Marlon Starling	USA	1987

IBF

Don Curry	USA	1984
Lloyd Honeyghan	Jam	1987

NBA

Johnny Bratton	USA	1951

OTHER CLAIMANTS

Harry Lewis	USA	1908
Jimmy Gardner	Ire	1908
Jimmy Clabby	USA	1910
Waldemar Holberg	Den	1914
Tom McCormick	Ire	1914
Matt Wells	GB	1914
Mike Glover	USA	1915
Jack Britton	USA	1915
Charley Shipes	USA	1966
Hedgemon Lewis	USA	1972

LIGHT-WELTERWEIGHT/
UNDISPUTED CHAMPIONS

Mushy Callahan	USA	1926
Jack 'Kid' Berg	GB	1931
Tony Canzoneri	USA	1931
Johnny Jaddick	USA	1932
Battling Shaw	Mex	1933
Tony Canzoneri	USA	1933
Barney Ross	USA	1933
Tippy Larkin	USA	1946
Carlos Ortiz	PR	1959
Duilio Loi	Ita	1960
Eddie Perkins	USA	1962
Duilio Loi	Ita	1962
Roberto Cruz	Phi	1963
Eddie Perkins	USA	1963
Carlos Hernandez	Ven	1965
Sandro Lopopolo	Ita	1966
Paul Fuji	Haw	1967

WBC

Pedro Adigue	Phi	1968
Bruno Arcari	Ita	1970
Perico Fernandez	Spa	1974
Saensak Muangsurin	Tha	1975
Miguel Velasquez	Spa	1976
Saensak Muangsurin	Tha	1976
Sang-Hyun Kim	S. Kor	1978
Saoul Mamby	Jam	1980
Leroy Haley	USA	1982
Bruce Curry	USA	1983

Billy Costello	USA	1984
Lonnie Smith	USA	1985
Rene Arredondo	Mex	1986
Tsuyoshi Hamad	Jap	1986
Rene Arredondo	Mex	1987

WBA

Nicolino Loche	Arg	1968
Alfonso Frazer	Pan	1972
Antonio Cervantes	Col	1972
Wilfred Benitez	USA	1976
Antonio Cervantes	Col	1977
Aaron Pryor	USA	1980
Johnny Bumphus	USA	1984
Gene Hatcher	USA	1984
Ubaldo Sacco	Arg	1985
Patrizio Oliva	Ita	1986
Juan Martin Coggi	Arg	1987

IBF

Aaron Pryor	USA	1984
Gary Hinton	USA	1986
Joe Louis Manley	USA	1986
Terry Marsh	GB	1987

NEW YORK STATE

Jack 'Kid' Berg	GB	1930

OTHER CLAIMANTS

Pinkey Mitchell	USA	1922

LIGHTWEIGHT
UNDISPUTED CHAMPIONS

Jack McAuliffe	Ire	1888
George 'Kid' Lavigne	USA	1896
Frank Erne	Swi	1899
Joe Gans	USA	1902
Battling Nelson	Den	1908
Ad Wolgast	USA	1910
Willie Ritchie	USA	1912
Freddie Welsh	GB	1914
Benny Leonard	USA	1917
Jimmy Goodrich	USA	1925
Rocky Kansas	USA	1925
Sammy Mandell	USA	1926
Al Singer	USA	1930
Tony Canzoneri	USA	1930
Barney Ross	USA	1933
Tony Canzoneri	USA	1935
Lou Ambers	USA	1936
Henry Armstrong	USA	1938
Lou Ambers	USA	1939
Sammy Angott	USA	1941
Ike Williams	USA	1947
Jimmy Carter	USA	1951
Lauro Salas	Mex	1952
Jimmy Carter	USA	1952
Paddy de Marco	USA	1954
Jimmy Carter	USA	1954
Wallace 'Bud' Smith	USA	1955
Joe Brown	USA	1956
Carlos Ortiz	PR	1962
Ismael Laguna	Pan	1965
Carlos Ortiz	PR	1965
Carlos Ortiz	PR	1967
Carlos Cruz	Dom	1968
Mando Ramos	USA	1969
Ismael Laguna	Pan	1970
Ken Buchanan	GB	1970
Roberto Duran	Pan	1978

WBC

Pedro Carrasco	Spa	1971
Mando Ramos	USA	1972
Chango Carmona	Mex	1972
Rodolfo Gonzalez	Mex	1972
Guts Ishimatsu	Jap	1974
Esteban de Jesus	PR	1976
Jim Watt	GB	1979
Alexis Arguello	Nic	1981
Edwin Rosario	PR	1983
Jose Luis Ramirez	Mex	1984
Hector Camacho	PR	1985
Jose Luis Ramirez	Mex	1987

WBA

Carlos Ortiz	PR	1966
Ken Buchanan	GB	1971
Roberto Duran	Pan	1972
Ernesto Espana	Ven	1979
Hilmer Kenty	USA	1980
Sean O'Grady	USA	1981
Claude Noel	Tri	1981
Arturo Frias	USA	1981
Ray Mancini	USA	1982
Livingstone Bramble	VI	1984
Edwin Rosario	PR	1986

IBF

Charlie 'Choo Choo' Brown	USA	1984
Harry Arroyo	USA	1984
Jimmy Paul	USA	1985
Greg Haugen	USA	1986
Vinny Pazienza	USA	1987

NBA

Sammy Angott	USA	1940
Sammy Angott	USA	1943
Juan Zurita	Mex	1944
Ike Williams	USA	1945

NEW YORK STATE

Lew Jenkins	USA	1940
Beau Jack	USA	1942
Bob Montgomery	USA	1943
Beau Jack	USA	1943
Bob Montgomery	USA	1944

OTHER CLAIMANTS

Jimmy Britt	USA	1902
Battling Nelson	Den	1905
Freddie Welsh	GB	1912
Luther 'Slugger' White	USA	1942
Kenny Lane	USA	1963

JUNIOR-LIGHTWEIGHT
UNDISPUTED CHAMPIONS

Johnny Dundee	Ita	1921
Jack Bernstein	USA	1923
Johnny Dundee	Ita	1923
Steve 'Kid' Sullivan	USA	1924
Mike Balerino	USA	1925
Tod Morgan	USA	1925
Benny Bass	USSR	1929
Kid Chocolate	Cuba	1931
Frankie Klick	USA	1933
Harold Gomes	USA	1959
Flash Elorde	Phi	1960

Yoshiaki Numata	Jap	1967
Hiroshi Kobayashi	Jap	1967

WBC

Rene Barrientos	Phi	1969
Yoshiaki Numata	Jap	1970
Ricardo Arredondo	Mex	1971
Kuniaki Shibata	Jap	1974
Alfredo Escalera	PR	1975
Alexis Arguello	Nic	1978
Rafael Limon	Mex	1980
Cornelius Boza-Edwards	Uga	1981
Rolando Navarette	Phi	1981
Rafael Limon	Mex	1982
Bobby Chacon	USA	1982
Hector Camacho	PR	1983
Julio Cesar Chavez	Mex	1984

WBA

Hiroshi Kobayashi	Jap	1969
Alfredo Marcano	Ven	1971
Ben Villaflor	Phi	1972
Kuniaki Shibata	Jap	1973
Ben Villaflor	Phi	1973
Sam Serrano	PR	1976
Yasutsune Uehara	Jap	1980
Sam Serrano	PR	1981
Roger Mayweather	USA	1983
Rocky Lockridge	USA	1984
Wilfredo Gomez	PR	1985
Alfredo Layne	Pan	1986
Brian Mitchell	SA	1986

IBF

Hwan-Kil Yuh	S. Kor	1984
Lester Ellis	Aus	1985
Barry Michael	GB	1985
Rocky Lockridge	USA	1987

OTHER CLAIMANTS

Sandy Saddler	USA	1949

FEATHERWEIGHT

UNDISPUTED CHAMPIONS

Ike Weir	GB	1889
Billy Murphy	NZ	1890
Young Griffo	Aus	1890
George Dixon	Can	1891
Solly Smith	USA	1897
Dave Sullivan	Ire	1898
George Dixon	Can	1898
Terry McGovern	USA	1900
Young Corbett II	USA	1901
Abe Attell	USA	1904
Johnny Kilbane	USA	1912
Eugene Criqui	Fra	1923
Johnny Dundee	Ita	1923
Louis 'Kid' Kaplan	USSR	1925
Benny Bass	USSR	1927
Tony Canzoneri	USA	1928
Andre Routis	Fra	1928
Battling Battalino	USA	1929
Henry Armstrong	USA	1937
Joey Archibald	USA	1939
Willie Pep	USA	1946
Sandy Saddler	USA	1948
Willie Pep	USA	1949
Sandy Saddler	USA	1950
Hogan 'Kid' Bassey	Ngr	1957

Davey Moore	USA	1959
Sugar Ramos	Cuba	1963
Vicente Saldivar	Mex	1964

WBC

Howard Winstone	GB	1968
Jose Legra	Cuba	1968
Johnny Famechon	Fra	1969
Vicente Saldivar	Mex	1970
Kuniaki Shibata	Jap	1970
Clemente Sanchez	Mex	1972
Jose Legra	Cuba	1972
Eder Jofre	Bra	1973
Bobby Chacon	USA	1974
Ruben Olivares	Mex	1975
David Kotey	Gha	1975
Danny Lopez	USA	1976
Salvador Sanchez	Mex	1980
Juan Laporte	PR	1982
Wilfredo Gomez	PR	1984
Azumah Nelson	Gha	1984

WBA

Raul Rojas	USA	1968
Sho Saijyo	Jap	1968
Antonio Gomez	Ven	1971
Ernesto Marcel	Pan	1972
Ruben Olivares	Mex	1974
Alexis Arguello	Nic	1974
Rafael Ortega	Pan	1977
Cecilio Lastra	Spa	1977
Eusebio Pedroza	Pan	1978
Barry McGuigan	Ire	1985
Steve Cruz	USA	1986
Antonio Esparragoza	Ven	1987

IBF

Min-Keum Oh	S. Kor	1984
Chung-Ki Yung	S. Kor	1985
Antonio Rivera	PR	1986

NBA

Tommy Paul	USA	1932
Freddie Miller	USA	1933
Petey Sarron	USA	1936
Leo Rodak	USA	1938
Petey Scalzo	USA	1940
Ritchie Lemos	USA	1941
Jackie Wilson	USA	1941
Jackie Callura	Can	1943
Phil Terranova	USA	1943
Sal Bartolo	USA	1944

NEW YORK STATE

Johnny Dundee	Ita	1922
Tony Canzoneri	USA	1927
Kid Chocolate	Cuba	1932
Baby Arizmendi	Mex	1934
Mike Belloise	USA	1936
Joey Archibald	USA	1938
Harry Jeffra	USA	1940
Joey Archibald	USA	1941
Chalky Wright	Mex	1941
Willie Pep	USA	1942

OTHER CLAIMANTS

Ben Jordan	GB	1898
Eddie Santry	USA	1899
Tommy Sullivan	USA	1904
Jim Driscoll	GB	1909
Tommy Noble	GB	1920

Dick 'Honeyboy' Finnegan	USA	1926
Maurice Holtzer	Fra	1937
Percy Bassett	USA	1952
Teddy 'Red Top' Davis	USA	1953

SUPER-BANTAMWEIGHT

UNDISPUTED CHAMPIONS

None

WBC

Rigoberto Riasco	Pan	1976
Royal Kobayashi	Jap	1976
Dong-Kyun Yum	S. Kor	1976
Wilfredo Gomez	PR	1977
Jaime Garza	USA	1983
Juan 'Kid' Meza	Mex	1984
Lupe Pintor	Mex	1985
Smart Payakaroon	Tha	1986
Jeff Fenech	Aus	1987

WBA

Soo-Hwan Hong	S. Kor	1977
Ricardo Cardona	Col	1978
Leo Randolph	USA	1980
Sergio Palma	Arg	1980
Leonardo Cruz	Dom	1982
Loris Stecca	Ita	1984
Victor Callejas	PR	1984
Louie Espinoza	USA	1987

IBF

Bobby Berna	Phi	1983
Seung-In Suh	S. Kor	1984
Chi-Wan Kim	S. Kor	1985
Seung-Hoon Lee	S. Kor	1987

OTHER CLAIMANTS

Jack Wolfe	USA	1922
Carl Duane	USA	1923

BANTAMWEIGHT

UNDISPUTED CHAMPIONS

George Dixon	Can	1890
Jimmy Barry	USA	1897
Terry McGovern	USA	1899
Harry Harris	USA	1901
Harry Forbes	USA	1901
Frankie Neil	USA	1903
Joe Bowker	GB	1904
Jimmy Walsh	USA	1905
Johnny Coulon	Can	1911
Kid Williams	Den	1914
Pete Herman	USA	1917
Joe Lynch	USA	1920
Pete Herman	USA	1921
Johnny Buff	USA	1921
Joe Lynch	USA	1922
Abe Goldstein	USA	1924
Eddie Martin	USA	1924
Charley Phil Rosenberg	USA	1925
Panama Al Brown	Pan	1929
Sixto Escobar	PR	1936
Harry Jeffra	USA	1937
Sixto Escobar	PR	1938
Lou Salica	USA	1940
Manuel Ortiz	USA	1942
Harold Dade	USA	1947

Manuel Ortiz	USA	1947
Vic Toweel	SA	1950
Jimmy Carruthers	Aus	1952
Robert Cohen	Alg	1954
Alphonse Halimi	Alg	1957
Joe Becerra	Mex	1959
Eder Jofre	Bra	1962
Fighting Harada	Jap	1965
Lionel Rose	Aus	1968
Ruben Olivares	Mex	1969
Jesus Castillo	Mex	1970
Ruben Olivares	Mex	1971
Rafael Herrera	Mex	1972
Enrique Pinder	Pan	1972

WBC

Rafael Herrera	Mex	1973
Rodolfo Martinez	Mex	1974
Carlos Zarate	Mex	1976
Lupe Pintor	Mex	1979
Albert Davila	USA	1983
Daniel Zaragoza	Mex	1985
Miguel Lora	Col	1985

WBA

Romeo Anaya	Mex	1973
Arnold Taylor	SA	1973
Soo-Hwan Hong	S. Kor	1974
Alfonso Zamora	Mex	1975
Jorge Lujan	Pan	1977
Julian Solis	PR	1980
Jeff Chandler	USA	1980
Richard Sandoval	USA	1984
Gaby Canizales	USA	1986
Bernardo Pinango	Ven	1986
Takuya Muguruma	Jap	1987
Chang-Yung Park	S.Kor	1987

IBF

Satoshi Shingaki	Jap	1984
Jeff Fenech	Aus	1985
Kelvin Seabrooks	USA	1987

NBA

Sixto Escobar	PR	1934
Lou Salica	USA	1935
Sixto Escobar	PR	1935
Georgie Pace	USA	1940
Raton Macias	Mex	1955
Eder Jofre	Bra	1960

NEW YORK STATE

Abe Goldstein	USA	1923
Bud Taylor	USA	1927
Bushy Graham	Ita	1928
Baltazar Sangchilli	Spa	1935
Tony Marino	USA	1936
Robert Cohen	Alg	1955
Mario D'Agata	Ita	1956
Alphonse Halimi	Alg	1957

OTHER CLAIMANTS

George Dixon	Can	1888
Tommy Kelly	USA	1888
Chappie Moran	GB	1889
Billy Plimmer	GB	1892
Jimmy Barry	USA	1894
Pedlar Palmer	GB	1895
Digger Stanley	GB	1904
Jimmy Walsh	USA	1904
Kid Murphy	USA	1907
Jimmy Walsh	USA	1908
Johnny Coulon	Can	1908
Monte Attell	USA	1908
Digger Stanley	GB	1909
Frankie Conley	Ita	1911
Charles Ledoux	Fra	1912
Eddie Campi	USA	1913
Johnny Ertle	Aut	1915
Joe Burman	GB	1919
Teddy Baldock	GB	1927
Willie Smith	SA	1927
Pete Sanstol	Nor	1931
Alphonse Halimi	Alg	1960
Johnny Caldwell	GB	1961

SUPER-FLYWEIGHT/ UNDISPUTED CHAMPIONS

None

WBC

Rafael Orono	Ven	1980
Chul-Ho Kim	S. Kor	1981
Rafael Orono	Ven	1982
Payao Poontarat	Tha	1983
Jiro Watanabe	Jap	1984
Gilberto Roman	Mex	1986
Santos Laciar	Arg	1987
Jesus Rojas	Col	1987

WBA

Gustavo Ballas	Arg	1981
Rafael Pedroza	Pan	1981
Jiro Watanabe	Jap	1982
Kaosai Galaxy	Tha	1984

IBF

Joo-Do Chun	S. Kor	1983
Ellyas Pical	Ina	1985
Cesar Polonco	Dom	1986
Ellyas Pical	Ind	1986
Tae-Il Chang	S.Kor	1986

FLYWEIGHT UNDISPUTED CHAMPIONS

Jimmy Wilde	GB	1916
Pancho Villa	Phi	1923
Fidel La Barba	USA	1925
Frankie Genaro	USA	1930
Benny Lynch	GB	1937
Peter Kane	GB	1938
Jackie Paterson	GB	1943
Rinty Monaghan	GB	1948
Terry Allen	GB	1950
Dado Marino	Haw	1950
Yoshio Shirai	Jap	1952
Pascual Perez	Arg	1954
Pone Kingpetch	Tha	1960
Fighting Harada	Jap	1962
Pone Kingpetch	Tha	1963
Hiroyuki Ebihara	Jap	1963
Pone Kingpetch	Tha	1964
Salvatore Burruni	Ita	1965

WBC

Salvatore Burruni	Ita	1965
Walter McGowan	GB	1966
Chartchai Chionoi	Tha	1966
Efren Torres	Mex	1969
Chartchai Chionoi	Tha	1970
Erbito Salavarria	Phi	1970
Betulio Gonzalez	Ven	1972
Venice Borkorsor	Tha	1972
Betulio Gonzalez	Ven	1973
Shoji Oguma	Jap	1974
Miguel Canto	Mex	1975
Chan-Hee Park	S.Kor	1979
Shoji Oguma	Jap	1980
Antonio Avelar	Mex	1981
Prudencio Cardona	Col	1982
Freddie Castillo	Mex	1982
Eleonceo Mercedes	Dom	1982
Charlie Magri	Tun	1983
Frank Cedeno	Phi	1983
Koji Kobayashi	Jap	1984
Gabriel Bernal	Mex	1984
Sot Chitalada	Tha	1984

WBA

Horacio Accavallo	Arg	1966
Hiroyuki Ebihara	Jap	1969
Bernabe Villacampo	Phi	1969
Berkrerk Chartvanchai	Tha	1970
Masao Ohba	Jap	1970
Chartchai Chionoi	Tha	1973
Susumu Hanagata	Jap	1974
Erbito Salavarria	Phi	1975
Alfonso Lopez	Pan	1976
Gustavo Espadas	Mex	1976
Betulio Gonzalez	Ven	1978
Luis Ibarra	Pan	1979
Tae-Shik Kim	S. Kor	1980
Peter Mathebula	SA	1980
Santos Laciar	Arg	1981
Luis Ibarra	Pan	1981
Juan Herrera	Mex	1981
Santos Laciar	Arg	1982
Hilario Zapata	Pan	1986
Fidel Bassa	Col	1987

IBF

Soon-Chun Kwon	S. Kor	1983
Chung-Bi Won	S.Kor	1986
Hi-Sop Shin	S.Kor	1986
Dodie Penalosa	Phi	1987
Chang-Ho Choi	S.Kor	1987

NBA

Albert Belanger	Can	1927
Frankie Genaro	USA	1928
Emile Pladner	Fra	1929
Frankie Genaro	USA	1929
Rinty Monaghan	GB	1947

NEW YORK STATE

Izzy Schwartz	USA	1927
Midget Wolgast	USA	1930
Small Montana	Phi	1935

OTHER CLAIMANTS

Sid Smith	GB	1913
Bill Ladbury	GB	1913
Percy Jones	GB	1914
Joe Symonds	GB	1914
Frankie Genaro	USA	1925
Johnny McCoy	USA	1927
Newsboy Brown	USSR	1928
Johnny Hill	GB	1928
Willie Le Morte	USA	1929

Young Perez	Tun	1931	Netrnoi Vorasingh	Tha	1978	Katsuo Tokashiki	Jap	1981
Jackie Brown	GB	1932	Sung-Jun Kim	S. Kor	1978	Lupe Madera	Mex	1983
Benny Lynch	GB	1935	Shigeo Nakajima	Jap	1980	Francisco Quiroz	Dom	1984
Valentin Angelmann	Fra	1937	Hilario Zapata	Pan	1980	Joey Olivo	USA	1985
			Amado Ursua	Mex	1982	Myung-Woo Yuh	S. Kor	1985

LIGHT-FLYWEIGHT/ UNDISPUTED CHAMPIONS

None

			Tadashi Tomori	Jap	1982	**IBF**		
			Hilario Zapata	Pan	1982			
			Chang-Jung Koo	S. Kor	1983	Dodie Penalosa	Phi	1983
						Chong-Hwan Choi	S.Kor	1986

WBC

Franco Udella	Ita	1975
Luis Estaba	Ven	1975
Freddie Castillo	Mex	1978

WBA

Jaime Rios	Pan	1975
Juan Guzman	Dom	1976
Yoko Gushiken	Jap	1976
Pedro Flores	Mex	1981
Hwan-Jin Kim	S. Kor	1981

MINI-FLYWEIGHT

IBF

Kyung-Yun Lee	S.Kor	1987

World champions—nation-by-nation

A total of 47 different countries have provided world champions. The following list is a nation-by-nation summary of all world champions. Claimants to titles are excluded. The year after each fighter's name is the year he first won a title. Fighters are listed according to country of birth.

ALGERIA

Marcel Cerdan (1948), Robert Cohen (1954), Alphonse Halimi (1957).

ANTIGUA

Maurice Hope (1979).

ARGENTINA

Pascual Perez (1954), Horacio Accavallo (1966), Nicolino Loche (1968), Carlos Monzon (1970), Victor Galindez (1974), Miguel Castellini (1976), Miguel Cuello (1977), Hugo Corro (1978), Sergio Palma (1980), Santos Laciar (1981), Gustavo Ballas (1981), Ubaldo Sacco (1985), Juan Martin Coggi (1987).

AUSTRALIA

Young Griffo (1890), Jimmy Carruthers (1952), Lionel Rose (1968), Jeff Fenech (1985).

AUSTRIA

Jack Root (1903), Johnny Ertle (1915).

BAHAMAS

Elisha Obed (1975).

BARBADOS

Joe Walcott (1901).

BRAZIL

Eder Jofre (1960), Miguel de Oliveira (1975).

CANADA

George LaBlanche (1889), George Dixon (1890), Tommy Burns (1906), Johnny Coulon (1910), Jack Delaney (1926), Albert Belanger (1927), Lou Brouillard (1931), Jackie Callura (1943), Matthew Hilton (1987).

COLOMBIA

Antonio Cervantes (1972), Rodrigo Valdes (1974), Ricardo Cardona (1978), Prudencio Cardona (1982), Miguel 'Happy' Lora (1985), Fidel Bassa (1987), Jesus Rojas (1987).

CUBA

Kid Chocolate (1931), Kid Gavilan (1951), Benny 'Kid' Paret (1960), Luis Rodriguez (1963), Sugar Ramos (1963), Jose Legra (1968), Jose Napoles (1969).

DENMARK

Battling Nelson (1908), Kid Williams (1914).

DOMINICAN REPUBLIC

Carlos Cruz (1968), Juan Jose Guzman (1976), Leonardo Cruz (1982), Eleoncio Mercedes (1982), Francisco Quiroz (1984), Cesar Polonco (1986).

FRANCE

Georges Carpentier (1920), Eugene Criqui (1923), Andre Routis (1928), Emile Pladner (1929), Marcel Thil (1932), Johnny Famechon (1969).

GERMANY

Max Schmeling (1930), Eckhard Dagge (1976).

GHANA

David Kotey (1975), Azumah Nelson (1984).

GREAT BRITAIN

Ike Weir (1889), Bob Fitzsimmons (1891), Joe Bowker (1904), Freddie Welsh (1914), Ted 'Kid' Lewis (1915), Jimmy Wilde (1916), Jack 'Kid' Berg (1930), Jackie Brown (1932), Benny Lynch (1935), Peter Kane (1938), Jackie Paterson (1943), Rinty Monaghan (1947), Freddie Mills (1948), Terry Allen (1950), Randolph Turpin (1951), Johnny Caldwell (1961), Terry Downes (1961), Walter McGowan (1966), Howard Winstone (1968), Ken Buchanan (1970), John Conteh (1974), John H. Stracey (1975), Jim Watt (1979), Alan Minter (1980), Murray Sutherland (1984), Barry Michael (1985), Lester Ellis (1985), Terry Marsh (1987).

GREECE

Anton Christoforidis (1941).

GUYANA

Dennis Andries (1986).

HAWAII
Dado Marino (1950), Carl 'Bobo' Olson (1953), Paul Fuji (1967).

INDONESIA
Ellyas Pical (1985).

IRELAND, REPUBLIC OF
Jack 'Nonpareil' Dempsey (1884), Jack McAuliffe (1888), Dave Sullivan (1898), George Gardner (1903), Mike McTigue (1923), Jimmy McLarnin (1933), Barry McGuigan (1985).

ITALY
Johnny Dundee (1921), Joe Dundee (1927), Bushy Graham (1928), Young Corbett III (1933), Primo Carnera (1933), Vince Dundee (1933), Mario D'Agata (1956), Duilio Loi (1960), Sandro Mazzinghi (1963), Salvatore Burruni (1965), Nino Benvenuti (1965), Sandro Lopopolo (1966), Bruno Arcari (1970), Carmen Bossi (1970), Franco Udella (1975), Rocky Mattioli (1977), Vito Antuofermo (1979), Loris Stecca (1984), Patrizio Oliva (1986).

JAMAICA
Saoul Mamby (1980), Mike McCallum (1984), Trevor Berbick (1986), Lloyd Honeyghan (1986).

JAPAN
Yoshio Shirai (1952), Fighting Harada (1962), Hiroyuki Ebihara (1963), Yoshiaki Numata (1967), Hiroshi Kobayashi (1967), Sho Saijyo (1968), Masao Ohba (1970), Kuniaki Shibata (1970), Koichi Wajima (1971), Guts Ishimatsu (1974), Shoji Oguma (1974), Susumu Hanagata (1974), Kazuo Kobayashi (1976), Yoko Gushiken (1976), Masashi Kudo (1978), Shigeo Nakajima (1980), Yasatsune Uehara (1980), Tadashi Mihara (1981), Katsuo Tokashiki (1981), Jiro Watanabe (1982), Tadashi Tomori (1982), Koji Kobayashi (1983), Satosi Singaki (1984), Tsuyoshi Hamada (1986), Takuya Muguruma (1987).

KOREA, SOUTH
Ki-Soo Kim (1966), Soo-Hwan Hong (1974), Jae-Do Yuh (1975), Dong-Kyun Yum (1976), Sung-Jun Kim (1978), Sang-Hyun Kim (1978), Chan-Hee Park (1979), Tae-Shik Kim (1980), Chul-Ho Kim (1980), Hwan-Jin Kim (1981), Chang-Jung Koo (1983), Ju-Do Chun (1983), Soon-Chun Kwon (1983), Chong-Pal Park (1984), Hwan-Kil Yuh (1984), Min-Keum Oh (1984), Seing-In Suh (1984), Chi-Won Kim (1984), Myung-Woo Yuh (1985), Chung-Ki Yung (1985), Chung-Bi Won (1986), Hi-Sop Shin (1986), Chong-Hwan Choi (1986), Chong-Hwan Choi (1986), Tae-Il Chang (1986), Seung-Hoon Lee (1987), Chang-Yung Park (1987), Kyung-Yun Lee (1987), Chang-Ho Choi (1987).

MEXICO
Battling Shaw (1933), Baby Arizmendi (1934), Chalky Wright (1941), Juan Zurita (1944), Lauro Salas (1952), Raton Macias (1955), Joe Becerra (1959), Vicente Saldivar (1964), Efren Torres (1969), Ruben Olivares (1969), Jesus Chucho Castillo (1970), Ricardo Arredondo (1971), Rafael Herrera (1972), Clemente Sanchez (1972), Erubey 'Chango' Carmona (1972), Rodolfo Gonzalez (1972), Romeo Anaya (1973), Rodolfo Martinez (1974), Miguel Canto (1975), Alfonso Zamora (1975), Carlos Zarate (1976), Carlos Palomino (1976), Jose Cuevas (1976), Guty Espadas (1976), Freddie Castillo (1978), Lupe Pintor (1979), Salvador Sanchez (1980), Rafael Limon (1980), Pedro Flores (1981), Antonio Avelar (1981), Juan Herrera (1981), Armado Ursua (1982), Lupe Madera (1983), Gabriel Bernal (1984), Julio-Cesar Chavez (1984), Jose-Luis Ramirez (1984), Juan 'Kid' Meza (1984), Daniel Zaragoza (1985), Gilberto Roman (1986), Rene

Arredondo (1986), Lupe Aquino (1987).

NEW ZEALAND
Billy Murphy (1890).

NICARAGUA
Alexis Arguello (1974), Eddie Gazo (1977).

NIGERIA
Hogan 'Kid' Bassey (1957), Dick Tiger (1962).

PANAMA
Panama Al Brown (1929), Ismael Laguna (1965), Alfonso Frazer (1972), Roberto Duran (1972), Enrique Pinder (1972), Ernesto Marcel (1972), Jaime Rios (1975), Alfonso Lopez (1976), Rigoberto Riasco (1976), Rafael Ortega (1977), Jorge Lujan (1977), Eusebio Pedroza (1978), Luis Ibarra (1979), Hilario Zapata (1980), Rafael Pedroza (1981), Alfredo Layne (1986).

PHILIPPINES
Pancho Villa (1923), Small Montana (1935), Ceferino Garcia (1939), Flash Elorde (1960), Roberto Cruz (1963), Pedro Adigue (1968), Rene Barrientos (1969), Bernabe Villacampo (1969), Erbito Salavarria (1970), Ben Villaflor (1972), Rolando Navarette (1981), Frank Cedeno (1983), Dodie Penalosa (1983).

PUERTO RICO
Sixto Escobar (1934), Carlos Ortiz (1959), Jose Torres (1965), Angel Espada (1975), Alfredo Escalera (1975), Esteban de Jesus (1976), Sam Serrano (1976), Wilfredo Gomez (1977), Julian Solis (1980), Carlos de Leon (1980), Ossie Ocasio (1982), Juan Laporte (1982), Edwin Rosario (1983), Hector Camacho (1983), Victor Callejas (1984), Carlos Santos (1984), Antonio Rivera (1986).

SENEGAL
Battling Siki (1922).

SOUTH AFRICA
Vic Toweel (1950), Arnold Taylor (1973), Peter Mathebula (1980), Gerrie Coetzee (1983), Piet Crous (1984), Brian Mitchell (1986).

SPAIN
Baltazar Sangchilli (1935), Pedro Carrasco (1971), Perico Fernandez (1974), Jose Duran (1976), Miguel Velasquez (1976), Cecilio Lastra (1977).

SWEDEN
Ingemar Johansson (1959).

SWITZERLAND
Frank Erne (1899).

THAILAND
Pone Kingpetch (1960), Chartchai Chionoi (1966), Berkrerk Chartvanchai (1970), Venice Borkorsor (1972), Saensak Muangsurin (1975), Netrnoi Vorasingh (1978), Payao Poontarat (1983), Sot Chitalada (1984), Kaosai Galaxy (1984), Samart Payakaroon (1986).

TRINIDAD
Claude Noel (1979), Leslie Stewart (1987).

TUNISIA
Young Perez (1931), Charlie Magri (1983).

UGANDA

Ayub Kalule (1979), Cornelius Boza-Edwards (1980).

USA

Paddy Duffy (1888), James J. Corbett (1892), Mysterious Billy Smith (1892), Tommy Ryan (1894), Charles 'Kid' McCoy (1896), George 'Kid' Lavigne (1896), Solly Smith (1897), Jimmy Barry (1897), James J. Jeffries (1899), Terry McGovern (1899), Rube Ferns (1900), Matty Matthews (1900), Harry Harris (1901), Harry Forbes (1901), Young Corbett II (1901), Joe Gans (1902), Frankie Neil (1903), Abe Attell (1904), Dixie Kid (1904), Marvin Hart (1905), Jimmy Walsh (1905), Philadelphia Jack O'Brien (1905), Honey Mellody (1906), Mike 'Twin' Sullivan (1907), Stanley Ketchel (1907), Billy Papke (1908), Jack Johnson (1908), Ad Wolgast (1910), Cyclone Johnny Thompson (1911), Johnny Kilbane (1912), Willie Ritchie (1912), Frank Klaus (1913), George Chip (1913), Al McCoy (1914), Jack Dillon (1914), Jess Willard (1915), Jack Britton (1916), Battling Levinsky (1916), Pete Herman (1917), Benny Leonard (1917), Mike O'Dowd (1917), Jack Dempsey (1919), Johnny Wilson (1920), Joe Lynch (1920), Johny Buff (1921), Dave Rosenberg (1922), Mickey Walker (1922), Jack Bernstein, (1923), Harry Greb (1923), Abe Goldstein (1923), Steve 'Kid' Sullivan (1924), Eddie 'Cannonball' Martin (1924), Charley Phil Rosenberg (1925), Mike Ballerino (1925), Paul Berlenbach (1925), Jimmy Goodrich (1925), Tod Morgan (1925), Rocky Kansas (1925), Tiger Flowers (1926), Pete Latzo (1926), Sammy Mandell (1926), Mushy Callahan (1926), Gene Tunney (1926), Fidel La Barba (1927), Bud Taylor (1927), Jimmy Slattery (1927), Tommy Loughran (1927), Corporal Izzy Schwartz (1927), Frankie Genaro (1928), Tony Canzoneri (1928), Jackie Fields (1929), Battling Battalino (1929), Midget Wolgast (1930), Maxie Rosenbloom (1930), Al Singer (1930), Young Jack Thompson (1930), Tommy Freeman (1930), Gorilla Jones (1931), Johnny Jadick (1932), George Nichols (1932), Tommy Paul (1932), Lou Scozza (1932), Jack Sharkey (1932), Ben Jeby (1932), Freddie Miller (1933), Barney Ross (1933), Frankie Klich (1933), Max Baer (1934), Teddy Yarosz (1934), Bob Olin (1934), James J. Braddock (1935), Lou Salica (1935), Ed 'Babe' Risko (1935), John Henry Lewis (1935), Petey Sarron (1936), Tony Marino (1936), Freddie Steele (1936), Lou Ambers (1936), Mike Belloise (1936), Joe Louis (1937), Harry Jeffra (1937), Henry Armstrong (1937), Fred Apostoli (1938), Al Hostak (1938), Joey Archibald (1938), Sol Kreiger (1938), Tiger Jack Fox (1938), Leo Rodak (1938), Melio Bettina (1939), Billy Conn (1939), Sammy Angott (1940), Lew Jenkins (1940), Petey Scalzo (1940), Tony Zale (1940), Fritzie Zivic (1940), Ken Overlin (1940), Billy Soose (1941), Gus Lesnevich (1941), Richie Lemos (1941), Freddie 'Red' Cochrane (1941), Jackie Wilson (1941), Manuel Ortiz (1942), Willie Pep (1942), Beau Jack (1942), Bob Montgomery (1943), Phil Terranova (1943), Sal Bartolo (1944), Ike Williams (1945), Marty Servo (1946), Tippy Larkin (1946), Sugar Ray Robinson (1946), Harold Dade (1947), Rocky Graziano (1947), Sandy Saddler (1948), Jack La Motta (1949), Ezzard Charles (1949), Joey Maxim (1950), Johnny Bratton (1951), Jimmy Carter (1951), Jersey Joe Walcott (1951), Rocky Marciano (1952), Archie Moore (1952), Paddy de Marco (1954), Johnny Saxton (1954), Tony de Marco (1955), Carmen Basilio (1955), Wallace 'Bud' Smith (1955), Joe Brown (1956), Floyd Patterson (1956), Gene Fullmer (1957), Virgil Atkins (1958), Don Jordan (1958), Davey Moore (1959), Harold Gomes (1959), Paul Pender (1960), Harold Johnson (1961), Eddie Perkins (1962), Sonny Liston (1962), Denny Moyer (1962), Ralph Dupas (1963), Willie Pastrano (1963), Joey Giardello (1963), Cassius Clay (1964), Ernie Terrell (1965), Curtis Cokes (1966), Joe Frazier (1968), Raul Rojas (1968), Jimmy Ellis (1968), Bob Foster (1968), Mando Ramos (1969), Freddie Little (1969), Billy Backus (1970), George Foreman (1973), Oscar Albarado (1974), Bobby Chacon (1974), Wilfred Benitez (1976), Danny Lopez (1976), Leon Spinks (1978), Larry Holmes (1978), Mike Rossman (1978), Marvin Johnson (1978), Matt Franklin (1979), John Tate (1979), Sugar Ray Leonard (1979), Hilmer Kenty (1980), Mike Weaver (1980), Marvin Camel (1980), Eddie Gregory (1980), Leo Randolph (1980), Thomas Hearns (1980), Aaron Pryor (1980), Marvin Hagler (1980), Jeff Chandler (1980), Sean O'Grady (1981), Michael Spinks (1981), Arturo Frias (1981), Dwight Braxton (1981), Davey Moore (1982), Ray Mancini (1982), Leroy Haley (1982), S.T. Gordon (1982), Mike Dokes (1982), Roger Mayweather (1983), Don Curry (1983), Alberto Davila (1983), Milton McCrory (1983), Bruce Curry (1983), Jaime Garza (1983), Bobby Berna (1983), Charlie 'Choo-Choo' Brown (1984), Johnny Bumphus (1984), Billy Costello (1984), Rocky Lockridge (1984), Mark Medal (1984), Tim Witherspoon (1984), Harry Aroyo (1984), Richard Sandoval (1984), Leroy Murphy (1984), Gene Hatcher (1984), Pinklon Thomas (1984), Greg Page (1984), Joey Olivo (1985), Jimmy Paul (1985), Tony Tubbs (1985), Alphonso Ratliff (1985), Lonnie Smith (1985), Bernard Benton (1985), J.B. Williamson (1985), Gaby Canizales (1986), Gary Hinton (1986), Buster Drayton (1986), Steve Cruz (1986), Evander Holyfield (1986), Bobby Czyz (1986), Rickey Parkey (1986), Joe Louis Manley (1986), Mike Tyson (1986), Duane Thomas (1986), Greg Haugen (1986), James Smith (1986), Louie Espinoza (1987), Mark Breland (1987), Kelvin Seabrooks (1987), Tony Tucker (1987), Vinny Pazienza (1987), Marlon Starling (1987), Virgil Hill (1987).

USSR

Louis 'Kid' Kaplan (1925), Benny Bass (1927).

VENEZUELA

Carlos Hernandez (1965), Vicente Paul Rondon (1971), Alfredo Marcano (1971), Antonio Gomez (1971), Betulio Gonzalez (1972), Luis Estaba (1975), Ernesto Espana (1979), Rafael Orono (1980), Bernardo Pinango (1986), Antonio Esparragoza (1987).

VIRGIN ISLANDS

Emile Griffith (1961), Livingstone Bramble (1984).

YUGOSLAVIA

Mate Parlov (1978), Slobodan Kacar (1985).

Records and Statistics

The first world title bout under Queensberry Rules was on 30 July 1884 and was a middleweight bout, at Great Kills, New York, between Jack Dempsey (Ire) v. George Fulljames (USA).

The first black world heavyweight champion was Jack Johnson (USA) who won the title from Tommy Burns (Can) in 1908).

The first all-negro world heavyweight title bout was between Jack Johnson (USA) and Jim Johnson (USA) on 19 December 1913.

The first man to win world titles in two weight divisions was George Dixon (Can) who won the bantamweight title in 1890 and the featherweight title in 1891.

The first man to win world titles at three different weights was Bob Fitzsimmons who won the middleweight title in 1891, the heavyweight in 1897 and the light-heavyweight in 1903.

The first man to regain a world title was Mysterious Billy Smith (USA) who regained the welterweight title 25 August 1898, five years after winning the title.

The first former champion to referee a world heavyweight title fight was James J. Jeffries on 3 July 1905 when he took charge of the Marvin Hart (USA) – Jack Root (Aut) bout.

The first referee to officiate inside the ring in England was Eugene Corri (Eng), when he controlled the world heavyweight title fight between Tommy Burns (Can) and Gunner Moir (GB) at the National Sporting Club, London, on 2 December 1907. This was also the first world heavyweight title fight to be held in England.

The first black world champion was George Dixon of Canada. He beat Nunc Wallace (GB) to win the bantamweight title in 1890.

The first southpaw world champion was Al McCoy (USA), middleweight champion 1914.

The first million-dollar gate was on 2 July 1921, when 80 183 people paid $1 789 238 to watch the world heavyweight contest between Jack Dempsey (USA) and Georges Carpentier (Fra) at Jersey City, USA.

The first 100 000 crowd was on 23 September 1926 when 120 757 witnessed the Gene Tunney (USA)–Jack Dempsey (USA) world heavyweight contest at the Sesquicentennial Stadium, Philadelphia, USA.

The first radio broadcast of a world title fight in its entirety was of the Jack Dempsey (USA) v. Georges Carpentier (Fra) heavyweight bout on 2 July 1921.

The first world title fight to be televised was the Willie Pep (USA)–Chalky Wright (Mex) featherweight contest from New York on 29 September 1944.

The first heavyweight title fight to be televised was the Joe Louis (USA)–Jersey Joe Walcott (USA) bout from New York on 5 December 1947.

The first world title fight to be broadcast in colour was the Emile Griffith (VI)–Manuel Gonzales (USA) welterweight fight from New York on 10 December 1965.

The first world championship fight to be televised in a country other than the United States was the Kid Gavilan (Cuba)–Billy Graham (USA) welterweight bout from Havana, Cuba on 5 October 1952.

The first live televising of a world title fight weigh-in took place on 30 May 1951 when Ezzard Charles (USA) and Joey Maxim (USA) weighed-in for their world heavyweight contest.

The first referee to be replaced during a world title fight was Ruby Goldstein. While refereeing the Ray Robinson (USA)–Joey Maxim (USA) light-heavyweight bout on 25 June 1952 he was overcome by the intense heat and had to be replaced by Ray Miller at the end of the 12th round. Robinson retired two rounds later, also suffering from the excessive heat.

The first stadium to be named after a former world champion was the Escobar Stadium in San Juan, Puerto Rico (opened 1955). It was named after Sixto Escobar, the world bantamweight champion, 1934–9.

The first occasion the same two men engaged in three successive world heavyweight title fights was between 26 June 1959 and 13 March 1961 when Floyd Patterson (USA) and Ingemar Johansson (Swe) engaged in three successive bouts, the American winning two fights to one.

The first time two titles changed hands on the same night was on 21 March 1963 when Luis Rodriguez (Cuba) defeated Emile Griffith (VI) to take the welterweight crown and Sugar Ramos (Cuba) beat Davey Moore (USA) to win the featherweight title.

The first time a four-roped ring was used for a world title fight was at Madison Square Garden, New York, on 8 June 1963 for the Emile Griffith (VI)–Luis Rodriguez (Cuba) welterweight fight. Prior to this either two or three roped rings were used.

The first WBC title fight was on 2 December 1965: Salvatore Burruni (Ita) KO –13 Rocky Gattelleri (Ita), flyweight (Sydney, Australia).

The first WBA title fight was on 5 March 1965: Ernie Terrell (USA) PTS-15 Eddie Machen (USA), heavyweight (Chicago, USA).

The first IBF title fight was on 21 May 1983: Marvin Camel (USA) KO–9 Rocky Sekorski (USA), cruiserweight (Billings, USA).

The first fighter from a communist country to win a world title was Mate Parlov (Yug) who won the world light-heavyweight title in 1978. Benny Bass and 'Kid' Kaplan, world title holders in the 1920s, were both born in Russia but were domiciled in the United States at the time of winning their titles.

The first world title fight to be held in a communist country was the middleweight contest between Nino Benvenuti (Ita) and Tom Bethea (USA) at Umag, Yugoslavia, on 23 May 1970.

The first woman judge to be used in a world heavyweight title fight was Eva Shain who officiated at the Muhammad Ali (USA)–Earnie Shavers (USA) contest on 29 September 1977.

The first time both champion and challenger entered the ring undefeated for a world title fight was on 15 November 1952 at Johannesburg, when the defending champion Vic Toweel (SA) met Jimmy Carruthers (Aus) for the bantamweight title. Toweel's record remained intact as he won in the 1st round.

First world title fights in each country

ARGENTINA
11 Jan 1956 *Fl* Pascual Perez v. Leo Espinosa (Phi)

AUSTRALIA
3 Sep 1890 *Fe* Young Griffo v. Billy Murphy (NZ)

BAHAMAS
28 Feb 1976 *LM(WBC)* Elisha Obed v. Tony Gardner (USA)

BRAZIL
25 Mar 1961 *B(NBA)* Eder Jofre v. Piero Rollo (Ita)

CANADA
24 Mar 1901 *W* Rube Ferns (USA) v. Matty Matthews (USA)

CHILE
30 Nov 1977 *FL(WBC)* Miguel Canto (Mex) v. Martin Vargas

COLOMBIA
27 Nov 1964 *B* Eder Jofre (Bra) v. Bernardo Carabello

Mate Parlov of Yugoslavia taken shortly after he became the first boxer from a Communist country to win a world title when he beat Miguel Angel Cuello (Arg) for the light-heavyweight title in 1978. Syndication International

COSTA RICA
29 Jan 1972 *JL(WBC)* Ricardo Arredondo (Mex) v. Jose Isaac Marin

CUBA
5 Apr 1915 *H* Jess Willard (USA) v. Jack Johnson (USA)

DENMARK
19 Aug 1972 *M* Carlos Monzon (Arg) v. Tom Bogs

DOMINICAN REPUBLIC
29 Jun 1968 *L* Carlos Cruz v. Carlos Ortiz (PR)

DUTCH WEST INDIES
4 May 1985 *B(WBC)* Daniel Zaragoza (Mex) v. Freddie Jackson (USA)

ECUADOR
15 Jan 1977 *JL(WBC)* Sam Serrano (PR) v. Alberto Herrera (WBA)

ENGLAND
27 Jun 1890 *B* George Dixon (Can) v. Nunc Wallace

FINLAND
17 Aug 1962 *Fe* Davey Moore (USA) v. Olli Makim

FRANCE
18 Apr 1908 *H* Tommy Burns (Can) v. Jewey Smith (GB)

GERMANY, Federal Republic of
23 Jun 1962 *LH* Harold Johnson (USA) v. Gustav Scholz

GHANA
9 May 1964 *Fe* 'Sugar' Ramos (Cuba) v. Floyd Robertson

HAWAII
30 May 1947 *B* Manuel Ortiz (USA) v. David Kui Kong Young

INDONESIA
29 Aug 1981 *LW(WBC)* Saoul Mamby (Jam) v. Thomas Americo

IRELAND, Northern
23 Mar 1948 *Fl* Rinty Monaghan (GB) v. Jackie Paterson (GB)

IRELAND, Republic of
17 Mar 1908 *H* Tommy Burns (Can) v. Jem Roche

ITALY
18 Mar 1933 *B* Panama Al Brown (Pan) v. Dom Bernasconi

IVORY COAST
24 Apr 1976 *LM(WBC)* Elisha Obed (Bah) v. Sea Robinson

JAMAICA
19 April 1964 *LW* Eddie Perkins (USA) v. Bunny Grant

JAPAN
19 May 1952 *Fl* Yoshio Shirai v. Dado Marino (Haw)

KOREA, South
25 June 1966 *LM* Ki-Soo Kim v. Nino Benvenuti (Ita)

MALAYSIA
1 July 1975 *H* Muhammad Ali (USA) v. Joe Bugner (GB)

MEXICO
1 Mar 1931 *W* Tommy Freeman (USA) v. Alfredo Gaona

MIDDLE EAST (Kuwait)
22 Feb 1986 *Fl (WBC)* Sot Chitalada (Tha) v. Freddie Castillo (Mex)

MONACO
8 May 1971 *M* Carlos Monzon (Arg) v. Nino Benvenuti (Ita)

NEW GUINEA
17 Nov 1979 *Fe(WBA)* Eusebio Pedroza (Pan) v. Johnny Aba

NICARAGUA
31 May 1975 *Fe(WBA)* Alexis Arguello v. Rigoberto Riasco (Pan)

NIGERIA
10 Aug 1963 *M* Dick Tiger v. Gene Fullmer (USA)

NORWAY
12 Dec 1975 *JL(WBC)* Alfredo Escalera (PR) v. Svein-Erik Paulsen

PANAMA
10 Apr 1965 *L* Ismael Laguna v. Carlos Ortiz (PR)

PHILIPPINES
23 Dec 1939 *M(NY)* Ceferino Garcia v. Glen Lee (USA)

PUERTO RICO
21 Feb 1937 *B* Sixto Escobar v. Lou Salica (USA)

ST VINCENT
22 Oct 1983 *Fe(WBA)* Eusebio Pedroza (Pan) v. Jose Caba (Dom)

Hogan 'Kid' Bassey became Nigeria's first world champion in 1957. The Photo Source

SCOTLAND
16 Sep 1936 *Fl(IBU)* Benny Lynch v. Pat Palmer

SOUTH AFRICA
4 Sep 1937 *Fe(NBA)* Petey Sarron (USA) v. Freddie Miller (USA)

SPAIN
7 Jul 1928 *W* Joe Dundee (Ita) v. Hilario Martinez

SWEDEN
14 Sep 1968 *H(WBA)* Jimmy Ellis (USA) v. Floyd Patterson (USA)

SWITZERLAND
27 Apr 1974 *Fl(WBA)* Chartchai Chionoi (Tha) v. Fritz Chervet

THAILAND
2 May 1954 *B* Jimmy Carruthers (Aus) v. Chamrern Songkitrat

UNITED STATES
30 Jul 1884 *M* Jack Dempsey (Ire) v. George Fulljames

URUGUAY
30 Jun 1956 *Fl* Pascual Perez (Arg) v. Oscar Suarez (Cuba)

VENEZUELA
19 Apr 1958 *Fl* Pascual Perez (Arg) v. Ramon Arias

WALES
4 Sep 1946 *L(NBA)* Ike Williams (USA) v. Ronnie James

YUGOSLAVIA
23 May 1970 *M* Nino Benvenuti (Ita) v. Tom Bethea (USA)

ZAIRE
30 Oct 1974 *H* Muhammad Ali (USA) v. George Foreman (USA)

Of the 50 countries that have staged world title fights the following 13 have not provided a world champion of their own: Chile, Costa Rica, Dutch West Indies, Ecuador, Finland, Ivory Coast, Malaysia, Monaco, New Guinea, Norway, St Vincent, Uruguay, Zaire.

Pascual Perez (Argentina, Uruguay and Venezuela) and Nino Benvenuti (Monaco, South Korea and Yugoslavia) have each figured in the first world title fight in three different countries.

Undefeated world champions

Only three world champions retired without suffering defeat during their entire career. They were:

Jimmy Barry (USA)
first professional fight: 1891
last professional fight: 1899
total bouts: 70 won: 59 drew: 9 ND: 2
World bantamweight champion 1897–9 (he claimed the title, however, in 1894)

Jack McAuliffe (Ire)
first professional fight: 1884
last professional fight: 1897
(McAuliffe fought a three-round exhibition in 1914 in his 48th year.)
total bouts: 53 won: 41 drew: 9 ND: 3
World lightweight champion 1887–96

Rocky Marciano (USA)
first professional fight: 1947
last professional fight: 1955
total bouts: 49 won: 49
World heavyweight champion 1952–6

Many world champions were undefeated at the time of winning their world title. The following is a list of all world heavyweight champions who were undefeated at the time of taking the title (figures in brackets indicate number of contests before winning title): James J. Corbett (16), James J. Jeffries (13), Rocky Marciano (42), Ingemar Johansson

Thailand's first world champion was Pone Kingpetch, who won the flyweight title from Pascual Perez in 1960. The Photo Source

(21), Cassius Clay (19), Joe Frazier (19), George Foreman (37), Leon Spinks (7), Larry Holmes (27), John Tate (19), Pinklon Thomas (25), Tony Tubbs (18), Mike Weaver (27), Mike Tyson (31). Leon Spinks holds the record for winning the world heavyweight crown in the least number of professional fights–eight.

The distinction of winning a world title in the fewest contests in any weight division belongs to Thailand's Saensak Muangsurin who, when he won the WBC light-welterweight title in 1975, was competing in his third professional bout. He had, however, fought as a professional Thai-kick boxer.

Longest reigning champions

The longest continuous reigns in each weight division have been:

HEAVYWEIGHT
Joe Louis (USA) – 11 years 252 days (22 Jun 1937 – 1 Mar 1949) – 25 defences.

CRUISERWEIGHT
Carlos de Leon (PR) – 1 year 334 days (17 Jul 1983 – 6 June 1985) – 3 defences.

LIGHT-HEAVYWEIGHT
Archie Moore (USA) – 9 years 55 days (17 Dec 1952 – 10 Feb 1962) – 9 defences.

MIDDLEWEIGHT
Tommy Ryan (USA) – 9 years 285 days (24 Oct 1898 – 5 Aug 1907) – 4 defences.

LIGHT-MIDDLEWEIGHT
Thomas Hearns (USA) – 3 years 315 days (3 Dec 1982 – 24 Oct 1986) – 4 defences.

WELTERWEIGHT
Red Cochrane (USA) – 4 years 187 days (29 Jul 1941 – 1 Feb 1946) – No defences.

LIGHT-WELTERWEIGHT
Bruno Arcari (Ita) – 4 years 191 days (31 Jan 1970 – 10 Aug 1974) – 8 defences.

LIGHTWEIGHT
Benny Leonard (USA) – 7 years 260 days (28 May 1917 – 15 Jan 1925) – 7 defences.

JUNIOR-LIGHTWEIGHT
Flash Elorde (Phi) – 7 years 91 days (16 Mar 1960 – 15 Jun 1967) – 10 defences.

FEATHERWEIGHT
Johnny Kilbane (USA) – 11 years 103 days (22 Feb 1912 – 2 Jun 1923) – 10 defences.

SUPER-BANTAMWEIGHT
Wilfredo Gomez (PR) – 5 years 336 days (21 May 1977 – 22 Apr 1983) – 17 defences.

BANTAMWEIGHT
Al Brown (Pan) – 5 years 348 days (18 Jun 1929 – 1 Jun 1935) – 9 defences.

SUPER-FLYWEIGHT
Kaosai Galaxy (Tha) – 2 years 273 days (21 Nov 1984 – 31 Aug 1987) – 5 defences (Reigning champion as at 31 August 1987).

FLYWEIGHT
Jimmy Wilde (GB) – 7 years 125 days (14 Feb 1916 – 18 Jun 1923) 4 defences.

LIGHT-FLYWEIGHT
Chang-Jung Koo (S.Kor) – 4 years 158 days (26 Mar 1983 – 31 Aug 1987) – 13 defences (Reigning champion as at 31 August 1987).

Shortest reigning champions

The shortest reigning world champion in each weight division has been:

HEAVYWEIGHT
Tony Tucker (USA) – 64 days (30 May – 2 Aug 1987)

CRUISERWEIGHT
Piet Crous (SA) and **Marvin Camel** (USA) – 239 days (1 Dec 1984 – 28 Jul 1985 (Crous)) (31 Mar – 25 Nov 1980 (Camel))

LIGHT-HEAVYWEIGHT
Jack Root (Aut) – 73 days (22 Apr – 4 Jul 1903)

MIDDLEWEIGHT
Randolph Turpin (GB) – 64 days (10 Jul – 12 Sep 1951)

LIGHT-MIDDLEWEIGHT
Tadashi Mihara (Jap) – 87 days (7 Nov 1981 – 2 Feb 1982)

WELTERWEIGHT
Johnny Bratton (USA) – 65 days (14 Mar – 18 May 1951)

Max Baer (USA) held the world heavyweight title for one day short of a year. He beat Primo Carnera (Ita) for the title on 14 June 1934 and lost it to James J. Braddock (USA), in his first defence, on 13 June 1935. The Photo Source

LIGHT-WELTERWEIGHT
Tony Canzoneri (USA) – 33 days (21 May – 23 Jun 1933)

LIGHTWEIGHT
Erubey Carmona (Mex) – 56 days (15 Sep – 10 Nov 1972)

JUNIOR-LIGHTWEIGHT
Rafael Limon (Mex) – 86 days (11 Dec 1980 – 8 Mar 1981)

FEATHERWEIGHT
Dave Sullivan (Ire) – 46 days (26 Sep – 11 Nov 1898)

SUPER-BANTAMWEIGHT
Royal Kobayashi (Jap) – 45 days (10 Oct – 24 Nov 1976)

BANTAMWEIGHT
Takuya Muguruma (Jap) – 56 days (29 Mar – 24 May 1987) NB: On 19 Oct 1923 Joe Lynch pulled out of his bantamweight contest against Joe Burman at the last minute. The New York Boxing Commission withdrew Lynch's crown from him and, at 3.00 p.m., awarded it to Burman. Abe Goldstein stepped in as a late replacement for the Madison Square Garden bill and at 11.00 p.m. he beat Burman to end Burman's eight-hour reign as world champion.

SUPER-FLYWEIGHT
Gustavo Ballas (Arg) – 84 days (12 Sep – 5 Dec 1981)
Santos Laciar (Arg) – 84 days (16 May – 8 Aug 1987)

FLYWEIGHT
Emile Pladner (Fra) 47 days (2 Mar – 18 Apr 1929)

LIGHT-FLYWEIGHT
Amado Ursua (Mex) – 66 days (6 Feb – 13 Apr 1982)

World champions at more than one weight

Winners of world titles at three different weights

Bob Fitzsimmons (GB)
middleweight (1891) heavyweight (1897) light-heavyweight (1903)

Tony Canzoneri (USA)
featherweight (1928) lightweight (1930) light-welterweight (1931)

Barney Ross (USA)
lightweight (1933) light-welterweight (1933) welterweight (1934)

Henry Armstrong (USA)
featherweight (1937) welterweight (1938) lightweight (1938)

Wilfred Benitez (USA)
light-welterweight (1976) welterweight (1979) WBC light-middleweight (1981)

Alexis Arguello (Nic)
WBA featherweight (1974) WBC junior-lightweight (1978) WBC lightweight (1981)

Roberto Duran (Pan)
lightweight (1972) welterweight (1980) WBA light-middleweight (1983)

Wilfredo Gomez (PR)
WBC super-bantamweight (1977) WBC featherweight (1984) WBA junior-lightweight (1985)

Thomas Hearns (USA)
WBA welterweight (1980) WBC light-middleweight (1982) WBC light-heavyweight (1987)

Sugar Ray Leonard (USA)
WBC welterweight (1979) WBA light-middleweight (1981) WBC middleweight (1987)

Winners of world titles at two different weights

George Dixon (Can)
bantamweight (1890) featherweight (1891)

Tommy Ryan (USA)
welterweight (1894) middleweight (1898)

Terry McGovern (USA)
bantamweight (1899) featherweight (1900)

Johnny Dundee (Ita)
junior-lightweight (1921) featherweight (1923)

Mickey Walker (USA)
welterweight (1922) middleweight (1926)

Benny Bass (USSR)
featherweight (1927) junior-lightweight (1929)

Kid Chocolate (Cuba)
junior-lightweight (1931) NY featherweight (1932)

Lou Brouillard (Can)
welterweight (1931) NY middleweight (1933)

Barney Ross (USA)
lightweight (1933) welterweight (1934)

Harry Jeffra (USA)
bantamweight (1937) NY featherweight (1940)

Joe Louis (right) and Jersey Joe Walcott (USA) chat at a Boxing Writer's Dinner in January 1948. Five months later the pair of them met in the ring — Louis won with an 11th-round knock-out. The Photo Source

Sugar Ray Robinson (USA)
welterweight (1946) middleweight (1951)

Carmen Basilio (USA)
welterweight (1955) middleweight (1957)

Carlos Ortiz (PR)
light-welterweight (1959) lightweight (1962)

Emile Griffith (VI)
welterweight (1961) middleweight (1966)
(Also claimed to be first light-middleweight champion, but
he only received recognition in Austria)

Fighting Harada (Jap)
flyweight (1962) bantamweight (1965)

Dick Tiger (Ngr)
middleweight (1963) light-heavyweight (1966)

Nino Benvenuti (Ita)
light-middleweight (1965) middleweight (1967)

Eder Jofre (Bra)
NBA bantamweight (1960) WBC featherweight (1973)

Kuniaki Shibata (Jap)
WBC featherweight (1970) WBC junior-lightweight (1974)

Ruben Olivares (Mex)
bantamweight (1969) WBA featherweight (1974)

Soo-Hwan Hong (S. Kor)
WBA bantamweight (1974) WBA super-bantamweight
(1977)

Freddie Castillo (Mex)
WBC light-flyweight (1978) WBC flyweight (1982)

Bobby Chacon (USA)
WBC featherweight (1974) WBC junior-lightweight (1982)

Dwight Qawi (USA) – formerly Dwight Braxton
WBC light-heavyweight (1981) WBA cruiserweight (1985)

Hector Camacho (PR)
WBC junior-lightweight (1983) WBC lightweight (1985)

Michael Spinks (USA)
WBA light-heavyweight (1981) IBF heavyweight (1985)
NB: Spinks is the only light-heavyweight champion to go on
and win the heavyweight crown.

Lupe Pintor (Mex)
WBC bantamweight (1979) WBA super-bantamweight
(1985)

Hilario Zapata (Pan)
WBC light-flyweight (1982) WBA flyweight (1986)

Jeff Fenech (Aus)
IBF bantamweight (1985) WBC super-bantamweight (1987)

Santos Laciar (Arg)
WBA flyweight (1981) WBC super-flyweight (1987)

Dodie Penalosa (Phi)
IBF light-flyweight (1983) WBC super-bantamweight (1987)

Most successful world title defences

The following have made the most successful defences in
one weight division.

25 – Joe Louis (USA) heavyweight 1937–48
20 – Larry Holmes (USA) heavyweight 1978–85
19 – Henry Armstrong (USA) welterweight 1938–40
19 – Manuel Ortiz (USA) bantamweight 1942–6, 1947–9
19 – Muhammad Ali (USA) heavyweight 1965–7, 1975–7
19 – Eusebio Pedroza (Pan) featherweight 1978–85
17 – Wilfredo Gomez (PR) super-bantamweight 1977–82
15 – George Dixon (Can) featherweight 1892–7, 1898–1900
(Some sources quote Dixon as having made up to 20
defences of the title, but several of his bouts were at a time
when his claim to the title was in doubt.)
15 – Joe Gans (USA) lightweight 1902–8

Some sources quote Abe Attell (USA) as having made 20
defences of the featherweight title (1904–12) but there was a
time during his reign that his claim was challenged and
consequently many of his 'title' fights were dubious in
status.

Most world title fights engaged in

27 – Joe Louis (USA) heavyweight 1937–50
25 – Henry Armstrong (USA) middleweight, welterweight,
lightweight, flyweight 1937–41
25 – Muhammad Ali (USA) heavyweight 1964–80
23 – Manuel Ortiz (USA) bantamweight 1942–50
23 – Larry Holmes (USA) heavyweight 1978–86
22 – Emile Griffith (VI) middleweight, light-middleweight,
welterweight 1961–76

The first man to regain the world heavyweight title, Floyd Patterson (USA). Svenskt Pressfoto

21 – Tony Canzoneri (USA) junior-lightweight, featherweight, bantamweight 1927–37
20 – Eusebio Pedroza (Pan) featherweight, bantamweight 1976–85

Regained world titles

Years when fighters have regained world titles in each weight division

HEAVYWEIGHT

Floyd Patterson (USA)	1960
Muhammad Ali (USA)	1974, 1981 WBA
Tim Witherspoon (USA)	1986 WBA

CRUISERWEIGHT

Carlos de Leon (PR)	1983 IBF
Carlos de Leon (PR)	1986 WBC

LIGHT-HEAVYWEIGHT

Victor Galindez (Arg)	1979 WBA
Marvin Johnson (USA)	1986 WBA

MIDDLEWEIGHT

Stanley Ketchell (USA)	1908
Billy Papke (USA)	1910
Gorilla Jones (USA)	1933 NBA
Marcel Thil (Fra)	1933 NBA
Al Hostak (USA)	1939 NBA
Tony Zale (USA)	1948
Sugar Ray Robinson (USA)	1951, 1955, 1957, 1958
Paul Pender (USA)	1962
Dick Tiger (Ngr)	1965

Emile Griffith (VI)	1967
Nino Benvenuti (Ita)	1968

LIGHT-MIDDLEWEIGHT

Sandro Mazzinghi (Ita)	1968
Koichi Wajima (Jap)	1975

WELTERWEIGHT

Mysterious Billy Smith (USA)	1898
Rube Ferns (USA	1901
Ted 'Kid' Lewis (GB)	1917
Jack Britton (USA)	1919
Young Jack Thompson (USA)	1931
Jackie Fields (USA)	1932
Jimmy McLarnin (Ire)	1934
Barney Ross (USA)	1935
Johnny Saxton (USA)	1956
Carmen Basilio (USA)	1956
Benny Paret (Cuba)	1961
Emile Griffith (VI)	1962, 1963
Jose Napoles (Cuba)	1971
Sugar Ray Leonard (USA)	1980 WBC

LIGHT-WELTERWEIGHT

Rene Arredondo (Mex)	1987 WBC
Tony Canzoneri (USA)	1933
Duilio Loi (Ita)	1962
Eddie Perkins (USA)	1963
Saensak Muangsurin (Tha)	1976 WBC
Antonio Cervantes (Col)	1977 WBA
Rene Arredondo (Mex)	1987 WBC

LIGHTWEIGHT

Jose Luis Ramirez (Mex)	1987 WBC
Tony Canzoneri (USA)	1935
Lou Ambers (USA)	1939
Beau Jack (USA)	1943 NY
Bob Montgomery (USA)	1944 NY
Jimmy Carter (USA)	1952, 1954
Carlos Ortiz (PR)	1965
Ismael Iaguna (Pan)	1970
Jose Luis Ramirez (Mex)	1987 WBC

JUNIOR-LIGHTWEIGHT

Johnny Dundee (Ita)	1923
Ben Villaflor (Phil)	1973 WBA
Sam Serrano (PR)	1981 WBA
Rafael Limon (Mex)	1982 WBC

FEATHERWEIGHT

George Dixon (Can)	1898
Joey Archibald (USA)	1941 NY
Willie Pep (USA)	1949
Sandy Saddler (USA)	1950
Vincente Saldivar (Mex) (had previously held the universal title)	1970 WBC
Jose Legra (Cuba)	1972 WBC

BANTAMWEIGHT

Pete Herman (USA)	1921
Joe Lynch (USA)	1922
Sixto Escobar (PR)	1935 NBA, 1938
Manuel Ortiz (USA)	1947
Ruben Olivares (Mex)	1971

SUPER-FLYWEIGHT

Rafael Orono (Ven)	1982 WBC
Ellyas Pical (Ina)	1986 IBF

FLYWEIGHT

Frankie Genaro (USA)	1929 NBA
Pone Kingpetch (Tha)	1963, 1964
Chartchai Chionoi (Tha)	1970 WBC
Betulio Gonzalez (Ven)	1973 WBC

Shoji Oguma (Jap)   1980 WBC
Santos Laciar (Arg)   1982 WBA

LIGHT-FLYWEIGHT
Hilario Zapata (Pan)   1982 WBC

Emile Griffith (VI) (middleweight and welterweight) and Tony Canzoneri (USA) (light-welterweight and lightweight) are the only men to have regained titles at two different weights.

Fighters who won different versions of the same title (other than universal)
(Only WBC, WBA or IBF included)

HEAVYWEIGHT
Tim Witherspoon (USA)   1984 WBC; 1986 WBA

CRUISERWEIGHT
Marvin Camel (USA)   1980 WBC; 1983 IBF

LIGHT-HEAVYWEIGHT
Marvin Johnson (USA)   1978 WBC; 1979 WBA; 1986 WBA

WELTERWEIGHT
Don Curry (USA)   1983 WBA; 1984 IBF

LIGHTWEIGHT
Edwin Rosario (PR)   1983 WBC; 1986 WBA

JUNIOR-LIGHTWEIGHT
Rocky Lockridge (USA)   1984 WBA; 1987 IBF

SUPER-FLYWEIGHT
Jiro Watanabe (Jap)   1982 WBA; 1984 WBC

Tony Canzoneri (USA), the first man to regain world titles at different weights — light-welterweight and lightweight. The Photo Source

World title fights that ended in round one

12 Sep 1899 *B* Terry McGovern (USA) beat Pedlar Palmer (GB)

12 May 1902 *L* Joe Gans (USA) beat Frank Erne (Swi)*

4 Jul 1907 *H* Tommy Burns (Can)* beat Bill Squires (Aus)

22 Feb 1908 *M* Stanley Ketchel (USA)* beat Mike 'Twin' Sullivan (USA)

17 Mar 1908 *H* Tommy Burns (Can)* beat Jem Roche (Ire)

7 Apr 1914 *M* Al McCoy (USA) beat George Chip (USA)*

31 Aug 1917 *W* Ted 'Kid' Lewis (GB)* beat Albert Badoud (Swe)

11 May 1922 *LH* Georges Carpentier (Fra)* beat Ted 'Kid' Lewis (GB)

2 Mar 1929 *Fl (NBA)* Emile Pladner (Fra) beat Frankie Genaro (USA)*

17 Jul 1930 *L* Al Singer (USA) beat Sammy Mandell (USA)*

14 Nov 1930 *L* Tony Canzoneri (USA) beat Al Singer (USA)*

19 Sep 1932 *B* Al Brown (Pan)* beat Emile Pladner (Fra)

29 May 1933 *W* Jimmy McLarnin (GB) beat Young Corbett III (Ita)*

17 Feb 1935 *Fe (NBA)* Freddie Miller (USA)* beat Jose Girones (Spa)

13 Oct 1936 *B* Sixto Escobar (PR)* beat Carlos Quintana (Pan)

22 Jun 1938 *H* Joe Louis (USA)* beat Max Schmeling (Ger)

26 Jul 1938 *M (NBA)* Al Hostak (USA) beat Freddie Steele (USA)*

25 Jan 1939 *H* Joe Louis (USA)* beat John Henry Lewis (USA)

16 Mar 1939 *W* Henry Armstrong (USA)* beat Lew Feldman (USA)

17 Apr 1939 *H* Joe Louis (USA)* beat Jack Roper (USA)

11 Dec 1939 *M (NBA)* Al Hostak (USA)* beat Eric Seelig (Ger)

9 Jan 1942 *H* Joe Louis (USA)* beat Buddy Baer (USA)

19 Jun 1943 *Fl* Jackie Paterson (GB) beat Peter Kane (GB)*

18 Sep 1946 *H* Joe Louis (USA)* beat Tami Mauriello (USA)

5 Mar 1948 *LH* Gus Lesnevich (USA) beat Billy Fox (USA)

15 Nov 1952 *B* Jimmy Carruthers (Aus) beat Vic Toweel (SA)*

15 May 1953 *H* Rocky Marciano (USA)* beat Jersey Joe Walcott (USA)

30 Mar 1957 *Fl* Pascual Perez (Arg)* beat Dai Dower (GB)

17 Aug 1960 *JL* Flash Elorde (Phi)* beat Harold Gomes (USA)

Marvin Hagler (USA) sweating it out in training for his fight with Thomas Hearns (USA). All Sport

8 Apr 1961 *Fe* Davey Moore (USA)* beat Danny Valdez (USA)

16 Dec 1961 *JL* Flash Elorde (Phi)* beat Sergio Caprari (Ita)

25 Sep 1962 *H* Sonny Liston (USA) beat Floyd Patterson (USA)*

21 Mar 1963 *LW* Roberto Cruz (Phi) beat Battling Torres (Mex)

22 Jul 1963 *H* Sonny Liston (USA)* beat Floyd Patterson (USA)

18 Sep 1963 *Fl* Hiroyuki Ebihara (Jap) beat Pone Kingpetch (Tha)*

25 May 1965 *H* Muhammad Ali (USA)* beat Sonny Liston (USA)

22 Jan 1969 *LH* Bob Foster (USA)* beat Frank de Paula (USA)

22 Apr 1969 *H (NY)* Joe Frazier (USA)* beat Davy Zyglewicz (USA)

3 Jun 1971 *Fe (WBC)* Kuniaki Shibata (Jap)* beat Raul Cruz (Mex)

5 Jun 1971 *LH (WBA)* Vicente Rondon (Ven)* beat Piero del Papa (Ita)

7 May 1972 *LM* Koichi Wajima (Jap)* beat Domenico Tiberia (Ita)

1 Sep 1973 *H* George Foreman (USA)* beat Joe Roman (PR)

17 Oct 1973 *JL (WBA)* Ben Villaflor (Phi) beat Kuniaki Shibata (Jap)*

21 Dec 1974 *L (WBA)* Roberto Duran (Pan)* beat Mastaka Takayama (Jap)

15 Oct 1976 *L (WBA)* Roberto Duran (Pan)* beat Alvaro Rojas (CR)

3 Jun 1978 *JL (WBC)* Alexis Arguello (Nic)* beat Diego Alcala(Pan)

7 Mar 1982 *M* Marvin Hagler (USA)* beat William 'Caveman' Lee (USA)

20 Mar 1982 *Fl (WBC)* Prudencio Cardona (Col) beat Antonio Avelar (Mex)*

8 May 1982 *L (WBA)* Ray Mancini (USA) beat Arturo Frias (USA)*

10 Dec 1982 *H* Mike Dokes (USA) beat Mike Weaver (USA)*

16 Jul 1983 *Fl (WBA)* Santos Laciar (Arg)* beat Shin-Hi Sop (S. Kor)

19 Aug 1983 *JL (WBA)* Roger Mayweather (USA)* beat Ben Villablanca (Chi)

12 Sep 1983 *W (WBA)* Don Curry (USA)* beat Roger Stafford (USA)

25 Feb 1984 *JL (WBA)* Rocky Lockridge (USA) beat Roger Mayweather (USA)*

17 Mar 1984 *L (WBC)* Edwin Rosario (PR)* beat Roberto Elizondo (USA)

17 Mar 1984 *SF (IBF)* Joo-Du Chun (S. Kor)* beat Diego de Villa (Phi)

3 Nov 1984 *SB (WBC)* Juan 'Kid' Meza (Mex) beat Jaime Garza (USA)*

8 Oct 1985 *SB (IBF)* Chi-Wan Kim (S. Kor)* beat Song-In Suh (S. Kor)

12 Oct 1985 *Fe (WBC)* Azumah Nelson (Gha)* beat Pat Cowdell (GB)

24 Jul 1986 *LW (WBC)* Tsuyoshi Hamada (Jap) beat Rene Arredondo (Mex)*

12 Dec 1986 *H (WBA)* James Smith (USA) beat Tim Witherspoon (USA)*

26 Dec 1986 *LH (IBF)* Bobby Czyz (USA)* beat David Sears (USA)

1 Mar 1987 *LF (WBA)* Myung-Woo Yuh (S. Kor)* beat Eduardo Tunon (Pan)

30 Aug 1987 *W (WBC/IBF)* Lloyd Honeyghan (Jam)* beat Gene Hatcher (USA)

*Defending champion

Men who have stopped two or more opponents in the first round in world title fights

5 – Joe Louis (USA) heavyweight
2 – Tommy Burns (Can) heavyweight
2 – Roberto Duran (Pan) lightweight
2 – Flashe Elorde (Phi) junior-lightweight
2 – Al Hostak (USA) middleweight
2 – Sonny Liston (USA) heavyweight
(Liston's opponent on each occasion was Floyd Patterson)

Patterson is the only man to have been stopped in the first round of two world title fights.

Men who have both stopped an opponent and been stopped in the first round of a world title fight

Ted 'Kid' Lewis (GB) welterweight, light-heavyweight
Sonny Liston (USA) heavyweight
Roger Mayweather (USA) junior-lightweight
Emile Pladner (Fra) flyweight, bantamweight
Kuniaki Shibata (Jap) featherweight, junior-lightweight
Al Singer (USA) lightweight

(Singer won the world title with a 1st round KO and lost the title by a 1st round KO.)

Shortest world title fights
Winner of each bout appears first.

45s Al McCoy (USA) v. George Chip (USA) middleweight 7 Apr 1914

45s Lloyd Honeyghan (Jam) v. Gene Hatcher (USA) WBC/IBF welterweight 30 Aug 1987

58s Emile Pladner (Fra) v. Frankie Genaro (USA) NBA flyweight 2 Mar 1929

1min 01s Jackie Paterson (GB) v. Peter Kane (GB) flyweight 19 Jun 1943

1min 01s Bobby Czyz (USA) v. David Sears (USA) IBF light-heavyweight 26 Dec 1986

1min 03s Michael Dokes (USA) v. Mike Weaver (USA) WBA heavyweight 10 Dec 1982

1min 06s Tony Canzoneri (USA) v. Al Singer (USA) lightweight 14 Nov 1930

1min 07s Marvin Hagler (USA) v. Caveman Lee (USA) middleweight 7 Mar 1982

1min 15s Terry McGovern (USA) v. Pedlar Palmer (GB) bantamweight 12 Sep 1899

1min 19s Santos Laciar (Arg) v. Shin-Hi Sop (S. Kor) WBA flyweight 16 Jul 1983

1min 20s Flash Elorde (Phi) v. Harold Gomes (USA) junior-lightweight 17 Aug 1960

1min 21s Al Hostak (USA) v. Eric Seeling (Ger) NBA middleweight 11 Dec 1939

Sugar Ray Robinson (USA) knocked out Jose Basora (USA) in 52s in a middleweight contest in 1950, but it was only recognized as a world title fight in Philadelphia.

Al Singer (USA) won the world lightweight title in 1930, stopping his opponent in 1min 46s. Four months later he lost the title when beaten in 1min 6s!

Al Hostak (USA) is the only man to have stopped two opponents (Eric Seelig (Ger) and Freddie Steele (USA)) in under two minutes in world title fights.

Disqualifications in world title fights

29 Mar 1889 *W* Paddy Duffy (USA) beat Tom Meadows (Aus)

11 Nov 1898 *Fe* George Dixon (Can) beat Dave Sullivan (Ire)*

15 Jan 1900 *W* Rube Ferns (USA) beat Mysterious Billy Smith (USA)*

30 Apr 1904 *W* Dixie Kid (USA) beat Joe Walcott (Bar)*

31 Oct 1904 *L* Joe Gans (USA)* beat Jimmy Britt (USA)

3 Sep 1906 *L* Joe Gans (USA)* beat Battling Nelson (Den)

28 Nov 1912 *L* Willie Ritchie (USA) beat Ad Wolgast (USA)*

5 Mar 1913 *M* Frank Klaus (USA) beat Billy Papke (USA)*

10 Sep 1915 *B* Johnny Ertle (Aut) beat Kid Williams)Den)*

4 Jul 1916 *L* Freddie Welsh (GB)* beat Ad Wolgast (USA)

18 Nov 1921 *JL* Johnny Dundee (Ita) beat George Chaney (USA)

26 Jun 1922 *W* Jack Britton (USA)* beat Benny Leonard (USA)

30 Nov 1922 *M (NY)* Mike O'Dowd (USA) beat Dave Rosenberg (USA)*

9 Jul 1926 *W* Pete Latzo (USA)* beat George Levine (USA)

20 Jul 1928 *Fl (NY)* Corporal Izzy Schwartz (USA)* beat Frisco Grande (Phi)

18 Apr 1929 *Fl (NBA)* Frankie Genaro (USA) beat Emile Pladner (Fra)*

25 Jul 1929 *W* Jackie Fields (USA)* beat Joe Dundee (Ita)

12 Jun 1930 *H* Max Schmeling (Ger) beat Jack Sharkey (USA)

11 Jun 1932 *M (NBA)* Marcel Thil (Fra) beat Gorilla Jones (USA)*

20 Jan 1936 *M (NBA)* Marcel Thil (Fra)* beat Lou Brouillard (Can)

23 May 1941 *H* Joe Louis (USA)* beat Buddy Baer (USA)

16 Nov 1963 *JL* Flash Elorde (Phi)* beat Love Allotey (Gha)

4 Oct 1969 *M* Nino Benvenuti (Ita)* beat Fraser Scott (USA)

10 Jul 1970 *LW (WBC)* Bruno Arcari (Ita)* beat Rene Roque (Fra)

5 Nov 1971 *L (WBC)* Pedro Carrasco (Spa) beat Mando Ramos (USA)

16 Feb 1974 *LW (WBC)* Bruno Arcari (Ita)* beat Tony Ortiz (Spa)

4 Apr 1975 *LF (WBC)* Franco Udella (Ita) beat Valentine Martinez (Mex)

30 Jun 1976 *LW (WBC)* Miguel Velasquez (Spa) beat Saensak Muangsurin (Tha)*

21 Oct 1978 *Fe (WBC)* Danny Lopez (USA)* beat Pel Clemente (Phi)

4 May 1985 *B (WBC)* Daniel Zaragoza (Mex) beat Freddie Jackson (USA)

*Defending champion

Ad Wolgast (USA) is the only person to have been disqualified in two world title fights

Joe Gans (USA), Marcel Thil (Fra) and Bruno Arcari (Ita) have all had two opponents disqualified in world title fights.

Drawn world title fights

16 Nov 1887 *L* Jack McAuliffe (Ire) D – 74 Jem Carney (GB). Declared a draw after the ring had been invaded by spectators who tried to prevent Carney from knocking out McAuliffe.

31 Mar 1889 *Fe* Ike Weir (GB) D – 80 Frank Murphy (GB). Police stopped fight.

26 Sep 1894 *Fe* George Dixon (Can) D – 20 Young Griffo (Aus)

27 May 1895 *W* Tommy Ryan (USA) D – 18 Mysterious Billy Smith (USA). Police stopped fight.

17 Mar 1898 *L* George 'Kid' Lavigne (USA) D – 20 Jack Daly (USA)

30 May 1898 *B* Jimmy Barry (USA) D – 20 Casper Leon (Ita)

28 Sep 1898 *L* George 'Kid' Lavigne (USA) D – 20 Frank Erne (Swi)

29 Dec 1898 *B* Jimmy Barry (USA) D – 20 Casper Leon (Ita)

30 Jun 1899 *W* Mysterious Billy Smith (USA) D – 20 Charley McKeever (USA)

11 Aug 1899 *Fe* George Dixon (Can) D – 20 Eddie Santry (USA)

4 Dec 1899 *L* Frank Erne (Swi) D – 25 Jack O'Brien (USA)

6 Sep 1900 *B* Harry Forbes (USA) D – 20 Casper Leon (Ita)

16 Oct 1903 *B* Frankie Neil (USA) D – 20 Johnny Reagan (USA)

12 May 1904 *W* Dixie Kid (USA) D – 20 Joe Walcott (Bar)

22 Feb 1905 *Fe* Abe Attell (USA) D – 15 Kid Goodman (USA)

28 Nov 1906 *H/LH* Tommy Burns (Can) D – 20 Philadelphia Jack O'Brien (USA)

1 Jan 1908 *Fe* Abe Attell (USA) D – 25 Owen Moran (GB)

7 Sep 1908 *Fe* Abe Attell (USA) D – 23 Owen Moran (GB)

21 May 1912 *Fe* Johnny Kilbane (USA) D – 12 Jimmy Walsh (USA)

29 Apr 1913 *Fe* Johnny Kilbane D – 20 Johnny Dundee (Ita)

19 Dec 1913 *H* Jack Johnson (USA) D – 20 Jim Johnson (USA)

6 Dec 1915 *B* Kid Williams (Den) D – 20 Frankie Burns (USA)

7 Feb 1916 *B* Kid Williams (Den) D – 29 Pete Herman (USA)

23 Aug 1920 *W* Jack Britton (USA) D – 12 Lou Bogash (USA)

17 Feb 1922 *W* Jack Britton (USA) D – 15 Dave Shade (USA)

27 Aug 1925 *Fe* Louis 'Kid' Kaplan (USSR) D – 15 Babe Herman (Por)

26 Mar 1927 *B (NBA)* Bud Taylor (USA) D – 10 Tony Canzoneri (USA)

26 Dec 1930 *Fl* Frankie Genaro (USA) D – 15 Midget Wolgast (USA)

25 Mar 1931 *Fl (NBA)* Frankie Genaro (USA) D – 15 Victor Ferrand (Spa)

17 Mar 1933 *M (NY)* Ben Jeby (USA) D – 15 Vince Dundee (Ita)

5 Feb 1934 *LH* Maxie Rosenbloom (USA) D – 15 Joe Knight (USA)

5 Mar 1934 *LW* Barney Ross (USA) D – 10 Frankie Klick (USA)

18 Jun 1934 *Fl (IBU)* Jackie Brown (GB) D – 15 Valentin Angelmann (Fra)

15 Oct 1934 *M (NBA)* Marcel Thil (Fra) D – 15 Carmelo Candel (Fra)

1 Mar 1940 *M (NY)* Ceferino Garcia (Phi) D – 10 Henry Armstrong (USA)

4 Mar 1940 *B (NBA)* Georgie Pace (USA) D – 15 Lou Salica (USA)

30 Sep 1949 *Fl* Rinty Monaghan (GB) D – 15 Terry Allen (GB)

3 Sep 1955 *B (NY)* Robert Cohen (Alg) D – 15 Willie Toweel (SA)

20 Apr 1960 *M (NBA)* Gene Fullmer (USA) D – 15 Joey Giardello (USA)

3 Dec 1960 *M (NBA)* Gene Fullmer (USA) D – 15 Sugar Ray Robinson (USA)

21 Oct 1961 *LW* Duilio Loi (Ita) D – 15 Eddie Perkins (USA)

23 Feb 1963 *M* Dick Tiger (Ngr) D – 15 Gene Fullmer (USA)

30 Mar 1968 *JL* Hiroshi Kobayashi (Jap) D – 15 Rene Barrientos (Phi)

29 Apr 1971 *LM* Carmen Bossi (Ita) D – 15 Jose Hernandez (Spa)

11 Nov 1971 *Fe (WBC)* Kuniaki Shibata (Jap) D – 15 Ernesto Marcel (Pan)

20 Nov 1971 *Fl (WBC)* Erbito Salavarria (Phi) D – 15 Betulio Gonzalez (Ven)

Frenchman Laurent Dauthuille was ahead on all three scorecards with just 13 seconds of his 1950 world middleweight title fight with Jake La Motta (USA) remaining when La Motta knocked him out!

'The Merthyr Matchstick' — Johnny Owen. This picture was taken in September 1980 just before he set off for America to fight Lupe Pintor (Mex) for the world bantamweight title. Seven weeks later he died from injuries received during the fight. Syndication International

5 Sep 1972 *JL (WBA)* Ben Villaflor (Phi) D – 15 Victor Echegaray (Arg)

9 Jan 1973 *LM* Koichi Wajima (Jap) D – 15 Miguel de Oliveira (Bra)

14 Mar 1974 *JL (WBA)* Ben Villaflor (Phi) D – 15 Apollo Yoshio (Jap)

17 Jun 1974 *LH* Bob Foster (USA) D – 15 Jorge Ahumada (Arg)

12 Sep 1974 *L (WBC)* Guts Ishimatsu (Jap) D – 15 Arturo Pineda (USA)

20 Sep 1975 *JL (WBC)* Alfredo Escalera (PR) D – 15 Leonel Hernandez (Ven)

13 Apr 1976 *JL (WBA)* Ben Villaflor (Phi) D – 15 Sam Serrano (PR)

15 Mar 1977 *LM (WBC)* Eckhard Dagge (FRG) D – 15 Maurice Hope (Ant)

29 Jan 1979 *Fl (WBA)* Betulio Gonzalez (Ven) D – 15 Shoji Oguma (Jap)

31 Mar 1979 *LF (WBC)* Sung-Jun Kim (S. Kor) D – 15 Ray Melandez (Dom)

9 Sep 1979 *Fl (WBC)* Chan-Hee Park (S. Kor) D – 15 Miguel Canto (Mex)

30 Nov 1979 *M* Vito Antuofermo (Ita) D – 15 Marvin Hagler (USA)

8 Dec 1979 *C (WBC)* Marvin Camel (USA) D – 15 Mate Parlov (Yug)

11 Jun 1980 *B (WBC)* Lupe Pintor (Mex) D – 15 Eijiro Murata (Jap)

28 Jul 1980 *SF (WBC)* Rafael Orono (Ven) D – 15 Willie Jensen (USA)

4 Apr 1981 *B (WBA)* Jeff Chandler (USA) D – 15 Eijiro Murata (Jap)

4 Jul 1982 *SF (WBC)* Chul-Ho Kim (S. Kor) D – 15 Raul Valdez (Mex)

16 Oct 1982 *Fe (WBA)* Eusebio Pedroza (Pan) D – 15 Bernard Taylor (USA)

19 Mar 1983 *W (WBC)* Milton McCrory (USA) D – 12 Colin Jones (GB)

9 Apr 1983 *LF (WBA)* Katsuo Tokashiki (Jap) D – 15 Lupe Madera (Mex)

20 May 1983 *H (WBA)* Mike Dokes (USA) D – 15 Mike Weaver (USA)

22 Jun 1985 *Fl (WBC)* Sot Chitalada (Tha) D – 12 Gabriel Bernal (Mex)

27 Mar 1987 *JL (WBA)* Brian Mitchell (SA) D-15 Jose Rivera (PR)

15 Aug 1987 *Fl(WBA)* Fidel Bassa (Col) D–15 Hilario Zapata (Pan)

The following fighters have all been involved in three drawn world title fights: Abe Attell (USA) featherweight; Casper Leon (Ita) bantamweight; Gene Fullmer (USA) middleweight; Ben Villaflor (Phi) junior-lightweight.

The following are the only instances of fighters drawing with each other twice in world title fights: Jimmy Barry (USA) v. Casper Leon (Ita) bantamweight (30 May 1898 and 29 Dec 1898); Abe Attell (USA) v. Owen Moran (GB) featherweight (1 Jan 1908 and 7 Sep 1908).

Most knockdowns in world title fights

Figures in brackets indicate the number of times fighter was floored. Winners of each fight is first named man.

14 – Vic Toweel (SA–0) v. Danny O. Sullivan (GB–14) bantamweight: 2 Dec 1950
11 – Mike O'Dowd (USA–2) v. Al McCoy (USA–9) middleweight: 14 Nov 1917
11 – Jack Dempsey (USA–2) v. Luis 'Angel' Firpo (Arg–9) heavyweight: 14 Sep 1923
11 – Max Baer (USA–0) v. Primo Carnera (Ita–11) heavyweight: 14 Jun 1934
10 – Benny Lynch (GB–0) v. Jackie Brown (GB–10) flyweight: 9 Sep 1935
10 – Jimmy Carter (USA–0) v. Tommy Collins (USA–10) lightweight: 24 Apr 1953

Bill Ladbury (GB) floored Bill Smith (GB) 16 times in a flyweight bout in 1913 but the fight was not universally recognised as being for the world title.

Most knockdowns in single round

Figures in brackets indicate the number of times fighter was floored. Winner of each fight is first named man.

9 – Jack Dempsey (USA–2) v. Luis 'Angel' Firpo (Arg–7) heavyweight, 14 Sep 1923, round one
8 – Vic Toweel (SA–0) v. Danny O'Sullivan (GB–8) bantamweight, 2 Dec 1950, round five

Floyd Patterson (USA) was floored more times (17) than any other man in world heavyweight title fights.

Fatalities in world title fights

Since the first world title fight under Queensberry Rules in 1884, there have been over 2000 world title fights. The number of fatalities is few in comparison to that number, with just seven men losing their life as a result of injuries received during a world title bout. The following is a full list of such casualties (the fighter concerned appears first):

6 Dec 1897 Walter Croot (GB) v. Jimmy Barry (USA) bantamweight

24 Jun 1947 Jimmy Doyle (USA) v. Sugar Ray Robinson (USA) welterweight

Cuban boxer Sugar Ramos (right) seen here beating Nigerian Rafiu King. Ramos won the world featherweight title in 1963 by defeating Davey Moore (USA) who died two days after the fight. The Photo Source

24 Mar 1962 Benny Paret (Cuba)* v. Emile Griffith (VI) welterweight

21 Mar 1963 Davey Moore (USA)* v. Sugar Ramos (Cuba) featherweight

19 Sep 1980 Johnny Owen (GB) v. Lupe Pintor (Mex) WBC bantamweight

13 Nov 1982 Duk-Koo Kim (S. Kor) v. Ray Mancini (USA) WBA lightweight

31 Aug 1983 Kiko Bejines (Mex) v. Albert Davila (USA) WBC bantamweight
*Defending champion

Record Purses

Sugar Ray Leonard (USA) received a reported $11 million when he beat Thomas Hearns (USA) for the undisputed world welterweight title at Las Vegas on 16 Sep 1981. When he came out of retirement to beat Marvin Hagler (USA) for the WBC middleweight title at Las Vegas on 6 Apr 1987 he collected a cheque, reported to be 'not less' than $11 million. These are the two biggest purses received by one boxer.

First $100 000 purse

To Jack Johnson (USA) when he beat Jim Jeffries (USA) on 4 Jul 1910 in a heavyweight title bout. Johnson actually received $120 000.

First $1 million purse

Sonny Liston (USA) and Floyd Patterson (USA) each received $1 434 000 for their world heavyweight title fight on 22 July 1963 at Las Vegas.

First $5 million purse

Muhammad Ali (USA) and George Foreman (USA) each received $5 million for their heavyweight title fight in Kinshasa, Zaire, on 30 Oct 1974.

Record purse — pre-television era

The large purses paid to fighters these days are aided by television rights. The record purse in pre-television days was the $990 445 paid to Gene Tunney (USA) for his second meeting with Jack Dempsey (USA) on 22 Sep 1927.

Most world title fights on one bill

4 – Superdrome New Orleans, USA 15 September 1978 Muhammad Ali (USA) v. Leon Spinks (USA) H (WBA); Mike Rossman (USA) v. Victor Galindez (Arg) LH (WBA); Danny Lopez (USA) v. Juan Malvarez (Arg) Fe (WBC); Jorge Lujan (Pan) v. Albert Davila (USA) Fe (WBA)

Most on one day

5 – 19 November 1977 and 31 March 1980.

The first time two world title fights were contested on the same day

26 September 1894
Bob Fitzsimmons v. Dan Creedon (middleweight) New Orleans, USA
George Dixon v. Young Griffo (featherweight) Boston, USA

Most in one year

95 – 1986
90 – 1980
89 – 1984
85 – 1985
75 – 1981
72 – 1982
70 – 1976

Most pre-1946
30 – 1933
29 – 1931
27 – 1939
27 – 1941

Most pre-1919
18 – 1899
16 – 1908
12 – 1898

The following shows how the number of world title fights per year has increased over the years.

Year	No. of fights
1886	2
1896	3
1906	3
1916	10
1926	12
1936	16
1946	17
1956	11
1966	30
1976	70
1986	95

Just four world title fights have been held on Boxing Day (26 December)

1908 Jack Johnson v. Tommy Burns (heavyweight)
1930 Frankie Genaro v. Midget Wolgast (flyweight)
1933 Frankie Klich v. Kid Chocolate (junior-lightweight)
1986 Bobby Czyz v. David Sears (IBF light-heavyweight)

The champions

Oldest champions

48 years 59 days
Archie Moore (USA) light-heavyweight
(Moore may only have been 45, there is some dispute as to his date of birth. He maintained he was born in 1916, his mother maintained it was 1913.)

42 years 208 days
Bob Fitzsimmons (GB) light-heavyweight

Oldest fighters at time of winning world titles

40 years 183 days
Bob Fitzsimmons (GB) light-heavyweight

39 years 4 days
Archie Moore (USA) light-heavyweight

37 years 168 days
Jersey Joe Walcott (USA) heavyweight
(Held title until 38 years 235 days)

Youngest champions

17 years 176 days
Wilfred Benitez (USA) light-welterweight

18 years 203 days
Pipino Cuevas (Mex) WBA welterweight

18 years 352 days
Tony Canzoneri (USA) featherweight

The youngest world heavyweight champion was Mike Tyson (GB) — 20 years 145 days when he won the WBC title.

Heaviest world champions (all heavyweights)

270lb – Primo Carnera (Ita), 1 Mar 1934
240lb – John Tate (USA), 20 Oct 1979
239½lb – Greg Page (USA), 29 Apr 1984
235lb – Tim Witherspoon (USA) 20 Jul 1986
230lb – Jess Willard (USA), 5 Apr 1915
230lb – Muhammad Ali (USA), 30 Apr 1976
232lb – Mike Weaver (USA), 31 Mar 1980

The heaviest unsuccessful challenger in a world heavyweight contest was Abe Simon (USA) who weighed 255½lb when he challenged Joe Louis in 1942.

Greatest weight difference in world heavyweight title bout

86lb – Primo Carnera (Ita) 270lb v. Tommy Loughran (USA) 184lb, 1 Mar 1934
58lb – Jack Dempsey (USA) 187lb v. Jess Willard (USA) 245lb, 4 Jul 1919
53¾ – Max Baer (USA) 209½lb v. Primo Carnera (Ita) 263¼lb, 14 Jun 1934
52½lb – Joe Louis (USA) 202lb v. Abe Simon (USA) 254½lb, 21 Mar 1941

Greatest tonnage in one world title bout

488¾lb – Primo Carnera (Ita) 259½lb v. Paulino Uzcudun (Spa) 229¼lb, 22 Oct 1933
472¾lb – Max Baer (USA) 209½lb v. Primo Carnera (Ita) 263¼lb, 14 Jun 1934
465½lb – Larry Holmes (USA) 211lb v. Leroy Jones (USA) 254½lb, 31 Mar 1980

Lightest world champions

96lb – Jimmy Wilde (GB) flyweight
106lb – Pascual Perez (Arg) flyweight
106½lb – Freddie Castillo (Mex) WBA light-flyweight

The lightest world heavyweight champion was Bob Fitzsimmons (GB). He weighed 167lb.

The lightest challenger in a world heavyweight contest was Charley Mitchell (GB) who weighed 158lb when he challenged James J. Corbett on 25 January 1894.

Tallest world champions (all heavyweights)

6ft 6¼in – Jess Willard (USA)
6ft 6in – Ernie Terrell (USA)
6ft 5¾in – Primo Carnera (Ita)
6ft 5in – Tony Tucker (USA)
6ft 4in – James Smith (USA)
6ft 4in – John Tate (USA)
6ft 3½in – Larry Holmes (USA)
6ft 3in – Muhammad Ali (USA)
6ft 3in – George Foreman (USA)
6ft 3in – Ken Norton (USA)
6ft 3in – Michael Dokes (USA)
6ft 3in – Tim Witherspoon (USA)
6ft 3in – Pinklon Thomas (USA)
6ft 3in – Greg Page (USA)

Shortest world champions

4ft 11in – Netrnoi Vorasingh (Tha) WBC light-flyweight
4ft 11½in – Pascual Perez (Arg) flyweight
4ft 11¾in – Johnny Coulon (Can) bantamweight

Shortest world heavyweight champions:
5ft 7in – Tommy Burns (Can)
5ft 10¼in – Rocky Marciano (USA)

Tommy Burns of Canada who engaged in seven world heavyweight title fights in 1908. He won the first six and then lost his title to Jack Johnson (USA) on Boxing Day. Syndication International

Venues

Most widely used for world title fights

183 – Madison Square Garden, New York
54 – Caesar's Palace, Las Vegas
30 – Yankee Stadium, New York
27 – Polo Grounds, New York

Leading British venues for world title fights

21 – Wembley Pool, London
20 – National Sporting Club, London
7 – Belle Vue, Manchester
6 – Royal Albert Hall, London
(many of the bouts at the NSC were not universally regarded as being world title fights)

Seven British football league grounds have been used to stage world title fights: Anfield Park, Liverpool FC (twice); Ibrox Stadium, Glasgow Rangers FC; Hampden Park, Queen's Park FC (twice); Highbury Stadium, Arsenal FC; Loftus Road, Queen's Park Rangers FC; Ninian Park, Cardiff City FC (twice); Shawfield Park, Clyde FC (twice).

Referees

Referees who have officiated in the most world heavyweight title fights

14 – Arthur Donovan (1933–46)
12 – Mills Lane (1978–)
7 – Ruby Goldstein (1947–59)
7 – Arthur Mercante (1960–76)

Former world champions who have refereed world heavyweight title fights

Mushy Callahan (USA)
1958 Floyd Patterson v. Roy Harris

Georges Carpentier (Fra)
1914 Jack Johnson v. Frank Moran (Carpentier was only 20 at the time!)

James J. Jeffries (USA)
1905 Marvin Hart v. Jack Root
1906 Tommy Burns v. Philadelphia Jack O'Brien
1907 Tommy Burns v. Bill Squires

Tommy Loughran (USA)
1957 Floyd Patterson v. Pete Rademacher

Jersey Joe Walcott (USA)
1961 Floyd Patterson v. Tom McNeeley
1965 Muhammad Ali v. Sonny Liston

Managers

Manager of most world champions

6 – Jack 'Doc' Kearns (USA)
He managed the following American world champions: Jack Dempsey (heavyweight), Joey Maxim (light-heavyweight), Archie Moore (light-heavyweight), Mickey Walker (middleweight), Benny Leonard (lightweight), Abe Attell (featherweight).

Manager of two world heavyweight champions

William A. Brady (USA) is the only person to have managed two world heavyweight champions — James J. Corbett and James J. Jeffries (both USA). The pair of them, incidentally, met for the world title on two occasions.

Doc Kearns (USA) (right) managed a record six world champions. He is seen here with one of them, Joey Maxim (USA). The Photo Source

Terry Lawless, the most successful British trainer, seen with one of his many champions, Frank Bruno. Syndication International

Trainers

Trainer of most world champions

Angelo Dundee (USA) has been, by far, the sport's most successful trainer. In his 40-year career he has been connected with no fewer than nine American world champions: Carmen Basilio (welterweight), Willie Pastrano (light-heavyweight), Ralph Dupas (light-middleweight), Luis Rodriguez (welterweight), Sugar Ramos (featherweight), Muhammad Ali (heavyweight), Jimmy Ellis (heavyweight), Jose Napoles (welterweight), Sugar Ray Leonard (welterweight).

Most successful British trainer

Terry Lawless holds the record, having trained four world champions: Maurice Hope (junior-middleweight), John H. Stracey (welterweight), Jim Watt (lightweight), Charlie Magri (flyweight).

The Heavyweight Champions

The following are career details of all world heavyweight champions. The weights indicated are the heaviest weight at which each man contested a world title fight. All details are correct as at August 1987.

James J. Corbett
Born: 1 Sep 1866 San Francisco, California, USA
Died: 18 Feb 1933 Bayside, New York, USA
Height: 6ft 1in   Weight: 190lb
Champion: 7 Sep 1892–17 Mar 1897   duration: 4 years 191 days
Heavyweight title fights: 5   won: 2   lost: 3
Career bouts: 19   won: 11 (KO–7)   drew: 2   ND/NC: 2   lost: 4

Bob Fitzsimmons
Born: 26 May 1863 Helston, Cornwall, England
Died: 22 Oct 1917 Chicago, Illinois, USA
Height: 6ft 0in   Weight: 172lb
Champion: 17 Mar 1897–9 Jun 1899   duration: 2 years 84 days
Heavyweight title fights: 3   won: 1   lost: 2
Career bouts: 62   won: 40 (KO–32) ND/NC: 11   lost: 11

James J. Jeffries
Born: 15 Apr 1875 Carroll, Ohio, USA
Died: 3 Mar 1953 Burbank, California, USA
Height: 6ft 2in   Weight: 220lb
Champion: 9 Jun 1899–13 May 1903   duration: 5 years 338 days
Heavyweight title fights: 9   won: 8   lost: 1
Career bouts: 21   won: 18 (KO–15)   drew: 2   lost: 1

Marvin Hart
Born: 16 Sep 1876 Jefferson County, Kentucky, USA
Died: 17 Sep 1931 Fern Creek, Kentucky, USA
Height: 5ft 11in   Weight: 190lb
Champion: 3 Jul 1905–23 Feb 1906   duration: 235 days
Heavyweight title fights: 2   won: 1   lost: 1
Career bouts: 47   won: 28 (KO–19)   drew: 4   ND/NC: 8   lost: 7

The greatest? Jack Dempsey (USA), who held the world heavyweight title from July 1919 to September 1926. The Photo Source

Tommy Burns
Born: 17 Jun 1881 Ontario, Canada
Died: 10 May 1955 Vancouver, Canada
Height: 5ft 7in   Weight: 184lb
Champion: 23 Feb 1906–26 Dec 1908   duration: 2 years
   306 days
Heavyweight title fights: 13   won: 11   drew: 1   lost: 1
Career bouts: 60   won: 46 (KO–36)   drew: 8   ND/NC: 1
   lost: 5

Jack Johnson
Born: 31 Mar 1878 Galveston, Texas, USA
Died: 10 Jun 1946 Raleigh, North Carolina, USA
Height: 6ft 1in   Weight: 221lb

Champion: 26 Dec 1908–5 Apr 1915   duration: 6 years
   110 days
Heavyweight title fights: 11   won: 5   drew: 1   ND: 4   lost: 1
Career bouts: 112   won: 78 (KO–45)   drew: 12   ND/NC: 14
   lost: 8

Jess Willard
Born: 29 Dec 1881 Pottawatomie County, Kansas, USA
Died: 15 Dec 1968 Los Angeles, California, USA
Height: 6ft 6¼in   Weight: 245lb
Champion: 5 Apr 1915–4 Jul 1919   duration: 4 years
   90 days
Heavyweight title fights: 3   won: 1   ND:1   lost: 1
Career bouts: 35   won: 24 (KO–21)   drew: 1   ND/NC: 4
   lost: 6

Jack Dempsey
Born: 24 Jun 1895 Manassa, Colorado, USA
Died: 31 May 1983 New York, USA
Height: 6ft 0in   Weight: 192lb
Champion: 4 Jul 1919–23 Sep 1926   duration: 7 years
   81 days
Heavyweight title fights: 8   won: 6   lost: 2
Career bouts: 78   won: 62 (KO–49)   drew: 10   lost: 6

Gene Tunney
Born: 25 May 1897 New York, USA
Died: 7 Nov 1978 Greenwich, Connecticut, USA
Height: 6ft 0in   Weight: 192lb
Champion: 23 Sep 1926–2 Aug 1928   duration: 1 year
   314 days
Heavyweight title fights: 3   won: 3   lost: 0
Career bouts: 83   won: 77 (KO–45)   drew: 3   ND/NC: 2
   lost: 1

Max Schmeling
Born: 28 Sep 1905 Brandenburg, Germany
Height: 6ft 1in   Weight: 189lb
Champion: 12 Jun 1930–21 Jun 1932   duration: 2 years
   9 days
Heavyweight title fights: 4   won: 2   lost: 2
Career bouts: 70   won: 56 (KO–38)   drew: 4   lost: 10

Jack Sharkey
Born: 26 Oct 1902 Binghampton, New York, USA
Height: 6ft 0in   Weight: 205lb
Champion: 21 Jun 1932–29 Jun 1933   duration: 1 year
   8 days
Heavyweight title fights: 3   won: 1   lost: 2
Career bouts: 55   won: 38 (KO–14)   drew: 3   ND/NC: 1
   lost: 13

Primo Carnera
Born: 26 Oct 1906 Sequals, Italy
Died: 29 Jun 1967 Sequals, Italy
Height: 6ft 5¾in   Weight: 270lb
Champion: 29 Jun 1933–14 June 1934   duration: 350 days
Heavyweight title fights: 4   won: 3   lost: 1
Career bouts: 103   won: 88 (KO–69)   ND/NC: 1   lost: 14

Max Baer
Born: 11 Feb 1909 Omaha, Nebraska, USA
Died: 21 Nov 1949 Hollywood, California, USA
Height 6ft 2in   Weight: 209lb
Champion: 14 Jun 1934–13 Jun 1935   duration: 364 days
Heavyweight title fights: 2   won: 1   lost: 1
Career bouts: 83   won: 70 (KO–52)   lost: 13

James J. Braddock
Born: 7 Jun 1906 New York, USA
Died: 29 Nov 1974 North Bergen, New Jersey, USA
Height: 6ft 3in   Weight: 197lb

Ezzard Charles (USA) had more professional fights, 122, than any other world heavyweight champion. The Photo Source

Champion: 13 Jun 1935–22 June 1937   duration: 2 years
   9 days
Heavyweight title fights: 2   won: 1   lost: 1
Career bouts: 86   won: 46 (KO–27)   drew: 4   ND/NC: 13
   lost: 23

Joe Louis
Born: 13 May 1914 Lafayette, Alabama, USA
Died: 12 Apr 1981 Las Vegas, Nevada, USA
Height: 6ft 1in   Weight: 218lb
Champion: 22 Jun 1937–1 Mar 1949   duration: 11 years
   252 days
Heavyweight title fights: 27   won: 26   lost: 1
Career bouts: 66   won: 63 (KO–49)   lost: 3

Ezzard Charles
Born: 7 Jul 1921 Lawrenceville, Georgia, USA
Died: 27 May 1975 Chicago, Illinois, USA
Height: 6ft 0in   Weight: 192lb
Champion: 22 Jun 1949–18 Jul 1951   duration: 2 years
   26 days
Heavyweight title fights: 13   won: 9   lost: 4
Career bouts: 122   won: 96 (KO–58)   drew: 1   lost: 25

Jersey Joe Walcott
Born: 31 Jan 1914 Merchantville, New Jersey, USA
Height: 6ft 0in   Weight: 197lb
Champion: 18 Jul 1951–23 Sep 1952   duration: 1 year
   67 days
Heavyweight title fights: 7   won: 2   lost: 5
Career bouts: 69   won: 50 (KO–30)   drew: 1   lost: 18

Rocky Marciano
Born: 1 Sep 1923 Brockton, Massachusetts, USA
Died: 31 Aug 1969 Newton, Iowa, USA
Height: 5ft 10¼in   Weight: 189lb
Champion: 23 Sep 1952–27 Apr 1956   duration: 3 years
   217 days
Heavyweight title fights: 7   won: 7   lost: 0
Career bouts: 49   won: 49 (KO–43)

Marciano (left) showing power and determination against Roland La Starza (USA) during their world heavyweight title bout at New York in 1953. Marciano retained his title with an 11th-round knock-out. The Photo Source

Floyd Patterson
Born: 4 Jan 1935 Waco, North Carolina, USA
Height: 5ft 11in   Weight: 194lb
Champion: 30 Nov 1956–26 Jun 1959
   20 Jun 1960–25 Sep 1962
   duration (1st reign): 2 years 208 days
      (2nd) reign): 2 years 97 days
      (total): 4 years 305 days
Heavyweight title fights: 13   won: 8   lost: 5
Career bouts: 64   won: 55 (KO–40)   drew: 1   lost: 8

Ingemar Johansson
Born: 16 Oct 1932 Gothenburg, Sweden

Moore is counted out in the ninth round of his world heavyweight title fight against Rocky Marciano (USA) in 1955. This was the first of two attempts light-heavyweight champion Moore had at the heavyweight crown. UPI/ Bettmann Newsphotos

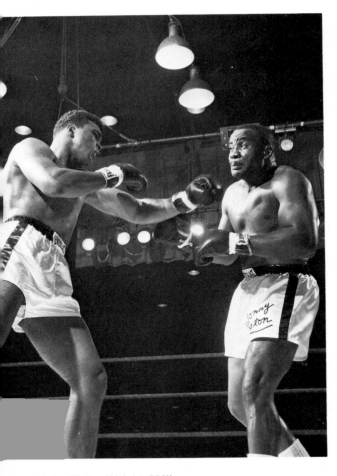

(Left) *Cassius Clay (left) in the sixth round of his first world title fight with Sonny Liston (USA). Liston failed to come out for the next round, giving the title to the 22-year-old Clay. This was Clay's only world title fight under his real name.* UPI/ Bettmann Newsphotos

Heavyweight title fights: 4 won: 3 lost: 1
Career bouts: 55 won: 46 (KO–21) lost: 9

Joe Frazier
Born: 12 Jan 1944 Beaufort, South Carolina, USA
Height: 5ft 11in Weight: 217lb
Champion: 4 Mar 1968–22 Jan 1973 duration: 4 years 324 days
Heavyweight title fights: 12 won: 10 lost: 2
Career bouts: 37 won: 32 (KO–27) drew: 1 lost: 4

Jimmy Ellis
Born: 24 Feb 1940 Louisville, Kentucky, USA
Height: 6ft 1in Weight: 201lb
Champion: 27 Apr 1968–16 Feb 1970 duration: 1 year 295 days
Heavyweight title fights: 3 won: 2 lost: 1
Career bouts: 53 won: 40 (KO–24) drew: 1 lost: 12

George Foreman
Born: 22 Jan 1948 Marshall, Texas, USA
Height: 6ft 3in Weight: 224lb
Champion: 22 Jan 1973–30 Oct 1974 duration: 1 year 281 days
Heavyweight title fights: 4 won: 3 lost: 1
Career bouts: 49 won: 47 (KO–44) lost: 2

Leon Spinks
Born: 11 Jul 1953 St Louis, Missouri, USA
Height: 6ft 1in Weight: 201lb
Champion: 15 Feb–15 Sep 1978 duration: 212 days
Heavyweight title fights: 3 won: 1 lost: 2
Career bouts: 27 won: 17 (KO–11) drew: 2 lost: 8

Ken Norton
Born: 9 Aug 1943 Jacksonville, Illinois, USA
Height: 6ft 3in Weight: 220lb
Champion: 29 Mar–9 Jun 1978 (never won title, proclaimed champion by the WBC) duration: 72 days
Heavyweight title fights: 3 won: 0 lost: 3
Career bouts: 50 won: 42 (KO–33) drew: 1 lost: 7

Larry Holmes
Born: 3 Nov 1949 Cuthbert, Georgia, USA
Height: 6ft 3½in Weight: 223lb
Champion: 9 Jun 1978–21 Sep 1985 duration: 7 years 104 days
Heavyweight title fights: 23 won: 21 lost: 2
Career bouts: 50 won: 48 (KO–34) lost: 2

Height: 6ft 0in Weight: 206lb
Champion: 26 Jun 1959–20 Jun 1960 duration: 360 days
Heavyweight title fights: 3 won: 1 lost: 2
Career bouts: 28 won: 26 (KO–17) lost: 2

Sonny Liston
Born: 8 May 1932 St Francis County, Arkansas, USA
Died: 30 Dec 1970 Las Vegas, Nevada, USA
Height: 6ft 1in Weight: 218lb
Champion: 25 Sep 1962–25 Feb 1964 duration: 1 year 153 days
Heavyweight title fights: 4 won: 2 lost: 2
Career bouts: 54 won: 50 (KO–39) lost: 4

Muhammad Ali
Born: 17 Jan 1942 Louisville, Kentucky, USA
Height: 6ft 3in Weight: 230lb
Champion: 25 Feb 1964–28 Apr 1967
　　　　　30 Oct 1974–15 Feb 1978
　　　　　15 Sep 1978–22 Jun 1979
duration: (1st reign): 3 years 63 days
　　　　　(2nd reign): 3 years 108 days
　　　　　(3rd reign): 284 days
　　　　　(total): 7 years 90 days
Heavyweight title fights: 25 won: 22 lost: 3
Career bouts: 61 won: 56 (KO–37) lost: 5

Ernie Terrell
Born: 4 Apr 1939 Chicago, Illinois, USA
Height: 6ft 6in Weight: 212lb
Champion: 5 Mar 1965–6 Feb 1967 duration: 1 year 343 days

Jean Terrell, sister of WBA heavyweight champion Ernie Terrell (USA), was a member of the famous Supremes pop group. She replaced Diana Ross in 1970.

John Tate
Born: 29 Jan 1955 Marion City, Arkansas, USA
Height: 6ft 4in Weight: 240lb
Champion: 20 Oct 1979–31 Mar 1980 duration: 162 days
Heavyweight title fights: 2 won: 1 lost: 1
Career bouts: 32 won: 30 (KO–21) lost: 2

Mike Weaver
Born: 14 Jun 1952 Gatesville, Texas, USA
Height: 6ft 1in Weight: 232lb
Champion: 31 Mar 1980–10 Dec 1982 duration: 2 years
254 days
Heavyweight title fights: 7 won: 3 drew: 1 lost: 3
Career bouts: 42 won: 29 (KO–20) drew: 1 lost: 12

Mike Dokes
Born: 10 Aug 1958 Akron, Ohio, USA
Height: 6ft 3in Weight: 223lb
Champion: 10 Dec 1982–23 Sep 1983 duration: 287 days
Heavyweight title fights: 3 won: 1 drew: 1 lost: 1
Career bouts: 31 won: 28 (KO–15) drew: 2 lost: 1

Gerrie Coetzee
Born: 4 Aug 1955 Boxsburg, Transvaal, South Africa
Height: 6ft 3in Weight: 226lb
Champion: 23 Sep 1983–1 Dec 1984 duration: 1 year
69 days
Heavyweight title fights: 4 won: 1 lost: 3
Career bouts: 35 won: 30 (KO–18) drew: 1 lost: 4

Tim Witherspoon
Born: 27 Dec 1957 Philadelphia, Pennsylvania, USA
Height: 6ft 3in Weight: 220lb
Champion: (1st reign) 9 Mar–31 Aug 1984 duration: 175
days (2nd reign) 17 Jan 1986 current WBA champion
Heavyweight title fights: 6 won: 3 lost: 3
Career bouts: 29 won: 26 (KO–18) lost: 3

Pinklon Thomas
Born: 10 Feb 1958 Pontiac, Michigan, USA
Height: 6ft 3in Weight: 216lb
Champion: 31 Aug 1984–current WBC champion
Heavyweight title fights: 4 won: 2 lost: 2
Career bouts: 31 won: 28 (KO–22) drew: 1 lost: 2

Greg Page
Born: 25 Oct 1958 Louisville, Kentucky, USA
Height: 6ft 3in Weight: 239½lb

Champion: 1 Dec 1984–29 Apr 1985 duration: 150 days
Heavyweight title fights: 3 won: 1 lost: 2
Career bouts: 33 won: 27 (KO–20) lost: 6

Tony Tubbs
Born: 15 Feb 1958 Cincinatti, Ohio, USA
Height: 6ft 3in Weight: 229lb
Champion: 29 Apr 1985–17 Jan 1986 duration: 263 days
Heavyweight title fights: 2 won: 1 lost: 1
Career bouts: 24 won: 23 (KO–14) lost: 1

Michael Spinks
Born: 13 Jul 1956 St Louis, Missouri, USA
Height: 6ft 2in Weight: 200lb
Champion: 21 Sep 1985–current IBF champion
Heavyweight title fights: 3 won: 3
Career bouts: 31 won: 31 (KO–21) lost: 0

Trevor Berbick
Born: 1 Aug 1952, Jamacia
Height: 6ft 3in Weight: 217lb
Champion: 22 Mar 1986–22 Nov 1986 duration: 245 days
Heavyweight title fights: 2 won: 1 lost: 1
Career bouts: 37 won: 31 (KO–23) lost: 5 drew: 1

Mike Tyson
Born: 30 Jun 1966, Brooklyn, New York, USA
Height: 5ft 11½in Weight: 219lb
Champion: 22 Nov 1986 – current undisputed champion
(Won WBC title 22 Nov 1986, WBA/WBC 7 Mar 1987,
Undisputed 2 Aug 1987)
Heavyweight title fights: 4 won: 4 lost: 0
Career bouts: 31 won: 31 (KO–27) lost: 0

James Smith
Born: 3 Apr 1954, Fayetville, North Carolina, USA
Height: 6ft 4in Weight: 228½lb
Champion: 12 Dec 1986–7 Mar 1987 duration: 84 days
Heavyweight title fights: 2 won: 1 lost: 1
Career bouts: 25 won: 19 (KO–14) lost: 6

Tony Tucker
Born: 28 Dec 1958, Grand Rapids, Michigan, USA
Height: 6ft 5in Weight: 221lb
Champion: 30 May 1987–2 Aug 1987 duration: 64 days
Heavyweight title fights: 2 won: 1 lost: 1
Career bouts: 36 won: 34 (KO–30) lost: 1 ND: 1

Madison Square Garden, New York, has seen many great occasions, and many great fighters. One of the greatest of them all was Muhammad Ali (USA) seen here suffering his first professional defeat, by 'Smokin' Joe Frazier (USA) in 1971. The Photo Source

The Queensberry Rules

John Sholto Douglas, the Eighth Marquess of Queensberry, is regarded as the 'Patron Saint' of boxing. His Queensberry Rules are the most famous piece of sporting legislation ever created.

A champion amateur lightweight, Douglas is known only to most people because of his boxing connections. But his first love was horses.

An expert horseman, he enjoyed riding with the hounds. He was also a first-class steeplechase jockey, proudly boasting that he completed the Grand National course every time he rode. That claim may have little credence because it was never made clear how many times he competed!

One horse that provided him with many National Hunt rules winners was 1886 Grand National winner Old Joe. The Marquess was scheduled to ride him in the big race, but it was felt that in view of his age (he was over 40 at the time) a younger, more experienced jockey should be brought in. Professional Tom Skelton was given the mount and duly won at 25–1!

George Stephenson, inventor of The Rocket, *once engaged in a prize-fight. It was against Ned Nelson at Newcastle upon Tyne: Stephenson won.*

Douglas' involvement in boxing started in his Cambridge University days. He spent a lot of time in London, and became a member of the Pelican Club, a famous sporting club of the day.

He left the 30 000-acre family home in Dumfriesshire and moved to the capital. The move, which was to boxing's ultimate advantage, hit the family fortune because the estate reduced considerably to maintain his lavish lifestyle!

Douglas, with his racing connections, felt a need to raise the standard of the noble art, just as the Jockey Club had done for horse racing. So, just after the end of the American Civil War, Douglas, and Salford-born John Chambers, a former lightweight champion of England and former Cambridge colleague, set sail for America. Their objective was to study prize-ring conditions and compare them with those in Britain.

When they returned they drew up the now famous Queensberry Rules. That was in 1867 and Douglas, just 22 years of age, had been successful in getting fighters both sides of the Atlantic to adopt his new code of rules.

The Eighth Marquess of Queensberry died in 1900 and, although he had given away a large part of the family estate, he had given boxing a legacy that is still honoured today, although his original rules have been slightly altered over the years.

Boxing's first set of rules as drawn up by Jack Broughton (GB) in 1743; it was over one hundred years later before the 8th Marquess of Queensberry drew up his now famous rules.
Mary Evans Picture Library

The Original Queensberry Rules

Rule 1. To be a fair stand-up boxing match in a twenty-four foot ring or as near that size as practicable.

Rule 2. No wrestling or hugging allowed.

Rule 3. The rounds to be of three minutes duration and one minute time between rounds.

Rule 4. If either man fall through weakness or otherwise, he must get up unassisted, ten seconds to be allowed him to do so, the other man meanwhile to return to his corner; and when the fallen man is on his legs the round to be resumed and continued till the three minutes have expired. If one man fails to come to the scratch in the ten seconds allowed, it shall be in the power of the referee to give his award in favour of the other man.

Rule 5. A man hanging on the ropes in a helpless state, with his toes off the ground, shall be considered down.

Rule 6. No seconds or any other person to be allowed in the ring during the rounds.

Rule 7. Should the contest be stopped by any unavoidable interference, the referee to name the time and place as soon as possible for finishing the contest, so that the match must be won and lost, unless the backers of the men agree to draw the stakes.

Rule 8. The gloves to be fair-sized boxing gloves of the best quality and new.

Rule 9. Should a glove burst, or come off, it must be replaced to the referee's satisfaction.

Rule 10. A man on one knee is considered down, and if struck is entitled to the stakes.

Rule 11. No shoes or boots with springs allowed.

Rule 12. The contest in all other respects to be governed by the revised rules of the London Prize Ring.

The first champion— James Figg

James Figg (or Fig as he was also known) was not only the first boxing champion, but he can also claim to be the first boxing coach, manager and promoter.

A master exponent of the cudgel and broadsword, he opened his school of arms at his amphitheatre on the corner of Tottenham Court Road and Oxford Road (now Oxford Street), London in 1719.

Figg was shrewd. As well as having the ability

Figg had his business card designed for him by one of the leading artists of the day, William Hogarth. Mary Evans Picture Library

to fight, he sought the services of one of the country's leading artists of the day — William Hogarth — to design a business card for him to promote his new arms school. It was Hogarth who painted 'Southwark Fair' in which Figg is depicted taking on all-comers in the boxing booth.

The ornate business card advertised the services offered by Figg at his amphitheatre and royalty regularly attended sword and single-stick exercises under his guidance.

Born at Thame, on the Oxfordshire/Buckinghamshire border, in 1695, he defeated Ned Sutton from Gravesend to claim the English title in 1720. The pair had met on two earlier occasions, winning one contest each, but they were classed as cudgel matches. Figg held the title until retiring undefeated in 1730.

Figg helped develop many young fighters at his amphitheatre. Two were George Taylor and Jack Broughton and they both succeeded Figg as champion. Broughton has his own place in boxing history as the man responsible for drawing up boxing's first set of rules in 1743. He was also the inventor of the gloves four years later.

Figg, the first public champion and 'Father of the Ring', died on 8 December 1740. The Figg legend continued long after his death. His grandson Jack Slack became champion in 1750 (defeating Broughton) and he was to remain champion for ten years.

Jimmy Wilde

Pound-for-pound, Jimmy Wilde was one of the best fighters ever to have been crowned world champion. Nicknamed the 'Mighty Atom', the 'Tylorstown Terror' and the 'Ghost with a hammer in his hand', Wilde held the flyweight title for a record seven years four months.

Tylorstown, a mining area of Wales around Pontypridd, was a tough place to live and it was from that background that Wilde became a great world champion.

Standing just over 5ft 2in and rarely fighting at more than 100lb, his first title was the European flyweight title which he won in 1914 at the expense of Frenchman Eugene Husson with a sixth-round knock-out.

His first British title did not come until 1916 when he knocked out the defending champion Joe Symonds in the 11th round. Within two months of winning the British title, Wilde had claimed the world flyweight title after beating American Johnny Rosner. Later that year he was universally acknowledged as the first world flyweight champion after knocking out Young Zulu Kid (USA) in the first bout to be held at London's Holborn Stadium.

One more title defence followed, against Englishman George Clark in 1917, before Wilde went into virtual retirement. In 1923, at the age of 31, he ended the 'retirement' to fight Filipino Pancho Villa for the world title. The nine-year gap was too much for Wilde and he was battered to defeat in seven rounds. That ended the 'Mighty Atom's' fighting career and, although he had only contested three officially recognized world flyweight titles, he held the title for a record length of time.

Wilde engaged in well over 800 bouts in his career, including fairground booth fights, losing just six. He died, in his native Wales, in 1969 just two months short of his 77th birthday. A broken man, he spent the last four years of his life in hospital, and was unaware that his wife had died two years before he did.

Jimmy Wilde relaxing at home in Wales with his wife and children. This picture was taken in 1921; he had only one more fight after it was taken. That was in 1923 when he lost his world flyweight title to Pancho Villa (Phi). BBC Hulton Picture Library

CAREER HIGHLIGHTS

Professional bouts:	153
Won:	132
Drew:	2
Lost:	6
No decision:	13

His 132 wins included a British-record 101 knock-outs.

Jimmy Wilde (left) beats Memphis Pal Moore in 1919, which avenged a third-round defeat the previous year. Syndication International

Joe Louis

A credit to the sport both in and out of the ring, Joe Louis reigned supreme as heavyweight champion of the world from 1937 to 1949 during which time he made a record 25 defences of his title.

The son of an Alabama cotton-picker, Joseph Louis Barrow was born in 1914. At the age of 20 he was beaten by Max Marek in the National Amateur Championships and after that defeat he decided to turn professional under managers John Roxborough and Julian Black.

His first professional fight was in Chicago on 4 July 1934 (Independence Day) when he knocked out Jack Kracken (USA) in the first round. The following year he came to prominence following knock-out wins over former world champions Primo Carnera (Ita) and Max Baer (USA). The win over Carnera was at the Yankee Stadium, the first of Louis's

CAREER HIGHLIGHTS
Professional bouts: 66
 Won: 63
 Lost: 3
The only men to defeat Louis were:
1936 Max Schmeling (KO—12)
1950 Ezzard Charles (PTS—15) – title fight
1951 Rocky Marciano (KO—8)

28 fights in New York. A win over another former champion, Jack Sharkey, in 1936, set up his first world title shot the following year.

Joe took the title at the first attempt when he came back from being floored early in the fight to beat James J. Braddock with an eighth-round knock-out.

In Louis' next 25 world title fights only three men took him the distance: Welshman Tommy Farr, American Jersey Joe Walcott and Chilean Arturo Godoy.

During the war years he served as a sergeant in the army and, apart from exhibition bouts which entertained troops in the United States and Britain, was inactive between 1942 and 1946. He did have two world title fights in 1942, before he joined the army, and donated both his purses to the army and navy relief funds. He returned to championship fighting in 1946 with an 8th-round win over Billy Conn (USA). Louis announced his retirement in March 1949 but made a comeback the

Joe Louis being watched by many young admirers at his training camp for his world title comeback against Ezzard Charles (USA) in 1950. The youngsters saw their idol lose his first-ever world title fight when he lost on points. The Photo Source

following year to challenge Ezzard Charles (USA) for the heavyweight title. He lost on points, thus suffering the second defeat of his career. His last fight was on 26 October 1951 when he was knocked out by future champion Rocky Marciano.

Joe Louis – 'The Brown Bomber' — died at Las Vegas on 12 April 1981. The best tribute paid to him came from Muhammed Ali, who said: 'I idolized him. I just give lip service to being the greatest. He *was* the greatest.'

(Right) *Thirty-seven years of age and nearing the end of his career, Joe Louis was still too good for Lee Savold (USA) in 1951, knocking him out in the 6th round.* The Photo Source

(Opposite) *Louis' last successful defence of his world title was against Jersey Joe Walcott (USA) in 1948. A powerful right stuns Walcott.* The Photo Source

93

Sugar Ray Robinson

(b. 1921)

One of the most skilful boxers of the 20th century, Sugar Ray Robinson had great speed, style and the ability to box with both hands. And his mastery of the defensive art meant that, after his 25-year professional career, he left the sport with an unblemished face.

Born as Walker Smith in Detroit in 1921, he enjoyed a very successful amateur career

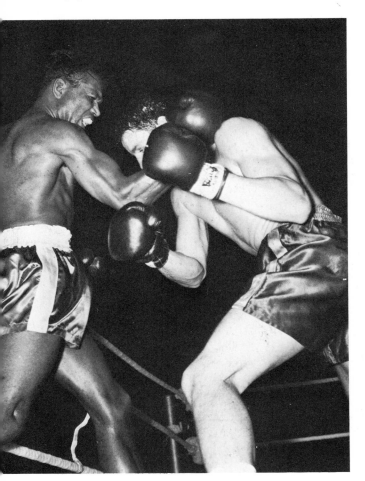

winning all 85 of his bouts, including two Golden Gloves titles.

He turned professional in 1940 and was victorious in his first 40 professional fights, but he came unstuck in number 41 when he was outpointed by Jake La Motta (USA) in 1943. Clearly the taste of defeat did not suit Robinson because he followed that reverse with 91 unbeaten bouts. Incidentally he subsequently overcame La Motta four times. Sweet revenge indeed.

In between, Robinson had won the world welterweight crown in December 1946 — beating Tommy Bell. And in 1951 he beat La Motta to win the middleweight title. The 92-win run ended on Robinson's European tour later that year.

Not fully fit he agreed, perhaps foolishly, to meet Randolph Turpin (GB) for the world title in London — just nine days after fighting in Italy.

Turpin took the crown from Robinson but, 64 days later, at New York's Polo Grounds, Robinson regained his title after a bruising affair.

Trying to emulate Bob Fitzsimmons and Henry Armstrong's feat of winning three different world titles, he challenged Joey Maxim (USA) for the light-heavyweight title in June 1952. The intense heat beat Robinson who, when well on top, had to retire at the end of the 13th round. He did better than referee Ruby Goldstein — he retired at the end of the tenth round!

Six months later Robinson announced his retirement to pursue a stage career. Fortunately

Although he appears to be on top, 41-year-old Robinson lost this ten-round contest to Britain's Terry Downes in 1962. Syndication International

94

for boxing, the new career was not very successful and after two years away from the ring Sugar Ray was back. Six fights after his return he had won the world middleweight title for the third time when he beat Carl 'Bobo' Olson in two rounds.

Aged 36, he subsequently lost and re-won the title against Gene Fullmer (USA). He performed the same feat against Carmen Basilio (USA), to win the title for the fifth time — just short of his 37th birthday.

He came close to winning the title for the sixth time when he drew with Fullmer for the NBA version of the title in 1960. By then Robinson was past his 40th birthday.

Retirement finally came in 1965 when he returned to the theatre and the movies.

In 201 professional bouts, Robinson was never knocked out or stopped by another boxer. Only the intense heat in the 1952 Maxim fight forced him to quit and cost him a chance to be a triple world champion.

CAREER HIGHLIGHTS

Professional bouts: 201
Won: 174
Drew: 6
Lost: 19
No contest: 2

Of his 174 wins, 109 were knock-outs. Ten of his defeats came after Robinson's 40th birthday.

(Above) *The stylish Robinson lands a left on former German middleweight champion Hans Stretz in December 1950.* The Photo Source

(Below) *Early morning tea . . . with Sugar! Robinson outside Blackpool's Imperial Hotel.* Syndication International

The Thrilla in Manila

On 1 October 1975 two men engaged in one of the hardest and most unrelenting heavyweight title bouts ever seen. The two central characters were Muhammad Ali, the defending champion, and Joe Frazier, who was trying to win back the crown he lost to George Foreman more than two years earlier.

This was the third meeting between these two great rivals, and each had a personal score to settle. Frazier had gained a unanimous points decision over Ali when he tried to regain his world title in 1971. But Ali gained revenge by winning on points over 12 rounds to regain his NABF title in 1974.

But this was the needle match and the pre-fight hype was as great as in any of Ali's previous world title fights, even though the contest was taking place in Manila. Ali wanted to win desperately, but so did Frazier. Both men attracted the kind of attention never before seen in the Philippines with more than 100,000 fans paying to watch them prepare for the fight in the weeks leading up to the bout.

Frazier's will to win stemmed from the fact that he disliked Ali who had humiliated him in public several times. He tried his own piece of 'physching' by referring to Ali by his pre-Muslim name, Cassius Clay. Ali, in return, was never short of a retort: 'Frazier's got two chances, slim and none', he said. He further added: 'It's gonna be a chilla and a thrilla when I get the gorilla in Manila'.

The atmosphere was electric at Quezon City's Araneta Coliseum as local referee Carlos Padilla called the fighters together for their pre-fight talk. More than 770 million watched the fight as it was beamed via closed circuit television to cinemas and stadiums all around the world. Ali tipped the scales at 224½ pounds, ten pounds heavier than Frazier. Ali

Round seven and it is still impossible to predict the winner. But that honour fell to Ali (right) at the end of 14 gruelling rounds. Popperfoto

gained an early advantage by taking the opening rounds, but Frazier then took control in the middle of the fight. Both men threw everything at each other. Both men *took* everything the other threw at them. Ali's two-handed ripostes scored points while Frazier's left hooks caused Ali trouble.

Ali regained control in the 12th round and he took the next two rounds, unleashing punch after punch upon the tiring body of his opponent. It was in the 14th round that Ali sent Frazier's gumshield from his mouth, which was followed by a gush of blood.

Frazier was not allowed out of his corner for the final round and an exhausted Muhammad Ali had regained his title. Despite the pre-fight verbal fisticuffs and antagonism, Ali was generous in victory when he had the honesty to acknowledge Frazier as: 'One hell of a fighter', and he rightly described the contest as 'one hell of a fight'.

96

Right *Muhammad Ali (on the ropes) came out of retirement in 1980 to fight Larry Holmes for the world heavyweight title in Las Vegas but Ali showed he had lost his old sparkle and Holmes won in 11 rounds. All Sport*

Above *Joe Bugner (Australia) used to be the top British heavyweight. He tried to prove he was still 'king' in 1987 when he fought Britain's Frank Bruno at White Hart Lane, but he succumbed to the new number one of British heavyweight boxing. All Sport*

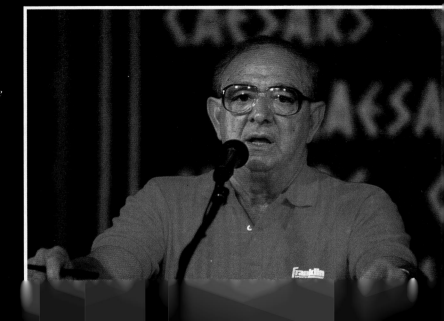

Right *The most successful trainer of all time, Angelo Dundee, the*

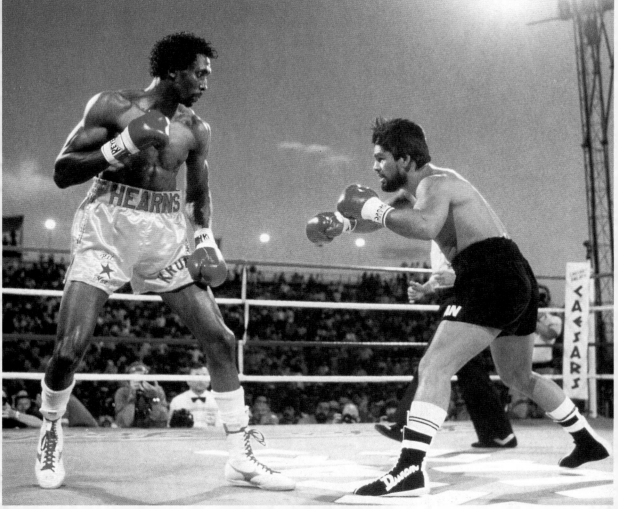

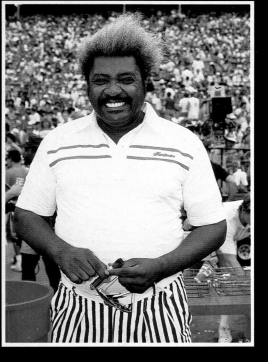

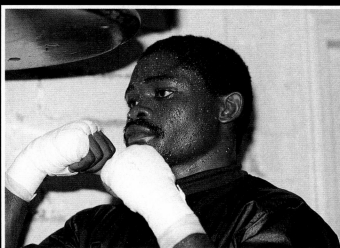

Above left   *The unmistakable sight of extrovert promoter Don King (USA).* All Sport

Above right   *Azumah Nelson (Ghana), the WBC featherweight champion since taking the title off Wilfredo Gomez (Puerto Rico) in 1984.* Sporting Pictures

Below right   *A happy looking Robert Dickie. On 29 October 1986 he beat John Feeney to win a Lonsdale Belt outright in the featherweight division in a record 203 days . . . three days better than Pat Cowdell's old record. A few months later Dickie was involved in a car accident that nearly ended his career but, happily, he made a successful comeback to the ring.* Sporting Pictures

Opposite above   *Canada's Matthew Hilton proudly holds aloft his championship belt after beating Buster Drayton (USA) to win the IBF junior-middleweight title in 1987.* Gamma Presse (Paris)

Opposite below   *Tommy Hearns (left) on his way to knocking out Roberto Duran (Panama) in the 2nd round of their junior-middleweight title bout in 1984. It was Hearns' second world title. In 1987 Hearns became the first man to win four different world titles when he beat Juan Roldan (Argentina) to win the WBC middleweight crown.* Sporting Pictures

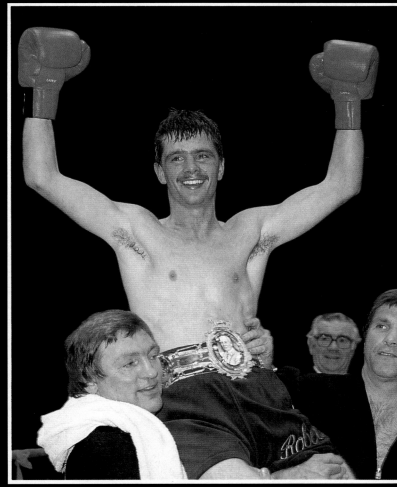

One of the cleverest of the bare-knuckle fighters, Daniel
Mendoza was also one of the sport's first managers and
promoters. Born in London in 1763 he died at the age of
73. Mary Evans

Georges Carpentier

Frenchman Georges Carpentier has one of boxing's most remarkable records. Not only is he the best boxer produced by his country but he won major titles at all weights from lightweight to heavyweight. But it was in the light-heavyweight division that the handsome Carpentier, known as the 'Orchid Man', excelled.

Born just outside Paris in 1894 he had his first professional bout when only 14, and was not quite 16 when he won his first French title, at lightweight. He progressed through the weight divisions winning the national, European and world light-heavyweight crowns.

In October 1911 he won his first European title when he stopped Young Joseph in 10 rounds for the welterweight crown. Four months later he knocked Jim Sullivan out to win the middleweight title in Monaco and by June 1913 he had added the European light-heavyweight and heavyweight titles to his already impressive list.

Just before the outbreak of the war Carpentier fought the American 'Gunboat' Ed Smith for the white version of the world heavyweight title. Smith was disqualified and the Frenchman collected his first world title, albeit unofficial.

During the war Carpentier served in the French Air Force and, despite winning military honours, was inactive as a boxer for five years, apart from the occasional bout. But once the hostilities were over he retained his European heavyweight title by beating the British light-heavyweight champion Dick Smith in Paris. In 1920 he stepped down a division to beat Battling Levinsky with a fourth round knock-out to win the world light-heavyweight title. The following year he had his one and only attempt at the official world heavyweight

Carpentier (left) throws a left to Dempsey's head but despite a brave effort the American retained his title with a 4th round knockout. Mary Evans Picture Library

crown when he challenged Jack Dempsey.

The fight has a special place in boxing history being the first to attract a $1 million dollar gate as 80,000 fight fans packed into the specially-built stadium promoter Tex Rickard had erected in Jersey City. Carpentier, despite conceding 16 pounds, put up a brave performance before losing in the fourth round. Carpentier then successfully defended his world light-heavyweight title against Ted 'Kid' Lewis before losing the title to Battling Siki of Senegal in 1922.

Just when it was thought the best of Georges Carpentier had been seen he beat Marcel Nilles in 1923 to win the French heavyweight title in his 101st professional bout. He had eight more bouts before ending his career in a four round exhibition against Jack Walker in 1927.

CAREER HIGHLIGHTS

Professional bouts:	109
Won:	88
Drew:	6
Lost:	14
ND:	1

Henry Cooper

(b. 1934)

Cassius Clay declared before his fight with Henry Cooper at Wembley in 1963: 'He's a bum. He's a cripple. I'll take him in five.' And so he did, but not before Clay had suffered one of the biggest scares of his career.

In the fourth round, Cooper floored the future world champion with his famous left hook. Only the intervention of the bell and subsequent damage to Clay's glove prevented Cooper gaining a famous victory.

Clay gained valuable 'breathing space' during the interval while his glove was replaced. Clay's trainer, Angelo Dundee, revealed several years later that the cut in the glove was not as big when Clay first came to his corner as it was when shown to the referee — he 'just helped it along a bit'.

The fight resumed, but was stopped in the fifth round when a badly cut eye caused the bloody-faced Cooper to quit. Henry was deprived of a memorable win, but Clay never called him a bum again.

When the pair of them met for the world title at Highbury Stadium in 1966 it was, again, Cooper's tendency to cut easily that caused the fight to be stopped in the sixth round.

Born in Bellingham, Kent, Henry is one of a pair of twins. The other half, George, also fought professionally (as Jim Cooper) but he never experienced Henry's success.

Henry was the ABA light-heavyweight champion in 1952 and 1953. He turned professional under the guidance of Jim Wicks — 'The Bishop' — in 1954 and by knocking out Brian London in 1959 won the British heavyweight title that he was to hold for a record ten years. During his reign he became the first, and only, boxer to win three Lonsdale Belts outright.

His reign as champion ended when he relinquished the title in 1969 after the British Boxing Board of Control refused to recognize his proposed WBA title fight with Jimmy Ellis (USA) as a world title fight. Ironically the Ellis fight never went ahead.

He regained the British title in 1970 before losing it on a controversial points decision to Joe Bugner in 1971. Cooper, just short of his 37th birthday, announced his retirement.

Henry Cooper remains as popular today as he did in his fighting days. As well as enjoying a game of golf he devotes a lot of his time to children and to charitable organisations. It is hardly surprising that Henry was honoured with the OBE in 1969.

A couple of young protégés looking on as Henry goes through his gym routine. All Sport

98

CAREER HIGHLIGHTS
Professional bouts: 55
           Won: 40
          Drew: 1
          Lost: 14
Cooper beat Joe Erskine (1961), Brian London
(1964) and Billy Walker (1967) to win his
Lonsdale Belts outright.

*Another happy customer. Mrs Durnford seems quite
pleased with 'Enery's coxes at his Wembley greengrocer's
shop in 1965. Syndication International*

Rocky Marciano

(1923–69)

It was Muhammad Ali who once said: 'All the great world heavyweight champions were black. There was Jack Johnson, Joe Louis, Jersey Joe Walcott, Rocky Marciano . . .!'

Whether or not that was a deliberate slip of the tongue from Ali, Marciano's record of 49 wins in 49 professional fights certainly puts him among the 'greats' of the world heavyweight championship scene. Out of the ring he was one of the sport's 'nice guys'.

Behind the unbeaten record, which included 43 knock-outs, there is to be found one of the hardest-hitting champions the heavyweight division has ever seen. Evidence of that was seen at the Philadelphia Stadium in 1952 when he took the title from Jersey Joe Walcott with a 13th-round knock-out. The punch he delivered to put the defending champion down was probably the hardest ever thrown by Marciano. The famed right-hand of Marciano's was nicknamed 'Suzi-Q'.

Born Rocco Francis Marchegiano, in Brockton, Massachusetts, the 'Brockton Blockbuster' did not engage in his first professional bout until the age of 24, and he was nearly 30 when manager Al Weill fixed up his first world title bout. The idea of taking up boxing is reported to have come to him while serving with the US forces in Britain during the war after he knocked out an Australian

(Above left) *Archie Moore (USA), right, seems to have the better of champion Rocky Marciano in the second round of their world heavyweight title bout in 1955, but seven rounds later Marciano had retained his title by knocking out the challenger.* UPI/Bettmann Newsphotos

(Left) *Joe Louis' last fight. He is sadly seen out of the ring after being knocked through the ropes by Rocky Marciano during their meeting in October 1951.* UPI/Bettmann Newsphotos

serviceman during a pub brawl!

Small for a heavyweight he stood under 5ft 11in and weighed 184lb. Today he would be more suited to the cruiserweight division.

Marciano's first defence of his world title was against Walcott (USA) in 1953 and, once more, the power of Marciano told as he knocked out the challenger after just 2 minutes 25 seconds of the contest.

Five more defences followed and in April 1956 he announced his retirement — seven months after his last defence against Archie Moore. Marciano left the ring as the only world heavyweight champion to remain undefeated throughout his career. Not until the emergence of Larry Holmes was there anybody likely to better his record. Holmes came unstuck one fight short of Marciano's record.

Rocky invested his ring earnings wisely and became a successful businessman. It was on his way to a business convention on 31 August 1969 that the light aircraft he was aboard crashed at Newton, Iowa. The following day would have been his 46th birthday which he was going to spend with his wife and two teenage children. They lost a husband and father; the boxing world lost one of its greatest heavyweight champions.

CAREER HIGHLIGHTS
Professional bouts: 49

Wins: 49

Forty-three of his wins were inside the distance. The only man to go the distance with him twice was Ted Lowry (USA) in 1949 and 1950.

Marciano (left) retired as undefeated world heavyweight champion in 1956, after 49 fights.

Madison Square Garden

The current Madison Square Garden — known affectionately as 'The Garden' — is the fourth such centre to bear that name.

Situated over Pennsylvania Station, on New York's 7th Avenue, the Madison Square Garden building is 13-storeys tall and contains the main arena, with seating capacity for around 20 000, an art gallery, a bowling centre, a cinema and theatre — and much more. The present complex was opened on 11 February, 1968.

Boxing was seen for the first time at the 'New' Garden on March 4 1968. It was a double world title bill when Nino Benvenuti of Italy took the middleweight title off Emile Griffith (VI), and Joe Frazier (USA) beat Buster Matthis (USA) to gain recognition by the New York State Commission as heavyweight champion of the world. The first contest seen, however, was a middleweight bout between Dennis Hefferman of Philadelphia and Tony Smith of the Bronx. Hefferman stopped Smith in the third round.

The first 'Garden' had its roots in the 1870s when an Irish musician called Gilmore used to give concerts from a disused railroad depot in Madison Square Park. This became known as 'Gilmore's Garden'.

Circus proprietor Barnum was a former owner. He took it over again in 1880, and renamed it Madison Square Garden. In 1890 the original buildings were pulled down and an impressive new building built on the site. This was later known as the 'Old Garden'.

The 'Old Garden' was demolished in 1925 to make way for insurance company offices. Sid Terris (USA) beat Johnny Dundee (Ita) in 12 rounds to win the last fight at the 'Old Garden'. The third garden was opened in December the same year, but it was some considerable distance away from the site of the first two, on 8th Avenue. Paul Berlenbach (USA) beat Jack Delaney (USA) on 11 December 1925 to retain his world light-heavyweight title in the first fight at the third Garden. The $160 000 Madison Square Bowl was added in 1932. It was an outdoor arena with seating for 80 000. The first fight staged at the Bowl was the world heavyweight title fight between Jack Sharkey (USA) and Max Schmeling (Ger) in June 1932. The last bout in that Bowl was in 1938. It was the world welterweight title fight between Henry Armstrong (USA) and Barney Ross (USA).

The current Garden, regarded by many as the world's most famous indoor stadium, was opened in 1968. It took nearly five years to construct at a cost of around $130 million.

(Top of page) *Nino Benvenuti (Ita), in the dark trunks, on his way to beating Virgin Islander Emile Griffith to win the world middleweight title on 4 March 1968. This was the first world title fight to be held at the fourth, and current, Madison Square Garden.* UPI/Bettmann Newsphotos

Bob Fitzsimmons

(1863–1917)

It seems strange calling Bob Fitzsimmons an English world champion when he never fought in England. But he *was* born in Cornwall and that is good enough for England to lay claim to its only world heavyweight champion.

Fitzsimmons was born in the town of Helston in 1863 but was still a baby when the family emigrated to Timaru in New Zealand. He never had ambitions to box as a youngster, being more interested in serving his apprenticeship as a blacksmith, until the legendary Jem Mace toured the country in 1880. Mace organized a boxing tournament and Bob Fitzsimmons thought he would enter. He went on to win and so began his 30 years in boxing.

Fitzsimmons moved to Australia to box professionally. Fighting around middleweight at that time, he had an unsuccessful attempt at the Australian title in 1890 before setting sail for the United States. The following year he beat Jack Dempsey to capture the world middleweight crown at the age of 27.

Never weighing more than 175 pounds Fitzsimmons still fought the top heavyweights of the day and fought them well. He wanted a crack at James J. Corbett's crown but Corbett would not accept Fitzsimmons' challenge because he was not an American, so Fitzsimmons took out US citizenship. The fight eventually took place in Carson City in 1897, and after being outclassed for 13 rounds Fitzsimmons threw a lethal punch to Corbett's stomach which left the champion counted out.

Fitzsimmons did not make his first defence of the title for two years, and succumbed to the younger and 39-pound heavier James J. Jeffries in 11 rounds. They had a return three years later but Fitzsimmons lost in eight rounds.

It looked as though the career of England's first world heavyweight champion was over but at San Francisco in November 1903 Fitzsimmons became the first man to win three world titles when he beat George Gardner over 20 rounds to capture the light-heavyweight crown. He lost his title to Philadelphia Jack O'Brien in 1905 when 42 years of age.

England's only world heavyweight champion, Bob Fitzsimmons, and the first man to win titles at three different weights. Hulton Picture Library.

CAREER HIGHLIGHTS

Professional bouts:	62
Won:	40
Lost:	11
ND/NC:	11

Jack Dempsey

One of the most popular heavyweight champions, Jack Dempsey was still regarded as 'The Champ' by the American people long after he had retired from the ring.

The respect and love of the American public was hard earned. In fact, he was very unpopular in the early part of his career because he had avoided national service.

Jack's real name was William Harrison Dempsey. He started fighting in 1914 under the name of Kid Blackie but took his new name after his older brother, who used to box under the name of the former middleweight champion, Jack Dempsey.

The fortunes of Dempsey improved in 1917 when he met manager Jack Kearns. He set about transforming the 'slugger' into one of the most polished heavyweights the world has seen.

Two years after teaming up with Kearns, Dempsey — known as the 'Manassa Mauler' — challenged Jess Willard (USA) for the heavyweight title at Toledo, Ohio.

Conceding over 57lb, and 5 inches in height and reach, Dempsey took the title with a third-round knock-out. Unfortunately, he never picked up any prize-money. Jack Kearns bet all his purse at 10–1 that he would stop the giant Willard in the first round!

Five more successful defences followed, and one of them against Argentinian Luis 'Angel' Firpo in 1923 was one of the most dramatic world heavyweight contests ever witnessed. It only lasted two rounds, but those two rounds saw more action than many fights that have gone 15 rounds or more.

After being put on the canvas seven times, Firpo got up and knocked Dempsey out of the ring — all in the first round. Had Dempsey not been pushed back into the ring by the fans, he could well have lost his title! Dempsey put Firpo down twice more in the second round before Firpo's bravery ran out.

Not regarded as a 'fighting' champion, Dempsey preferred to engage himself in exhibition bouts, and took his skills around the United States. People attended in vast numbers and Dempsey's bank balance swelled.

He lost his title in front of 120 757 fans at the Sesquicentennial Stadium, Philadelphia in 1926 when Gene Tunney (USA) gained a ten-round points decision. The following year, the pair of them engaged in the famous 'Battle of the Long Count' in which Dempsey nearly regained the title.

Dempsey retired in 1940 having earned in excess of $10 million from the sport. He had taken up refereeing — boxing and wrestling — shortly before he retired, and continued to make money from that. He was paid a reputed $10 000 for refereeing the first world title fight in the Philippines, between Ceferino Garcia (Phi) and Glen Lee (USA), in 1939.

A successful businessman, Dempsey opened his famous restaurant on New York's Broadway — a meeting place for many former boxers and fight fans. The 'champ' lost his last battle on 31 May 1983 when he died at the age of 87.

Dempsey (left) with leading promoter Tex Rickard in 1927. Syndication International

CAREER HIGHLIGHTS
Professional bouts: 78
Won: 62
Drew: 10
Lost: 6

Dempsey knocked out 49 of his 78 opponents, 25 of them in the first round.

(Opposite) *Jack Dempsey with his wife Hannah and his mother at Jack's restaurant, on one of the rare occasions his mother visited New York.* The Photo Source

Henry Armstrong

(b. 1912)

Henry Armstrong, born Henry Jackson and known as 'Homicide Hank', is immortalized in boxing history as the only man to hold three world titles simultaneously. Between October 1937 and August 1938 he won the featherweight, welterweight and lightweight crowns.

Born in Columbus, Mississippi, Armstrong hailed from a deprived background. All he knew was fighting. So, at the age of 19, he left home and made for Los Angeles to seek his fortune. He was very effective as an amateur and one man he impressed was singer Al Jolson, who put him in touch with his first manager, Eddie Mead. He had his first professional fight in 1931; it resulted in a knock-out defeat for Armstrong, who fought under the name of Melody Jackson. That was one of only two knock-outs he suffered in his entire professional career.

Six years later his first world title arrived, when he beat Petey Sarron (USA) to win the featherweight title. Barney Ross (USA) was Armstrong's victim when he won the welterweight title at the Madison Square Bowl in May 1938, and his next fight saw him lift the lightweight crown, beating Lou Ambers (USA) on a split decision in one of the best fights seen in the division for many years.

Unable to make the featherweight limit he relinquished that title a month after the Ambers fight, without having made a defence. He lost his lightweight crown in the rematch with Ambers, but in the welterweight division he was outstanding.

Between May 1938, when he beat Ross to take the title, and September 1940, he made 19 successful defences. Also during that period he had an attempt at winning the middleweight

Dr William Walker checks Armstrong's eyes during the weigh-in before his world welterweight title fight against Fritzie Zivic (right) in January 1941. Zivic (USA) won with a 12th-round knock-out, and it turned out to be Armstrong's last world title fight. The Photo Source

crown but narrowly failed after fighting a ten-round draw with Ceferino Garcia (Phi) in Los Angeles.

Altogether Armstrong took part in 26 world title bouts winning 22, drawing one, and losing three. His only defeats in the welterweight division were by Fritzie Zivic (USA), when Zivic took the title from him in 1940, and again three months later when the referee stepped in to prevent Armstrong from taking heavy punishment.

Regarded as one of the best fighters of the inter-war years, Armstrong had great speed, an aggressive style, and was a fine attacking boxer with a great deal of stamina. Sadly, like many fighters who found fame and fortune from the sport, he left it almost penniless. He turned to drink with his life in tatters — but, seeing the error of his ways, subsequently turned to religion, being ordained a Baptist Minister in 1951.

Armstrong in training for his world title fight with Britain's Ernie Roderick at Harringay Arena in 1939. The Photo Source

. . . and the result of his effort. Armstrong receives the world title trophy as a battered Roderick looks on. The Photo Source

CAREER HIGHLIGHTS

Professional bouts: 174
Won: 145
Drew: 9
Lost: 20

Between 1 January 1937 and 25 May 1939, Armstrong went 46 consecutive bouts without defeat.

Battle of the Long Count

In 1926 a record crowd of more than 120 000 paid to see American Gene Tunney take the world heavyweight title off Jack Dempsey. Twelve months later, another 100 000-plus crowd went to the Soldier's Field Stadium in Grant Park, Chicago, to see if Dempsey could regain the title. They did not see that, but they were to witness one of the most controversial incidents in world heavyweight championship history.

The first six rounds of the return bout saw Tunney well on top. Dempsey had won just one round, the sixth. The next round was to become one of the most talked-about in the sport's history.

Dempsey had taken two quick punches from Tunney. He retaliated with a left and a right to Tunney's jaw. The punches were reminiscent of Dempsey in his heyday: Tunney was floored.

Thinking his man was out, Dempsey stood over Tunney waiting for the count to start. Timekeeper Beeler started the count but referee Dave Barry was frantically waving Dempsey away to a neutral corner.

Barry would not start the count until Dempsey moved. Dempsey was unaware of Barry's actions, he was too busy looking at the dazed Tunney who had fallen near to Dempsey's corner.

Under the Illinois State Athletic Commission's rules a boxer had to retreat to the neutral corner furthest away from the fallen boxer. When Dempsey eventually retreated Barry started the count but Tunney had already been on the canvas five, six or possibly seven seconds.

Tunney rose on the count of nine. The official time given was 14 seconds. Some said it was as long as 18 seconds. Dempsey maintains he

Tunney is floored by Dempsey. Referee Barry refused to start the count until Dempsey went to a neutral corner. Tunney eventually got up, and went on to gain a unanimous points decision. UPI/Bettmann Newsphotos

should have won, Tunney reckons he was able to get up at five but was told to stay down until the count of nine by his corner.

No matter which account is correct, the fight continued and Tunney took command of the final three rounds to gain a unanimous points decision.

Such was the impact of the contest, it was reported that 12 people died in the United States while listening to the contest — seven of them in the seventh round!

Dempsey lodged a complaint to the Illinois Athletic Commission, to no avail. At the end of the day he only had himself to blame. His refusal to observe, or ignorance of, the rules prevented him from being the first man to regain the world heavyweight crown.

Archie Moore (b. 1916/13?)

Archibald Lee Wright — better known as Archie Moore — was the oldest man to hold a world title at any weight. When he was stripped of his world light-heavyweight title in February 1962 he was in his 49th year. His date of birth has never been clarified: some records show he was born in 1913, some in 1916. Even if it was 1916 he would still be the oldest world champion.

He won the light-heavyweight crown four days after his 39th (or 36th) birthday, by beating Joey Maxim at St Louis in 1952, and held it for a record nine years, remaining undefeated. One man who came close to taking his title off him was Canadian Yvon Durelle who floored Moore three times in the opening round of their fight in 1958. Moore came back to knock Durelle out in the 11th round.

Having the ability to put on, or lose, weight quite easily, he twice fought for the world heavyweight crown. The first occasion was in 1955 when he was knocked out in the ninth round by Rocky Marciano. Moore had the defending champion down in the second round, and Moore maintained that the referee assisting Marciano cost him his chance of supreme glory.

His second crack at the heavyweight title came in 1956 when he was knocked out by Floyd Patterson in their contest for the vacant title. Patterson was just 21 at the time, Moore was 40 (or 43).

A keep-fit fanatic, Moore used to do 250 press-ups per day to develop his arm muscles. Those exercises paid dividends because Moore became known as a knock-out specialist — 145 of his 234 opponents were stopped by him.

Archie Moore used to sport a gold and purple dressing robe as he entered the ring. When he fought Britain's Yolande Pompey at Harringay in 1956 (Moore's only fight in Britain) he presented the robe to the British Boxing Board of Control in appreciation of the way he had been treated in England.

After being stripped of his title Moore entered the world of films and television in 1964, only returning to the ring for an exhibition bout in 1965.

One of the 145 men to have been knocked out by Archie Moore, Yolande Pompey (GB) (left) fell to the American in ten rounds at Harringay Arena in 1956. The Photo Source

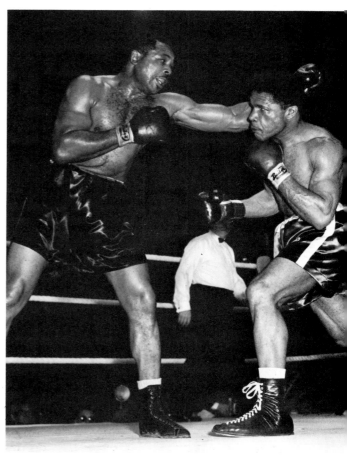

CAREER HIGHLIGHTS

Professional bouts: 234
Won: 199
Drew: 8
Lost: 26
No contest: 1

Moore knocked-out 145 opponents, 21 of them in the first round.

Mike Tyson

(b. 1966)

Mike Tyson's arrival was like a breath of fresh air to the heavyweight boxing scene and the interest he generated in the division was reminiscent of Muhammad Ali's early days.

Abandoned by his father before he was born, Tyson was brought up by his mother in Brooklyn. At the age of 11 he turned to robbery but, as he says: 'That's not so bad, some guys did murder at 11 . . .' He ended up in a home for juvenile delinquents at the age of 13.

One of the guards at the home was ex-boxer Bobby Stewart who was a great believer in getting the boys to channel their aggression into boxing. Tyson was prepared to give it a try and Stewart soon recognized the making of a good, if not aggressive, fighter. Tyson was released into the custody of Cus d'Amato, the man who

styled Floyd Patterson, and he was moulded into his next world heavyweight champion. Ironically, Tyson was to succeed Patterson as the youngest holder of boxing's supreme crown.

Tyson's first payday was in March 1985 when he picked up $500 for beating Hector Mercedes. As opponent-after-opponent fell to Tyson's lethal uppercut, the man from Brooklyn suddenly became boxing's hottest property. He got his first crack at the world title in November 1986 when he fought the Jamaican-born Canadian, Trevor Berbick, for the WBC title. Tyson went into the fight as the heaviest-backed challenger since Joe Louis against Jim Braddock in 1937. The bookmakers got the odds right as Berbick went

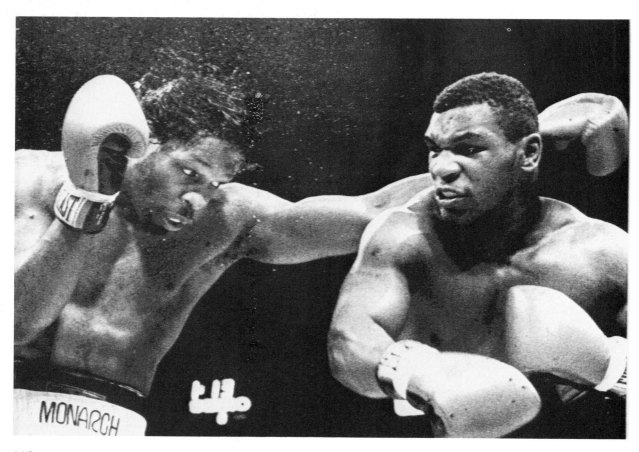

the same way as 25 of Tyson's previous 27 opponents, when referee Mills Lane stopped the fight in the second round. At 20 years and 145 days he was a year and a half younger than Patterson when he won the world title in 1956. Sadly, Cus d'Amato died in 1985 and did not witness the arrival of his second great champion.

The 'Typhoon' whirled on and in March 1987 he captured the WBA version of the world title when he won a unanimous points decision against James 'Bonecrusher' Smith, the champion of less than three months. Tyson put his two titles at stake two months later when he fought the former WBC champion Pinklon Thomas at the Las Vegas Hilton. Tyson came out with a flourish and three consecutive early punches in the opening round would have stopped a less determined man than Thomas. Thomas hung on bravely however, before the end came in the sixth round and he became Tyson's 30th victim.

Tyson still wanted to become the youngest

undisputed heavyweight champion and his chance came in August 1987 when he fought the IBF champion Tony Tucker. Tucker was a 15-1 outsider. Once more the bookies had it right, but even they did not expect Tucker would become the fourth man to take Tyson the distance, which he did. Tyson won the unanimous decision to become the first undisputed champion since Leon Spinks in 1978, and the youngest by nearly a year.

What next for Tyson? To retire undefeated and with a better record than Rocky Marciano is an obvious goal. Mike Tyson has, however, been a 'working' champion, and it is up to his co-managers Jim Jacobs and Bill Cayton to make sure he is not pushed too hard, otherwise he could become a victim of his own talent.

(Above) Tyson and 'Bonecrusher' Smith during their WBA fight. (Left) Tyson and Mitch Green. Green lost on points after 10 rounds. Popperfoto

CAREER HIGHLIGHTS
Professional bouts: 31
Won: 31
Lost: 0
Only four men have gone the distance with Tyson, they are Mitch Green, James Tillis, James 'Bonecrusher' Smith and Tony Tucker.

Sugar Ray Leonard

Sugar Ray Leonard left the sport with his good looks intact and a healthy bank balance! All Sport

When Muhammed Ali faded away from the limelight in the late seventies and early eighties, boxing was fortunate to have a ready-made successor in Sugar Ray Leonard. Flamboyant and a teaser like Ali, Leonard also had the skills of the master, including an explosive punch.

From Palmer Park, Maryland, Ray Charles Leonard (the names Ray Charles were given to him because his parents were both great fans of singer Ray Charles) won the 1976 Olympic light-welterweight title, beating Britain's Clinton McKenzie on his way to the final.

Shortly after his Olympic triumph he turned professional and engaged in his first paid fight on 5 February 1977. That was a six-round points decision over Luis Vega (USA) in Baltimore. Two years later Leonard was world welterweight champion.

He took the WBC version of the title when he stopped Wilfred Benitez (USA) six seconds from the end of the contest. A successful defence against Britain's Dave 'Boy' Green was followed by his first professional defeat when he lost a classic encounter, on points, to Roberto Duran (Pan). Despite losing he still collected over $8 million for the fight.

The return bout, eagerly awaited, was not the classic of the first meeting, but Leonard regained the crown when Duran surrendered his title at the end of the eighth round by staying in his corner when the bell went for round nine.

After making one more defence of his welterweight title, Leonard beat Ayub Kalule (Uga) to take the WBA version of the light-middleweight title in 1981. He gave that away a couple of months later to concentrate on the welterweight division.

That decision was proved correct in Las Vegas on 16 September 1981 when he took the biggest purse in boxing history — approximately $11 million — and beat Thomas Hearns (USA) for the undisputed title. Leonard stopped Hearns in the 14th round after hauling himself back from the brink of defeat.

He made only one more defence of his title before announcing his retirement in November 1982.

His decision to retire was made after an eye operation on a detached retina. Perhaps his decision was aided by his wife Juanita who told him she'd 'Break all his fingers' if he didn't quit.

The lure of the spotlight forced him to make a comeback in May 1984. He had no need to come back for financial reasons: his wise investments were yielding him in the region of $3000 per day. Although he beat Kevin Howard with a ninth-round knockout, Leonard was floored for the first time in his professional career and that led him immediately to pronounce: 'that's it for good'. But no, it wasn't . . .

The chance to fight Marvin Hagler for the world middleweight crown was too tempting, not to mention the $11 million it would add to his bank account. When promoter Bob Arum set up the fight in 1987 at Ceasar's Palace, Las Vegas, it was an instant sell out. Leonard defied the bookies, who made Hagler the 3-1 on favourite, by gaining a split decision over 12 rounds. Seven weeks later Leonard announced his third retirement from the ring.

CAREER HIGHLIGHTS

Professional bouts: 35
Won: 34
Drew: 0
Lost: 1

Leonard's first and only defeat came in his 28th contest, and was at the hands of Roberto Duran.

Panamanian Roberto Duran (left) and Sugar Ray Leonard exchanging punches during their world welterweight contest at Montreal in 1980. Duran took Leonard's title off him with a unanimous points decision. Even though he lost the fight Leonard picked up a reported $8.5 million. UPI/Bettmann Newsphotos

Britain's Dave 'Boy' Green was no match for Leonard in 1980 when the American made the first successful defence of his world welterweight title. Syndication International

The Terry Lawless Stable

The atmosphere at Terry Lawless's gymnasium above the Royal Oak pub, Canning Town, in the heart of London's dockland, is more reminiscent of a Boy's Club than a boxing gymnasium.

Fifty-year-old East Ender Lawless believes in getting his fighters in the right frame of mind as much as building them up physically. And a friendly environment is the best place to start those preparations. 'We don't have prima donnas. Everyone is equal—world champion or six-rounder', he once said. A visit to the premises will soon confirm that.

Terry is just one half of the success story, the other is his wife of 28 years, Sylvie. She is like a mother to the fighters and many of them confide in her with their personal problems, sometimes without the knowledge of Terry. Fighters quite often share the Lawless household, in the stockbroker belt of Essex, before big fights, but Sylvie never objects.

The family atmosphere has certainly paid dividends for Terry who has been the most successful British manager/trainer. He has turned Maurice Hope, John H. Stracey and Charlie Magri into world champions and his latest hopeful, Frank Bruno, stands every chance of being added to that list.

Gifted, Terry has the ability to turn an ordinary fighter into a champion. One such case was John L. Gardner whom he turned from a raw amateur into British, European and Commonwealth heavyweight champion.

Before a fight Terry admits he gets very nervous, but he never lets his fighters see those nerves. Like soccer's Bill Shankly, Terry convinces his fighters that they are the best. He has often been accused of being 'too involved' with his fighters. That may be the case, but his

Deep in thought — Britain's most successful trainer Terry Lawless. All Sport

success over the years has proved it certainly works for the Terry Lawless stable.

THE LAWLESS WORLD CHAMPIONS

John H. Stracey (GB)	– WBC welterweight
Maurice Hope (Ant)	– WBC junior-middleweight
Jim Watt (GB)	– WBC lightweight
Charlie Magri (Tun)	– WBC flyweight

Jack Johnson

(1878–1968)

James J. Jeffries failed to wrest the world title from Johnson. Mary Evans Picture Library

Jack Johnson is shown as the first Negro to win the world heavyweight title, and that was the crux of his troubles – he was a Negro.

Born in Texas in 1878, Johnson first boxed professionally when he was 19. A very clever and defensive fighter, he was a true innovator of modern techniques and was way ahead of his time. He reached the peak of his career at a time when Negro boxers were unacceptable in the United States – unless they were defeated.

It was apparent Johnson would never get a title fight in the United States so when the champion, Canadian Tommy Burns, set off on tour to Australia, Johnson followed him. Burns eventually agreed to meet Johnson for the title in Sydney on Boxing Day, 1908, the offer of a £6,000 purse, win, lose or draw, being a big temptation. Johnson wore the champion down before stopping him in the 14th round.

Jack Johnson was the champion at last, but he was certainly not liked. Outside the ring his antics upset many people. His arrogance and association with white women, something unheard of in those days, were far from popular. Johnson became the most hated man in the United States. The boxing authorities desperately wanted a white champion but they could find no likely contender.

The former middleweight champion Stanley Ketchel was seen as the first of many 'Great White Hopes' to win back the crown, but he failed. He managed to put Johnson on the canvas but the champ responded by knocking out Ketchel and collecting two of his teeth in his glove in the process. Even James J. Jeffries came out of a six-year retirement to try and win the crown, but 15 rounds of destruction from Johnson saw him beaten.

Outside the ring Johnson still had his problems. In 1913 he was charged with importing a white woman for immoral purposes. To avoid a prison sentence he fled to Europe. He agreed to return and put his title at stake if the sentence was dropped. Nobody in America would stage the fight for fear of race riots so in Cuba, in April 1915, he fought the mighty Jess Willard.

Johnson was 37 years of age by then. Willard was three years younger and had the advantage of five inches in height and 25 pounds in weight. Willard won in the 26th round. Johnson maintained that he was forced to throw the fight, a claim which is still unsubstantiated. Johnson eventually served his prison sentence and carried on boxing until he was 50.

CAREER HIGHLIGHTS

Professional bouts:	112
Won:	78
Drew:	12
Lost:	8
ND/NC:	14

Of all the world heavyweight champions only Ezzard Charles (122) had more professional bouts than Johnson.

Ali's Three World Titles

Between 1892, when James J. Corbett (USA) beat John L. Sullivan (USA) for the first title, and 1974, only one man — Floyd Patterson (USA) — had successfully regained the world heavyweight title.

On 30 October 1974, in the early hours of the morning at Kinshasa, Zaire, Muhammad Ali beat George Foreman (USA) to share Patterson's distinction. Four years later Ali proved himself, in his own words, 'The Greatest', when he won the title for the third time by outpointing champion Leon Spinks.

The Muhammad Ali phenomenon started at the Convention Hall, Miami Beach in 1964. Ali (then known as Cassius Clay) was given no chance against Sonny Liston — his odds were 8–1 against him winning.

Doctor Robbin, who examined both boxers before the fight said of Clay: 'He is emotionally unbalanced. He acts like a man in mortal fear of death. Judging by his pulse rate he's burning up energy at an enormous rate.'

Clay held some in reserve for the fight, forcing Liston to stay in his corner at the end of

The determination to win back the title is clearly visible on Ali's face as he throws a left to the face of George Foreman (USA). Ali regained the title for the first time with an eighth round knock-out.
UPI/ Bettmann Newsphotos

Ali, well away from harm, as Leon Spinks (USA) fails to make contact with a right. Ali went on to gain a unanimous 15-round points decision to regain the title a second time. UPI/Bettmann Newsphotos

the sixth round. The fight was over and Cassius Marcellus Clay, 1960 Olympic light-heavyweight winner, was world heavyweight champion.

After that fight he changed his name to Muhammad Ali and successfully defended his title nine times before having the title stripped from him by the boxing authorities in 1967 for refusing to be inducted into the US Armed Forces.

His next world title fight was against Joe Frazier in 1971 which he lost. But in Kinshasa he returned to winning ways beating George Foreman with an eighth round knock-out. Ali never liked anything that was ordinary and he defied the pundits who claimed that if he won, 'It would be the biggest upset in the history of the planet!'

He beat Foreman because the champion lacked experience. The same happened to Leon Spinks (USA) whom Ali beat at New Orleans in September 1978 to win his third world heavyweight crown.

Spinks let himself down with poor defence as Ali went on to win on points. Ali reckoned he 'danced' round the ring for 15 rounds, putting his younger opponent to shame, but it was more a display of energy conservation by the 36-year-old superstar. Nevertheless, he had

regained boxing's most prized title for the second time.

Right from the start the young Clay had been telling the world he was the greatest. After the win over Spinks he asked the media: 'Am I the greatest of all time?' stressing the 'all time'. Perhaps for once they just had to agree.

The first of his three titles, and boy is he pleased at stopping the 'Big Ugly Bear' Sonny Liston (USA) in 1964. The Photo Source

Larry Holmes (b. 1949)

When Larry Holmes entered the ring for his 49th professional fight, against Michael Spinks (USA) in 1985, there was not only the heavyweight championship of the world at stake, but Holmes had a personal goal. That goal was to emulate the great Rocky Marciano (USA) and become only the second heavyweight champion to win 49 successive fights.

Holmes felt as though he had lived in the shadow of Muhammad Ali for too long and that if he could emulate Marciano's feat this would change. But it was not to be.

In an uninspiring 15-round contest at Las Vegas's Riviera Hotel Holmes lost his 48-fight unbeaten record. His retirement, which had been pending from his previous three or four fights, was immediately announced. And the

son of a Georgia cropper (he was one of 11 children) also announced that he was going to enjoy his family and the 'bright lights' he had turned his back on for 17 years.

Those years had been ones of real blood, sweat and tears for Holmes, who turned professional in 1973. Despite knocking out opponent after opponent in his early days he still failed to gain recognition. And, although he was used by Muhammad Ali and Joe Frazier as a sparring partner, he was still not recognized as a potential champion.

He was given his world title chance in 1978 but, even after he won the WBC title from Ken Norton (USA), there was still a shortage of backers for the 6ft 3in fighter with two powerful fists and a tremendous left jab. The boxing world eventually took notice of the 'Black Cloud' after his next eight world title opponents, of which one was Ali, were all stopped by him.

Holmes, who relinquished his WBC title to become the IBF's first heavyweight champion in 1984, certainly went on to become a great champion and has, rightly so, been talked about in the same breath as Ali, Joe Louis and Rocky Marciano.

Holmes tried to win back his crown in April 1986 but strange scoring by the judges resulted in Michael Spinks retaining his title. Despite an appeal to the IBF's grievance committee Larry Holmes could not get the title back. However, the 18 years of toil paid off financially for Holmes and he wisely invested his estimated $50 million earnings – unlike many heavyweight champions of the past.

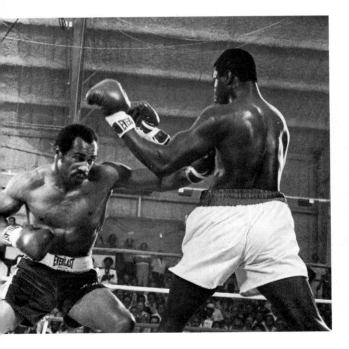

Ken Norton (USA) (left) lands a punch to Larry Holmes' stomach during their meeting for the WBC heavyweight title at Caesars Palace, Las Vegas, in 1978. Holmes became the new champion with a 15-round split decision. UPI/Bettmann Newsphotos

CAREER HIGHLIGHTS
Professional bouts: 50
Won: 48
Lost: 2
Holmes stopped 15 of his 23 world title fight opponents.

Larry Holmes after making his second successful defence of the IBF heavyweight title against Carl 'The Truth' Williams (USA) at Reno, Nevada in May 1985.
The Photo Source

British Champions

Since the early days of boxing there have always been claimants to 'British titles'. The following is a list of all recognized champions since 5 March 1891 when the National Sporting Club was accepted as the controlling body.

HEAVYWEIGHT

Ted Pritchard	1891
Jem Smith	1895
George Crisp	1897
Jack Palmer	1903
Gunner Jim Moir	1906
William 'Iron' Hague	1909
Bombardier Billy Wells	1911
Joe Beckett	1919
Frank Goddard	1919
Joe Beckett	1919
Frank Goddard	1923
Phil Scott	1926
Reggie Meen	1931
Jack Petersen	1932
Len Harvey	1933
Jack Petersen	1934
Ben Foord	1936
Tommy Farr	1937
Len Harvey	1938
Jack London	1944
Bruce Woodcock	1945
Jack Gardner	1950
Johnny Williams	1952
Don Cockell	1953
Joe Erskine	1956
Brian London	1958
Henry Cooper	1959
Jack Bodell	1969
Henry Cooper	1970
Joe Bugner	1971
Jack Bodell	1971
Danny McAlinden	1972
Bunny Johnson	1975
Richard Dunn	1975
Joe Bugner	1976
John L. Gardner	1978
Gordon Ferris	1981
Neville Meade	1981
David Pearce	1983
Hughroy Currie	1985
Horace Notice	1986

CRUISERWEIGHT

Sammy Reeson	1985
Andy Straughn	1985
Roy Smith	1987
Tee Jay	1987

LIGHT-HEAVYWEIGHT

Dick Smith	1914
Harry Reeve	1916
Dick Smith	1918
Boy McCormick	1919
Jack Bloomfield	1922
Tom Berry	1925
Gipsy Daniels	1927
Frank Moody	1927
Harry Crossley	1929
Jack Petersen	1932
Len Harvey	1933
Eddie Phillips	1935
Jock McAvoy	1937
Len Harvey	1938
Freddie Mills	1942
Don Cockell	1950
Randolph Turpin	1952
Dennis Powell	1953
Alex Buxton	1953
Randolph Turpin	1955
Ron Barton	1956
Randolph Turpin	1956
Chick Calderwood	1960
John 'Young' McCormack	1967
Eddie Avoth	1969
Chris Finnegan	1971
John Conteh	1973
Johnny Frankham	1975
Chris Finnegan	1975
Tim Wood	1976
Bunny Johnson	1977
Tom Collins	1982
Dennis Andries	1984
Tom Collins	1987

MIDDLEWEIGHT

Ted Pritchard	1891
Tony Diamond	1898
Pat O'Keefe	1906
Tom Thomas	1906
Jim Sullivan	1910
Jack Harrison	1912
Pat O'Keefe	1914
Bandsman Blake	1916
Pat O'Keefe	1918
Ted 'Kid' Lewis	1920
Tom Gummer	1920
Gus Platts	1921
Johnny Basham	1921
Ted 'Kid' Lewis	1921
Roland Todd	1923
Tommy Milligan	1926
Frank Moody	1927
Alex Ireland	1928
Frank Moody	1928
Alex Ireland	1928
Len Harvey	1929
Jock McAvoy	1933
Ernie Roderick	1945
Vince Hawkins	1946
Dick Turpin	1948
Albert Finch	1950
Randolph Turpin	1950
Johnny Sullivan	1954
Pat McAteer	1955
Terry Downes	1958
John 'Cowboy' McCormack	1959
Terry Downes	1959
George Aldridge	1962
Mick Leahy	1963
Wally Swift	1964
Johnny Pritchett	1965
Les McAteer	1969
Mark Rowe	1970
Bunny Sterling	1970
Kevin Finnegan	1974
Bunny Sterling	1975
Alan Minter	1975
Kevin Finnegan	1977
Alan Minter	1977
Tony Sibson	1979
Kevin Finnegan	1979
Roy Gumbs	1981
Mark Kaylor	1983
Tony Sibson	1984
Herol Graham	1985
Brian Anderson	1986
Tony Sibson	1987

LIGHT-MIDDLEWEIGHT

Larry Paul	1973
Maurice Hope	1974
Jimmy Batten	1977
Pat Thomas	1979
Herol Graham	1981
Prince Rodney	1983
Jimmy Cable	1984
Prince Rodney	1985
Chris Pyatt	1986
Lloyd Hibbert	1987

WELTERWEIGHT

Pat O'Keefe	1903
Charlie Allum	1903
Charlie Knock	1906
Curley Watson	1906
Andrew Jeptha	1907
Joe White	1907
Curley Watson	1907
Joe White	1908
Young Joseph	1908
Arthur Evernden	1911
Johnny Summers	1912
Tom McCormick	1914
Matt Wells	1914
Johnny Basham	1914
Ted 'Kid' Lewis	1920
Tommy Milligan	1924
Hamilton Johnny Brown	1925
Harry Mason	1925
Jack Hood	1926
Harry Mason	1934
Pat Butler	1934
Dave McCleave	1936
Jake Kilrain	1936
Ernie Roderick	1939
Henry Hall	1948
Eddie Thomas	1949
Wally Thom	1951
Cliff Curvis	1952
Wally Thom	1953
Peter Waterman	1956

Tommy Molloy	1958
Wally Swift	1960
Brian Curvis	1960
Johnny Cooke	1967
Ralph Charles	1968
Bobby Arthur	1972
John H. Stracey	1973
Pat Thomas	1975
Henry Rhiney	1976
Kirkland Laing	1979
Colin Jones	1980
Lloyd Honeyghan	1983
Kostas Petrou	1985
Sylvester Mittee	1985
Lloyd Honeyghan	1985
Kirkland Laing	1987

JUNIOR-WELTERWEIGHT

Des Rae	1968
Vic Andreetti	1969

Division abolished 1969, revived 1973 as light-welterweight

LIGHT-WELTERWEIGHT

Des Morrison	1973
Pat McCormack	1974
Joey Singleton	1974
Dave Green	1976
Colin Power	1977
Clinton McKenzie	1978
Colin Power	1979
Clinton McKenzie	1979
Terry Marsh	1984
Tony Laing	1985
Tony McKenzie	1986
Lloyd Christie	1987

LIGHTWEIGHT

Dick Burge	1891
Tom Causer	1897
Dick Burge	1897
Jabez White	1899
Jack Goldswain	1906
Johnny Summers	1908
Freddie Welsh	1909
Matt Wells	1911
Freddie Welsh	1912
Bob Marriott	1919
Ernie Rice	1921
Seaman James Hall	1922
Harry Mason	1923
Ernie Izzard	1924
Harry Mason	1925
Sam Steward	1928
Fred Webster	1929
Al Foreman	1930
Johnny Cuthbert	1932
Harry Mizler	1934
Jack 'Kid' Berg	1934
Jimmy Walsh	1936
Dave Crowley	1938
Eric Boon	1938
Ronnie James	1944
Billy Thompson	1947
Tommy McGovern	1951
Frank Johnson	1952
Joe Lucy	1953

Bombardier Billy Wells knocks out Bandsman Blake in the fourth round to retain his British heavyweight title in 1914. Wells made a record 13 successful defences of the title. Syndication International

Frank Johnson	1955
Joe Lucy	1956
Dave Charnley	1957
Maurice Cullen	1965
Ken Buchanan	1968
Willie Reilly	1972
Jim Watt	1972
Ken Buchanan	1973
Jim Watt	1975
Charlie Nash	1978
Ray Cattouse	1980
George Feeney	1982
Tony Willis	1985

JUNIOR-LIGHTWEIGHT

(Division abolished 1969 but reinstated 1986)

Jimmy Anderson	1968
John Doherty	1986

Pat Cowdell	1986
Najib Daho	1986

FEATHERWEIGHT

Fred Johnson	1895
Ben Jordan	1897
Jack Roberts	1901
Ben Jordan	1902
Joe Bowker	1905
Johnny Summers	1906
Jim Driscoll	1906
Johnny Summers	1906
Frank 'Spike' Robson	1906
Jim Driscoll	1907
Ted 'Kid' Lewis	1913
Llew Edwards	1915
Charlie Hardcastle	1917
James 'Tancy' Lee	1917

Five former British champions. From left to right: Dave Charnley (lightweight), Jack Petersen (light-heavyweight and heavyweight), Charlie Nash (lightweight), Henry Cooper (heavyweight) and Howard Winstone (featherweight). Syndication International

Mike Honeyman	1920	Andrew Tokell	1902
Joe Fox	1921	Harry Ware	1902
George McKenzie	1924	Joe Bowker	1902
Johnny Curley	1925	Digger Stanley	1910
Johnny Cuthbert	1927	Billy Beynon	1913
Harry Corbett	1928	Digger Stanley	1913
Johnny Cuthbert	1929	Con 'Curley' Walker	1914
Nel Tarleton	1931	Joe Fox	1915
Seaman Tommy Watson	1932	Tommy Noble	1918
Nel Tarleton	1934	Walter Ross	1919
Johnny McGrory	1936	Jim Higgins	1920
Jim 'Spider' Kelly	1938	Tommy Harrison	1922
Johnny Cusick	1939	Bugler Harry Lake	1923
Nel Tarleton	1940	Johnny Brown	1923
Ronnie Clayton	1947	Alf 'Kid' Pattenden	1928
Sammy McCarthy	1954	Teddy Baldock	1928
Billy 'Spider' Kelly	1955	Alf 'Kid' Pattenden	1928
Charlie Hill	1956	Teddy Baldock	1929
Bobby Neill	1959	Dick Corbett	1931
Terry Spinks	1960	Johnny King	1932
Howard Winstone	1961	Dick Corbett	1934
Jimmy Revie	1969	Johnny King	1935
Evan Armstrong	1971	Jackie Paterson	1947
Tommy Glencross	1972	Stan Rowan	1949
Evan Armstrong	1973	Danny O'Sullivan	1949
Vernon Sollas	1975	Peter Keenan	1951
Alan Richardson	1977	John Kelly	1953
Dave Needham	1978	Peter Keenan	1954
Pat Cowdell	1979	Freddie Gilroy	1959
Steve Sims	1982	John Caldwell	1964
Barry McGuigan	1983	Alan Rudkin	1965
Robert Dickie	1986	Walter McGowan	1966
		Alan Rudkin	1968
		Johnny Clark	1973
		Dave Needham	1974
		Paddy Maguire	1975
		Johnny Owen	1977
		John Feeney	1981

BANTAMWEIGHT

Billy Plimmer	1891
Pedlar Palmer	1895
Harry Ware	1900

Hugh Russell	1983
David Larmour	1983
John Feeney	1983
Ray Gilbody	1985
Billy Hardy	1987

FLYWEIGHT

Sid Smith	1911
Bill Ladbury	1913
Percy Jones	1914
Joe Symonds	1914
Tancy Lee	1914
Joe Symonds	1915
Jimmy Wilde	1916
Elky Clark	1924
Johnny Hill	1927
Jackie Brown	1929
Bert Kirby	1930
Jackie Brown	1931
Benny Lynch	1935
Jackie Paterson	1939
Rinty Monaghan	1948
Terry Allen	1951
Teddy Gardner	1952
Terry Allen	1952
Dai Dower	1955
Frankie Jones	1957
John Caldwell	1960
Jackie Brown	1962
Walter McGowan	1963
John McCluskey	1967
Charlie Magri	1977
Kelvin Smart	1982
Hugh Russell	1984
Duke McKenzie	1985
Dave McAuley	1986

Len Harvey — holder of British titles at middleweight, light-heavyweight and heavyweight. Syndication International

Title holders at three weights

Len Harvey
(middleweight, light-heavyweight, heavyweight)
Ted 'Kid' Lewis
(featherweight, welterweight, middleweight)
Johnny Summers
(featherweight, lightweight, welterweight)

Longest reigning champions

12 years — Jock McAvoy (middleweight) 1933–45

11 years 9 months — Johnny King (bantamweight) 1935–47

10 years 8 months — John McCluskey (flyweight) 1967–77

10 years 5 months — Henry Cooper (heavyweight) 1959–69

Shortest reigning champions

24 days – Frank Goddard (heavyweight) 25 May–17 June 1919

37 days – Pat Cowdell (Junior-lightweight) 17 April–24 May 1986

41 days – Dave McCleave (welterweight) 23 April–2 June 1936

43 days – Hamilton Johnny Brown (welterweight) 8 October–19 November 1925

Most successful defences

13 – Bombadier Billy Wells (heavyweight)
8 – Henry Cooper (heavyweight)

8 – William 'Iron' Hague (heavyweight)
6 – Brian Curvis (welterweight)
6 – Len Harvey (middleweight)
6 – Howard Winstone (featherweight)

Shortest contest

40s – Dave Charnley knocked out Darkie Hughes (lightweight) at Nottingham on 20 November 1961

Lonsdale Belts

The original Lonsdale Belts were given to the National Sporting Club by the 5th Earl of Lonsdale in 1909. These belts were replaced by redesigned belts in 1936 which were issued by the British Boxing Board of Control. A belt is awarded to a fighter who wins three title fights, not necessarily in succession, in any one weight division. Winners: (weight division appears in brackets)

30 Jan 1911	Jim Driscoll (Fe)
11 Nov 1912	Freddie Welsh (L)
27 Oct 1913	Digger Stanley (B)
1 May 1916	Johnny Basham (W)
18 Dec 1916	Bombardier Billy Wells (H)
11 Mar 1917	Jimmy Wilde (Fl)
25 Jun 1917	Joe Fox (B)
28 Jan 1918	Pat O'Keefe (M)
25 Feb 1918	Dick Smith (LH)
24 Feb 1919	Tancy Lee (Fe)
31 Jan 1921	Jim Higgins (B)
19 Oct 1925	Johnny Brown (B)
22 May 1930	Len Harvey (M)
22 May 1930	Johnny Cuthbert (Fe)
13 Mar 1933	Jack Hood (W)
12 Jul 1933	Jack Petersen (H)
11 Dec 1933	Jackie Brown (Fl)
12 Dec 1934	Nel Tarleton (Fe)
24 June 1935	Jock McAvoy (M)
31 May 1937	Johnny King (B)
9 Dec 1939	Eric Boon (L)
29 Sep 1941	Ernie Roderick (W)
19 Jun 1943	Jackie Paterson (Fl)
23 Feb 1945	Nel Tarleton (Fe)
11 Jul 1950	Billy Thompson (L)
28 Nov 1950	Ronnie Clayton (Fe)
28 Jan 1953	Peter Keenan (B)
12 May 1953	Ronnie Clayton (Fe)
16 Feb 1954	Terry Allen (Fl)
19 Oct 1954	Wally Thom (W)
26 Jun 1956	Joe Lucy (L)
26 Nov 1956	Randolph Turpin (LH)
22 May 1957	Peter Keenan (B)
5 Sep 1957	Pat McAteer (M)
2 Jul 1958	Charlie Hill (Fe)
5 Jul 1960	Terry Downes (M)
21 Mar 1961	Henry Cooper (H)
31 Oct 1961	Brian Curvis (W)
3 Mar 1962	Freddie Gilroy (B)
30 May 1962	Howard Winstone (Fe)
20 May 1963	Dave Charnley (L)
30 Jul 1963	Chic Calderwood (LH)
9 Dec 1963	Howard Winstone (Fe)
24 Feb 1964	Henry Cooper (H)
28 Jul 1964	Brian Curvis (W)
Nov 1966	Walter McGowan (Fl)

McGowan was awarded a belt three years after winning the title. No worthy challengers could be found for him

6 Jun 1966	Maurice Cullen (L)
20 Feb 1967	Johnny Pritchett (M)
7 Nov 1967	Henry Cooper (H)
25 Feb 1969	Jimmy Anderson (JL)

9 Jun 1969	Alan Rudkin (B)
7 Dec 1971	Ralph Charles (W)
17 Jan 1973	Bunny Sterling (M)
29 Jan 1973	Ken Buchanan (L)
17 Sep 1973	Evan Armstrong (Fe)
14 Oct 1974	John McCluskey (Fl)
14 Oct 1975	Chris Finnegan (LH)
11 Nov 1975	Joey Singleton (LW)
20 Apr 1976	Maurice Hope (LM)
14 Sep 1976	Alan Minter (M)
21 Feb 1977	Jim Watt (L)
12 Sep 1978	Jimmy Batten (LM)
6 Feb 1979	Colin Power (LW)
13 Jun 1979	Johnny Owen (B)
6 Nov 1979	Kevin Finnegan (M)
27 Feb 1980	Bunny Johnson (LH)
29 May 1980	Pat Cowdell (Fe)
16 Sep 1980	Pat Thomas (LM)
6 Jan 1981	Clinton McKenzie (LW)
24 Apr 1981	Colin Jones (W)
18 Feb 1982	Roy Gumbs (M)
8 Apr 1983	Clinton McKenzie (LW)
3 Sep 1983	Tom Collins (LH)
10 Feb 1984	George Feeney (L)
10 Oct 1984	Dennis Andries (LH)
6 Sep 1985	Prince Rodney (LM)
27 Nov 1985	Lloyd Honeyghan (W)
24 May 1986	Tony Willis (L)
29 Oct 1986	Robert Dickie (Fe)
16 Sep 1987	Tony Sibson (M)

Winners of two or more Lonsdale Belts

Ronnie Clayton (Fe)	1950, 1953
Henry Cooper (H)	1961, 1964, 1967
Brian Curvis (W)	1961, 1964
Peter Keenan (B)	1953, 1957
Clinton McKenzie (LW)	1981, 1983
Nel Tarleton (Fe)	1934, 1945
Howard Winstone (Fe)	1962, 1963

(Tarleton is the only man to have won National Sport Club and British Boxing Board of Control Belts outright.)

The only occasion that two fighters won Lonsdale Belts outright on the same bill was on 22 May 1930 at London's Olympia. Len Harvey beat Steve McCall to win a belt in the middleweight division and Johnny Cuthbert beat Dom Volante to win one in the featherweight division.

Outright winners in shortest time

203 days – Robert Dickie (9 Apr 1986–29 Oct 1986)
206 days – Pat Cowdell (6 Nov 1979–29 May 1980)
259 days – Dennis Andries (26 Jan–10 Oct 1984)

Outright winners in longest time

8 years 159 days – Tony Sibson (10 Apr 1979–16 Sep 1987)
7 years 273 days – John McCluskey (16 Jan 1967–14 Oct 1974)
6 years 287 days – Jack Hood (31 May 1926–13 Mar 1933)
6 years 42 days – Dave Charnley (9 Apr 1957–20 May 1963)

American Champions

Over the years there have been numerous claimants to American titles. Such a list would be virtually impossible to compile since different states recognized their own champions. The formation of the North American Boxing Federation (NABF) in 1969, and the United States Boxing Association (USBA) in 1979, has helped standardize American champions. The following is a full list of champions since 1969.

HEAVYWEIGHT

Leotis Martin	1969	NABF
Muhammad Ali	1972	NABF
Ken Norton	1973	NABF
Muhammad Ali	1973	NABF
Ken Norton	1975	NABF
Leroy Jones	1978	NABF
Mike Weaver	1979	USBA
Greg Page	1981	USBA
Lynn Ball	1981	NABF
Michael Dokes	1982	NABF
Tim Witherspoon	1983	NABF
James Broad	1984	NABF
David Bey	1984	USBA
Tim Witherspoon	1985	NABF
Trevor Berbick	1985	USBA
Tony Tucker	1986	USBA
Larry Alexander	1987	NABF
Carl Williams	1987	USBA

CRUISERWEIGHT

Marvin Camel	1979	NABF
S. T. Gordon	1980	NABF
Bashiru Ali	1980	USBA
Marvin Camel	1981	USBA
Leon Spinks	1982	NABF
Anthony Davis	1984	NABF
Bernard Benton	1984	USBA
Bashiru Ali	1985	NABF
Boone Pultz	1985	USBA
Stanley Ross	1985	USBA
Henry Tillman	1986	NABF
Joe Cooper	1986	NABF
Boone Pultz	1986	USBA
Sherman Griffin	1987	USBA

LIGHT-HEAVYWEIGHT

Jimmy Dupree	1970	NABF
Mike Quarry	1971	NABF
Lonnie Bennett	1974	NABF
Matt Franklin	1977	NABF
Jerry Martin	1979	NABF
Jerry Martin	1979	USBA
Murray Sutherland	1980	USBA
Eddie Davis	1982	USBA
Willie Edwards	1982	NABF
Pete McIntyre	1982	USBA
Willie Edwards	1983	NABF
Marvin Johnson	1985	USBA
Charles Williams	1987	NABF
Tony Willis	1986	USBA

SUPER-MIDDLEWEIGHT

Murray Sutherland	1984	USBA
Lindell Holmes	1986	USBA

MIDDLEWEIGHT

Denny Moyer	1970	NABF
Nate Williams	1970	NABF
Art Hernandez	1970	NABF
Denny Moyer	1971	NABF
Art Hernandez	1972	NABF
Bennie Briscoe	1973	NABF
Rodrigo Valdez	1973	NABF
George Cooper	1975	NABF
Sugar Ray Seales	1976	NABF
Ronnie Harris	1977	NABF
Curtis Parker	1980	USBA
Sammy Nesmith	1980	NABF
Sugar Ray Seales	1981	NABF
Frank Fletcher	1981	USBA
James Shuler	1982	NABF
Wilford Scypion	1983	USBA
Alex Ramos	1984	USBA
James Kinchen	1984	USBA
John Collins	1985	USBA
Thomas Hearns	1986	NABF
Robbie Sims	1986	USBA
Frank Tate	1987	USBA

LIGHT-MIDDLEWEIGHT

Ralph Palladin	1977	NABF
Edgar Ross	1978	NABF
Tony Chiaverini	1979	USBA
Nick Ortiz	1979	NABF
Steve Delgado	1980	NABF
Rocky Mosley, Jnr	1980	NABF
Rocky Fratto	1981	NABF
Gary Guiden	1981	USBA
David Braxton	1983	NABF
Duane Thomas	1983	USBA
Milton McCrory	1987	NABF
Don Curry	1987	USBA

WELTERWEIGHT

Armando Muniz	1971	NABF
Eddie Perkins	1973	NABF
Pete Ranzany	1976	NABF
Sugar Ray Leonard	1979	NABF
Thomas Hearns	1980	USBA
Greg Stephens	1980	NABF
Pepe Dominguez	1980	NABF
Babilah McCarthy	1981	USBA
Bruce Finch	1981	NABF
Kevin Morgan	1981	USBA
Donald Curry	1982	NABF
Marlon Starling	1982	USBA
Donald Curry	1982	USBA
Marlon Starling	1983	NABF
Marlon Starling	1983	USBA
Pedro Vilella	1984	NABF
Maurice Blocker	1985	NABF
Johnny Bumphus	1986	USBA
Tommy Ayers	1987	NABF

LIGHT-WELTERWEIGHT

Rollin Williams	1987	NABF
Adolfo Viruet	1975	NABF
Monroe Brooks	1977	NABF
Bruce Curry	1978	NABF
Willie Rodriguez	1979	USBA
Johnny Bumphus	1981	USBA
Leroy Haley	1981	NABF
Bruce Curry	1982	NABF
Ronnie Shields	1983	NABF
Gary Hinton	1984	USBA
Harold Brazier	1986	NABF
Frankie Warren	1986	USBA

LIGHTWEIGHT

Jimmy Robertson	1971	NABF
Erubey Carmona	1972	NABF
Esteban de Jesus	1973	NABF
Vicente Saldivar Mijares	1976	NABF
Andrew Ganigan	1978	NABF
Sean O'Grady	1979	USBA
Jorge Morales	1980	NABF
Ray Mancini	1981	NABF
Curtis Harris	1981	USBA
Ruben Munoz	1982	USBA
Roger Mayweather	1982	USBA
Jose Luis Ramirez	1982	NABF
Jimmy Paul	1983	USBA
Hector Camacho	1985	NABF
Greg Haugen	1986	NABF
Frankie Randall	1986	USBA
Terrence Ali	1986	USBA
Pernell Whitaker	1987	USBA
Pernell Whitaker	1987	NABF

JUNIOR-LIGHTWEIGHT

Ray Lunny III	1975	NABF
Tyrone Everett	1975	NABF
Rafael Limon	1978	NABF
Robert Mullins	1980	USBA
Johnny Sato	1981	NABF
Rolando Navarrete	1981	NABF
John Verderosa	1981	USBA
Blaine Dickson	1981	NABF
Hector Camacho	1981	NABF
Guy Villegas	1983	NABF
Refugio Rojas	1983	USBA
Dennis Cruz	1984	NABF
Kenny Baysmore	1984	USBA
Roger Mayweather	1985	USBA
Dwight Pritchett	1986	NABF
Kenny Baysmore	1986	USBA
Marion Miranda	1987	NABF
Harold Knight	1987	USBA

FEATHERWEIGHT

Antonio Gomez	1970	NABF
Ruben Olivares	1973	NABF
Tyrone Everett	1976	NABF
Ron McGarvey	1977	NABF

Mike Ayala	1978	NABF	
Rocky Lockridge	1980	USBA	
Nicky Perez	1980	NABF	
Juan Laporte	1981	USBA	
Jackie Beard	1982	NABF	
Refugio Rojas	1982	USBA	
Refugio Rojas	1983	USBA	
(Title declared vacant April–December 1983)			
Irving Mitchell	1984	USBA	
Calvin Grove	1985	USBA	
Baby Joe Ruelaz	1985	NABF	
Bernard Taylor	1986	NABF	

SUPER-BANTAMWEIGHT

Mike Ayala	1977	NABF
Rodolfo Martinez	1977	NABF
Earl Large	1978	NABF
Javier Flores	1978	NABF
Nicky Perez	1978	NABF
Mike Ayala	1980	NABF
Oscar Muniz	1984	USBA
Greg Richardson	1986	USBA
Daniel Zaragoza	1986	NABF

BANTAMWEIGHT

Jesus 'Chucho' Castillo	1970	NABF
Rafael Herrera	1971	NABF
Rodolfo Martinez	1972	NABF
Joe Guevara	1975	NABF
Roberto Rubaldino	1975	NABF
Jeff Chandler	1979	USBA
Jeff Chandler	1980	NABF
Johnny Carter	1980	USBA
Oscar Muniz	1981	NABF
Gaby Canizales	1982	USBA
Harold Petty	1982	NABF
Greg Richardson	1984	NABF
Hurley Snead	1985	USBA
Freddie Jackson	1985	USBA
Frankie Duarte	1986	NABF

FLYWEIGHT

Alberto Morales	1973	NABF
Antonio Avelar	1980	NABF

Willie Jensen	1981	USBA	
Freddy Castillo	1981	NABF	
Henry Brent	1982	USBA	
Mario Savala	1983	NABF	
Candido Tellez	1983	NABF	
Joey Olivo	1983	USBA	
Alonzo Gonzalez	1984	NABF	
Paul Gonzales	1986	NABF	

LIGHT-FLYWEIGHT

Juan Alvarez	1978	NABF
Guadalupe Madera	1978	NABF
Joey Olivo	1979	NABF
Wildebaldo Salazar	1987	NABF

Holders of both USBA and NABF titles in same weight division

Marvin Camel	–	cruiserweight
Bashiru Ali	–	cruiserweight
Jerry Martin	–	light-heavyweight
Donald Curry	–	welterweight
Marlon Starling	–	welterweight
Jeff Chandler	–	bantamweight

Holders of USBA and NABF titles simultaneously

Jerry Martin (light-heavyweight)
Nov 1979–Oct 1980
Jeff Chandler (bantamweight)
Feb–Nov 1980
Donald Curry (welterweight)
Oct 1982–Feb 1983
Marlon Starling (welterweight)
Apr 1983–Jun 1984
Pernell Whitaker (lightweight)
July 1987–

Title holders at two weights

– Murray Sutherland (light-heavyweight, super-middleweight)
– Hector Camacho (junior-lightweight, lightweight)
– Roger Mayweather (lightweight, junior-lightweight)
– Refugio Rojas (featherweight, junior-lightweight)
– Mike Ayala (super-bantamweight, featherweight)
– Nicky Perez (super-bantamweight, featherweight)
– Rodolfo Martinez (bantamweight, super-bantamweight)
– Tyrone Everett (junior-lightweight, featherweight)
– Oscar Muniz (bantamweight, super-bantamweight)
– Joey Olivo (light-flyweight, flyweight)
– Johnny Bumphus (light-welterweight, welterweight)
– Greg Richardson (bantamweight, super-bantamweight)
– Don Curry (welterweight, light-welterweight)

Longest reigning champion

7 years 3 months – Alberto Morales (NABF flyweight) May 1973 – August 1980.

Shortest reigning champion

28 days – Tyrone Everett (NABF featherweight) 10 February–11 March 1976

Commonwealth Champions

Although several fighters claimed to be champion of the British Empire in the early part of the 20th century, it was not until Jim Driscoll won the featherweight title in 1908 that records were started. A governing body, the British Commonwealth and Empire Boxing Championships Committee, was set up in 1954. Their aim was to control championship bouts. They still exist today although their name has been changed to the Commonwealth Boxing Championships Committee.

HEAVYWEIGHT

Tommy Burns	Canada	1910
Matthew Curran	England	1911
Bombardier Billy Wells	England	1911

Joe Beckett	England	1919
Phil Scott	England	1926
Larry Gains	Canada	1931
Len Harvey	England	1934
Jack Petersen	Wales	1934
Ben Foord	South Africa	1936
Tommy Farr	Wales	1937
Len Harvey	England	1939
Jack London	England	1944
Bruce Woodcock	England	1945
Jack Gardner	England	1950
Johnny Williams	Wales	1952
Don Cockell	England	1953
Joe Bygraves	Jamaica	1956

Joe Erskine	Wales	1957
Brian London	England	1958
Henry Cooper	England	1959
Joe Bugner	England	1971
Jack Bodell	England	1971
Danny McAlinden	N. Ireland	1972
Bunny Johnson	England	1975
Richard Dunn	England	1975
Joe Bugner	England	1976
John L. Gardner	England	1978
Trevor Berbick	Canada	1981
Horace Notice	England	1986

CRUISERWEIGHT

Stewart Lithgo	England	1984
Chisandra Mutti	Zambia	1984
Glenn McCrory	England	1987

LIGHT-HEAVYWEIGHT

Jack Bloomfield	England	1923
Tom Berry	England	1927
Billy 'Gypsy' Daniels	Wales	1927
Len Harvey	England	1939
Freddie Mills	England	1942
Randolph Turpin	England	1952
Gordon Wallace	Canada	1956
Yvon Durelle	Canada	1957
Mike Holt	South Africa	1960
Chic Calderwood	Scotland	1960
Bob Dunlop	Australia	1968
Eddie Avoth	Wales	1970
Chris Finnegan	England	1971
John Conteh	England	1973
Steve Aczel	Australia	1975
Tony Mundine	Australia	1975
Gary Summerhays	Canada	1978
Lotte Mwale	Zambia	1979
Leslie Stewart	Trinidad	1985
Willie Featherstone	Canada	1987

MIDDLEWEIGHT

Ted 'Kid' Lewis	England	1922
Roland Todd	England	1923
Tommy Milligan	Scotland	1926
Alex Ireland	Scotland	1928
Len Harvey	England	1929
Jock McAvoy	England	1933
Ron Richards	Australia	1940
Bos Murphy	New Zealand	1948
Dick Turpin	England	1948
Dave Sands	Australia	1949
Randolph Turpin	England	1952
Johnny Sullivan	England	1954
Pat McAteer	England	1955
Dick Tiger	Nigeria	1958
Wilf Greaves	Canada	1960
Dick Tiger	Nigeria	1960
Gomeo Brennan	Bahamas	1963
Tuna Scanlan	New Zealand	1964
Gomeo Brennan	Bahamas	1964
Blair Richardson	Canada	1966
Milo Calhoun	Jamaica	1967
Johnny Pritchett	England	1967
Les McAteer	England	1969
Mark Rowe	England	1970
Bunny Sterling	Jamaica	1970
Tony Mundine	Australia	1972
Monty Betham	New Zealand	1975
Al Korovou	Australia	1978
Ayub Kalule	Uganda	1978
Tony Sibson	England	1980

Roy Gumbs	England	1983
Mark Kaylor	England	1983
Tony Sibson	England	1984

LIGHT-MIDDLEWEIGHT

Charkey Ramon	Australia	1972
Maurice Hope	England	1976
Kenny Bristol	Guyana	1979
Herol Graham	England	1981
Ken Salisbury	Australia	1984
Nick Wilshire	England	1985
Lloyd Hibbert	England	1987
Troy Waters	Australia	1987

WELTERWEIGHT

Johnny Summers	England	1913
Tom McCormick	England	1914
Matt Wells	England	1914
Johnny Basham	Wales	1919
Ted 'Kid' Lewis	England	1920
Tommy Milligan	Scotland	1924
Eddie Thomas	Wales	1951
Wally Thom	England	1951
Cliff Curvis	Wales	1952
Gerald Dreyer	South Africa	1952
Barry Brown	New Zealand	1954
George Barnes	Australia	1954
Darby Brown	Australia	1956
George Barnes	Australia	1956
Johnny van Rensburg	South Africa	1958
George Barnes	Australia	1958
Brian Curvis	Wales	1960
Johnny Cooke	England	1967
Ralph Charles	England	1968
Clyde Gray	Canada	1973
Chris Clarke	Canada	1979
Clyde Gray	Canada	1979
Colin Jones	Wales	1981
Sylvester Mittee	England	1984
Lloyd Honeyghan	England	1985
Wilf Gentzen	Australia	1987

LIGHT-WELTERWEIGHT

Joe Tetteh	Ghana	1972
Hector Thompson	Australia	1973
Baby Cassius Austin	Australia	1977
Hector Thompson	Australia	1977
Baby Cassius Austin	Australia	1977
Jeff Malcolm	Australia	1978
Obisia Nwankpa	Nigeria	1979
Billy Famous	Nigeria	1983

LIGHTWEIGHT

Hughie Mehegan	Australia	1912
Freddie Welsh	Wales	1912
Al Foreman	Canada	1930
Jimmy Kelso	Australia	1933
Laurie Stevens	South Africa	1936
Arthur King	Canada	1948
Frank Johnson	England	1953
Pat Ford	Australia	1953
Ivor Germain	Barbados	1954
Pat Ford	Australia	1954
Johnny van Rensburg	South Africa	1955
Willie Toweel	South Africa	1956
Dave Charnley	England	1959
Bunny Grant	Jamaica	1962
Manny Santos	New Zealand	1967
Love Allotey	Ghana	1967
Percy Hayles	Jamaica	1968
Jonathan Dele	Nigeria	1975

Joe Bugner regained the British, Commonwealth and European titles with this first-round knock-out of Richard Dunn in 1976. Syndication International

Lennox Blackmore	Guyana	1977
Hogan Jimoh	Nigeria	1978
Langton Tinago	Zimbabwe	1980
Barry Michael	Australia	1981
Claude Noel	Trinidad	1982
Graham Brooke	Australia	1984
Barry Michael	Australia	1985
Langton Tinago	Zimbabwe	1986
Mo Hussein	England	1987

JUNIOR LIGHTWEIGHT

Billy Moeller	Australia	1975
Johnny Aba	Papua New Guinea	1977
Langton Tinago	Zimbabwe	1983
John Sichula	Zambia	1984
Lester Ellis	Australia	1984
John Sichula	Zambia	1985
Sam Akromah	Ghana	1987
John Sichula	Zambia	1987

FEATHERWEIGHT

Jim Driscoll	Wales	1908
Llew Edwards	Wales	1915
Johnny McGrory	Scotland	1936
Jim 'Spider' Kelly	N. Ireland	1938
Johnny Cusick	England	1939
Nel Tarleton	England	1940
Al Phillips	England	1947
Ronnie Clayton	England	1947
Roy Ankrah	Ghana	1951
Billy 'Spider' Kelly	N. Ireland	1954
Hogan Bassey	Nigeria	1955
Percy Lewis	Trinidad	1957
Floyd Robertson	Ghana	1960
John O'Brien	Scotland	1967
Johnny Famechon	Australia	1967
Toro George	New Zealand	1970
Bobby Dunne	Australia	1972
Evan Armstrong	Scotland	1974

David 'Poison' Kotey	Ghana	1974
Eddie Ndukwu	Nigeria	1977
Pat Ford	Guyana	1980
Azumah Nelson	Ghana	1981
Tyrone Downes	Barbados	1986

BANTAMWEIGHT

Jim Higgins	Scotland	1920
Tommy Harrison	England	1922
Bugler Harry Lake	England	1923
Johnny Brown	England	1923
Teddy Baldock	England	1928
Dick Corbett	England	1930
Johnny King	England	1932
Dick Corbett	England	1934
Jim Brady	Scotland	1941
Jackie Paterson	Scotland	1945
Stan Rowan	England	1949
Vic Toweel	South Africa	1949
Jimmy Carruthers	Australia	1952
Peter Keenan	Scotland	1955
Freddie Gilroy	N. Ireland	1959
John Caldwell	N. Ireland	1964
Alan Rudkin	England	1965
Walter McGowan	Scotland	1966
Alan Rudkin	England	1968
Lionel Rose	Australia	1969
Alan Rudkin	England	1970
Paul Ferreri	Australia	1972
Sulley Shittu	Ghana	1977
Johnny Owen	Wales	1978
Paul Ferreri	Australia	1981
Ray Minus jnr	Bahamas	1986

FLYWEIGHT

Elky Clark	Scotland	1924
Jackie Paterson	Scotland	1940
Rinty Monaghan	N. Ireland	1948
Teddy Gardner	England	1952

Jake Tuli	South Africa	1952
Dai Dower	Wales	1954
Frankie Jones	Scotland	1957
Dennis Adams	South Africa	1957
Jackie Brown	Scotland	1962
Walter McGowan	Scotland	1963
John McCluskey	Scotland	1970
Henry Nissen	Australia	1971
Big Jim West	Australia	1974
Patrick Mambwe	Zambia	1976
Ray Amoo	Nigeria	1980
Stephen Muchoki	Kenya	1980
Keith Wallace	England	1983
Richard Clarke	Jamaica	1986

Longest reigning champion

12 years 2 months – Henry Cooper (Eng) heavyweight, January 1959–March 1971

Shortest reigning champion

36 days – Richard Dunn (Eng) heavyweight, 30 September–4 November 1975

First winners from each country

Australia	1912 Hughie Mehegan (lightweight)
Bahamas	1963 Gomeo Brennan (middleweight)
Barbados	1954 Ivor Germain (lightweight)
Canada	1910 Tommy Burns (heavyweight)
England	1911 Matthew Curran (heavyweight)
Ghana	1951 Roy Ankrah (featherweight)
Guyana	1977 Lennox Blackmore (lightweight)
Jamaica	1956 Joe Bygraves (heavyweight)
Kenya	1980 Stephen Muchoki (flyweight)
New Zealand	1948 Bos Murphy (middleweight)
Nigeria	1955 Hogan Bassey (featherweight)
Northern Ireland	1938 Jim 'Spider' Kelly (featherweight)
Papua New Guinea	1977 Johnny Aba (junior-lightweight)
Scotland	1920 Jim Higgins (bantamweight)
South Africa	1936 Laurie Stevens (lightweight)
Trinidad	1957 Percy Lewis (featherweight)
Uganda	1978 Ayub Kalule (middleweight)
Wales	1908 Jim Driscoll (featherweight)
Zambia	1976 Patrick Mambwe (flyweight)
Zimbabwe	1980 Langton Tinago (lightweight)

Title holder at three weights

Len Harvey (Eng)
(heavyweight, light-heavyweight, middleweight)

Most successful defences

10 – Henry Cooper (Eng) heavyweight
7 – Brian Curvis (Wal) welterweight
7 – Paul Ferreri (Aus) bantamweight
7 – Clyde Gray (Can) welterweight
6 – Johnny Aba (PNG) junior-lightweight
6 – Len Harvey (Eng) middleweight

Shortest contest

55 s – Matt Curran (Eng) beat Bill Lang (Aus) 18 January 1911, heavyweight, London.

Fighters who have regained Commonwealth titles

HEAVYWEIGHT
Len Harvey (Eng)	1939
Joe Bugner (Eng)	1976

MIDDLEWEIGHT
Dick Tiger (Ngr)	1960
Gomeo Brennan (Bah)	1964
Tony Sibson (Eng)	1984

WELTERWEIGHT
George Barnes (Aus)	1956, 1958
Clyde Gray (Can)	1979

LIGHT-WELTERWEIGHT
Hector Thompson (Aus)	1977
Baby Cassius Austin (Aus)	1977

LIGHTWEIGHT
Al Foreman (Can)	1933
Pat Ford (Aus)	1954
Barry Michael (Aus)	1985
Langton Tinago (Zim)	1986

JUNIOR LIGHTWEIGHT
John Sichula (Zam)	1985

BANTAMWEIGHT
Dick Corbett (Eng)	1934
Alan Rudkin (Eng)	1968, 1970
Paul Ferreri (Aus)	1981

Warwickshire County cricketer Anton Ferreira once fought former WBA heavyweight champion Gerrie Coetzee (SA). Ferreira, whose father has been involved with amateur boxing in South Africa for over 45 years, won the 1971 Northern Transvaal heavyweight title and, at the same time, maintained his unbeaten record. Coetzee won the Eastern Transvaal title and the pair of them met at Elsburg, Germiston, for the Transvaal title. Ferreira's unbeaten record disappeared in round one!

European Champions

The International Boxing Union (IBU) was formed in Paris in 1911. One of its duties was to control championship bouts for European titles. The IBU changed its name in 1946 to the European Boxing Union (EBU). N.B. All Germany's post 1945 are West Germany.

HEAVYWEIGHT

Gunner Moir	Great Britain	1906
Iron Hague	Great Britain	1909
Bombadier Billy Wells	Great Britain	1911
Georges Carpentier	France	1913
Battling Siki	Senegal	1922
Erminio Spalla	Italy	1923
Paolino Uzcudun	Spain	1926
Pierre Charles	Belgium	1929
Hein Muller	Germany	1931
Pierre Charles	Belgium	1932
Paolino Uzcudun	Spain	1933
Primo Carnera	Italy	1933
Pierre Charles	Belgium	1935
Arno Kolblin	Germany	1937
Heinz Lazek	Austria	1938
Adolph Heuser	Germany	1939
Max Schmeling	Germany	1939
Olle Tandberg	Sweden	1943
Karel Sys	Belgium	1943
Bruce Woodcock	Great Britain	1946
Jo Weidin	Austria	1950
Jack Gardner	Great Britain	1951
Hein Ten Hoff	Germany	1951
Karel Sys	Belgium	1952
Heinz Neuhaus	Germany	1952
Franco Cavicchi	Italy	1955
Ingemar Johansson	Sweden	1956
Dick Richardson	Great Britain	1960
Ingemar Johansson	Sweden	1962
Henry Cooper	Great Britain	1964
Karl Mildenberger	Germany	1964
Henry Cooper	Great Britain	1968
Peter Weiland	Germany	1969
Jose Urtain	Spain	1970
Henry Cooper	Great Britain	1970
Joe Bugner	Great Britain	1971
Jack Bodell	Great Britain	1971
Jose Urtain	Spain	1971
Jurgen Blin	Germany	1972
Joe Bugner	Great Britain	1972
Richard Dunn	Great Britain	1976
Joe Bugner	Great Britain	1976
Jean-Pierre Coopman	Belgium	1977
Lucien Rodriguez	France	1977
Alfredo Evangelista	Spain	1977
Lorenzo Zanon	Italy	1979
John L. Gardner	Great Britain	1980
Lucien Rodriguez	France	1981
Stefan Tangstad	Norway	1984
Anders Eklund	Sweden	1985
Frank Bruno	Great Britain	1985
Steffen Tangstad	Norway	1986
Alfredo Evangelista	Spain	1987
Anders Eklund	Sweden	1987

CRUISERWEIGHT

Sammy Reeson	Great Britain	1987

LIGHT-HEAVYWEIGHT

Georges Carpentier	France	1913
Battling Siki	France	1922
Emile Morelle	France	1923
Raymond Bonnel	France	1923
Luis Clement	Switzerland	1924
Herman van T'Hof	Holland	1926
Fernand Delarge	Belgium	1926
Max Schmeling	Germany	1927
Michele Bonaglia	Italy	1929
Ernst Pistulla	Germany	1931
Adolph Heuser	Germany	1932
John Andersson	Sweden	1933
Martinez de Alfara	Spain	1934
Marcel Thil	France	1934
Merlo Preciso	Italy	1935
Heinz Lazek	Austria	1935
Gustav Roth	Belgium	1936
Adolph Heuser	Germany	1938
Luigi Musina	Italy	1942
Freddie Mills	Great Britain	1947
Albert Yvel	France	1950
Don Cockell	Great Britain	1951
Conny Rux	Germany	1952
Jacques Hairabedian	France	1953
Gerhard Hecht	Germany	1954
Willi Hoepner	Germany	1955
Gerhard Hecht	Germany	1955
Artimio Calzavara	Italy	1957
Willi Hoepner	Germany	1958
Erich Schoppner	Germany	1958
Giulio Rinaldi	Italy	1962
Gustav Scholz	Germany	1964
Giulio Rinaldi	Italy	1965
Piero del Papa	Italy	1966
Lothar Stengel	Germany	1967
Tom Bogs	Denmark	1968
Yvan Prebeg	Yugoslavia	1969
Piero del Papa	Italy	1970
Connie Velensek	Germany	1971
Chris Finnegan	Great Britain	1972
Rudiger Schmidtke	Germany	1972
John Conteh	Great Britain	1973
Domenico Adinolfi	Italy	1974
Mate Parlov	Yugoslavia	1976
Aldo Traversaro	Italy	1977
Rudi Koopmans	Holland	1979
Richard Caramanolis	France	1984
Alex Blanchard	Holland	1984

MIDDLEWEIGHT

Georges Carpentier	France	1912
Ercole Balzac	France	1920
Gus Platts	Great Britain	1921
Johnny Basham	Great Britain	1921
Ted 'Kid' Lewis	Great Britain	1921
Roland Todd	Great Britain	1923
Bruno Frattini	Italy	1924
Tommy Milligan	Great Britain	1925
Rene Devos	Belgium	1926
Mario Bosisio	Italy	1928
Leoni Jacovacci	Italy	1928
Marcel Thil	France	1929

Mario Bosisio	Italy	1930
Poldi Steinbach	Austria	1931
Hein Domgorgen	Germany	1931
Ignacio Ara	Spain	1932
Gustav Roth	Belgium	1933
Marcel Thil	France	1934
Edouard Tenet	France	1938
Bep van Klavaren	Holland	1938
Anton Christoforidis	Greece	1938
Edouard Tenet	France	1939
Josef Besselmann	Germany	1942
Marcel Cerdan	France	1947
Cyrille Delannoit	Belgium	1948
Marcel Cerdan	France	1948
Cyrille Delannoit	Belgium	1948
Tiberio Mitri	Italy	1949
Randolph Turpin	Great Britain	1951
Tiberio Mitri	Italy	1954
Charles Humez	France	1954
Gustav Scholz	Germany	1958
John McCormack	Great Britain	1961
Chris Christensen	Denmark	1962
Laszlo Papp	Hungary	1962
Nino Benvenuti	Italy	1965
Juan Carlos Duran	Italy	1967
Tom Bogs	Denmark	1969
Juan Carlos Duran	Italy	1970
Jean-Claude Boutier	France	1971
Tom Bogs	Denmark	1973
Elio Calcabrina	Italy	1973
Jean-Claude Boutier	France	1974
Kevin Finnegan	Great Britain	1974
Gratien Tonna	France	1975
Bunny Sterling	Great Britain	1976
Angelo Jacopucci	Italy	1976
Germano Valsecchi	Italy	1976
Alan Minter	Great Britain	1977
Gratien Tonna	France	1977
Alan Minter	Great Britain	1978
Kevin Finnegan	Great Britain	1980
Matteo Salvemini	Italy	1980
Tony Sibson	Great Britain	1980
Louis Acaries	France	1982
Tony Sibson	Great Britain	1984
Ayub Kalule	Denmark	1985
Herol Graham	Great Britain	1986
Sambu Kalambay	Italy	1987

LIGHT-MIDDLEWEIGHT

Bruno Visintin	Italy	1964
Bo Hogberg	Sweden	1966
Yolande Leveque	France	1966
Sandro Mazzinghi	Italy	1966
Remo Golfarini	Italy	1968
Gerhard Piaskowy	Germany	1969
Jose Hernandez	Spain	1970
Juan Carlos Duran	Italy	1972
Jacques Kechichian	France	1973
Jose Duran	Spain	1974
Eckhard Dagge	Germany	1975
Vito Antuofermo	Italy	1976
Maurice Hope	Great Britain	1976
Gilbert Cohen	France	1978
Marijan Benes	Yugoslavia	1979
Luis Arcaries	France	1981
Luigi Minchillo	Italy	1981
Herol Graham	Great Britain	1983
Jimmy Cable	Great Britain	1984
Georg Steinherr	Germany	1984
Said Skouma	France	1985
Chris Pyatt	Great Britain	1986
Gianfranco Rosi	Italy	1987

WELTERWEIGHT

Young Joseph	Great Britain	1910
Georges Carpentier	France	1911
Albert Badoud	Switzerland	1915
Ted 'Kid' Lewis	Great Britain	1920
Piet Hobin	Belgium	1921
Mario Bosisio	Italy	1925
Alf Genon	Belgium	1928
Gustav Roth	Belgium	1929
Adrien Aneet	Belgium	1932
Jack Hood	Great Britain	1933
Gustav Eder	Germany	1934
Felix Wouters	Belgium	1936
Saverio Turiello	Italy	1938
Marcel Cerdan	France	1939
Ernie Roderick	Great Britain	1946
Robert Villemain	France	1947
Livio Minelli	Italy	1949
Michel Palermo	Italy	1950
Eddie Thomas	Great Britain	1951
Charles Humez	France	1951
Gilbert Lavoine	France	1953
Wally Thom	Great Britain	1954
Idrissa Dione	France	1955
Emilio Marconi	Italy	1956
Peter Waterman	Great Britain	1958
Emilio Marconi	Italy	1958
Duilio Loi	Italy	1959
Fortunato Manca	Italy	1964
Jean Josselin	France	1966
Carmelo Bossi	Italy	1967
Fighting Mack	Holland	1968
Silvano Bertini	Italy	1969
Jean Josselin	France	1969
Johann Orsolics	Austria	1969
Ralph Charles	Great Britain	1970
Roger Menetrey	France	1971
John H. Stracey	Great Britain	1974
Marco Scano	Italy	1976
Jorgen Hansen	Denmark	1977
Jorg Eipel	Germany	1977
Alain Marion	France	1977
Jorgen Hansen	Denmark	1978
Josef Pachler	Austria	1978
Henry Rhiney	Great Britain	1978
Dave 'Boy' Green	Great Britain	1979
Jorgen Hansen	Denmark	1979
Hans-Henrik Palm	Denmark	1982
Colin Jones	Great Britain	1982
Gilles Elbilia	France	1983
Gianfranco Rossi	Italy	1984
Lloyd Honeyghan	Great Britain	1985
Jose Varelo	Germany	1986
Alfonso Redondo	Spain	1987
Mauro Martelli	Switzerland	1987

LIGHT-WELTERWEIGHT

Olli Maki	Finland	1964
Juan Sombrita Albornoz	Spain	1965
Willi Quatuor	Germany	1965
Conny Rudhof	Germany	1967
Johann Orsolics	Austria	1967
Bruno Arcari	Italy	1968
Rene Roque	France	1970
Pedro Carrasco	Spain	1971
Roger Zami	France	1972
Cemal Kamaci	Turkey	1972
Toni Ortiz	Spain	1973
Perico Fernandez	Spain	1974
Jose Ramon Gomez Fouz	Spain	1975
Cemal Kamaci	Turkey	1975

Dave 'Boy' Green	Great Britain	1976
Primo Bandini	Italy	1977
Jean-Baptiste Piedvache	France	1977
Colin Power	Great Britain	1978
Fernando Sanchez	Spain	1978
Jose Luis Heredia	Spain	1979
Jo Kimpuani	France	1979
Giuseppe Martinese	Italy	1980
Antonio Guinaldo	Spain	1980
Clinton McKenzie	Great Britain	1981
Robert Gambini	France	1982
Patrizio Oliva	Italy	1983
Terry Marsh	Great Britain	1985
Tek N'Kalankete	France	1986

LIGHTWEIGHT

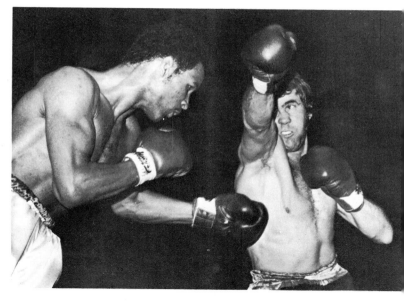

Freddie Welsh	Great Britain	1909
Matt Wells	Great Britain	1911
Freddie Welsh	Great Britain	1912
Bob Marriott	Great Britain	1919
Georges Papin	France	1920
Ernie Rice	Great Britain	1921
Seaman Hall	Great Britain	1922
Harry Mason	Great Britain	1923
Fred Bretonnel	France	1924
Lucien Vinez	France	1924
Luis Rayo	Spain	1927
Alme Raphael	France	1928
Francois Sybille	Belgium	1929
Alf Howard	Great Britain	1930
Francois Sybille	Belgium	1930
Bep van Klaveren	Holland	1931
Cleto Locatelli	Italy	1932
Francois Sybille	Belgium	1932
Cleto Locatelli	Italy	1933
Francois Sybille	Belgium	1934
Carlo Orlandi	Italy	1934
Enrico Venturi	Italy	1935
Vittorio Tamagnini	Italy	1936
Maurice Arnault	France	1937
Gustave Humery	France	1937
Aldo Spoldi	Italy	1938
Karl Blaho	Austria	1940
Bruno Bisterzo	Italy	1941
Ascenzo Botta	Italy	1941
Bruno Bisterzo	Italy	1941
Ascenzo Botta	Italy	1942
Roberto Proietti	Italy	1942
Bruno Bisterzo	Italy	1943
Roberto Proietti	Italy	1946
Emile Dicristo	France	1946
Kid Dussart	Belgium	1947
Roberto Proietti	Italy	1947
Billy Thompson	Great Britain	1948
Kid Dussart	Belgium	1949
Roberto Proietti	Italy	1949
Pierre Montane	France	1951
Elis Ask	Finland	1951
Jorgen Johansen	Denmark	1952
Duilio Loi	Italy	1954
Mario Vecchiatto	Italy	1959
Dave Charnley	Great Britain	1960
Conny Rudhof	Germany	1963
Willi Quatuor	Germany	1964
Franco Brondi	Italy	1965
Maurice Tavant	France	1965
Borge Krogh	Denmark	1966
Pedro Carrasco	Spain	1967
Miguel Velazquez	Spain	1970
Antonio Puddu	Italy	1971
Ken Buchanan	Great Britain	1974
Fernand Roelands	Belgium	1976

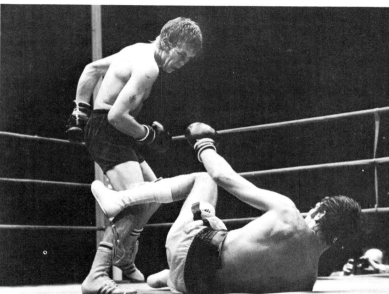

Chris Finnegan in action against John Conteh in 1973, and (below) his brother Kevin on his way to beating Jean-Claude Bouttier in 1974. Both of them held British and European titles: Chris at light-heavyweight and Kevin at middleweight. Chris also held the Commonwealth title. The Photo Source

Perico Fernandez	Spain	1976
Jim Watt	Great Britain	1977
Charlie Nash	Great Britain	1979
Francisco Leon	Spain	1980
Charlie Nash	Great Britain	1980
Joey Gibilisco	Italy	1981
Licio Cusma	Italy	1983
Rene Weller	Germany	1984
Gert Bo Jacobsen	Denmark	1986

JUNIOR-LIGHTWEIGHT

Tommaso Galli	Italy	1971
Lothar Abend	Germany	1972

Sven-Erik Paulsen	Norway	1974
Roland Cazeaux	France	1976
Natale Vezzoli	Italy	1976
Carlos Hernandez	Spain	1979
Rodolfo Sanchez	Spain	1979
Carlos Hernandez	Spain	1979
Cornelius Boza-Edwards	Great Britain	1982
Roberto Castanon	Spain	1982
Alfredo Raininger	Italy	1983
Jean-Marc Renard	Belgium	1984
Pat Cowdell	Great Britain	1984
Jean Marc Renard	Belgium	1986
Salvatore Curcetti	Italy	1987

FEATHERWEIGHT

Jim Driscoll	Great Britain	1912
Ted 'Kid' Lewis	Great Britain	1913
Louis de Ponthieu	France	1919
Arthur Wyns	Belgium	1920
Eugene Criqui	France	1922
Edouard Mascart	France	1923
Charles Ledoux	France	1924
Henry Hebrans	Belgium	1924
Antonio Ruiz	Spain	1925
Luigi Quadrini	Italy	1928
Knud Larsen	Denmark	1929
Jose Girones	Spain	1929
Maurice Holtzer	France	1935
Phil Dolhem	Belgium	1938
Lucien Popescu	Romania	1939
Ernst Weiss	Austria	1941
Gino Bondavalli	Italy	1941
Ermanno Bonetti	Italy	1945
Al Phillips	Great Britain	1947
Ronnie Clayton	Great Britain	1947
Ray Famechon	France	1948
Jean Sneyers	Belgium	1953
Ray Famechon	France	1954
Fred Galiana	Spain	1955
Cherif Hamia	France	1957
Sergio Caprari	Italy	1958
Gracieux Lamperti	France	1959
Alberto Serti	Italy	1962
Howard Winstone	Great Britain	1963
Jose Legra	Spain	1967
Manuel Calvo	Spain	1968
Tommaso Galli	Italy	1969
Jose Legra	Spain	1970
Gitano Jiminez	Spain	1973
Elio Cotena	Italy	1975
Nino Jiminez	Spain	1976
Manuel Masso	Spain	1977
Roberto Castanon	Spain	1977
Salvatore Melluzzo	Italy	1981
Pat Cowdell	Great Britain	1982
Loris Stecca	Italy	1983
Barry McGuigan	Great Britain	1983
Jim McDonnell	Great Britain	1985
Valerio Nati	Italy	1987

BANTAMWEIGHT

Joe Bowker	Great Britain	1910
Digger Stanley	Great Britain	1910
Charles Ledoux	France	1912
Tommy Harrison	Great Britain	1921
Charles Ledoux	France	1922
Harry Lake	Great Britain	1923
Johnny Brown	Great Britain	1923
Henry Scillie	Belgium	1925
Domenico Bernasconi	Italy	1929
Carlos Flix	Spain	1929
Lucien Popescu	Romania	1931
Domenico Bernasconi	Italy	1932
Nicholas Biquet	Belgium	1932
Maurice Dubois	Switzerland	1935
Joseph Decico	France	1936
Aurel Toma	Romania	1936
Nicholas Biquet	Belgium	1937
Aurel Toma	Romania	1938
Ernst Weiss	Austria	1939
Gino Cattaneo	Italy	1939
Gino Bondavalli	Italy	1941
Jackie Paterson	Great Britain	1946
Theo Medina	France	1946
Peter Kane	Great Britain	1947
Guido Ferracin	Italy	1948
Luis Romero	Spain	1949
Peter Keenan	Great Britain	1951
Jean Sneyers	Belgium	1952
Peter Keenan	Great Britain	1953
John Kelly	Great Britain	1953
Robert Cohen	France	1954
Mario D'Agata	Italy	1955
Piero Rollo	Italy	1958
Freddie Gilroy	Great Britain	1959
Pierre Cossemyns	Belgium	1961
Piero Rollo	Italy	1962
Alphonse Halimi	France	1962
Piero Rollo	Italy	1962
Mimoun Ben Ali	Spain	1963
Risto Luukkonen	Finland	1963
Mimoun Ben Ali	Spain	1965
Tommaso Galli	Italy	1965
Mimoun Ben Ali	Spain	1966
Salvatore Burruni	Italy	1968
Franco Zurlo	Italy	1969
Alan Rudkin	Great Britain	1971
Agustin Senin	Spain	1971
Johnny Clark	Great Britain	1973
Bob Allotey	Spain	1974
Daniel Trioulaire	France	1975
Salvatore Fabrizio	Italy	1976
Franco Zurlo	Italy	1977
Juan Francisco Rodriguez	Spain	1978
Johnny Owen	Great Britain	1980
Valerio Nati	Italy	1980
Giuseppe Fossati	Italy	1982
Walter Giorgetti	Italy	1983
Ciro de Leva	Italy	1984
Antoine Montero	France	1986
Louis Gomis	France	1987

FLYWEIGHT

Sid Smith	Great Britain	1913
Billy Ladbury	Great Britain	1913
Percy Jones	Great Britain	1914
Tancy Lee	Great Britain	1914
Jimmy Wilde	Great Britain	1916
Michel Montreuil	Belgium	1923
Elky Clark	Great Britain	1925
Victor Ferrand	Spain	1927
Emile Pladner	France	1928
Johnny Hill	Great Britain	1928
Emile Pladner	France	1929
Eugene Huat	France	1929
Kid Oliva	France	1930
Lucien Popescu	Romania	1930
Jackie Brown	Great Britain	1931
Praxile Gyde	France	1932
Kid David	Belgium	1935
Ernst Weiss	Austria	1936
Valentin Angelmann	France	1936

Georges Carpentier (Fra) who held European titles at four different weights. Syndication International

Enrico Urbinati	Italy	1938	Belgium	1920 Arthur Wyns (featherweight)	
Raoul Degryse	Belgium	1946	Denmark	1929 Knud Larsen (featherweight)	
Maurice Sandeyron	France	1947	Finland	1951 Elis Ask (lightweight)	
Rinty Monaghan	Great Britain	1949	France	1911 Georges Carpentier (welterweight)	
Terry Allen	Great Britain	1950	Germany	1927 Max Schmeling (light-heavyweight)	
Jean Sneyers	Belgium	1950			
Teddy Gardner	Great Britain	1952	Great Britain	1906 Gunner Moir (heavyweight)	
Louis Skena	France	1953	Greece	1938 Anton Christoforidis (middleweight)	
Nazzareno Giannelli	Italy	1954			
Dai Dower	Great Britain	1955	Holland	1926 Herman van T'Hof (light-heavyweight)	
Young Martin	Spain	1955			
Risto Luukkonen	Finland	1959	Hungary	1962 Laszlo Papp (middleweight)	
Salvatore Burruni	Italy	1961	Italy	1923 Erminio Spalla (heavyweight)	
Rene Libeer	France	1965	Norway	1974 Sven-Erik Paulsen (junior-lightweight)	
Fernando Atzori	Italy	1967			
Fritz Chervet	Switzerland	1972	Romania	1930 Lucien Popescu (flyweight)	
Fernando Atzori	Italy	1973	Spain	1925 Antonio Ruiz (featherweight)	
Fritz Chervet	Switzerland	1973	Sweden	1933 John Andersson (light-heavyweight)	
Franco Udella	Italy	1974			
Charlie Magri	Great Britain	1979	Switzerland	1915 Albert Badoud (welterweight)	
Antoine Montero	France	1983	Turkey	1972 Cemal Kamaci (light-welterweight)	
Charlie Magri	Great Britain	1984	Yugoslavia	1969 Yvan Prebeg (light-heavyweight)	
Franco Cherchi	Italy	1985			
Charlie Magri	Great Britain	1985			
Duke McKenzie	Great Britain	1986			

First winners from each country

Austria   1931 Poldi Steinbach (middleweight)

Title holder at most weights

4 – Georges Carpentier (Fra) heavyweight, light-heavyweight, middleweight, welterweight

Longest reigning champion

9 years 7 months – Georges Carpentier (Fra) light-heavyweight
(Carpentier also reigned 9 years 3 months in the heavyweight division)

Shortest reigning champion

31 days – Ernst Weiss (Aus) featherweight

Most successful defences

12 – Gustave Roth Bel (welterweight)
11 – Roberto Castanon (Spa) (featherweight)
10 – Rudi Koopmans Hol (light-heavyweight)
 9 – Fernando Atzori Ita (flyweight)
 8 – Ray Famechon Fra (featherweight)
 8 – Carlos Hernandez Spa (junior-lightweight)
 8 – Duilio Loi Ita (lightweight)
 8 – Franco Udella Ita (flyweight)
 8 – Natale Vezzoli Ita (junior-lightweight)
 8 – Franco Zurlo Ita (bantamweight)

Shortest contest

20s – Georges Carpentier (Fra) beat Joe Beckett (GB) 4 December 1919, heavyweight

Fighters who have regained European titles

Many fighters have regained European titles; the following is a list of fighters who have regained a title more than once.

HEAVYWEIGHT

Pierre Charles Bel	1932, 1935
Henry Cooper GB	1968, 1970
Joe Bugner GB	1972, 1976

WELTERWEIGHT

Jorgen Hansen Den	1978, 1979

LIGHTWEIGHT

Francois Sybille Bel	1930, 1932, 1934
Bruno Bisterzo Ita	1941, 1943
Roberto Proietti Ita	1946, 1947, 1949

BANTAMWEIGHT

Piero Rollo Ita	1962 (twice)
Mimoun Ben Ali Spa	1965, 1966

FLYWEIGHT

Charlie Magri GB	1984, 1985

The Olympic Games

Boxing has been included in the Olympic programme since 1904 and has been included every year since, with the exception of 1912 (the Games were held in Sweden where boxing was outlawed at the time). Since 1952 each losing semi-finalist has received a bronze medal.

Twelve weight divisions were contested at the 1984 Los Angeles Olympics. The year each was first seen in the programme is as follows:
1904 heavyweight, middleweight, welterweight, lightweight, featherweight, bantamweight, flyweight; 1920 light-heavyweight; 1952 light-middleweight, light-welterweight; 1968 light-flyweight; 1984 super-heavyweight.

SUPER-HEAVYWEIGHT

1984 Tyrell Biggs (USA) beat Francesco Damiani (Ita) PTS
Most gold medals   1 – USA
Most medals: 1 – GB, Italy, USA, Yugoslavia

HEAVYWEIGHT

1904 Samuel Berger (USA) beat Charles Mayer (USA) PTS
1908 A. L. Oldham (GB) beat S. C. H. Evans (GB) KO –1
1920 Ronald Rawson (GB) beat Soren Petersen (Den) PTS
1924 Otto von Porat (Nor) beat Soren Petersen (Den) PTS
1928 Arturo Jurado (Arg) beat Nils Ramm (Swe) RSF –1
1932 Santiago Lovell (Arg) beat Luigi Rovati (Ita) PTS
1936 Herbert Runge (Ger) beat Guillermo Lovell (Arg) PTS
1948 Rafael Iglesias (Arg) beat Gunnar Nilsson (Swe) KO –2
1952 Edward Sanders (USA) beat Ingemar Johansson (Swe) DIS –2
1956 Peter Rademacher (USA) beat Lev Mukhin (USSR) RSF –1

1960 Franco de Piccoli (Ita) beat Daniel Bekker (SA) KO –1
1964 Joe Frazier (USA) beat Hans Huber (FRG) PTS
1968 George Foreman (USA) beat Ionas Chepulis (USSR) RSF –2
1972 Teofilio Stevenson (Cuba) beat Ion Alexe (Rom) DEF
1976 Teofilio Stevenson (Cuba) beat Mircea Simon (Rom) KO –3
1980 Teofilio Stevenson (Cuba) beat Pyotr Zaev (USSR) PTS
1984 Henry Tillman (USA) beat Willie DeWitt (Can) PTS

Most gold medals: 6 – USA
Most medals: 10 – USA

LIGHT-HEAVYWEIGHT

1920 Eddie Eagan (USA) beat Sverre Sorsdal (Nor) PTS
1924 Harry Mitchell (GB) beat Thyge Petersen (Den) PTS
1928 Victor Avendano (Arg) beat Ernst Pistulla (Ger) PTS
1932 David Carstens (SA) beat Gino Rossi (Ita) PTS
1936 Roger Michelot (Fra) beat Richard Vogt (Ger) PTS
1948 George Hunter (SA) beat Donald Scott (GB) PTS
1952 Norvel Lee (USA) beat Antonio Pacenza (Arg) PTS
1956 James Boyd (USA) beat Gheorghe Negrea (Rom) PTS
1960 Cassius Clay (USA) beat Zbigniew Pietrzykowski (Pol) PTS
1964 Cosimo Pinto (Ita) beat Aleksey Kisselyov (USSR) PTS
1968 Dan Poznyak (USSR) beat Ion Monea (Rom) DEF
1972 Mate Parlov (Yug) beat Gilberto Carrillo (Cuba) RSF –2
1976 Leon Spinks (USA) beat Sixto Soria (Cuba) RSF –3
1980 Slobodan Kacar (Yug) beat Pawel Skrzeck (Pol) PTS
1984 Anton Jospovic (Yug) beat Kevin Barry (NZ) DEF

Most gold medals: 5 – USA
Most medals: 6 – Poland, USA

MIDDLEWEIGHT

1904 Charles Mayer (USA) beat Ben Spradley (USA) RSF –3
1908 John Douglas (GB) beat Reginald Baker (Aus) PTS
1920 Harry Mallin (GB) beat Georges Prudhomme (Can) PTS
1924 Harry Mallin (GB) beat John Elliott (GB) PTS
1928 Piero Toscani (Ita) beat Jan Hermanek (Cz) PTS
1932 Carmen Barth (USA) beat Amado Azar (Arg) PTS
1936 Jean Despeaux (Fra) beat Henry Tiller (Nor) PTS
1948 Laszlo Papp (Hun) beat John Wright (GB) PTS
1952 Floyd Patterson (USA) beat Vasile Tita (Rom) KO –1
1956 Genaddy Schatkov (USSR) beat Ramon Tapia (Chi) KO –1
1960 Edward Crook (USA) beat Tadeusz Walasek (Pol) PTS
1964 Valery Popenchenko (USSR) beat Emil Schultz (FRG) RSF –1
1968 Chris Finnegan (GB) beat Aleksey Kisselyov (USSR) PTS
1972 Vyacheslav Lemechev (USSR) beat Reima Virtanen (Fin) KO –1
1976 Michael Spinks (USA) beat Rufat Riskiev (USSR) RSF –3
1980 Jose Gomez (Cuba) beat Viktor Savchenko (USSR) PTS
1984 Sin-Joon Sup (S. Kor) beat Virgil Hill (USA) PTS

Most gold medals: 5 – USA
Most medals: 8 – USA

LIGHT-MIDDLEWEIGHT

1952 Laszlo Papp (Hun) beat Theunis van Schalkwyk (SA) PTS
1956 Laszlo Papp (Hun) beat Jose Torres (USA) PTS
1960 Wilbert McClure (USA) beat Carmelo Bossi (Ita) PTS
1964 Boris Lagutin (USSR) beat Joseph Gonzales (Fra) PTS
1968 Boris Lagutin (USSR) beat Rolando Garbey (Cuba) PTS
1972 Dieter Kottysch (FRG) beat Wieslaw Rudkowski (Pol) PTS
1976 Jerzy Rybicki (Pol) beat Tadija Kacar (Yug) PTS
1980 Armando Martinez (Cuba) beat Alexsandr Koshkin (USSR) PTS
1984 Frank Tate (USA) beat Shawn O'Sullivan (Can) PTS

Most gold medals: 2 – Hungary, USSR, USA
Most medals: 6 – USSR

WELTERWEIGHT

1904 Albert Young (USA) beat Harry Spanger (USA) PTS
1908 Not held
1920 Albert Schneider (Can) beat Alex Ireland (GB) PTS
1924 Jean Delarge (Bel) beat Hector Mendez (Arg) PTS
1928 Edward Morgan (NZ) beat Raul Landini (Arg) PTS
1932 Edward Flynn (USA) beat Erich Campe (Ger) PTS
1936 Sten Suvio (Fin) beat Michael Murach (Ger) PTS
1948 Julius Torma (Cz) beat Horace Herring (USA) PTS
1952 Zygmunt Chychla (Pol) beat Sergei Scherbakov (USSR) PTS
1956 Nicolae Linca (Rom) beat Frederick Tiedt (Ire) PTS
1960 Giovanni Benvenuti (Ita) beat Yuri Radonyak (USSR) PTS
1964 Marian Kasprzyk (Pol) beat Ritschardas Tamulis (USSR) PTS
1968 Manfred Wolke (GDR) beat Joseph Bessala (Cam) PTS
1972 Emilio Correa (Cuba) beat Janos Kajdi (Hun) PTS
1976 Jochen Bachfeld (GDR) beat Pedro Gamarro (Ven) PTS
1980 Andres Aldama (Cuba) beat John Mugabi (Uga) PTS
1984 Mark Breland (USA) beat An-Yung Soo (S. Kor) PTS

Most gold medals: 3 – USA
Most medals: 9 – USA

LIGHT-WELTERWEIGHT

1952 Charles Adkins (USA) beat Viktor Mednov (USSR) PTS
1956 Vladimir Yengibaryan (USSR) beat Franco Nenci (Ita) PTS
1960 Bohumil Nemecek (Cz) beat Clement Quartey (Gha) PTS
1964 Jerzy Kulej (Pol) beat Yevgeny Frolov (USSR) PTS
1968 Jerzy Kulej (Pol) beat Enrique Regueiferos (Cuba) PTS
1972 Ray Seales (USA) beat Angel Angelov (Bul) PTS

The gold and silver medallists in the middleweight division at the 1908 London Olympics were a versatile pair.

Gold medallist J. W. H. T. Douglas captained the England cricket team on 18 occasions and during his first-class career scored 24 530 runs and took 1894 wickets. He also played amateur soccer for England and the Corinthians.

Silver medallist Reginald 'Snowy' Baker competed in the springboard diving competition at the same Olympics! Baker was regarded as the best-ever all-round Australian sportsman. He won the lightweight, welterweight, middleweight and heavyweight boxing championships of Australia. In a 50-year sporting career he competed in nearly 30 different sports, including: soccer, cricket, rugby, polo, water polo, hockey, rowing, running, yachting, weightlifting, fencing and horse racing — flat and steeplechase!

Chris Finnegan (GB) proudly shows his Olympic gold medal to his four-year-old daughter Pearl upon returning to his Buckinghamshire home from Mexico in 1968.
The Photo Source

1976 Ray Leonard (USA) beat Andres Aldama (Cuba) PTS
1980 Patrizio Oliva (Ita) beat Serik Konakbaev (USSR) PTS
1984 Jerry Page (USA) beat Dhawee Umponmaha (Tha) PTS

Most gold medals: 4 – USA
Most medals: 6 – USA

LIGHTWEIGHT

1904 Harry Spanger (USA) beat James Eagan (USA) PTS
1908 Frederick Grace (GB) beat Frederick Spiller (GB) PTS
1920 Samuel Mosberg (USA) beat Gotfred Johansen (Den) PTS
1924 Hans Nielsen (Den) beat Alfredo Copello (Arg) PTS
1928 Carlo Orlando (Ita) beat Stephen Halaiko (USA) PTS
1932 Lawrence Stevens (SA) beat Thure Ahlqvist (Swe) PTS
1936 Imre Harangi (Hun) beat Nikolai Stepulov (Est) PTS
1948 Gerald Dreyer (SA) beat Joseph Vissers (Bel) PTS
1952 Aureliano Bolognesi (Ita) beat Aleksy Antkiewicz (Pol) PTS
1956 Dick McTaggart (GB) beat Harry Kurschat (FRG) PTS
1960 Kazimierz Pazdzior (Pol) beat Sandro Lopopolo (Ita) PTS
1964 Jozef Grudzien (Pol) beat Velikton Barannikov (USSR) PTS
1968 Ron Harris (USA) beat Jozef Grudzien (Pol) PTS
1972 Jan Szczepanski (Pol) beat Laszlo Orban (Hun) PTS
1976 Howard Davis (USA) beat Simion Cutov (Rom) PTS
1980 Angel Herrera (Cuba) beat Viktor Demianenko (USSR) RSF –3
1984 Pernell Whitaker (USA) beat Luis Ortiz (PR) RSF –2

Most gold medals: 5 – USA
Most medals: 11 – USA

FEATHERWEIGHT

1904 Oliver Kirk (USA) beat Frank Haller (USA) PTS
1908 Richard Gunn (GB) beat C. W. Morris (GB) PTS
1920 Paul Fritsch (Fra) beat Jean Gachet (Fra) PTS
1924 John Fields (USA) beat Joseph Salas (USA) PTS
1928 Lambertus van Klavaren (Hol) beat Victor Peralta (Arg) PTS
1932 Carmelo Robledo (Arg) beat Josef Schleinkofer (Ger) PTS
1936 Oscar Casanovas (Arg) beat Charles Catterall (SA) PTS
1948 Ernesto Formenti (Ita) beat Dennis Shephard (SA) PTS
1952 Jan Zachara (Cz) beat Sergio Caprari (Ita) PTS
1956 Vladimir Safronov (USSR) beat Thomas Nicholls (GB) PTS
1960 Francesco Musso (Ita) beat Jerzy Adamski (Pol) PTS
1964 Stanislav Stepashkin (USSR) beat Anthony Villanueva (Phi) PTS
1968 Antonio Roldan (Mex) beat Albert Robinson (USA) DIS –2
1972 Boris Kousnetsov (USSR) beat Philip Waruinge (Ken) PTS
1976 Angel Herrera (Cuba) beat Richard Nowakowski (GDR) KO –2
1980 Rudi Fink (GDR) beat Adolfo Horta (Cuba) PTS
1984 Meldrick Taylor (USA) beat Peter Konyegwachie (Ngr) PTS

Most gold medals: 3 – USSR, USA
Most medals: 9 – USA

BANTAMWEIGHT

1904 Oliver Kirk (USA) beat George Finnegan (USA) RSF –3
1908 Henry Thomas (GB) beat John Condon (GB) PTS
1920 Clarence Walker (SA) beat Chris Graham (Can) PTS
1924 William Smith (SA) beat Salvatore Tripoli (USA) PTS
1928 Vittorio Tamagnini (Ita) beat John Daley (USA) PTS
1932 Horace Gwynne (Can) beat Hans Ziglarski (Ger) PTS
1936 Ulderico Sergo (Ita) beat Jack Wilson (USA) PTS
1948 Tibor Csik (Hun) beat Giovanni Zuddas (Ita) PTS
1952 Pentti Hamalainen (Fin) beat John McNally (Ire) PTS
1956 Wolfgang Behrendt (FRG) beat Soon-Chun Song (S. Kor) PTS

1960 Oleg Grigoryev (USSR) beat Primo Zamparini (Ita) PTS
1964 Takao Sakurai (Jap) beat Shin-Cho Chung (S. Kor) RSF –2
1968 Valery Sokolov (USSR) beat Eridari Mukwanga (Uga) RSF –2
1972 Orlando Martinez (Cuba) beat Alfonso Zamora (Mex) PTS
1976 Yong-Jo Gu (N. Kor) beat Charles Mooney (USA) PTS
1980 Juan Hernandez (Cuba) beat Bernardo Pinango (Ven) PTS
1984 Maurizio Stecca (Ita) beat Hector Lopez (Mex) PTS

Most gold medals: 3 – Italy
Most medals: 7 – USA

FLYWEIGHT

1904 George Finnegan (USA) beat Miles Burke (USA) RSF –1
1908 Not held
1920 Frank Di Gennara (USA) beat Anders Petersen (Den) PTS
1924 Fidel La Barba (USA) beat James McKenzie (GB) PTS
1928 Antal Kocsis (Hun) beat Armand Appell (Fra) PTS
1932 Istvan Enekes (Hun) beat Francisco Cabanas (Mex) PTS
1936 Willi Kaiser (Ger) beat Gavino Matta (Ita) PTS
1948 Pascual Perez (Arg) beat Spartaco Bandinelli (Ita) PTS
1952 Nathan Brooks (USA) beat Edgar Basel (FRG) PTS
1956 Terry Spinks (GB) beat Mircea Dobrescu (Rom) PTS
1960 Gyula Torok (Hun) beat Sergey Sivko (USSR) PTS
1964 Fernando Atzori (Ita) beat Artur Olech (Pol) PTS
1968 Ricardo Delgado (Mex) beat Artur Olech (Pol) PTS
1972 Georgi Kostadinov (Bul) beat Leo Rwabwogo (Uga) PTS
1976 Leo Randolph (USA) beat Ramon Duvalov (Cuba) PTS
1980 Peter Lessov (Bul) beat Viktor Miroshnichenko (USSR) RSF –2
1984 Steve McCrory (USA) beat Redzed Redzepovski (Yug) PTS

Most gold medals: 6 – USA
Most medals: 11 – USA

LIGHT-FLYWEIGHT

1968 Francisco Rodriguez (Ven) beat Yong-Ju Jee (S. Kor) PTS
1972 Gyorgy Gedo (Hun) beat U-Gil Kim (N. Kor) PTS
1976 Jorge Hernandez (Cuba) beat Byong-Uk Li (N. Kor) PTS
1980 Shamil Sabyrov (USSR) beat Hipolito Ramos (Cuba) PTS
1984 Paul Gonzales (USA) beat Salvatore Todisco (Ita) DEF

Most gold medals: 1 – Cuba, Hungary, USSR, USA, Venezuela
Most medals: 3 – N. Korea

The first man to go the distance with Teofilio Stevenson (Cuba) in Olympic competition was Istvan Levai (Hun) in the semi-final of the 1980 heavyweight competition. Levai was Stevenson's tenth Olympic opponent, all previous nine had been knocked out by the Cuban. Levai's delight at lasting three rounds, even though he lost the contest, was reminiscent of a man winning the gold medal.

Medal-winning nations

	Gold	Silver	Bronze	Total
USA	42	17	26	85
USSR	13	18	15	46
Great Britain	12	10	19	41
Italy	13	12	13	38
Poland	8	9	21	38
Cuba	12	8	5	25
Argentina	7	7	9	23
Germany, Federal Republic of (inc. Germany)	4	10	8	22
South Africa	6	4	9	19
Romania	1	7	10	18
Hungary	9	2	3	14
Finland	2	1	10	13
France	3	3	6	12
Canada	2	4	5	11
Denmark	1	5	5	11
Yugoslavia	3	2	5	10
German Democratic Republic	3	1	6	10
Mexico	2	3	5	10
Korea, South	1	4	5	10
Bulgaria	2	1	6	9
Sweden	–	4	5	9
Ireland	–	2	5	7
Czechoslovakia	3	1	2	6
Norway	1	2	2	5
Venezuela	1	2	2	5
Kenya	–	1	4	5
Korea, North	1	2	1	4
Belgium	1	1	2	4
Uganda	–	3	1	4
Australia	–	1	3	4
Nigeria	–	1	3	4
Puerto Rico	–	1	3	4
Japan	1	–	2	3
Netherlands	1	–	2	3
Chile	–	1	2	3
Ghana	–	1	2	3
New Zealand	1	1	–	2
Cameroon	–	1	1	2
Philippines	–	1	1	2
Algeria	–	–	2	2
Colombia	–	–	2	2
Turkey	–	–	2	2
Estonia	–	1	–	1
Thailand	–	1	–	1
Bermuda	–	–	1	1
Brazil	–	–	1	1
Dominican Republic	–	–	1	1
Egypt	–	–	1	1
Guyana	–	–	1	1
Spain	–	–	1	1
Trinidad	–	–	1	1
Tunisia	–	–	1	1
Uruguay	–	–	1	1
Zambia	–	–	1	1

Leading nations at each celebration

Year	Total weight divs	Most gold medals	Most medals
1904 St Louis, USA	7	7–USA	19–USA
1908 London, England	5	5–GB	14–GB
1920 Antwerp, Belgium	8	3–USA	6–GB
1924 Paris, France	8	2–USA, GB	6–USA
1928 Amsterdam, Netherlands	8	3–Italy	4–Argentina, Italy
1932 Los Angeles, USA	8	2–Argentina, South Africa, USA	5–USA
1936 Berlin, Germany	8	2–France, Germany	5–Germany
1948 London, England	8	2–Argentina, Hungary, South Africa	5–Italy
1952 Helsinki, Finland	10	5–USA	6–USSR
1956 Melbourne, Australia	10	3–USSR	7–USSR
1960 Rome, Italy	10	3–Italy, USA	7–Italy, Poland
1964 Tokyo, Japan	10	3–Poland, USSR	9–USSR
1968 Mexico City, Mexico	11	3–USSR	7–USA
1972 Munich, FRG	11	3–Cuba	5–Cuba
1976 Montreal, Canada	11	5–USA	8–Cuba, USA
1980 Moscow, USSR	11	6–Cuba	10–Cuba
1984 Los Angeles, USA	12	9–USA	11–USA

Gold medal winning nations at the most consecutive celebrations

7–Hungary 1928–60
7–USA   1952–76

Host nations that failed to win a gold medal

1920 Belgium;   1924 France;   1948 Great Britain;
1956 Australia;   1976 Canada

Host nations that failed to win any medal

1920 Belgium;   1976 Canada

Laszlo Papp of Hungary, one of only two men to win three Olympic gold medals. He is seen here winning his first title at London in 1948, beating Great Britain's John Wright in the middleweight final. All Sport

Winners of more than one Olympic title

3 – Laszlo Papp (Hun)
M 1948; *LM* 1952, 1956

3 – Teofilio Stevenson (Cuba)
H 1972, 1976, 1980

2 – Angel Herrera (Cuba)
Fe 1976; *L* 1980

2 – Oliver Kirk (USA)
B 1904; *Fe* 1904

2 – Jerzy Kulej (Pol)
LW 1964, 1968

2 – Boris Lagutin (USSR)
LM 1964, 1968

2 – Harry Mallin (GB)
M 1920, 1924

The only man to win two titles at the same Olympic Games is Oliver Kirk (USA) when he won the bantamweight and the featherweight in 1904.

Fighters disqualified in finals

Ingemar Johansson (Swe) v. Edward Sanders
1952 – heavyweight

Albert Robinson (USA) v. Antonio Roldan (Mex)
1968 – featherweight

Brothers who won gold medals

Michael Spinks (USA) 1976 – middleweight
Leon Spinks (USA) 1976 – light-heavyweight

Oldest champion

37 years 254 days – Richard Gunn (GB), 1908 – featherweight

Youngest champion

16 years 162 days – Jackie Fields (USA), 1924 – featherweight

Olympic champions who went on to win professional world titles

Giovanni (Nino) Benvenuti (Ita)
1960 Olympic welterweight
1965 World light-middleweight
1967 World middleweight

Mark Breland (USA)
1984 Olympic welterweight
1987 World welterweight

Cassius Clay (USA)
1960 Olympic light-heavyweight
1964 World heavyweight

Jackie Fields (USA)
1924 Olympic featherweight
1929 World welterweight

George Foreman (USA)
1968 Olympic heavyweight
1973 World heavyweight

Joe Frazier (USA)
1964 Olympic heavyweight
1968 World heavyweight

Frankie Genaro (USA)
1920 Olympic flyweight
1928 World flyweight

Slobodan Kacar (Yug)
1980 Olympic light-heavyweight
1985 World middleweight

Fidel La Barba (USA)
1924 Olympic flyweight
1925 World flyweight

'Sugar' Ray Leonard (USA)
1976 Olympic light-welterweight
1979 World light-middleweight
1981 World welterweight

Patrizio Oliva (Ita)
1980 Olympic light-welterweight
1986 World light-welterweight

Mate Parlov (Yug)
1972 Olympic light-heavyweight
1978 World light-heavyweight

Floyd Patterson (USA)
1952 Olympic middleweight
1956 World heavyweight

Pascual Perez (Arg)
1948 Olympic flyweight
1954 World flyweight

Leo Randolph (USA)
1976 Olympic flyweight
1980 World light-flyweight

Willie Smith (USA)
1924 Olympic bantamweight
1927 World bantamweight (British version of title only)

Leon Spinks (USA)
1976 Olympic light-heavyweight
1978 World heavyweight

Michael Spinks (USA)
1976 Olympic middleweight
1981 World light-heavyweight and
1985 World heavyweight

VAL BARKER TROPHY

Instituted in 1936, the Val Barker Trophy is awarded, by the International Amateur Boxing Association (IABA), to the most stylish boxer of each Olympic competition. Winners:

1936 Louis Lauria (USA) *Fl
1948 George Hunter (SA) LH
1952 Norvel Lee (USA) LH
1956 Dick McTaggart (GB) L
1960 Giovanni Benvenuti (Ita) W
1964 Valeriy Popentschenko (USSR) M
1968 Philip Waruingi (Ken) *Fe
1972 Teofilo Stevenson (Cuba) H
1976 Howard Davis (USA) L
1980 Patrizio Oliva (Ita) LW
1984 Paul Gonzales (USA) LF

* bronze medal only

Commonwealth Games

The first Empire Games, as they were then called, were held at Hamilton, Ontario, Canada in 1930, and every four years since, with the exception of the war years. Boxing was included in the first Games, and has been included in all 11 celebrations since. The 11 current weight divisions were introduced as follows: 1930 heavyweight, light-heavyweight, middleweight, welterweight, lightweight, featherweight, bantamweight, flyweight; 1954 light-middleweight, light-welterweight; 1970 light-flyweight.

Since 1958 the losing semi-finalists have each received bronze medals.

SUPER-HEAVYWEIGHT

1986 L. Lewis (Can)

HEAVYWEIGHT

1930 V. Stuart (Sco)
1934 H. P. Floyd (Eng)
1938 T. Osborne (Can)
1950 F. Creagh (NZ)
1954 B. Harper (Eng)
1958 D. Becker (SA)
1962 G. Oywello (Uga)
1966 W. Kini (NZ)
1970 B. Masanda (Uga)
1974 N. Meade (Eng)
1978 J. Awome (Eng)
1982 W. DeWitt (Can)
1986 J. Peau (NZ)

Most gold medals: 9–England
Most medals: 8–England

LIGHT-HEAVYWEIGHT

1930 J. W. Goyder (Eng)
1934 G. J. Brennan (Eng)
1938 N. Wolmarans (SA)

1950 D. Scott (Eng)
1954 P. van Vauuren (SA)
1958 A. Madigan (Aus)
1962 A. Madigan (Aus)
1966 R. Tighe (Eng)
1970 F. Ayinla (Ngr)
1974 W. Knight (Eng)
1978 R. Fortin (Can)
1982 F. Sani (Fiji)
1986 J. Moran (Eng)

Most gold medals: 6–England
Most medals: 9–England

MIDDLEWEIGHT

1930 F. Mallin (Eng)
1934 A. Shawyer (Eng)
1938 D. P. Reardon (Wal)
1950 T. van Schackwyk (SA)
1954 J. van der Kolff (SA)
1958 T. Milligan (N. Ire)
1962 C. Coloquhoun (Jam)
1966 J. Darkey (Gha)
1970 J. Conteh (Eng)
1974 F. Lucas (St. Vin)
1978 P. McElwaine (Aus)
1982 J. Price (Eng)
1986 R. Douglas (Eng)

Most gold medals: 5–England
Most medals: 10–England

LIGHT-MIDDLEWEIGHT

1954 W. Greaves (Can)
1958 A. G. Webster (SA)
1962 H. Mann (Can)
1966 M. Rowe (Eng)
1970 T. Imrie (Sco)
1974 L. Mwale (Zam)
1978 K. Perlette (Can)
1982 S. O'Sullivan (Can)
1986 D. Sherry (Can)

Most gold medals: 5–Canada
Most medals: 6–Canada

WELTERWEIGHT

1930 L. Hall (SA)
1934 D. McCleave (Eng)
1938 W. Smith (Aus)
1950 T. Ratcliffe (Eng)
1954 N. Gargano (Eng)
1958 J. A. Greyling (SA)
1962 W. Coe (NZ)
1966 E. Blay (Gha)
1970 E. Ankudey (Gha)
1974 M. Muruli (Uga)
1978 M. McCallum (Jam)
1982 C. Pyatt (Eng)
1986 D. Dyer (Eng)

Most gold medals: 4–England
Most medals: 8–England

LIGHT-WELTERWEIGHT

1954 M. Bergin (Can)
1958 H. J. Loubscher (SA)
1962 C. Quartey (Gha)
1966 J. McCourt (N. Ire)
1970 M. Muruli (Uga)
1974 O. Nwankpa (Nig)
1978 W. Braithwaite (Guy)
1982 C. Ossai (Ngr)
1986 H. Grant (Can)

Most gold medals: 2–Canada
                   2–Ghana
                   2–Nigeria
Most medals: 5–Canada

LIGHTWEIGHT

1930 J. Rolland (Sco)
1934 L. Cook (Aus)
1938 H. Groves (Eng)
1950 R. Latham (Eng)

1954 P. Vanstaden (S. Rho)
1958 R. McTaggart (Sco)
1962 E. Blay (Gha)
1966 A. Andeh (Ngr)
1970 A. Adeyemi (Ngr)
1974 A. Kalule (Uga)
1978 G. Hamill (N. Ire)
1982 H. Khalili (Ken)
1986 Asif Dar (Can)

Most gold medals: 2–England
2–Nigeria
2–Scotland
Most medals: 9–England

FEATHERWEIGHT

1930 F. Meacham (Eng)
1934 C. Catterall (SA)
1938 A. W. Henricus (Cey)
1950 H. Gilliland (Sco)
1954 L. Leisching (SA)
1958 W. R. Taylor (Aus)
1962 J. McDermott (Sco)
1966 P. Waruinge (Ken)
1970 P. Waruinge (Ken)
1974 E. Ndukwu (Ngr)
1978 N. Azumah (Gha)

1982 P. Konyegwachie (Ngr)
1986 B. Downey (Can)

Most gold medals: 2–Kenya
2–Nigeria
2–Scotland
2–South Africa
Most medals: 7–England

BANTAMWEIGHT

1930 H. Mizler (Eng)
1934 F. Ryan (Eng)
1938 W. H. Butler (Eng)
1950 J. van Rensburgh (SA)
1954 J. Smillie (Sco)
1958 H. Winstone (Wal)
1962 J. Dynevor (Aus)
1966 E. Ndukwu (Ngr)
1970 S. Shittu (Gha)
1974 P. Cowdell (Eng)
1978 F. McGuigan (N. Ire)
1982 J. Orewa (Ngr)
1986 S. Murphy (Eng)

Most gold medals: 5–England
Most medals: 7–England

FLYWEIGHT

1930 J. N. Smith (SA)
1934 P. Palmer (Eng)
1938 J. Joubert (SA)
1950 H. Riley (Sco)
1954 R. Currie (Sco)
1958 J. Brown (Sco)
1962 R. Mallon (Sco)
1966 S. Shittu (Gha)
1970 D. Needham (Eng)
1974 D. Larmour (N. Ire)
1978 M. Irungu (Ken)
1982 M. Mutua (Ken)
1986 J. Lyon (Eng)

Most gold medals: 4–Scotland
Most medals: 7–Scotland

LIGHT-FLYWEIGHT

1970 J. Odwori (Uga)
1974 S. Muchoki (Ken)
1978 S. Muchoki (Ken)
1982 I. Bilale (Ken)
1986 S. Olsen (Can)

Most gold medals: 3–Kenya
Most medals: 3–Kenya

Medal-winning nations

	Gold	Silver	Bronze	Total
England	33	17	28	78
Canada	14	11	25	50
Scotland	10	13	21	44
Australia	7	13	19	39
Northern Ireland	5	6	20	31
South Africa	14	6	8	28
Kenya	8	6	12	26
Ghana	8	9	5	22
Wales	2	11	9	22
Uganda	6	8	7	21
New Zealand	4	5	11	20
Nigeria	9	2	8	19
Zambia	1	5	10	16
Rhodesia (inc. N. and S.)	1	7	3	11
Jamaica	2	3	2	7
India	–	1	4	5
Ceylon (Sri Lanka)	1	2	1	4
Western Samoa	–	–	4	4
Fiji	1	–	2	3
Malawi	–	–	3	3
Guyana	1	–	1	2
Papua New Guinea	–	1	1	2
Swaziland	–	1	1	2
Tanzania	–	1	1	2
Jersey	–	–	2	2
St. Vincent	1	–	–	1
Bahamas	–	–	1	1
Pakistan	–	–	1	1
Singapore	–	–	1	1

Gold medallists who have won two titles

Eddie Blay (Gha)
L 1962; *W* 1966

Tony Madigan (Aus)
LH 1958, 1962

Stephen Muchoki (Ken)
LF 1974, 1978

Mohammad Muruli (Uga)
LW 1970; *W* 1974

Eddie Ndukwu (Ngr)
B 1966; *Fe* 1974

Sulley Shittu (Gha)
Fl 1966; *B* 1970

Phillip Waruinge (Ken)
Fe 1966, 1970

Gold medallists who went on to win professional world titles

John Conteh (Eng)
1970 Commonwealth middleweight
1974 World light-heavyweight

Ayub Kalule (Uga)
1974 Commonwealth lightweight
1979 World light-middleweight

Mike McCallum (Jam)
1978 Commonwealth welterweight
1984 World junior-middleweight

Finbar (Barry) McGuigan (N. Ire)
1978 Commonwealth bantamweight
1985 World featherweight

Azumah Nelson (Gha)
(formerly Nelson Azumah)
1978 Commonwealth featherweight
1984 World featherweight

Howard Winstone (Wal)
1958 Commonwealth bantamweight
1968 World featherweight

The first record of a prize-fight dates to 1184 BC when Euryalus beat Epeus (described as a 'big bully').

The World Amateur Championships

The first World Amateur Championships were held at Havana, Cuba, in 1974 and are held every four years on an Olympic-style competition. However, after the 1982 championships, the world ruling body ordered that seven of the new champions would have to defend their titles in March 1983 at Reno, Nevada against a series of challengers. A further challenge series was organized at Tokyo in May 1983 for the remaining five 1982 champions. Because those series only involved two fighters in each weight division, the respective champions are not included in the list of medal-winning nations.

The venues for the four championships have been: 1974 Havana, Cuba; 1978 Belgrade, Yugoslavia; 1982 Munich, West Germany; 1986 Reno, Nevada, USA.

The Champions

SUPER HEAVYWEIGHT

1982 T. Biggs (USA)
1983 T. Biggs (USA)
1986 T. Stevenson (Cub)

HEAVYWEIGHT

1974 T. Stevenson (Cub)
1978 T. Stevenson (Cub)
1982 A. Lagubkin (USSR)
1983 W. Dewitt (Can)
1986 F. Savon (Cub)

LIGHT-HEAVYWEIGHT

1974 M. Parlov (Yug)
1978 S. Soria (Cub)
1982 P. Romero (Cub)
1983 P. Romero (Cub)
1986 P. Romero (Cub)

MIDDLEWEIGHT

1974 R. Riskiyev (USSR)
1978 J. Gomez (Cub)
1982 B. Comas (Cub)
1983 B. Comas (Cub)
1986 D. Allen (USA)

LIGHT-MIDDLEWEIGHT

1974 R. Garbey (Cub)
1978 V. Savchenko (USSR)
1982 A. Koshkin (USSR)
1983 S. O'Sullivan (Can)
1986 A. Espinosa (Cub)

WELTERWEIGHT

1974 E. Correa (Cub)
1978 V. Rachkov (USSR)
1982 M. Breland (USA)
1983 M. Breland (USA)
1986 K. Gould (USA)

LIGHT-WELTERWEIGHT

1974 A. Kalule (Uga)
1978 V. Lvov (USSR)
1982 C. Garcia (Cub)
1983 C. Garcia (Cub)
1986 V. Shishov (USSR)

LIGHTWEIGHT

1974 V. Solomin (USSR)
1978 A. Davison (Ngr)
1982 A. Herrera (Cub)
1983 P. Whitaker (USA)
1986 A. Horta (Cub)

FEATHERWEIGHT

1974 H. Davis (USA)
1978 A. Herrera (Cub)
1982 A. Horta (Cub)
1983 A. Horta (Cub)
1986 K. Banks (USA)

BANTAMWEIGHT

1974 W. Gomez (PR)
1978 A. Horta (Cub)
1982 F. Favors (USA)
1983 F. Favors (USA)
1986 Sung-Kil Moon (S. Kor)

FLYWEIGHT

1974 D. Rodriquez (Cub)
1978 H. Srednicki (Pol)
1982 Y. Alexandrov (USR)
1983 S. McCrory (USA)
1986 P. Reyes (Cub)

LIGHT-FLYWEIGHT

1974 J. Hernandez (Cub)
1978 S. Muchoki (Ken)
1982 I. Mustafov (Bul)
1983 R. Saiz (Cub)
1986 J. Torres (Cub)

Most titles

4 – Adolfo Horta (Cub)
B 1978; Fe 1982, 1983; L 1986

3 – Teofilio Stevenson (Cub)
H 1974, 1978, SH 1986

3 – Pablo Romero (Cub)
LH 1982, 1983, 1986

Medal-winning nations

	Gold	Silver	Bronze	Total
Cuba	22	7	5	34
USSR	9	5	11	25
USA	7	6	6	19
East Germany	–	4	13	17
Yugoslavia	1	6	9	16
Bulgaria	1	1	9	11
Poland	1	1	6	8
Venezuela	–	4	4	8
South Korea	1	1	3	5
Romania	–	2	3	5
West Germany	–	–	4	4
Puerto Rico	1	1	1	3
Nigeria	1	–	2	3
Kenya	1	1	–	2
Uganda	1	–	1	2
Finland	–	2	–	2
Holland	–	1	1	2
France	–	–	2	2
Sweden	–	–	2	2
Italy	–	1	–	1
North Korea	–	1	–	1
Mongolia	–	1	–	1
Canada	–	1	–	1
Ghana	–	1	–	1
Ireland	–	–	1	1
Japan	–	–	1	1
Panama	–	–	1	1
Spain	–	–	1	1
Hungary	–	–	1	1
Brazil	–	–	1	1
Turkey	–	–	1	1

World amateur champions who went on to win professional world titles

Mate Parlov (Yug)
1974 Amateur light-heavyweight;
1978 WBC light-heavyweight

Ayub Kalule (Uga)
1974 Amateur light-welterweight;
1979 WBA light-middleweight

Wilfredo Gomez (PR)
1974 Amateur bantamweight;
1977 WBC super-bantamweight;
1984 WBC featherweight

Mark Breland (USA)
1982/1983 Amateur welterweight;
1987 WBA welterweight

No Great Britain boxer has won a medal at the championships. The only British Isles fighter to win a medal is Ireland's Tommy Corr who won a bronze in the light-middleweight division in 1982.

ABA Champions

The Amateur Boxing Association (ABA) was formed in England in 1880 as a result of a meeting arranged by R. Frost-Smith. The first championships were held the following year and Frost-Smith was the Assocation's first heavyweight champion.

To reach an ABA final a fighter has to win a series of divisional eliminators. Reaching the final is the highlight of an amateur fighter's career in Britain.

The different weight divisions were first contested as follows: 1881 heavyweight, middleweight, lightweight, featherweight; 1884 bantamweight; 1920 light-heavyweight, welterweight, flyweight; 1951 light-middleweight, light-welterweight; 1971 light-flyweight; 1982 super-heavyweight.

Winners since 1975

SUPER-HEAVYWEIGHT

1982 A. Elliott
1983 K. Ferdinand
1984 R. Wells
1985 G. Williamson
1986–7 J. Oyebola

HEAVYWEIGHT

1975 G. McEwan
1976 J. Rafferty
1977 G. Adair
1978 J. Awome
1979 A. Palmer
1980 F. Bruno
1981 A. Elliott
1982 H. Hylton
1983 H. Notice
1984 D. Young
1985 H. Hylton
1986 E. Cardouza
1987 J. Moran

LIGHT-HEAVYWEIGHT

1975 M. Heath
1976 G. Evans
1977 C. Lawson
1978 V. Smith
1979–81 A. Straughn
1982 G. Crawford
1983–4 A. Wilson
1985 J. Beccles
1986 J. Moran
1987 J. Beccles

MIDDLEWEIGHT

1975 D. Odwell
1976 E. Burke
1977 R. Davies
1978 H. Graham
1979 N. Wilshire
1980 M. Kaylor
1981 B. Schumacher
1982 J. Price
1983 T. Ford
1984 B. Schumacher
1985 D. Cronin
1986 N. Benn
1987 R. Douglas

LIGHT-MIDDLEWEIGHT

1975 A. Harrison
1976 W. Lauder
1977 C. Malarkey
1978 E. Henderson
1979 D. Brewster
1980 J. Price
1981 E. Christie
1982 D. Milligan
1983–5 R. Douglas
1986 T. Vellinor
1987 N. Brown

WELTERWEIGHT

1975 W. Bennett
1976–7 C. Jones
1978 E. Byrne
1979 J. Frost
1980–1 T. Marsh
1982 C. Pyatt
1983 R. McKenley
1984 M. Hughes
1985 E. McDonald
1986 D. Dyer
1987 M. Elliott

LIGHT-WELTERWEIGHT

1975 J. Zeraschi

1976 C. McKenzie
1977 J. Douglas
1978 D. Williams
1979 E. Copeland
1980–1 A. Willis
1982 T. Adams
1983 D. Dent
1984 D. Griffiths
1985 I. Mustafa
1986 J. Alsop
1987 A. Holligan

LIGHTWEIGHT

1975 P. Cowdell
1976 S. Mittee
1977 G. Gilbody
1978 T. Marsh
1979–81 G. Gilbody
1982 J. McDonnell
1983 K. Willis
1984 A. Dickson
1985 E. McCauley
1986 J. Jacobs
1987 M. Ayers

FEATHERWEIGHT

1975 R. Beaumont
1976–7 P. Cowdell
1978 M. O'Brien
1979 P. Hanlon
1980 M. Hanif
1981 P Hanlon
1982 H. Henry
1983 P. Bradley
1984 K. Taylor
1985 F. Havard
1986 P. Hodgkinson
1987 P. English

Harry Mallin (left) was ABA middleweight champion five times between 1919 and 1923. His brother Fred (with trophy) won the same title in the five years between 1928 and 1932. He is seen here after winning the title for the third successive year in 1930. BBC Hulton Picture Library

BANTAMWEIGHT

1975 S. Ogilvie
1976 J. Bambrick
1977–8 J. Turner
1979 R. Ashton
1980 R. Gilbody
1981 P. Jones
1982 R. Gilbody
1983–4 J. Hyland
1985–6 S. Murphy
1987 J. Sillitoe

FLYWEIGHT

1975–7 C. Magri
1978 G. Nickels
1979 R. Gilbody
1980–1 K. Wallace
1982 J. Kelly
1983 S. Nolan
1984–5 P. Clinton
1986–7 J. Lyon

LIGHT-FLYWEIGHT

1975 M. Lawless
1976–7 P. Fletcher

1978–9 J. Dawson
1980 T. Barker
1981–4 J. Lyon
1985–7 M. Epton

Most titles

6–J. Steers 1890–1903
heavyweight, middleweight
6–J. Lyon 1981–7
light-flyweight, flyweight
5–G. Baker 1912–21
featherweight
5–G. Gilbody 1974–81
lightweight, featherweight
5– R. McTaggart 1956–65
light-welterweight, lightweight
5–F. Mallin 1928–32
middleweight
5–H. Mallin 1919–23
middleweight
5–T. Pardoe 1929–33
flyweight
5–F. Parks 1899–1906
heavyweight

5–T. Waller 1967–74
welterweight, light-welterweight,
lightweight
5–R. Warnes 1899–1910
middleweight

Most consecutive titles

5–H. Mallin 1919–23
middleweight
5–F. Mallin 1928–32
middleweight
5–T. Pardoe 1929–33
flyweight

Longest span between first and last titles

17 years–H. Floyd 1929–46
heavyweight–won four titles

Golden Gloves Champions

The first Golden Gloves tournament was organized by the *New York Daily News* in 1927. It was the largest boxing tournament ever contested at the time and consisted of 494 bouts in 16 classes. The following year the sister newspaper of the *Daily News*, the *Chicago Tribune*, also ran a Golden Gloves tournament. The New York and Chicago champions then met to decide the Inter-City champions.

As the tournaments grew, regional competitions were held under the auspices of the *Daily News* and *Tribune*. These regional tournaments were called the Eastern (and Western) Tournament of Champions. The winners, again, met for the Inter-City titles. These regional tournaments were discontinued in 1962 when an organization called Golden Gloves of America, Inc was formed. Since then they have organized the annual National Golden Gloves Championships. The *Daily News* and *Tribune* resumed their Inter-City competition (without the regional tournaments) in 1977, but discontinued them in 1982. Both Chicago and New York, however, still have their own annual Golden Gloves Championships.

National Golden Gloves Champions (since 1962)

SUPER-HEAVYWEIGHT

1962–81 Not contested
1982 Warren Thompson
1983 Craig Payne
1984 Michael Williams
1985 James Pritchard
1986 Kevin George
1987 Nathaniel Fitch

HEAVYWEIGHT

1962 Ben Black
1963 Harley Cooper
1964 Wyce Westbrook
1965 Jerry Quarry
1966 James Howard
1967 Clay Hodges
1968 Al Wilson
1969 Walt Moore
1970 Bill Thompson
1971 Ronnie Draper

1972 Duane Bobick
1973 Johnny Hudson
1974–5 Jim Chapman
1976 Michael Dokes
1977 James Clark
1978 Greg Page
1979 Marvis Frazier
1980 Michael Arms
1981 Joe Thomas
1982 Earl Lewis
1983 Olian Alexander
1984 Michael Tyson
1985 Jerry Goff
1986 Orlin North
1987 Dave Sherbrooke

LIGHT-HEAVYWEIGHT

1962 Billy Joiner
1963 Ted Gullick
1964 Harley Cooper
1965 Larry Charleston

1966 Gerry Pate
1967 Grady Bredzeale
1968 Len Hutchins
1969 Dave Matthews
1970 Felton Woods
1971 Marvin Johnson
1972 Verbie Garland
1973 D. C. Barker
1974 Bobby Stewart
1975 Frank Williams
1976–7 Rick Jester
1978 Charley Singleton
1979 Leroy Murphy
1980 Steve Eden
1981 Johnny Williams
1982 Keith Vining
1983 Ricky Womack
1984 Evander Holyfield
1985 Donald Stephens
1986 Harvie Richards
1987 Terry McGroom

Thomas Hearns, the 1977 National Golden Gloves welterweight champion. All Sport

MIDDLEWEIGHT

1962 Gary Brown
1963 Billy Douglas
1964 Roy McMillan
1965 Al Jones
1966 Joe Hopkins
1967 Paul 'Bad' Horse
1968 Roy Dale
1969 Roosevelt Molden
1970 Larry Ward
1971 Jerry Dobbs
1972 Marvin Johnson
1973 Roy Hollis
1974 Vonzell Johnson
1975 Tommy Sullivan
1976 Michael Spinks
1977 Keith Broome
1978 Wilford Scypion
1979 Tony Ayala
1980 Lamont Kirkland
1981 Donnie Lee
1982 Arthel Lawhorn
1983 Arthur Jimmerson
1984 Virgil Hill
1985 William Guthrie
1986 Domani Parker
1987 Fabian Williams

LIGHT-MIDDLEWEIGHT

1962–6 Not contested
1967 Jesse Valdez
1968 Bill Beeler
1969 Morris Jorden
1970 Bill Beeler
1971 Sammy Nesmith
1972 Lamont Lovelady

1973 Dale Grant
1974 Michael Spinks
1975 Ray Phillips
1976 Don Carbin
1977 Curtis Parker
1978 Donnie Bowers
1979–80 James Shuler
1981 Al Mayes
1982 Sanderline Williams
1983 Frank Tate
1984 Ronnie Essett
1985 Mylon Watkins
1986 Mylon Watkins
1987 Roy Jones

WELTERWEIGHT

1962 Rory O'Shea
1963 Wade Smith
1964–5 DonCobbs
1966 Hedgemon Lewis
1967 Pat O'Connor
1968 Richie Royal
1969 Dave Oropeza
1970 Mel Dennis
1971 Larry Carlisle
1972 Jesse Valdez
1973 Hal Beal
1974–6 Clint Jackson
1977 Thomas Hearns
1978 Jeff Stoudemire
1979 Mike McCallum
1980 Donald Curry
1981 Manny Vallejo
1982 Roman George
1983 Louis Howard
1984 Mylon Watkins
1985 Anthony Stephens

1986 Ralph Miles
1987 Roger Turner

LIGHT-WELTERWEIGHT

1962–6 Not contested
1967 Willie Richardson
1968 Harold Beal
1969 Ed Beauford
1970 Larry Bonds
1971 Wiley Johnson
1972 Ray Seales
1973 Larry Bonds
1974 Ray Leonard
1975 Paul Sherry
1976 Ronnie Shields
1977 Mike McCallum
1978 Ronnie Shields
1979 Lemuel Steeples
1980 Terry Silver
1981 Henry Hughes
1982 Timmy Rabon
1983 Roderick Moore
1984 Timmy Rabon
1985 Robert Guy
1986 Roy Jones
1987 Todd Foster

LIGHTWEIGHT

1962 Eddie Ellis
1963 Perry Bennett
1964 Hedgemon Lewis
1965 Frank Anderson
1966 Marcus Anderson
1967 Quincy Daniels
1968 Ronnie Harris
1969 Eddie Murry
1970 Norman Goins
1971–2 James Busceme
1973 Ray Leonard
1974 Curtis Harris
1975–6 Aaron Pryor
1977 Sammy Ayala
1978 Davey Armstrong
1979 Johnny Bumphus
1980 Melvin Paul
1981 Primo Ramos
1982 Robert Byrd
1983 Jesse Lopez
1984 Marvin Chambers
1985 Vincent Phillips
1986 Lavell Singer
1987 Skipper Kelp

FEATHERWEIGHT

1962 George Foster
1963 Nick Petrecca
1964–5 Marcus Anderson
1966 Dick Gillis
1967 Brooks Byrd
1968 Lorenzo Trujillo
1969–70 James Busceme
1971–2 Louis Self
1973 Maury Watkins
1974 Bill Berry
1975 Ronnie Shields
1976 Davey Armstrong
1977–8 Bernard Taylor
1979 Roland Cooley
1980 Bernard Taylor
1981 Rodney Watts
1982 Shelton LeBlanc

1983 Andrew Minsker	1980 Myron Taylor	1977 Orlando Maldonado
1984 Victor Levine	1981 Steve Cruz	1978 Bill Johnson
1985 Kelcie Banks	1982 Meldrick Taylor	1979–80 Jerome Coffee
1986 William Little	1983 Jess Benavides	1981 Ronnie Rentz
1987 Donald Stokes	1984 Robert Shannon	1982 Jess Benavides
	1985 Eugene Speed	1983 Todd Hickman
	1986 Fernando Rodriguez	1984 Les Fabri
	1987 Fernando Rodriguez	1985 Johnny Tapia
		1986 Anthony Wilson
		1987 Carl Daniels

BANTAMWEIGHT

1962 Jimmy Moon
1963 Manny Stewart
1964 Manny Navarro
1965 Mel Miller
1966 Johnny North
1967–8 Earl Large
1969 Oliver James
1970 Dave Kibby
1971 Johnny Moreno
1972 Ray Theragood
1973 Jimmy Martinez
1974 Don Hermisillo
1975 Mike Ayala
1976 Bernard Taylor
1977 Wayne Lynumm
1978 Jackie Beard
1979 Kenny Baysmore

FLYWEIGHT

1962 Ray Jutras
1963 Freddie Garcia
1964 Donnie Broadway
1965 Roland Miller
1966 Nick Priola
1967 Roland Miller
1968 Rudy Barrientos
1969–70 Tony Moreno
1971 Jimmy Martinez
1972 Greg Lewis
1973 Mike Ayala
1974 Greg Richardson
1975 Leo Randolph
1976 Julio Rodriguez

LIGHT-FLYWEIGHT

1962–74 Not contested
1975 Claudell Atkins
1976 Louis Curtis
1977 Not contested
1978–9 Richard Sandoval
1980 Steve McCrory
1981 Jess Benavides
1982 Jose Rosario
1983 Johnny Tapia
1984 Israel Acosta
1985 Arthur Johnson
1986 Mike Carbajal
1987 Eric Griffin

Most wins

4–Bernard Taylor
bantamweight 1976; featherweight 1977–8, 1980

4–James Busceme
featherweight 1969–70; lightweight 1971–2

Most titles at different weights

3–Jesse Benavides
light-flyweight 1981; flyweight 1982; bantamweight 1983

Winners who went on to win professional world titles

Johnny Bumphus
Golden Gloves lightweight 1979
WBA light-welterweight 1984

Don Curry
Golden Gloves welterweight 1980
WBA welterweight 1983

Steve Cruz
Golden Gloves bantamweight 1981
WBA featherweight 1986

Michael Dokes
Golden Gloves heavyweight 1976
WBA heavyweight 1982

Thomas Hearns
Golden Gloves welterweight 1977
WBA welterweight 1980
WBC light-middleweight 1984

Evander Holyfield
Golden Gloves light-heavyweight 1984
WBA cruiserweight 1986
IBF cruiserweight 1987

Marvin Johnson
Golden Gloves middleweight 1972, light-heavyweight 1971
WBC light-heavyweight 1978
WBA light-heavyweight 1979

Sugar Ray Leonard
Golden Gloves lightweight 1973, light-welterweight 1974
WBC World welterweight 1979
WBA World light-middleweight 1981

Hedgemon Lewis
Golden Gloves lightweight 1964, welterweight 1966
NY welterweight 1972

Mike McCallum
Golden Gloves light-welterweight 1977, welterweight 1979
WBA light-middleweight 1984

Leroy Murphy
Golden Gloves light-heavyweight 1979
IBF cruiserweight 1984

Greg Page
Golden Gloves heavyweight 1978
WBA heavyweight 1984

Aaron Pryor
Golden Gloves lightweight 1975–6
WBA light-welterweight 1980
IBF light-welterweight 1984

Leo Randolph
Golden Gloves flyweight 1975
WBA super-bantamweight 1980

Richard Sandoval
Golden Gloves light-flyweight 1978–9
WBA bantamweight 1984

Michael Spinks
Golden Gloves light-middleweight 1974, middleweight 1976
WBA light-heavyweight 1981
IBF heavyweight 1985

Mike Tyson
Golden Gloves heavyweight 1984
WBC heavyweight 1986
WBA/IBF heavyweight 1987

In September 1975 the WBC declared the light-flyweight title vacant and matched Luis Estaba (Ven) and Rafael Lovera (Par) for the vacant title. The Venezuelan won with a fourth-round knock-out. It was later learned that Lovera had never previously boxed as a professional.

Nicknames, real names and name changes

Nicknames

Nickname	Ring name
Ageless Archie	– Archie Moore
Ambling Alp	– Primo Carnera
Astoria Assassin	– Paul Berlenbach
Baby Face	– Jimmy McLarnin
Barbados Demon	– Joe Walcott
Basque Woodchopper	– Paolino Uzcudun
Bazooka	– Rafael Limon
Black Cloud	– Larry Holmes
Black Hercules	– Mike Weaver
Black Mamba	– Roger Mayweather
Black Uhlan	– Max Schmeling
Boilermaker	– Jim Jeffries
Boom-Boom	– Ray Mancini
Boston Gob	– Jack Sharkey
Boston Tar Baby	– Sam Langford
Boxing Marvel	– Jack Britton
Box O'Tricks	– Pedlar Palmer
Brockton Blockbuster	– Rocky Marciano
Bronx Bull	– Jake la Motta
Brown Bomber	– Joe Louis
Bump City	– Johnny Bumphus
California Grizzly Bear	– James J. Jeffries
Camden Buzzsaw	– Dwight Qawi (Braxton)
Cannonball	– Eddie Martin
Casablanca Clouter	– Marcel Cerdan
Cincinnati Cobra	– Ezzard Charles
Cinderella Man	– James J. Braddock
Cleveland Rubber Man	– Johnny Risko
Clones Cyclone	– Barry McGuigan
Clutch	– Sammy Angott
Cobra	– Don Curry
Corkscrew Kid	– Charles 'Kid' McCoy
Cuban Hawk	– Kid Gavilan
Durable Dane	– Battling Nelson
Fighting Marine	– Gene Tunney
Fish	– Benny Bass
Flame	– Eddie Mustafa Muhammad (Gregory)
Freckled Bob	– Bob Fitzsimmons
Galveston Giant	– Jack Johnson
Garfield Gunner	– Tippy Larkin
Gentleman Jim	– James J. Corbett
Georgia Deacon	– Tiger Flowers
Ghetto Wizard	– Benny Leonard
Ghost with a hammer in his hand	– Jimmy Wilde
Hard Rock from Down Under	– Tom Heeney
Harlem Spider	– Tommy Kelly
Havana Bon Bon	– Kid Chocolate
Hawk	– Kid Gavilan
Herkimer Hurricane	– Lou Ambers
Homicide Hank	– Henry Armstrong
Human Windmill	– Harry Greb
Illinois Thunderbolt	– Billy Papke
Jack the Giant Killer	– Jack Dillon
Jaws	– Ossie Ocasio
Kansas Rube	– Jim Ferns
King of the Canebrakes	– Young Stribling
Little Artha	– Jack Johnson
Little Chocolate	– George Dixon
Livermore Larruper	– Max Baer
Louisville Lip	– Muhammad Ali
Macho Man	– Hector Camacho
Mad Dog	– Gene Hatcher
Madcap Maxie	– Max Baer
Manassa Mauler	– Jack Dempsey (heavyweight)
Man of Steel	– Tony Zale
Marvellous Marvin	– Marvin Hagler
Michigan Assassin	– Stanley Ketchel
Michigan Wildcat	– Ad Wolgast
Mighty Atom	– Jimmy Wilde
Motor City Cobra	– Thomas Hearns
Nonpareil	– Jack Dempsey (middleweight)
Old Bones	– Joe Brown
Old Master	– Joe Gans
Old Mongoose	– Archie Moore
Orchid Man	– Georges Carpentier
Peerless Jim	– Jim Driscoll
Perpetual Motion	– Henry Armstrong
Pittsburgh Kid	– Billy Conn
Poison	– David Kotey
Pottawatomie Giant	– Jess Willard
Pride of the Ghetto	– Barney Ross
Rochdale Thunderbolt	– Jock McAvoy
Ruby Robert	– Bob Fitzsimmons
Saginaw Kid	– George 'Kid' Lavigne
St Paul Cyclone	– Mike O'Dowd
Scotch Wop	– Johnny Dundee
Shotgun	– Oscar Albarado
Slapsie Maxie	– Maxie Rosenbloom
Smokin' Joe	– Joe Frazier
Spider	– Emile Pladner
Stonefist	– Roberto Duran
Sugar Ray	– Ray Leonard
Sugar Ray	– Ray Robinson
Terrible Terry	– Terry McGovern
Terrible Tim	– Tim Witherspoon
Toy Bulldog	– Mickey Walker
Two Ton	– Tony Galento
Tylerstown Terror	– Jimmy Wilde
Welsh Wizard	– Freddie Welsh
Whitechapel Whirlwind	– Jack 'Kid' Berg
Wild Bull of the Pampas	– Luis Firpo
Will o' the Wisp	– Willie Pep

Real names

Ring name	Real name
Ali, Muhammad	– Cassius Marcellus Clay, Jnr
Allen, Terry	– Edward Albert Govier
Ambers, Lou	– Louis D'Ambrosio
Angott, Sammy	– Samuel Engotti
Armstrong, Henry	– Henry Jackson
Bartolo, Sal	– Salvatore Interbartolo
Bassey, Hogan 'Kid'	– Okon Bassey Asuquo

Two of heavyweight boxing's greats: (above left) 'The Manassa Mauler' — Jack Dempsey (USA) and (right) 'The Brown Bomber' — Joe Louis (USA). The Photo Source

(Above) *Jimmy Wilde (GB) was known as: 'The Tylorstown Terror', 'The Ghost With a Hammer in his Hand' and more commonly 'The Mighty Atom'. In this picture he looks more like 'The Cheerful Caddie'!* Syndication International

(Far left) *Easy to see why he is called the 'Louisville Lip'!* Syndication International

(Left) *World featherweight champion Willie Pep (USA) was born Guglielmo Papaleo.* The Photo Source

Becerra, Joe	– Jose Becerra Covarrubias	Dundee, Vince	– Vincent Lazzaro
Berg, Jack 'Kid'	– Judah Bergman	Duran, Roberto	– Manos de Piedra
Bernstein, Jack	– John Dodick	Espadas, Guty	– Gustavo Hernan Espadas Cruz
Borkorsor, Venice	– Pravas Polchiangkwang	Fields, Jackie	– Jacob Finkelstein
Bowker, Joe	– Tommy Mahon	Gavilan, Kid	– Gerardo Gonzalez
Britton, Jack	– William J. Breslin	Giardello, Joey	– Carmine Orlando Tilelli
Brown, Newsboy	– David Montrose	Glover, Mike	– Michael J. Cavanaugh
Brown, Panama Al	– Alphonse Theo Brown	Goodrich, Jimmy	– James Edward Moran
Buff, Johnny	– John Lesky	Graham, Bushy	– Angelo Geraci
Burns, Tommy	– Noah Brusso	Graziano, Rocky	– Thomas Rocco Barbella
Callahan, Mushy	– Vincent Morris Scheer	Griffo, Young	– Albert Griffiths
Carmona, Erubey		Guzman, Juan	– Juan Antonio Guzman Batista
'Chango'	– Eudibiel Guillen Chapin	Herman, Pete	– Peter Gulotta
Chip, George	– George Chipulonis	Herrera, Juan	– Juan Antonio Herrera Marrufo
Chocolate, Kid	– Eligio Sardinias		
Coetzee, Gerrie	– Gerhardus Christian Coetzee		
Corbett II, Young	– William H. Rothwell		
Corbett III, Young	– Ralph Capabianca Giordano		
Cuevas, Pipino	– Isidro Pipino Cuevas Gonzalez		
Dado, Little	– Eleveterio Zapanta		
Delaney, Jack	– Ovila Chapdelaine		
DeMarco, Tony	– Leonard Liotta		
Dempsey, Jack			
(Nonpareil)	– John Kelly		
Dillon, Jack	– Ernest Cutler Price		
Dundee, Joe	– Samuel Lazzaro		
Dundee, Johnny	– Joseph Carrora		

The referee of the Bob Fitzsimmons (GB)— Tom Sharkey (Ire) non-title bout in 1896 was none other than Wyatt Earp. Quite useful with the gun, he was forced to draw it on Fitzsimmons who protested violently after his disqualification.

Jack, Beau	– Sidney Walker	Saldivar, Vicente	– Vincente Samuel Saldivar Garcia
Jeby, Ben	– Morris Jebaltowski	Sangchilli, Baltazar	– Baltasar Belenguer Hevoas
Jeffra, Harry	– Ignacius Pasquali Guiffi	Schmeling, Max	– Maxmillian Adolph Otto Siegfried Schmeling
Jenkins, Lew	– Elmer Verlin Jenks		
Kansas, Rocky	– Rocco Tozzo	Servo, Marty	– Mario Severino
Ketchel, Stanley	– Stanislaus Kiecal	Sharkey, Jack	– Joseph Paul Cukoschay
Kid, Dixie	– Aaron L. Brown	Shaw, Battling	– Jose Perez Flores
Larkin, Tippy	– Antonio Pilleteri	Siki, Battling	– Louis Phal
Leonard, Benny	– Benjamin Leiner	Smith, Mysterious Billy	– Amos Smith
Leonard, Sugar Ray	– Ray Charles Leonard	Tiger, Dick	– Richard Ihetu
Levinsky, Battling	– Barney Lebrowitz	Villa, Pancho	– Francisco Guilledo
Lewis, Ted 'Kid'	– Gershon Mendeloff	Walcott, Jersey Joe	– Arnold Raymond Cream
Louis, Joe	– Joseph Louis Barrow	Welsh, Freddie	– Frederick Hall Thomas
McCoy, Al	– Al Rudolph	Williams, Kid	– Johnny Gutenko
McCoy, Charles 'Kid'	– Norman Selby	Wilson, Johnny	– John Panica
Madera, Lupe	– Jorge Guadalupe Madera Pacheco	Zale, Tony	– Anthony Florian Zaleski
Mandell, Sammy	– Samuel Mandella		
Marciano, Rocky	– Rocco Francis Marchegiano		
Maxim, Joey	– Guiseppe Antonio Berardinelli		
Moore, Archie	– Archibald Lee Wright		
Morgan, Tod	– Bert Morgan Pilkington		
Muangsurin, Saensak	– Boonsong Mansri		
Muhammad, Eddie Mustafa	– Eddie Dee Gregory		
Muhammad, Matthew Saad	– Maxwell Antonio Loach		
Obed, Elisha	– Everrett Oswald Ferguson		
O'Brien, Philadelphia Jack	– Joseph Francis Hagen		
Paul, Tommy	– Gaetano Alfonso Pappa		
Pep, Willie	– Guglielmo Papaleo		
Qawi, Dwight Muhammad	– Dwight Braxton		
Ramos, Sugar	– Ultimo Ramos Zaqueira		
Risko, Eddie	– Henry L. Pylkowski		
Ritchie, Willie	– Gerhardt A. Steffen		
Robinson, Ray	– Walker Smith		
Root, Jack	– Janos Ruthaly		
Rosenberg, Charley	– Charles Green		
Ross, Barney	– Beryl David Rosofsky		
Rossman, Mike	– Albert Michael DiPiano		
Roth, Gustave	– Gustave Scillie		
Ryan, Tommy	– Joseph Youngs		

Fighters who have changed their name during their career

New name	Original ring name
Muhammad Ali	– Cassius Clay
Henry Armstrong	– Melody Jackson
Wilfred Benitez	– Wilfredo Benitez
Jack Dempsey (heavyweight)	– Kid Blackie
Guts Ishimatsu	– Ishimatsu Susuki
Brian London	– Brian Harper
Eddie Mustapha Muhammad	– Eddie Gregory
Matthew Saad Muhammad	– Matt Franklin
Waruinge Nakayama	– Philip Waruinge
Azumah Nelson	– Nelson Azumah
Dwight Muhammad Qawi	– Dwight Braxton
Ed 'Babe' Risko	– Henry Polaski
Alonzo B. Strongbow	– Alonso Gonzalez
Barney Williams	– Battling Levinsky

(Levinsky used the name Barney Williams for just one fight, against Jack Dillon 17 April 1913)

Hall of Fame

Instituted by *The Ring* in 1954, there were 24 founder members of the Hall of Fame. Since then, at least three new members have been elected each year, with the exception of 1979 when there were no new entrants.

The men elected belong to one of four groups: The Pioneer Group — for men who were active in the bare-knuckle days;

The Old Timers Group — for men who were active before 1919; The Modern Group — for men who fought after 1919, but have been retired at least two years; and the Meritous Service to Boxing Group.

The full list of members, with their year of election, is as follows:

The Pioneer Group

Barney Aaron	1967	Dick Curtis	
Bendigo (William Thompson)	1955	Jack Dempsey	
Jack Broughton	1954	Dan Donnelly	
James Burke	1966	Mike Donovan	
Arthur Chambers	1954	James Figg	
Tom Chandler	1972	Joe Goss	
Nobby Clark	1971	John Gully	
Sam Collyer	1964	John C. Heenan	
Tom Cribb	1954	Jacob Hyer	
		Tom Hyer	
		Thomas Jackling	
		John Jackson	

	1974	Peter Jackson	1956
	1954	Jake Kilrain	1965
	1960	Tom King	1976
	1970	Nat Langham	1986
	1954	Jack McAuliffe	1954
	1969	Jem Mace	1954
	1959	Daniel Mendoza	1954
	1954	Charlie Mitchell	1957
	1968	Tom Molineaux	1958
	1954	John Morrissey	1954
	1985	Henry Pearce	1987
	1954	Ned Price	1962

William Richmond	1955
Paddy Ryan	1973
Tom Sayers	1954
Tom Spring	1961
John L. Sullivan	1954
Jem Ward	1963
Young Dutch Sam	1975
Young Griffo	1954

The Old Timers Group

Abe Atell	1955
Paul Berlenbach	1971
Jimmy Britt	1976
Panama Al Brown	1985
Charley Burley	1983
Tommy Burns	1960
Georges Carpentier	1964
George 'KO' Chaney	1974
Joe Choynski	1960
James J. Corbett	1954
Young Corbett II	1965
Johnny Coulon	1965
Les Darcy	1957
Jack Delaney	1973
Jack Dillon	1959
George Dixon	1956
Jem Driscoll	1956
Jackie Fields	1977
Bob Fitzsimmons	1954
Tiger Flowers	1971
Joe Gans	1954
Frankie Genaro	1973
Mike Gibbons	1958
Tom Gibbons	1963
Pete Herman	1959
Leo Houck	1969
Joe Jeannette	1967
Harry Jeffra	1982
James J. Jeffries	1954
Jack Johnson	1954
Stanley Ketchel	1954
Dixie Kid	1975
Johnny Kilbane	1960
Frank Klaus	1974
Fidel LaBarba	1972
Sam Langford	1955
George Lavigne	1959
Battling Levinsky	1966
Ted 'Kid' Lewis	1964
Benny Lynch	1986
Charles 'Kid' McCoy	1957
Packey McFarland	1957
Terry McGovern	1955
Sam McVey	1986
Peter Maher	1978
Owen Moran	1965
Battling Nelson	1957
Philadelphia Jack O'Brien	1968

Harry Greb (USA), the only man to beat world heavyweight champion Gene Tunney (USA), was elected to the Hall of Fame in 1955. BBC Hulton Picture Library

Billy Papke	1972
Willie Ritchie	1962
Jack Root	1961
Tommy Ryan	1958
Jack Sharkey	1980
Tom Sharkey	1959
Jeff Smith	1969
Charles (Bud) Taylor	1986
Pancho Villa	1961
Joe Walcott	1955
Freddy Welsh	1960
Jimmy Wilde	1959
Jess Willard	1977
Kid Williams	1970
Harry Willis	1970
Ad Wolgast	1958

The Modern Group

Muhammad Ali	1987
Lou Ambers	1964
Sammy Angott	1973
Fred Apostoli	1978
Henry Armstrong	1954
Max Baer	1968
Carmen Basilio	1969
Jack 'Kid' Berg	1975
James J. Braddock	1964
Jack Britton	1960
Tony Canzoneri	1956
Marcel Cerdan	1962
Ezzard Charles	1970
Kid Chocolate	1959
Billy Conn	1965
Jack Dempsey	1954
Johnny Dundee	1957
Sixto Escobar	1975
Bob Foster	1983

Joe Frazier	1980
Gene Fullmer	1974
Ceferino Garcia	1977
Eder Jofre	1986
Kid Gavilan	1966
Rocky Graziano	1971
Harry Greb	1955
Emile Griffith	1981
Beau Jack	1972
Lew Jenkins	1976
Eder Jofre	1986
Jake LaMotta	1985
Benny Leonard	1955
Gus Lesnevich	1973
Tommy Loughran	1956
Joe Louis	1954
Jimmy McLarnin	1956
Rocky Marciano	1959
Joey Maxim	1975
Carlos Monzon	1983
Archie Moore	1966
Jose Napoles	1985
Manuel Ortiz	1985
Floyd Patterson	1976
Willie Pep	1963
Pascual Perez	1977
Billy Petrolle	1962
Sugar Ray Robinson	1967
Maxie Rosenbloom	1972
Barney Ross	1956
Sandy Saddler	1971
Max Schmeling	1970
Yoshio Shirai	1977
William (Young) Stribling	1985
Lew Tendler	1961
Dick Tiger	1974
Gene Tunney	1955
Jersey Joe Walcott	1969
Mickey Walker	1955
Ike Williams	1978
Chalky Wright	1976
Tony Zale	1958
Fritzie Zivic	1972

Meritous Service to Boxing Group

Ray Arcel (trainer)	1982
Jack Blackburn (trainer)	1982
John Chambers (Rules Author)	1986
Dan Daniel (writer)	1977
Arthur Donovan (referee)	1981
Nat Fleischer	1975
(founder of *The Ring*)	
Jack Kearns (manager)	1981
Lord Lonsdale (5th Earl)	1985
(Lonsdale belts)	
Tex Rickard (promoter)	1980
Sam Taub (writer)	1978

In 1938, Ireland's Jack Doyle, while fighting Eddie Phillips, swung a blow at Thomas, missed, fell out of the ring, and was counted out. This is probably the only instance in ring history of a boxer knocking himself out!

On 19 March 1983 at Reno, Nevada the McCrory brothers of the United States were in action. Steve was winning the world amateur flyweight title while Milton was drawing with Colin Jones (GB) in his bid to win the vacant WBC welterweight title.

Fighters of the Year

The Ring Fighter of the Year

First instituted in 1928, the American magazine, *The Ring*, has nominated a 'Fighter of the Year' every year since, except 1933 and 1966. While the nominated fighter does not have to be a champion, all winners have, in fact, been world champions.

Winners of the gold medal, issued by the magazine, have been (USA unless stated otherwise):

1928 Gene Tunney
1929 Tommy Loughran
1930 Max Schmeling (Ger)
1931 Tommy Loughran
1932 Jack Sharkey
1933 No award
1934 Barney Ross
     Tony Canzoneri
1935 Barney Ross
1936 Joe Louis
1937 Henry Armstrong
1938–9 Joe Louis
1940 Billy Conn
1941 Joe Louis
1942 Sugar Ray Robinson
1943 Fred Apostoli
1944 Beau Jack
1945 Willie Pep
1946 Tony Zale
1947 Gus Lesnevich
1948 Ike Williams
1949–50 Ezzard Charles
1951 Sugar Ray Robinson
1952 Rocky Marciano
1953 Carl 'Bobo' Olson
1954–5 Rocky Marciano
1956 Floyd Patterson
1957 Carmen Basilio

1958–9 Ingemar Johansson (Swe)
1960 Floyd Patterson
1961 Joe Brown
1962 Dick Tiger (Ngr)
1963 Cassius Clay
1964 Emile Griffith
1965 Dick Tiger (Ngr)
1966 No award
1967 Joe Frazier
1968 Nino Benvenuti (Ita)
1969 Jose Napoles (Cuba)
1970–1 Joe Frazier
1972 Muhammad Ali
     Carlos Monzon (Arg)
1973 George Foreman
1974–5 Muhammad Ali
1976 George Foreman
1977 Carlos Zarate (Mex)
1978 Muhammad Ali
1979 Sugar Ray Leonard
1980 Thomas Hearns
1981 Sugar Ray Leonard
     Salvador Sanchez (Mex)
1982 Larry Holmes
1983 Marvin Hagler
1984 Thomas Hearns
1985 Don Curry and Marvin Hagler
1986 Mike Tyson

Most Wins

5– Muhammad Ali (Cassius Clay) 1963, 1972*, 1974, 1975, 1978
4– Joe Louis 1936, 1938, 1939, 1941
3– Rocky Marciano 1952, 1954, 1955
3– Joe Frazier 1967, 1970, 1971
*shared

British Fighter of the Year

In Britain, the leading award is the Geoffrey Simpson Award that goes to the best young boxer of the year. The award was first made in 1951 upon the institution of the Boxing Writer's Club and is named after the club's first chairman, the late Geoffrey Simpson of the *Daily Mail*.

1951 Randolph Turpin
1952 Sammy McCarthy
1953 John Kelly
1954 Dai Dower
1955 Joe Erskine
1956 Bobby Neill
1957 Terry Spinks
1958 Terry Downes
1959 Freddie Gilroy
1960 Brian Curvis
1961 Howard Winstone
1962 Frankie Taylor
1963 Walter McGowan
1964 Alan Rudkin
1965 Johnny Pritchett
1966 Ken Buchanan
1967 John McCluskey
1968 Johnny Clark
1969 Joe Bugner
1970 Bunny Sterling
1971 Jackie Turpin
1972 John H. Stracey
1973 John Conteh
1974 Dave Needham
1975 Vernon Sollas
1976 Dave 'Boy' Green
1977 Charlie Magri
1978 Johnny Owen
1979 Tony Sibson
1980 Colin Jones
1981 Herol Graham
1982 Keith Wallace
1983 Barry McGuigan
1984 Errol Christie
1985 Frank Bruno
1986 Dennis Andries

Miscellanea

The first boxing stadium was Figg's Amphitheatre, Oxford Road, London, England. It opened in 1719.

The first championship fight in Britain was in 1720 between James Figg and Ned Sutton in London. (Although Figg was generally recognized as the first champion a year earlier, this was the first championship contest.)

The first championship fight in America was in 1816 between Americans Jacob Hyer and Tom Beasley.

The first set of boxing rules was drawn up in 1743 by Jack Broughton in England. They were published at his Tottenham Court Road amphitheatre on 16 August.

The first gloves were devised by Jack Broughton (GB) in London, February 1747.

The first negro to win a prize-fight was Joe Lashley (USA) who beat Tom Treadway (GB) at St Mary-le-Bone Fields, London, on 13 June 1791.

The first boxing club was formed by 'Gentleman' John Jackson on 22 May 1814. It was the Pugilistic Club, London.

The first prize-fight with gloves took place at Aix-la-Chapelle, Germany, 8 October 1818, and was between two unnamed English fighters.

The first grandstand to be erected for a fight was at Worcester, England for the contest between Tom Spring and Jack Langan, 7 January 1824.

The first heavyweight champion of the world was Tom King (GB) who beat John C. Heenan (USA) at Wadhurst, England, 8 December 1863.

The first fighter to employ the services of a manager, Billy Madden, was John L. Sullivan (USA).

The first heavyweight title fight to be fought with gloves was between John L. Sullivan (USA) and Dominick McCaffery (USA) at Cincinatti, USA, 29 August 1885.

The first purpose-built open-air arena was built at Carson City, Nevada, USA for the Bob Fitzsimmons (GB)–James J. Corbett (USA) world heavyweight title fight, 17 March 1897.

The first boxer regularly to wear a gum shield was Ted 'Kid' Lewis of England. It had been invented by London dentist Jack Marles in 1902.

The first fight to have its result broadcast over the radio was the Jack Dempsey–Jess Willard (both USA) world heavyweight title fight from Toledo, Ohio, USA, 4 July 1919.

The first boxing commentary in Great Britain was made via Station 2LO on 11 May 1922 and covered the Ted 'Kid' Lewis (GB)–Georges Carpentier (Fra) world light-heavyweight bout from Olympia, London.

The first boxing match was televised in 1931. It was a contest between Mickey Walker and Benny Leonard from the CBS Studios, New York.

The first professional fight for general viewing by a British television audience was the Eric Boon–Arthur Danahar British lightweight title fight from Harringay Arena, London, 23 February 1939.

The first fight to be shown on closed-circuit television was the Joe Louis–Lee Savold American non-title fight in 1951. The fight was held in New York and shown at six other United States centres.

The first fight to be shown on closed-circuit television in Britain was the Terry Downes (GB)–Willie Pastrano (USA) world light-heavyweight title fight 30 November 1964. The fight took place in Manchester and was shown on closed-circuit television at the Phoenix Theatre, London.

The first fighter from a communist country to fight professionally was Laszlo Papp of Hungary. He turned professional in 1957 after a successful amateur career in which he won three Olympic titles. Kid Kaplan and Benny Bass (both USSR) fought professionally in the 1920s but they were both domiciled in the United States.

The first woman to be granted a referee's licence was 'Baby Bear' James who was issued with a licence at Kansas City in 1978.

Career earnings

Muhammad Ali (formerly Cassius Clay) holds the record for the greatest career earnings. In 61 professional bouts between 1960 and 1981 he earned in excess of $69 million.

Not far behind Ali is another heavyweight, Larry Holmes. His estimated ring earnings after his last fight, against Michael Spinks in 1985, were estimated at around $55 million. His earnings came in 49 professional fights spanning 12 years.

Sugar Ray Leonard (welterweight, light-middleweight and middleweight champion) won an estimated $40 million in his 10-year career to make him the biggest earner outside the heavyweight division. Remarkably, he was inactive for nearly five years during his career.

Attendances
Record attendance

135 132 – Tony Zale (USA) v. Billy Pryor (USA), middleweight

In a sport that requires maximum physical stamina, it is strange to find vegetarians. Yet two world champions are known to have been vegetarians — Freddie Welsh (Wal) and Eder Jofre (Bra).

(Opposite left) *Max Schmeling (Ger) was* The Ring Fighter of the Year *for 1930. The next European to win the award was Ingemar Johansson (Swe) nearly 30 years later.* The Photo Source

(Opposite right) *Sugar Ray Leonard (USA) (right), twice winner of* The Ring Fighter of the Year *award, seen with Errol Christie, the 1984 British Young Boxer of the Year.* Syndication International

contest (non-title), 18 August 1941. The contest, at Juneau Park, Milwaukee, Wisconsin, USA, was organized by the Fraternal Order of Eagles and admission was free.

Record paying attendance

120 757 – Gene Tunney (USA) v. Jack Dempsey (USA), world heavyweight title fight, 23 September 1926 at the Sesquicentennial Stadium, Philadelphia, Pennsylvania, USA.

Record paying attendance (non-heavyweight)

100 000 – Danny Lopez (USA) v. David Kotey (Gha), WBC featherweight title fight, 5 November 1976 at Accra, Ghana.

Record indoor attendance

63 350 – Muhammad Ali (USA) v. Leon Spinks (USA), world heavyweight title fight, 15 September 1978 at the New Orleans Superdrome, USA.

Record British attendance

82 000 – Len Harvey v. Jock McEvoy for the British, Empire, and British version of the world light-heavyweight title at White City, London on 10 July 1939. Some sources quote the crowd as being 90 000.

Smallest attendance for a world heavyweight title fight

2434 – Muhammad Ali (USA) v. Sonny Liston (USA) at Lewiston, Maine, USA, 25 May 1965.

Smallest attendance at any world title fight

25 – Jack Dempsey (Ire) v. Johnny Reagan (USA), middleweight, 13 December 1887. The contest started at Huntington, Long Island, USA but, due to flooding of the ring, the bout was finished 25 miles away.

Other large attendances

104 943 – Gene Tunney (USA) v. Jack Dempsey (USA), world heavyweight title fight, 22 September 1927 at Soldier's Field, Chicago, USA.

88 150 – Joe Louis (USA) v. Max Baer (USA), non-title heavyweight contest, 24 September 1935 at New York.

82 000 – Jack Dempsey (USA) v. Luis Firpo (Arg) world heavyweight title fight, 14 September 1923 at the New York Polo Grounds. (This is the record attendance for the Polo Grounds.)

80 183 – Jack Dempsey (USA) v. Georges Carpentier (Fra), world heavyweight title fight, 2 July 1921 at Boyles Thirty Acres, Jersey City, New York.

80 000 – Luis Firpo (Arg) v. Jess Willard (USA), non-title heavyweight bout, 12 July 1923 at Jersey City, New York.

79 222 – Max Schmeling (Ger) v. Jack Sharkey (USA), world heavyweight title fight, 12 June 1930 at Yankee Stadium, New York.

75 000 – Jack Dempsey (USA) v. Jack Sharkey (USA), non-title heavyweight bout, 21 July 1927 at Yankee Stadium, New York.

Most fights

1309 – Abe Hollandersky (Abe the Newsboy) (USA) 1905–18. Many of them were exhibition bouts.

1024 – Bobby Dobbs (USA) 1875–1914. Again, many of his contests were exhibition bouts. (See note on page 154 about Dobbs' date of birth.)
864 (approx.) – Jimmy Wilde (GB) 1910–23 (over 700 of these contests were boxing-booth bouts).

Most fights (excluding exhibitions and boxing booth bouts)

463 – Len Wickwar (USA) 1928–47
350 (approx.) – Jack Britton (USA) 1905–30
330 – Johnny Dundee (Ita) 1910–32

Most professional bouts – world champions

350 (approx.) – Jack Britton (USA) 1905–30
330 – Johnny Dundee (Ita) 1910–32
294 – Harry Greb (USA) 1913–26

Most professional bouts by a world heavyweight champion

122 – Ezzard Charles (USA) 1940–59

Most meetings between same two boxers

23 – Sam Langford (Can) and Harry Wills (USA) 1914–22

20 – Ted 'Kid' Lewis (GB) and Jack Britton (USA) 1915–21 (this figure includes five world title fights)

15 – Sam Langford (Can) and Sam McVey (USA) 1911–20

Most wins
Most wins in professional career

222 – Young Stribling (USA) 1921–33
210 – Maxie Rosenbloom (USA) 1923–39
194 – Archie Moore (USA) 1936–63
174 – Sugar Ray Robinson (USA) 1940–65

Most consecutive wins

83 – Pedro Carrasco (Spa) won 83 consecutive fights between April 1964 and November 1970. The run came to an end when he was held to a draw by Joe Tetteh (Gha). His unbeaten run stretched to 93 bouts when, in February 1972, he lost his world lightweight title to Mando Ramos (USA).

Longest unbeaten record

183 – Hal Bagwell (GB) went 183 bouts without defeat between 1938–48 (five drawn) until beaten by Morry Jones of Liverpool. As most of Bagwell's fights were during the war, his record is often regarded as sketchy.

Longest unbeaten record of any boxer with complete records

97 – Packey McFarland (USA) 1905–15. After losing to Dusty Miller (USA) in 1904, McFarland remained unbeaten in the remaining 97 fights of his career.

94 – Fred Dyer (USA) was unbeaten in the first 94 fights of his career, 1908–12.

93 – Pedro Carrasco (Spa): see above

91 – Sugar Ray Robinson (USA) went 91 fights without defeat between 19 February 1943 and 10 July 1951. Britain's Randolph Turpin ended the run.
(Nino Benvenuti (Ita) suffered his first professional defeat

The late Peter Waterman, the undefeated British welterweight champion 1956–8 was the older brother of Dennis Waterman, who plays 'minder' Terry McCann (retired boxer) in the popular television series Minder (Thames).

on 25 June 1966 to Ki-Soo Kim of South Korea. It ended a consecutive run of 65 professional and 120 amateur contests without defeat.)

Knock-outs

Most knock-outs in a career

145 – Archie Moore (USA) 1936–63
126 – Young Stribling (USA) 1921–33
125 – Billy Bird (USA) 1920–48
114 – George Odwell (USA) 1930–45
109 – Sugar Ray Robinson (USA) 1940–65
108 – Banty Lewis (USA) 1909–22
103 – Sandy Saddler (USA) 1944–56

Most consecutive knock-outs

44 – Lamar Clark (USA) 1958–60
43 – Billy Fox (USA) 1943–6

Most world title fight knock-outs

22 – Joe Louis (USA) heavyweight 1937–48

Best percentage of knock-outs to career bouts

87.7 per cent Rocky Marciano (USA) 43 knockouts, 49 fights

Worst percentage of knock-outs to career bouts

6.2 per cent Maxie Rosenbloom (USA) 18 knockouts, 289 fights

Oldest man to score a knock-out

Walter Edgerton (USA) was 63 years old when he knocked out John Henry Johnson (USA) at the Broadway Athletic Club, Philadelphia in February 1916.

Most knock-outs in one night

6 – Lamar Clark (USA) knocked out six opponents (five in the first round) on the evening of 1 December 1958.

Most one-round knock-outs

42 – Young Otto (USA) 1903–23

Hardest punch

The hardest knock-out punch delivered is believed to be that thrown by Jack Johnson (USA) when he knocked out Stanley Ketchel (USA) to retain his world heavyweight title at Colma, California, USA on 16 October 1909.

Johnson was floored by middleweight champion Ketchel in the 12th round. He was so annoyed he got up, threw a left, and suddenly Ketchel's dream of winning the world heavyweight title was over. By the time he got up Johnson was on his way back to the dressing-room, removing two of Ketchel's teeth that had become embedded in his glove!

Another punch reckoned to be the hardest thrown in a world heavyweight title fight was the one thrown, also in anger, by Argentine Luis 'Angel' Firpo in his battle with Jack Dempsey (USA) in 1923.

Having been knocked down seven times in the first round Firpo, infuriated, threw an almighty punch which put the champion through the ropes. And, had it not been for helping spectators who pushed Dempsey back into the ring to beat the count, he would have lost his title.

Worst records

Most defeats in career

146 – Arnold Sheppard (USA) 1926–39

Most defeats suffered by world champions during their career

65 – Fritzie Zivic (USA) 1931–47
56 – Johnny Dundee (Ita) 1910–32
52 – Lauro Salas (Mex) 1944–61
51 – Johnny Jadick (USA) 1927–37
45 – Jimmy Goodrich (USA) 1919–30

Joey Archibald (USA), with 41 defeats in 106 professional fights, has the worst percentage record.

The most defeats suffered by a world heavyweight champion is 25 by Ezzard Charles (USA). The worst percentage is 23 defeats suffered by James J. Braddock (USA) in 86 contests.

Bob Foster (USA) — light-heavyweight champion 1968–74 — lost his first seven fights as an amateur.

Henry Cooper — British, Commonwealth and European heavyweight champion — lost the first three title fights he contested. All three were in 1957 and were for each of the three titles he was later to win.

Longest contests

Longest fights with gloves

7hr 19min – Andy Bowen (USA) v. Jack Burke (USA) at New Orleans, USA, 6–7 April 1893. The contest started at 9.15 p.m. and finished 110 rounds later at 4.34 a.m. The contest was declared a draw, both fighters unable to continue.

6hr 40min – Danny Needham v. Patsy Kerrigan at San Francisco, USA, 27 February 1890.

The best record by any British boxer in the United States is held by Jack 'Kid' Berg. He fought 74 times in the States, losing on just 13 occasions.

Most recorded rounds

276 – Jack Jones (GB) and Patsy Tunney (GB) fought 276 rounds over 4hr 30min at Cheshire, England in 1825. N.B. Under London Prize Ring rules, a round ended when a contestant was floored. The fight recommenced after a 30-second interval.

Most recorded rounds with gloves

110 – Andy Bowen v. Jack Burke at New Orleans, USA, 6–7 April 1893 (see above).

106 – Jake Kilrain (GB) v. Jem Smith (GB) at Isle des Souverains, France, 19 December 1887. Contest declared a draw because of darkness.

100 – Danny Needham v. Patsy Kerrigan at San Francisco, USA, 27 February 1890.

Last scheduled 45-round contest

5 April 1915 – Jess Willard (USA) KO–26 Jack Johnson (USA) at Havana, Cuba.

Last scheduled 25-round contest

27 August 1941 – Bill Poland (USA) KO–4 Eddie Blunt (USA) at Washington DC, USA.

Last scheduled 20-round contest

1 June 1971 – Kelly Burden (USA) KO–10 Alonzo Harris (USA) at Oklahoma City, USA.

Last scheduled 20-round world title fight

21 March 1941 – heavyweight: Joe Louis (USA) KO–13 Abe Simon (USA) at Detroit, USA.

Last world title fight to go more than 15 rounds

17 March 1923 – Mike McTigue (Ire) beat Battling Siki (Sen) on points over 20 rounds in Dublin, Ireland, to win the world light-heavyweight title.

Shortest contests

(see also p. 77)

7s – Al Carr (USA) beat Lew Massey (USA) at New Haven, USA, 3 April 1936.

10s – Teddy Barker (GB) beat Bob Roberts (Ngr) at Maesteg, Wales, 2 September 1957.

During a Golden Gloves contest (amateur) on 4 November 1947, at Minneapolis, USA, Mike Collins floored Pat Brownson with the first punch of the contest. The referee immediately stopped the bout without taking up the count. It officially ended after four seconds!

The shortest fight in which a professional title was at stake was in New Zealand in 1923 when Jim O'Sullivan knocked out Bill Bartlett in 11 seconds for the New Zealand heavyweight championship.

Longest careers

The following fighters have enjoyed long professional careers:

39 Years – Bobby Dobbs (USA) 1875–1914. Dobbs was in his 56th year when he had his last fight. This may be a dubious claim because Dobbs' birth certificate is believed to have been found recently and it shows his date of birth as 1869, which means he was six when he had his first contest!

35 years – 'Gypsy' Jem Mace (GB) 1855–90. Between 1871–90 he only engaged in one fight. His last contest was while he was in his 59th year. He also fought an exhibition bout when he was 63.

35 years – Tom Faulkner (GB) 1756–91. It may be that Faulkner's first fight was not until 1758 thus reducing his career by two years, but records are not clear.

32 years – Kid Azteca (Mex) 1929–61.

The following is a list of all world champions who enjoyed a professional ring career in excess of 25 years:

31 – Bob Fitzsimmons (GB) 1883–1914
31 – Jack Johnson (USA) 1897–1928
28 – Archie Moore (USA) 1935–63
(Moore fought an exhibition bout in 1965)
28 – Pedlar Palmer (GB) 1891–1919
(Palmer was only a world title claimant)
27 – Joe Brown (USA) 1943–70
26 – Billy Murphy (NZ) 1881–1907
26 – Willie Pep (USA) 1940–66
25 – Young Griffo (Aus) 1886–1911
25 – Charles 'Kid' McCoy (USA) 1891–1916
25 – Jack Britton (USA) 1905–30
25 – Sugar Ray Robinson (USA) 1940–65
25 – Harold Johnson (USA) 1946–71

Shortest careers

The following world champions enjoyed a ring career of less than five years (active fighters are not included):

2 years 2 months Leo Randolph (USA) 1978–80
3 years 9 months Percy Jones (GB) 1912–15
(Jones was only a world title claimant)
3 years 10 months Tom McCormick (Ire) 1912–15
(McCormick was only a world title claimant)
3 years 10 months Billy Soose (USA) 1938–42
4 years 5 months Tadashi Tomori (Jap) 1978–82
4 years 8 months Miguel Cuello (Arg) 1973–8
4 years 10 months Jaime Rios (Pan) 1973–8
4 years 10 months Mate Parlov (Yug) 1975–80
4 years 10 months Shigeo Nakajima (Jap) 1976–81

The shortest professional career of any world heavyweight champion was 7 years 9 months by George Foreman (USA) — 1969–77.

Pete Scalzo (USA) had a professional career lasting just 7 years 4 months, but in that time he took part in 111 contests.

Fatalities

(See also pp. 79–80)

Since the first world title fight under Queensberry Rules, in 1884, there have been approximately 500 ring deaths. In comparison to the total number of contests, amateur and professional, the world over, that figure is relatively small.

The worst years for fatalities were:

1953 — 22 deaths
1949 — 18 deaths
1952 — 17 deaths

First recorded fatality

George Stevenson (GB) (24 April 1741) v. Jack Broughton (GB) at Tottenham Court Road, London, England.

First recorded fatality in the United States

Tom McCoy (USA) (13 September 1842) v. Chris Lilly (GB) at Yonkers, New York.

World champions who lost their lives as a result of injuries sustained in the ring (not necessarily in title fights)

Pancho Villa (Phi) engaged in his last fight, a non-title bout, against Jimmy McLarnin (Ire) at Oakland, USA, 4 July 1925. The day before the contest Villa had a wisdom tooth removed. Against the dentist's advice he still engaged in the contest, which he lost on points over ten rounds. He took so much punishment that he developed an abscess. He refused to have any more teeth out and died on the operating table ten days after the fight.

Tony Marino (USA) suffered a cerebral haemorrhage and died the day after his non-title bantamweight contest against Indian Quintana at Brooklyn, USA, 30 January 1937.

Benny 'Kid' Paret (Cuba) lost his world welterweight title to Emile Griffith (VI) at New York, USA, 24 March 1962. Ten days later Paret died from injuries received.

Davey Moore (USA) died two days after losing his world featherweight title to Sugar Ramos (Cuba) at Los Angeles, USA, 21 March 1963.

Men who died while a current world champion

Paddy Duffy (USA) died 19 July 1890. He was the reigning welterweight champion at the time.

Stanley Ketchel (USA) was shot and killed on 15 October 1910, four months after his last successful defence of the world middleweight crown.

Les Darcy (Aus) was recognized only in Australia as the world middleweight champion. But in 1917 he came to America to fight Al McCoy (USA) for universal recognition as champion. However, he developed pneumonia, and died at Memphis, Tennessee on 24 May 1917, before the fight.

Masao Ohba (Jap) lost his life in an automobile accident at Tokyo, Japan, 24 January 1973. Three weeks earlier he had made his fifth successful defence of the WBA flyweight title against Chartchai Chionoi (Tha).

Salvador Sanchez (Mex) was killed in an automobile accident in Mexico, 12 August 1982, just three weeks after successfully defending his WBC featherweight title against Azumah Nelson (Gha).

The first British super-featherweight title fight in 1986 involved two fighters with the same name – Pat Doherty of Croydon lost to Bradford's John Doherty, who was also known as Pat.

One of the biggest men to box professionally, Primo Carnera (Ita), displaying his strength by picking up two British lightweights, Bert Kirby and George Appleton.
BBC Hulton Picture Library

Oldest fighters

(See also p. 81)

The following fighters took part in bona fide contests at the ages given. There have been other fighters who engaged in exhibition bouts at greater ages but these are not included.

63 years – Walter Edgerton (USA) when he fought John Henry Johnson (USA) 4 December 1916.

58 years 305 days – 'Gypsy' Jem Mace (GB) when he fought Charley Mitchell (GB) 7 February 1890.

56 years 364 days – Daniel Mendoza (GB) when he fought Tom Owen (GB) 4 July 1820.

Greatest combined ages of two fighters

108 years – Walter Edgerton (USA) was aged 63 when he knocked out John Henry Johnson (USA), aged 45, at the Broadway Athletic Club, New York, USA, 4 December 1916.

When Jack Johnson and Joe Jeannette (both USA) met in an exhibition bout at New York, USA on 27 November 1945 Johnson was 67 and Jeannette 66, giving a combined age of 133 years!

Oldest fighter to make his professional debut

46 years – Herbert Odom (USA) v. Eddie Partee (USA), aged 19, 20 July 1979. Odom won in two rounds.

American Johnny Buff (bantamweight) is the oldest world champion to make his professional debut. He was aged 30 when he had his first pro contest in 1918.

World champions who fought beyond the age of 40

The following former world champions all engaged in bouts after the age of 40 (exhibition bouts excluded).

		Date of last fight
50 years 270 days	Bob Fitzsimmons (GB)	20 Feb 1914
50 years 45 days	Jack Johnson (USA)	15 May 1928
49 years 92 days	Archie Moore (USA)	15 Mar 1963
(Moore may have only been 46 years 92 days; there are conflicting reports about his date of birth)		
45 years 35 days	Jack Dempsey (USA)	29 Jul 1940
44 years 206 days	Jack Britton (USA)	8 May 1930

155

Frenchman Georges Carpentier who won eight French, European and world titles. He won French titles at lightweight, welterweight and heavyweight. The Photo Source

44 years 191 days	Sugar Ray Robinson (USA)	10 Nov 1965
43 years 341 days	Joe Brown (USA)	24 Apr 1970
43 years 296 days	Charles 'Kid' McCoy (USA)	4 Aug 1916
43 years 278 days	Billy Murphy (NZ)*	8 Aug 1907
43 years 178 days	Willie Pep (USA)	16 Mar 1966
43 years 33 days	Max Schmeling (Ger)	31 Oct 1948
42 years 233 days	Harold Johnson (USA)	30 Mar 1971
42 years 163 days	Young Griffo (Aus)	25 Sep 1911
42 years 111 days	Pedlar Palmer (GB)*	10 Mar 1919
41 years 195 days	Jess Willard (USA)	12 Jul 1923
41 years 133 days	Adolf Heuser (FRG)*	13 Feb 1949
40 years 335 days	Dick Tiger (Ngr)	15 Jul 1970
40 years 196 days	Eder Jofre (Bra)	8 Oct 1976
40 years 152 days	Panama Al Brown (Pan)	4 Dec 1942
40 years 67 days	Mysterious Billy Smith (USA)	21 Jul 1911
40 years 48 days	Eddie Cotton (USA)*	2 Aug 1967
40 years 19 days	George 'Kid' Lavigne (USA)	25 Dec 1909

*title claimant only

Youngest fighters

(See also p. 81)

The following champions all fought professionally under the age of 14:

		Date of first fight
12 years 175 days	Len Harvey (GB)	2 Jan 1920
12 years 298 days	Teddy Baldock (GB)	14 Mar 1921
13 years 208 days	Baby Arizmendi (Mex)	17 Mar 1914
13 years 336 days	Rodolfo Gonzalez (Mex)	17 Nov 1959

Georges Carpentier was just 15 years 344 days when he beat Paul Til on 22 December 1909 to claim the French lightweight title. Carpentier is also the youngest person to win a European title. He was 17 years 284 days when he beat Young Joseph (GB) for the welterweight title on 23 October 1911. Before he was 20, Carpentier had taken part in 82 professional fights and lost only nine. He had, during that time, won the French lightweight and welterweight titles. He had also won the European welterweight, middleweight, light-heavyweight and heavyweight titles.

The champions

(See also p. 81)

Heaviest men to fight professionally

360lb – Jimmy Black (USA)
340lb – Clyde Bickerstaff (USA)
340lb – Claude McBride (USA)
335lb – Ewart Potgieter (SA)
327lb – Gogea Mitu (Rom)
320lb – Charles Freeman (USA)
315lb – Leo Batiste (USA)
302lb – Big Ben Moroz (USA)
300lb – Ed Dunkhorst (USA)

The greatest combined weight of two fighters engaged in one contest was 700lb when Claude McBride (340lb) knocked out Jimmy Black (360lb) on 1 June 1971.

Lightest men to fight professionally

96lb – Jimmy Wilde (GB) 1910–23
100lb – Georges Carpentier (Fra) when he had his first professional fight in 1908: He later fought for the world heavyweight title!
106lb – Pascual Perez (Arg) 1952–64
106½lb – Freddie Castillo (Mex) 1971–

The greatest weight difference between two fighters in a senior contest was 140lb when Bob Fitzsimmons (172lb) knocked out Ed Dunkhorst (312lb) at Brooklyn, USA on 30 April 1900.

Tallest men to fight professionally

7ft 4in – Gogea Mitu (Rom)
7ft 4in – Jim Cully (Ire)
7ft 4in – John Rankin (USA)
7ft 3in – Charles Freeman (USA)
7ft 2in – Henry Johnson (Can)
7ft 2in – Ewart Potgieter (SA)

Shortest men to fight professionally

4ft 11in – Netrnoi Vorasingh (Tha) 1975–82
4ft 11½in – Pascual Perez (Arg) 1952–64
4ft 11¾in – Johnny Coulon (Can) 1905–20

Only four sets of brothers have won world titles: Joe and Vince Dundee, Leon and Michael Spinks, Ricardo and Rene Arredondo and Don and Bruce Curry. The Currys stand alone as the only pair to simultaneously hold titles which they did between 20 May 1983 and 29 January 1984.

Index

Numbers in *italics* refer to illustrations and their captions; *col* refers to the colour plates. Names of title-holders only mentioned in the tables will not be found in the index

Ager, Alex 10
Agnello, Judge 96
Albermarle, Duke of 5
Ali, Muhammad 116–17, *116, 117,* 118, *147,* 151, *see also* Clay, Cassius
Ali, Muhammad 74, 83, 86, 87, *93,* 96, *96, 100*
Amateur Boxing Association (ABA) 6, 142
Ambers, Lou 106
Appleton, George *155*
Archer, Joe 37
Armstrong, Henry 23, 94, 102, 106–7, *106, 107*
Association Internationale de Boxe Amateur (AIBA) 8
attendances 7, 67, 151–2
    largest 7, 96
Ayala, Mike 48

Baer, Max 72, 84, 92
Bagwell, Hal 152
Baker, Reginald 'Snowy' 135
bare-knuckle fighting 5, 8–9
    last fight 5, 10, *11 see also* prize-fighting
Barry, Dave 108
Barry, Jimmy 70
Basilio, Carmen 95
Bassey, Hogan 'Kid' *70*
'Battle of the Long Count' 18, 105, 108
Beasley, Tom 5
Bell, Tommy 94
belts, championship prizes 10
Benitez, Wilfred 112
Benvenuti, Nino 70, 102, *102,* 138
Berbick, Trevor 110
Berg, Jack 'Kid' *155*
Berlenbach, Paul 102
Bernard, George 15
'Big Ugly Bear' *117*
birthday, title wins on 69
Black, Julian 92
'Black Cloud' 118
Bodell, Jack *123*
Bouttier, Jean-Claude *131*
Boxing 6
Boxing News 6
Boxing Writer's Club 150
Braddock, James J. 72, 84–5, *93,* 110
Brady, William A. 82
British Boxing Board of Control (BBB of C) 1, 6, 7, 109, 110

British Commonwealth & Empire Boxing Championships Cttee 125
'Brockton Blockbuster' 100
brothers 10, 131, 149
Broughton, John (Jack) 5, *5,* 8, *89,* 90
'Brown Bomber' 93
Bruno, Frank *83*
Bugner, Joe 98, *127, col*
Bumphus, Johnny 145
Burman, Joe 72
Burns, Frankie 17
Burns, Tommy 82, 84, 115

Canzoner, Tony *75*
career earnings 151
careers
    longest 154
    shortest 154
Carnera, Primo *18, 19,* 72, 84, 92, *155*
Carpentier, Georges, 6, *6, 17,* 97, *97, 133,* 156, *156*
Carrasco, Pedro 152
Cayton, Bill 111
Chambers, John 88
champions
    American 124–5
    at more than one weight 67, 72–3, 75, 122, 125, 128, 133, 140
    black 67
    British 120–4
    Commonwealth 125–8
        later world champions 140
    Commonwealth Games 139–40
    European 129–34
    first 151
    first British 6, 9
    first heavyweight 6, *68*
    first world 6, 10
    Golden Gloves 143–5
        later world champions 145
    heaviest 81, 156
    heavyweight 6, 83–7
    lightest 81, 156
    longest reigning 10, 71, 122, 124, 125, 128
    most defenses 73, 128, 134
    most married 14
    most recently married 17
    most titles 143, 145
    most wins 145
    Olympic
        later world champions 138–9
        more than one title 138
    overcoming physical disabilities

29, 127
    recognition of 7
    regaining titles 10, *33, 67, 74, 75,* 116, 128, 134
    shortest 81–2, 156
    shortest reigning 10, 71–2, 122, 125, 128, 134
    tallest 81, 156
    world
        fatalities 155
        fewest contests 71
        grandfather 64
        left-handed 67
        most defeats 153
        most fights 152
        nation-by-nation 65–7
        previously amateur champions 138–9, 140, 141, 145
        as referees 82
        undefeated 70–1
        weight divisions 60–4
    World Amateur, later world champions 141
    youngest 81, 138, 156
championships *see* title fights
Charles, Ezzard 26, 85, *85,* 93, *93,* 115
Charnley, Dave *121*
Christie, Errol *150*
claimants to world titles 56–9
Clark, George 91
Clay, Cassius *35,* 86, 98, 116–17, 138, *see also* Ali, Muhammad
Coetzee, Gerrie 87, 128
Commonwealth Boxing Championships Committee 125
Commonwealth Games 110
Conn, Billy 93
Conteh, John *131,* 140
contests *see* fights, title fights
Cooper, George (Jim) 98
Cooper, Henry 98–9, *98, 99, 121, 123*
Corbett, Harry 7
Corbett, James J. 6, 83, 103, 116
Corr, Tommy 141
Criqui, Eugene 29
crowds, record 96, *see also* attendances
Cuello, Miguel Angel 69
Curley, Johnny 7
Currie, Hughroy 123
Curry, Don 145

D'Agata, Mario 29

Dalby, Barrington 22
D'Amato, Gus 110
Darcy, Les 155
Dauthuille, Laurent 78
de Marco, Tony 103
deaths 10, 79–80, 115, 154–5
defeats 153
Delaney, Jack 102
Dempsey, Jack 6, 6, 7, 13, 17, 18, 84, 84, 97, 103, 104, 104–5, 105, 108, 108, 147, 153
Dempsey, Mrs 105
di Carini, Tito Alberto 5
Dickie, Robert col
Dokes, Mike 87, 145
Douglas, J.W.H.T. 135
Douglas, John Sholto, Marquess of Queensberry 88
Downes, Terry 94
Doyle, Jack 149
Driscoll, Jim 125
Duffy, Paddy 155
Dundee, Angelo 83, 98
Dundee, Joe 103
Dundee, Johnny 6, 102
Dunn, Richard 127
Duran, Roberto 112, 113, col
Durell, Yvon 109

Earp, Wyatt 147
Ellis, Jimmy 86, 98
Empire Games 6, 139 see also Commonwealth Games
Epeus ('big bully') 140
Erskine, Joe 99
Estabe, Luis 43
European Amateur Championships 6
European Amateur Junior Championships 6
European Boxing Union (EBU) 7, 129
Euryalus 140

Farr, Tommy 41, 93
fatalities 10, 79–80, 115, 154–5
'Father of the Ring' 90
Feeney, John col
Ferreira, Anton 128
Fields, Jackie 138
Figg, James 5, 8, 90, 90
'Fight of the Century' 96
fighters
    with disabilities 29, 127
    disqualified in Olympics 138
    from communist countries 68, 151
    oldest 81, 138, 151, 155
    youngest 81, 138, 156
    see also champions
Fighters of the Year 150
    British 150
fights
    first professional 31, 43
    longest 153–4
    most 152
    shortest 10, 154
    see also title fights
Finnegan, Chris 131, 135

Finnegan, Kevin 131
Firpo, Luis 'Angel' 105, 153
firsts 67–8, 151
Fitzsimmons, Bob 83, 94, 103, 103, 147
Fleischer, Nat 6
Foreman, George 69, 86–7, 116, 116, 117, 138
Frawley Law (New York) 6
    last bout 16
Frazier, Joe 86, 87, 96, 96, 102, 117, 118, 138
Fullmer, Gene 95

Galindez, Victor 45
Garcia, Ceferino 105, 106
Gardner, John L. 114
gates 67
    first $1 million 6
Genaro, Frankie 138
Geoffrey Simpson Award 150
gloves 90, 151
Godoy, Arturo 93
gold medals
    Olympics 137
    World Amateur Championships 141
Goldberg, William 6
Golden Gloves Championships 115, 143
Goldstein, Abe 72
Goldstein, Ruby 94
Gomez, Wilfredo 141, col
Greb, Harry 29, 149
Green, Dave 'Boy' 112, 113
Green, Mitch 111
Griffith, Emile 37, 102, 102
Gully, John 7
gum shields 151

Hagler, Marvin 57, 76
Hall of Fame 148–9
Hart, Marvin 83
Harvey, Len 122
Hearns, Thomas 57, 76, 112, 145, col
heaviest champions 81, 156
Hefferman, Dennis 102
Herdman, Martin 123
Herman, Pete 17
Hilton, Matthew col
history 5–11
    United States 5, 6
Hogarth, William 90
Holmes, Larry 87, 101, 118, 118, 119, 151
'Homicide Hank' 106
Hope, Maurice 114
Horton Law (New York) 6
Howard, Kevin 113
Husson, Eugene 91
Hyer, Jacob 5

international boxing 5
International Boxing Federation (IBF) 7

International Boxing Union (IBU) 6, 7, 129

Jackson, Melody 106
Jacobs, Jim 111
Jeffries, James J. 15, 83, 103, 115, 115
Johansson, Ingemar 33, 85–6
Johnson, Jack 15, 68, 82, 84, 100, 115, 115, 153
Johnson, Marvin 145
Jolson, Al 106
Jones, Colin 149
Jordan, Don 32
judges 145
    women 68

Kacar, Slobodan 138
Kalule, Ayub 112, 140, 141
Kane, Peter 22
Kates, Richie 45
Kearns, Jack 'Doc' 82, 83, 104
Ketchel, Stanley 115, 153, 155
Kid Blackie 104
Kilrain, Jake 5, 11
King Rafiu 79
Kingpetch, Pone 71
Kirby, Bert 155
knock-outs 77, 78, 91, 92, 93, 95, 104, 105, 109, 149, 153
    at the last second 45
    two in one fight 48
knockdowns 79, 108, 113
Kracken, Jack 92

La Barba, Fidel 138
La Motta, Jake 78, 94
La Starza, Roland 85
Ladbury, Bill 79
Lawless, Sylvie 114
Lawless, Terry 83, 83, 114, 114
Lawson, Jim 10
Lee, Glen 105
Leonard, Sugar Ray 80, 112–13, 112, 113, 138, 145, 150, 151
Leslie, Jock 29
Lesnevich, Gus 25
Levai, Istvan 136
Lewis, Hedgemon 145
Lewis, Ted 'Kid' 97, 156
lightest champions 81, 156
Liston, Sonny 35, 86, 86, 116, 117
London, Brian 98
longest fights 10, 153–4
Lonsdale Belts 98, 99, 123
Lopez, Danny 48
Louis, Joe 41, 73, 85, 92–3, 93, 100, 100, 110, 147
Lovera, Rafael 43
Lowry, Ted 101
Lynch, Benny 22

McAuliffe, Jack 70
McAvoy, Jock 124
McCallum, Mike 140, 145
McCoy, Al 16

McCoy, Charles 'Kid' 14
McCrory, Milton 149
McCrory, Steve 149
Mace, Jem 9, 103
McGowan, Walter 123
McGuigan, Barry 58, 111, 140
McKenzie, Clinton 112
Madden, Billy 151
Madison Square Garden 102
magazines 6
Magri, Charlie 114
Mallin, Fred 142
Mallin, Harry 142
managers 82, 151
'Manassa Mauler' 104
Marciano, Rocky 70, 85, 85, 93,
    100–1, 100, 101, 109, 118
Marek, Max 92
Marino, Tony 155
Matthis, Buster 102
Maxim, Joey 26, 28, 83, 94, 109
Mead, Eddie 106
Mendoza, Daniel col
Mildenberger, Karl 31
Mills, Freddie 25, 26
Mitchell, Charley 6, 81
Monaghan, Rinty 156
Moore, Archie 30, 81, 85, 100, 101,
    109, 109
Moore, Davey 79, 155
Moore, Memphis Pal 91
Muangsurin, Saensak 71
Murphy, Leroy 145

names and nicknames 146–8
Napoles, Jose 44
Nash, Charlie 121
National Boxing Association (NBA)
    7
National Sporting Club 6, 120, 123
Nelson, Azumah 140, col
    Ned 88
New York laws 6
New York State Athletic Commission
    6, 7
nicknames 10, 146
North American Boxing Federation
    (NABF) 7, 124
Norton, Ken 74, 87, 118, 118

O'Dowd, Mike 16
Ohba, Masao 155
oldest fighters 81, 138, 151, 155
Olson, Carl 'Bobo' 95
Olympic Games 6, 97, 110, 134–9
Owen, Johnny 79

Padilla, Carlos 48
Page, Greg 87, 145
Palomino, Carlos 44
Papke, Billy 15
Papp, Laszlo 138
Paret, Benny 32, 155
Parlov, Mate 69, 138, 141
Patterson, Floyd 30, 31, 33, 74, 85,
    109, 110, 116, 138

Pedroza, Eusebio 58
Pelican Club 6, 88
Pep, Willie 29, 29, 147
Perez, Pascual 70, 71, 183
Petersen, Jack 121
Pintor, Lupe 79
Pompey, Yolande 109, 109
prize-fighting 5, 8–9
prize-fights, first 140
Pryor, Aaron 145
Pugilistic Club 5, 6, 8
purses 80
    largest 10, 112

Queensberry, Marquis of 88
Queensberry Rules 5, 6, 88–9

Rademacher, Pete 31, 31
radio, firsts 6–7, 67, 151
Raiteri, Lauri 7
Ramos, Sugar 80
Randolph, Leo 138, 145
Ray, Johnny 6
Reagan, Johnny 13
referees 67, 68, 82, 105, 145, 147
    women 151
Riasco, Rigoberto 145
Rickard, Tex 97, 105
Ring, The 148, 150
Ring Magazine 6
rings 68
Rivers, Joe 77
Robinson, Sugar Ray 28, 77, 94–5,
    94, 95
Roderick, Ernie 107
Rodriguez, Felipe 130
Rodriguez, Lucien 130
Rosner, Johnny 91
Ross, Barney 102, 106
Rowlandson, Thomas col
Roxborough, John 92
Rozadilla, Larry 145
rules 8, 90, 151
    London Prize Ring 5
    Queensberry 5, 6, 88–9

safety 6, 151
Saldivar, Vincente 37
Sanchez, Salvador 155
Sandoval, Richard 145
Sarron, Petey 106
Savold, Lee 93
Schmeling, Max 84, 93, 102, 150
Sexton, Archie 7, 124
Sexton, Dave 124
Shankley, Bill 114
Sharkey, Jack 84, 93, 102
Sharkey, Tom 147
shortest champions 81–2, 156
shortest fights 10,
    77, 154
shortest reigning champions 10,
    71–2, 122, 125, 128
Simon, Abe 81
Singer, Al 77

Skelton, Tom 88
Slack, Jack 90
Smith, James 'Bonecrusher' 111, 111
Smith, Tony 102
Smith, Willie 138
Spinks, Leon 71, 87, 110, 116, 117,
    117, 138
Spinks, Michael 87, 118, 138, 145
stadiums 68
stakes, bare-knuckle fighting 10
Stephenson, George 88
Stewart, Bobby 110
Stevenson, George 5
Stevenson, Teofilio 136
Stracey, John H. 44, 114
Stretz, Hans 95
Sullivan, John L. 5, 6, 11, 116
Sutton, Ned 5, 8, 90
'Suzi-Q' 100
Symonds, Joe 91

tallest champions 81, 156
Tarleton, Nel 124, 127
Tate, John 87
Taylor, George 90
Tyson, Mike 110–111, 111
television, firsts 7, 67, 68, 151
Terrell, Ernie 39, 86
Terrell, Jean 39
Terris, Sid 102
Thomas, Eddie 149
Thomas, Pinklon 87, 111
'Thrilla In Manila' 96
title fights
    firsts 5, 6, 7, 9, 31, 43, 68, 69, 151
    heavyweight, most dramatic 105
    longest 153–4
    most 152
    over ten rounds 18
    shortest 10, 123, 134, 154
    world 6, 7, 12–87
    world heavyweight, first all-
        European 20, 21
Tillis, James 111
titles
    British, most defenses 122
    most 143, 156
    Olympic 97, 138–9
    regained 10, 33, 67, 74, 75, 128,
        134
    see also champions
Tournament of Champions 143
trainers 83, 103, 114
Tubbs, Tony 87
Tucker, Tony 111
Tunney, Gene 7, 18, 84, 105, 108,
    108, 149
Turpin, Randolph 94

unbeaten records 152
United States Boxing Association
    International (USBAI) 7
United States Boxing Association
    (USBA) 7, 124
Uzcudun, Paulino 20, 21

Val Barker Trophy 139
Vega, Luis 112
vegetarians, stamina of 151
venues 32, 82
Villa, Pancho 91, 155

Walcott, Jersey Joe *26*, *73*, *85*, *93*, *93*,
   100, 101
Walker, Billy 99
Walker, Dr William 106
Ward, Jem *col*
Watt, Jim 114
Weaver, Mike 87
weight divisions 7, 8
   ABA 142
   Commonwealth Games 139
   Olympics 134
Weill, Al 100
Wells, Bombadier Billy *121*
'White Heavyweight' title *56*
'White Lightweight' title *59*
Whittaker, Bob *5*
Wicks, Jim 'The Bishop' 98
Wilde, Jimmy 91, *91*, *147*
Willard, Jess 84, 104, 115
Williams, Carl 'The Truth' *119*
wins, most 152
Winstone, Howard *37*, *121*, 140
Witherspoon, Tim 87

Wolgas, Ad 77
World Amateur Championships 6,
   141
World Boxing Association 7
World Boxing Council (WBC) 7
world champions
   at more than one weight 72–3, 75
   bare-knuckle 9
   divisions 60–4
   fatalities 155
   fewest contests 71
   grandfather 64
   heaviest 81
   left-handed 67
   lightest 81
   most defeats 153
   most fights 152
   nation-by-nation 65–7
   oldest 81
   previously Commonwealth
      champions 140
   previously Golden Gloves
      champions 145
   previously Olympic champions
      138–9
   previously World Amateur
      champions 141
   as referees 82
   shortest 81–2

   tallest 81
   undefeated 70–71
      youngest 81
world championships, first 67
world title fights 7
   first 6, 7
   results 12–56
   shortest 77
   when held 80–1
world titles
   deaths 79–80
   disqualifications 77–8
   drawn 78–9
   first fights in each country 68–70
   knockdowns 79
   most defenses 73
   most fights 73
   notable claimants 56–9
   purses 80
   regained 67, 74–5, 116
   in round one 75–7
Wright, John *138*

Young Zulu Kid 91
youngest fighters 81, 138, 156
Yum, Dong-Kyun 145

Zivic, Fritzie 106, *106*

Index compiled by Margaret Cooter